VOLUME THREE

The Age
of
Revolution

A HISTORY OF THE
ENGLISH-SPEAKING PEOPLES

The Age
of
Revolution

Winston S. Churchill

DODD, MEAD & COMPANY · NEW YORK

1957

ACKNOWLEDGMENTS

I desire to record my thanks again to Mr. F. W. Deakin and Mr. G. M. Young for their assistance before the Second World War in the preparation of this work; to Dr. J. H. Plumb of Christ's College, Cambridge, Mr. Steven Watson of Christ Church, Oxford, Professor Asa Briggs of Leeds University, Professor Frank Freidel, now of Stanford University, California, who have scrutinised the text in the light of subsequent advances in historical knowledge; and to Mr. Alan Hodge, Mr. Denis Kelly, and Mr. C. C. Wood. I have also to thank many others who have kindly read these pages and commented upon them.

In the opening chapters of this volume I have, with the permission of Messrs. George G. Harrap and Co. Ltd., followed the character of my *Marlborough: His Life and Times* (1933–38), summarising where necessary, but also using phraseology and making quotations.

Preface

DURING the period described in this volume, namely, from 1688 to 1815, three revolutions profoundly influenced mankind. They occurred within the space of a hundred years, and all of them led to war between the British and the French. The English Revolution of 1688 expelled the last Catholic king from the British Isles, and finally committed Britain to a fierce struggle with the last great King of France, Louis XIV. The American Revolution of 1775 separated the English-speaking peoples into two branches, each with a distinctive outlook and activity, but still fundamentally united by the same language, as well as by common traditions and common law. In 1789, by force of arms and a violent effort, unequalled in its effects until the Bolshevik Revolution of 1917, France proclaimed to Europe the principles of equality, liberty, and the rights of man. Beneath these political upheavals, and largely unperceived at the time, other revolutions in science and manufacture were laying the foundations of the Industrial Age in which we live to-day. The religious convulsions of the Reformation had at last subsided. Henceforward Britain was divided for practical purposes by Party and not by Creed, and henceforward Europe disputed questions of material power and national pre-eminence. Whereas the older conceptions had been towards a religious unity, there now opened European struggles for national aggrandisement, in which religious currents played a dwindling part.

When this tale begins the English Revolution had just been accomplished. King James II had fled, and the Dutch Prince of

Orange, soon to be King William III, had arrived in England. He was immediately involved in mortal combat with France. France tried to bring Europe again into a frame, and under an hegemony which Charlemagne had scarcely attained, and for an example of which we must look back to Roman times. This vehement French aspiration found its embodiment in Louis XIV. The ruin of Germany by the Thirty Years' War, and the decay of Spain, favoured his ambitions.

Meanwhile the rise of the Dutch Republic had brought into existence a Protestant state which though small in numbers was by valour, sea-power, and trade one of the Great Powers of the Continent. The alliance of England and Holland formed the nucleus of the resistance to France. Aided by the political interest of the Holy Roman Empire, the two maritime countries of the North Sea faced the genius and glory centred at Versailles. By the swords of William III, Marlborough, and Prince Eugene the power of Louis XIV was broken. Thereafter England, under the Hanoverian Dynasty, settled into acceptance of Whig conceptions. These gathered up all the fundamental English inheritance from Magna Carta and primitive times, and outlined in their modern form the relations of the State to religion and the subordination of the Crown to Parliament.

All this time the expansion of British overseas possessions grew. The British Islands were united, and though inferior in numbers exercised a noticeable guiding influence upon Europe. But they pursued a development separate and distinct from the Continent. Under the elder Pitt vast dominions were secured in the New World and in India, and the first British Empire came into being.

The ever-growing strength of the American colonies, uncomprehended by British Governments, led to an inevitable schism with the Mother Country. By the War of Independence, better known to Americans as the Revolutionary War, the United States were founded. France and Western Europe combined against Britain, and although the Island command of the sea was unsubdued the first British Empire came to an end.

Upon these changes in world-power there came the next decisive, liberating movement since the Reformation. The Reformation had over broad areas established liberty of conscience. The French Revolution sought to proclaim the equality of man, and at least set forth the principle of equality of opportunity irrespective of rank or wealth. During the great war against Napoleon Britain contended with almost the whole of Europe, and even with the United States of America. Napoleon was unable to found a United States of Europe. The Battle of Waterloo, a far-sighted Treaty of Peace, and the Industrial Revolution in England established Britain for nearly a century at or around the summit of the civilised world.

W.S.C.

Chartwell
   Westerham
     Kent
December 24, 1956

CONTENTS

CONTENTS

BOOK IX
NAPOLEON

MAPS AND GENEALOGICAL TABLE

MAPS AND TABLE

BOOK SEVEN

ENGLAND'S ADVANCE TO WORLD POWER

William of Orange

FROM his earliest years the extraordinary Prince who in the general interest robbed his father-in-law of the British throne had dwelt under harsh and stern conditions. William of Orange was fatherless and childless. His life was loveless. His marriage was dictated by reasons of State. He was brought up by a termagant grandmother, and in his youth was regulated by one Dutch committee after another. His childhood was unhappy and his health bad. He had a tubercular lung. He was asthmatic and partly crippled. But within this emaciated and defective frame there burned a remorseless fire, fanned by the storms of Europe, and intensified by the grim compression of his surroundings. His greatest actions began before he was twenty-one. From that age he had fought constantly in the field, and toiled through every intrigue of Dutch domestic politics and of the European scene. For four years he had been the head of the English conspiracy against the Catholic King James II.

Women meant little to him. For a long time he treated his loving, faithful wife with indifference. Later on, towards the end of his reign, when he saw how much Queen Mary had helped him in the English sphere of his policy, he was sincerely grateful to her, as to a faithful friend or Cabinet officer who had maintained the Government. His grief at her death was unaffected.

In religion he was of course a Calvinist; but he does not seem to have derived much spiritual solace from the forbidding doctrines of the sect. As a sovereign and commander he was entirely without religious prejudices. No agnostic could have displayed more philosophic impartiality. Protestant, Catholic, Jew, or infidel were all the same to him. He dreaded and hated Gallican Catholicism less because it was to him idolatrous than because it was French. He employed Catholic officers without hesitation when they would serve his purpose. He used religious questions as counters in his political combinations. While he beat the Protestant drum in England and Ireland, he had potent influence with the Pope, with whom his relations were at all times a model of comprehending statesmanship. It almost seemed that a being had been created for the sole purpose of resisting the domination of France and her "Great King."

It was the natural consequence of such an upbringing and of such a mission that William should be ruthless. Although he had not taken part in the conspiracy to murder the Dutch statesmen, the De Witts, in 1672, he had rejoiced at it, profited by it, and protected and pensioned the murderers. He had offered to help James II against the Protestant Duke of Monmouth, but took no trouble to hamper Monmouth's sailing from his refuge in Holland. The darkest stain upon his memory was to come from Scotland. A Highland clan whose chief had been tardy in making his submission was doomed to destruction by William's signed authority. Troops were sent to Glencoe "to extirpate that den of thieves." But the horror with which this episode has always been regarded arises from the treacherous breach of the laws of hospitality by which it was accomplished. The royal soldiers lived for weeks in the valley with the clansmen, partaking of their rude hospitality under the guise of friendship. Suddenly, on a freezing winter night, they turned upon their hosts and murdered them by the score while they slept or fled from their huts. The King had not prescribed the method, but he bears the indelible shame of the deed.

William was cold, but not personally cruel. He wasted no

time on minor revenges. His sole quarrel was with Louis XIV. For all his experience from a youth spent at the head of armies, and for all his dauntless heart, he was never a great commander. He had not a trace of that second-sight of the battlefield which is the mark of military genius. He was no more than a resolute man of good common sense whom the accident of birth had carried to the conduct of war. His inspiration lay in the sphere of diplomacy. He has rarely been surpassed in the sagacity, patience, and discretion of his statecraft. The combinations he made, the difficulties he surmounted, the adroitness with which he used the time factor or played upon the weakness of others, his unerring sense of proportion and power of assigning to objectives their true priorities, all mark him for the highest repute.

His paramount interest was in the great war now begun throughout Europe, and in the immense confederacy he had brought into being. He had regarded the English adventure as a divagation, a duty necessary but tiresome, which had to be accomplished for a larger purpose. He never was fond of England, nor interested in her domestic affairs. Her seamy side was what he knew. He required the wealth and power of England by land and sea for the European war. He had come in person to enlist her. He used the English public men who had been his confederates for his own ends, and rewarded them for their services, but as a race he regarded them as inferior in fibre and fidelity to his Dutchmen.

Once securely seated on the English throne he scarcely troubled to disguise these sentiments. It was not surprising that such manners, and still more the mood from which they evidently arose, gave deep offence. For the English, although submissive to the new authority of which they had felt the need, were as proud as any race in Europe. No one relishes being an object of aversion and contempt, especially when these affronts are unstudied, spontaneous, and sincere. The great nobles and Parliamentarians who had made the Revolution and were still rigidly set upon its purpose could not but muse upon the easy gaiety and grace of the Court of Charles II. William's unsociable disposition, his greediness at table, his silence and surliness in company, his indifference to women, his dislike of London, all prejudiced him with polite society. The ladies voted him "a low Dutch bear." The English Army too was troubled in its soul. Neither officers nor men could dwell without a sense of humiliation upon the military aspects of the Revolution. They did not like to see all the most important commands entrusted to Dutchmen. They eyed sourly the Dutch infantry who paced incessantly the sentry-beats of Whitehall and St James's, and contrasted their shabby blue uniforms with the scarlet pomp of the 1st Guards and Coldstreamers, now banished from London. As long as the Irish war continued, or whenever a French invasion threatened, these sentiments were repressed; but at all other times they broke forth with pent-up anger. The use of British troops on the Continent became unpopular, and the pressure upon William to dismiss his Dutch Guards and Dutch favourites was unceasing.

* * * * *

As soon as he learned on the afternoon of December 23, 1688, that by King James's flight he had become undisputed master of England the Prince of Orange took the step for which he had come across the water. The French Ambassador was given twenty-four hours to quit the Island and England was committed to the general coalition against France. This opened a war which, with an uneasy interlude, gripped Europe for twenty-five years, and was destined to bring low to the ground the power of Louis XIV.

The whole British nation had been united in the expulsion of James. But there was now no lawful Government of any kind. A Convention Parliament was summoned by the Prince on the advice of the statesmen who had made the Revolution. As soon as it was elected it became involved in points of constitutional propriety; and the national non-party coalition which was responsible for summoning William to England broke under the stress of creating a settled Government for the country. Personal ambitions and party creeds shot through the complicated manœuvres which led to the final constitutional arrangements. King Charles's former Minister, the Earl of Danby, had much to hope for from these weeks of chaos. It was he who had created the Tory Party from the Anglican gentry and the Established Church after the breakdown of the Cabal. The intrigues of Charles with France and the Popish Plot had wrecked his political career. To save him from the malice of his enemies the King had incarcerated him in comfort in the Tower. He had been released towards the end of the reign, and now in the 1688 Revolution he saw his chance to remake his fortunes. His position as a great landowner in the North had enabled him to raise the gentry and provide a considerable military force at a critical and decisive moment. With the prestige of this achievement behind him he had arrived in London. Loyal Tories were alarmed by the prospect of disturbing the Divine Right in the Stuart succession. Danby got in touch with Princess Mary. An obvious solution which would please many Tories was the accession of Mary in her own right. In this way the essential basis of the Tory creed could be preserved, and for this Danby now fought in the debates of the hastily assembled Lords. But other Tories, including Mary's uncle, the Earl of Clarendon, favoured the appointment of William as Regent, James remaining titular King. This cleavage of ideas helped the Whigs to prevail.

The Whigs, for their part, looked on the Revolution as the vindication of their own political belief in the idea of a contract between Crown and people. It now lay with Parliament to settle the succession. The whole situation turned upon the decision of William. Would he be content with the mere title of honorary consort to his wife? If so the conscience of the Tories would not be violated and the Whig share in the Revolution would be obscured. The Whigs themselves had lost their leaders in the Rye House Plot, and it was a single politician who played their game for them and won, while they reaped the benefit.

George Savile, Marquis of Halifax, "the Trimmer" as he was proud to be called, was the subtlest and most solitary statesman of his day. His strength in this crisis lay in his knowledge of William's intention. He had been sent by James to treat with the invading prince in the days before the King's flight. He knew that William had come to stay, that the Dutchman needed a secure and sovereign position in England in order to meet the overshadowing menace of French aggression in Europe. The suggestion that William should be Regent on behalf of James was rejected in the Lords, but only by 51 votes to 49. After protracted debates in the Convention Halifax's view was accepted that the Crown should be jointly vested in the persons of William and Mary. His triumph was complete, and it was he who presented the Crown and the Declaration of Rights to the two sovereigns on behalf of both Houses. But his conception of politics was hostile to the growing development of party. In a time of high crisis he could play a decisive rôle. He possessed no phalanx of partisans behind him. His moment of power was brief; but the Whig Party owed to him their revival in the years which followed.

Step by step the tangle had been cleared. By the private advice of John and Sarah Churchill, Princess Anne, Mary's younger sister, surrendered in favour of William her right to succeed to the throne should Mary predecease him. Thus William gained without dispute the crown for life. He accepted this Parliamentary decision with good grace. Many honours and promotions at the time of the coronation rewarded the Revolutionary leaders. Churchill, though never in William's immediate circle, was confirmed in his rank of Lieutenant-General, and employed virtually as Commander-in-Chief to reconstitute the English Army. He was created Earl of Marlborough, and when in May 1689 war was formally declared against France, and William was detained in England and later embroiled in Ireland, Marlborough led the English contingent of eight thousand men against the French in Flanders.

The British Islands now entered upon a most dangerous war crisis. The exiled James was received by Louis with every mark of consideration and sympathy which the pride and policy of the Great King could devise. Ireland presented itself as the obvious immediate centre of action. James, sustained by a disciplined French contingent, many French officers, and large supplies of French munitions and money, had landed in Ireland in March. He was welcomed as a deliverer. He reigned in Dublin, aided by an Irish Parliament, and was soon defended by a Catholic army which may have reached a hundred thousand men. The whole island except the Protestant settlements in the North passed under the control of the Jacobites, as they were henceforth called. While William looked eastward to Flanders and the Rhine the eyes of his Parliament were fixed upon the opposite quarter. When he reminded Parliament of Europe they vehemently drew his attention to Ireland. The King made the time-honoured mistake of meeting both needs inadequately. The defence of Londonderry and its relief from the sea was the one glorious episode of the campaigning season of 1689.

Cracks speedily appeared in the fabric of the original National Government. The Whigs considered that the Revolution belonged to them. Their judgment, their conduct, their principles, had been vindicated. Ought they not then to have all the offices? But William knew that he could never have gained the crown of England without the help of the Cavaliers and High Churchmen, who formed the staple of the Tory Party. Moreover, at this time, as a king he liked the Tory mood. Here was a Church devoted to hereditary monarchy. William felt that Whig principles would ultimately lead to a republic. Under the name of Stadtholder he was almost King of Holland; he had no desire under the name of King to be only Stadtholder of England. He was therefore ready to dissolve the Convention Parliament which had given him the crown while, as the Whigs said, "its work was all unfinished." At the election of February 1690 the Tories won.

It may seem strange that the new King should have turned to the inscrutable personality of the Earl of Sunderland, who had been King James's chief adviser. But James and Sunderland had now irrevocably quarrelled, and the Jacobites held the Earl mainly responsible for the Revolution. Sunderland was henceforth bound to William's interest, and his knowledge of the European political scene was invaluable to his sovereign's designs. After a brief interval he reappeared in England, and gained a surprising influence. He did not dare seek office for himself, but he made and marred the greatest fortunes. The actual government was entrusted to the statesmen of the middle view—the Duke of Shrewsbury, Sidney Godolphin, and Marlborough, and, though now, as always, he stood slightly aloof from all parties, Halifax. All had served King James. Their notion of party was to use both or either of the factions to keep themselves above water and to further the royal service. Each drew in others. "Shrewsbury was usually hand-in-glove with Wharton; Godolphin and Marlborough shared confidences with Admiral Russell." [1] Of these men it was Godolphin during the next twenty years who

[1] K. G. Feiling, *A History of the Tory Party, 1640–1714* (1924).

stood closest to Marlborough. Great political dexterity was combined in him with a scrupulous detachment. He never thrust forward for power, but he was seldom out of office. He served under four sovereigns, and with various colleagues, but no one questioned his loyalty. He knew how to use a well-timed resignation, or the threat of it, to prove his integrity. Awkward, retiring, dreamy by nature, he was yet heart and soul absorbed by the business of government.

*   *   *   *   *

Had William used his whole strength in Ireland in 1689 he would have been free to carry it to the Continent in 1690; but in the new year he found himself compelled to go in person with his main force to Ireland, and by the summer took the field at the head of thirty-six thousand men. Thus the whole power of England was diverted from the main theatre of the war. The Prince of Waldeck, William's Commander in the Low Countries, suffered a crushing defeat at the skilful hands of Marshal Luxembourg in the Battle of Fleurus. At the same time the French Fleet gained a victory over the combined fleets of England and Holland off Beachy Head. It was said in London that "the Dutch had the honour, the French had the advantage, and the English the shame." The command of the Channel temporarily passed to the French under Admiral Tourville, and it seemed that they could at the same time land an invading army in England and stop William returning from Ireland.

Queen Mary's Council, of which Marlborough was a member, had to face an alarming prospect. They were sustained by the loyalty and spirit of the nation. The whole country took up what arms they could find. With a nucleus of about six thousand regular troops and the hastily improvised militia and yeomanry, Marlborough stood ready to meet the invasion. However, on July 11 King William gained a decisive victory at the Boyne and drove King James out of Ireland back to France. The appeals of the defeated monarch for a French army to conquer England were not heeded by Louis. The French King had his eyes on Germany. The anxious weeks of July and August passed by without more serious injury than the burning of Teignmouth by French raiders. By the winter the French Fleet was dismantled, and the English and Dutch Fleets were refitted and again at sea. Thus the danger passed. Late as was the season, Marlborough was commissioned by Queen Mary's Council and King William to lead an expedition into Ireland, and in a short and brilliant campaign he captured both Cork and Kinsale and subdued the whole of the Southern Irish counties. The end of 1690 therefore saw the Irish War ended and the command of the sea regained. William was thus free after two years to proceed in person to the Continent with strong forces and to assume command of the main armies of the Alliance. He took Marlborough with him at the head of the English troops. But no independent scope was given to Marlborough's genius, already discerned among the captains of the Allies, and the campaign, although on the greatest scale, was indecisive.

Thereafter a divergence grew between the King and Marlborough. When the commands for the next year's campaign were being assigned William proposed to take Marlborough to Flanders as Lieutenant-General attached to his own person. Marlborough demurred at this undefined position. He did not wish to be carried round Flanders as a mere adviser, offering counsel that was not taken, and bearing responsibility for the failures that ensued. He asked to remain at home unless required to command the British troops, as in the past year. But the King had offered them to one of his Dutch generals, Baron Ginkel, fresh from Irish victories at Aughrim and Limerick. In the Commons a movement was on foot for an address on the employment of foreigners. Marlborough was known to be sympathetic, and he proposed himself to move a similar motion in the House of Lords.

Widespread support was forthcoming, and it even appeared at one time likely that the motion would be carried by majorities in both Houses. Moreover, Marlborough's activities did not end with Parliament. He was the leading British general, and many officers of various ranks resorted to him and loudly expressed their resentment at the favour shown to the Dutch.

At this time almost all the leading men in England resumed relations with James, now installed at Saint-Germain, near Paris. Godolphin also cherished sentiments of respectful affection towards the exiled Queen. Shrewsbury, Halifax, and Marlborough all entered into correspondence with James. King William was aware of this. He still continued to employ these men in great offices of State and confidence about his person. He accepted their double-dealing as a necessary element in a situation of unexampled perplexity. He tolerated the fact that his principal English counsellors were reinsuring themselves against a break-up of his Government or his death on the battlefield. He knew, or at least suspected, that Shrewsbury was in touch with Saint-Germain through his mother; yet he insisted on his keeping the highest offices. He knew that Admiral Russell had made his peace with James; yet he kept him in command of the Fleet. If he quarrelled with Marlborough it was certainly not because of the family contacts which the General preserved with his nephew, King James's son the Duke of Berwick, or his wife Sarah with her sister, the Jacobite Duchess of Tyrconnel. The King probably knew that Marlborough had obtained his pardon from James by persuading the Princess Anne to send a dutiful message to her father. There was talk of the substitution of Anne for William and Mary, and at the same time the influence of the Churchills with Princess Anne continued to be dominating. Any rift between Anne and her sister, Queen Mary, must sharpen the already serious differences between the King and Marlborough. The ill-feeling between the royal personages developed rapidly. William treated Anne's husband, Prince George of Denmark, with the greatest contempt. He excluded him from all share in the wars. He would not take him to Flanders, nor allow him to go to sea with the Fleet. Anne, who dearly loved her husband, was infuriated by these affronts.

As often happens in disputes among high personages, the brunt fell on a subordinate. The Queen demanded the dismissal of Sarah Churchill from Anne's household. Anne refused with all the obstinate strength of her nature. The talk became an altercation. The courtiers drew back distressed. The two sisters parted in the anger of a mortal estrangement. The next morning at nine o'clock Marlborough, discharging his functions as Gentleman of the Bedchamber, handed the King his shirt, and William preserved his usual impassivity. Two hours later the Earl of Nottingham, Secretary of State, delivered to Marlborough a written order to sell at once all the offices he held, civil and military, and consider himself as from that date dismissed from the Army and all public employment and forbidden the Court. No reasons were given officially for this important stroke. Marlborough took his dismissal with unconcern. His chief associates, the leading counsellors of the King, were offended. Shrewsbury let his disapproval be known; Godolphin threatened to retire from the Government. Admiral Russell, now Commander-in-Chief of the Navy, went so far as to reproach King William to his face with having shown ingratitude to the man who had "set the crown upon his head." The Queen now forbade Sarah to come to Court, and Anne retorted by quitting it herself. She left her apartments in the Cockpit at Whitehall and retired to Syon House, offered her by the Duke of Somerset. No pressure would induce Anne to part with her cherished friend, and in these fires of adversity and almost persecution links were forged upon which the destinies of England were presently to hang.

Continental War

NO sooner had King William set out upon the Continental war than the imminent menace of invasion fell upon the Island he had left denuded of troops. Louis XIV now planned a descent upon England. King James was to be given his chance of regaining the throne. The exiled Jacobite Court at Saint-Germain had for two years oppressed the French War Office with their assertion that England was ripe and ready for a restoration. An army of ten thousand desperate Irishmen and ten thousand French regulars was assembled around Cherbourg. The whole French Fleet, with a multitude of transports and store-ships, was concentrated in the Norman and Breton ports.

It was not until the middle of April 1692 that the French designs became known to the English Government. Fevered but vigorous preparations were made for defence by land and sea. As upon the approach of the Spanish Armada, all England was alert. But everything turned upon the Admiral. Russell, like Marlborough, had talked with the Jacobite agents: William and Mary feared, and James fervently believed, that he would play the traitor to his country and his profession. Jacobite sources admit however that Russell plainly told their agent that, much as he loved James and loathed William's Government, if he met the French Fleet at sea he would do his best to destroy it, "even though King James himself were on board." He kept his word. "If your officers play you false," he said to the sailors on the day of battle, "overboard with them, and myself the first."

On May 19–20 the English and Dutch Fleets met Tourville

with the main French naval power in the English Channel off Cape La Hogue. Russell's armada, which carried forty thousand men and seven thousand guns, was the stronger by ninety-nine ships to forty-four. Both sides fought hard, and Tourville was decisively beaten. Russell and his admirals, all of whom were counted on the Jacobite lists as pledged and faithful adherents of King James, followed the beaten Navy into its harbours. During five successive days the fugitive warships were cut out under the shore batteries by flotillas of English row-boats. The whole apparatus of invasion was destroyed under the very eyes of the former King whom it was to have borne to his native shore.

The Battle of Cape La Hogue, with its consequential actions, effaced the memories of Beachy Head. It broke decisively for the whole of the wars of William and Anne all French pretensions to naval supremacy. It was the Trafalgar of the seventeenth century.

On land the campaign of 1692 unrolled in the Spanish Netherlands, which we now know as Belgium. It opened with a brilliant French success. Namur fell to the French armies. But worse was to follow. In August William marched by night with his whole army to attack Marshal Luxembourg. The French were surprised near Steinkirk in the early morning. Their advanced troops were overwhelmed and routed, and for an hour confusion reigned in their camp. But Luxembourg was equal to the emergency and managed to draw out an ordered line of battle. The British infantry formed the forefront of the Allied attack. Eight splendid regiments, under General Mackay, charged and broke the Swiss in fighting as fierce as had been seen in Europe in living memory. Luxembourg now launched the Household troops of France upon the British division, already strained by its exertions, and after a furious struggle, fought mostly with cold steel, beat it back. Meanwhile from all sides the French advanced

THE
NETHERLANDS
1689-1714

UNITED
PROVINCES

The Hague

Nimwegen

Ostend
Bruges
Ghent
Antwerp
Calais
SPANISH
Scheldt
Oudenarde
Maastricht
Steinkirk
Brussels
Liege
Lille
Ramillies
Namur
Meuse
Cologne
Bonn
Malplaquet
NETHERLANDS
Rhine
FRANCE
Treves
Moselle

MILES

0   50   100

and their reinforcements began to reach the field. Count Solms, the Dutch officer and William's relation, who had replaced Marlborough in command of the British contingent, had already earned the cordial dislike of its officers and men. With the remark, "Now we shall see what the bulldogs can do!" he refused to send Mackay the help for which he begged. The British lost two of their best generals and half their numbers killed and wounded, and would not have escaped but for the action of a subordinate Dutch general, Overkirk, afterwards famous in Marlborough's campaigns. William, who was unable to control the battle, shed bitter tears as he watched the slaughter, and exclaimed, "Oh, my poor English!" By noon the whole of the Allied army was in retreat, and although the losses of seven or eight thousand men on either side were equal the French proclaimed their victory throughout Europe.

These events infuriated the English Parliament. The most savage debates took place upon the conduct of Count Solms. The House of Lords carried an address that no English general should be subordinated to a Dutchman, whatever his rank. It was with difficulty that the Government spokesmen persuaded the Commons that there were no English officers fit to be generals in a Continental campaign. Against great opposition supplies were voted for another mismanaged and disastrous year of war. In July 1693 was fought the great Battle of Landen, unmatched in Europe for its slaughter except by Malplaquet and Borodino for over two hundred years. The French were in greatly superior strength. Nevertheless the King determined to withstand their attack, and constructed almost overnight a system of strong entrenchments and palisades in the enclosed country along the Landen stream, within the windings of the Geet. After an heroic resistance the Allies were driven from their position by the French with a loss of nearly twenty thousand men, the attackers losing less than half this total. William rallied the remnants of his army, gathered reinforcements, and, since Luxembourg neglected to pursue his victory, was able to maintain himself in the field. In 1694 he planned an expedition upon Brest, and, according to the Jacobites, Marlborough betrayed this design to the enemy. At any rate Tollemache, the British commander on land, was received by heavy fire from prepared positions, was driven back to his ships with great loss, and presently died of his wounds. There is no doubt that the letter on which the charge against Marlborough was based is a forgery. There is no proof that he gave any information to the French, and it is also certain that they were fully informed from other sources.

*   *   *   *   *

The primitive finances of the English State could ill bear the burden of a European war. In the days of Charles II England was forced to play a minor and sometimes ignominious rôle in foreign affairs largely for lack of money. The Continental ventures of William III now forced English statesmen to a reconstruction of the credit and finances of the country.

The first war Government formed from the newly organised Whig Party possessed in the person of Charles Montagu a first-rate financier. It was he who was responsible for facing this major problem. The English troops fighting on the Continent were being paid from day to day. The reserves of bullion were being rapidly depleted and English financial agents were obsessed by the fear of a complete breakdown. The first essential step was the creation of some national organ of credit. The Dutch had for some years possessed a National Bank which worked in close collaboration with their Government, and the intimate union of the two countries naturally brought their example to the attention of the Whigs. In collaboration with the Scottish banker William Paterson,

Montagu, now Chancellor of the Exchequer, started the Bank of England in 1694 as a private corporation. This institution, while maintaining the principle of individual enterprise and private joint-stock company methods, was to work in partnership with the Government, and was to provide the necessary means for backing the Government's credit.

Montagu was not content merely to stop here. With the help of the philosopher John Locke, and William Loundes of the Treasury, he planned a complete overhaul of the coinage. Within two years the recoinage was carried out, and with this solidly reconstructed financial system the country was able in the future not only to bear the burden of King William's wars, but to face the prolonged ordeal of a conflict over the Spanish Succession. It is perhaps one of the greatest achievements of the Whigs.

At the end of 1694 Queen Mary had been stricken with smallpox, and on December 28 she died, unreconciled to her sister Anne, mourned by her subjects, and lastingly missed by King William. Hitherto the natural expectation had been that Mary would long survive her husband, upon whose frail, fiery life so many assaults of disease, war, and conspiracy had converged. An English Protestant Queen would then reign in her own right. Instead of this, the crown now lay with William alone for life, and thereafter it must come to Anne. This altered the whole position of the Princess, and with it that of the redoubtable Churchills, who were her devoted intimates and champions. From the moment that the Queen had breathed her last Marlborough's interest no longer diverged from William's. He shared William's resolve to break the power of France; he agreed with the whole character and purpose of his foreign policy. A formal reconciliation was effected between William and Anne. Marlborough remained excluded for four more years from all employment, military or civil, at the front or at home; but with his profound gift of patience and foresight upon the drift of events he now gave a steady support to William.

In 1695 the King gained his only success. He recovered Namur in the teeth of the French armies. This event enabled the war to be brought to an inconclusive end in 1696. It had lasted for over seven years. England and Holland—the Maritime Powers as they were called—and Germany had defended themselves successfully, but were weary of the struggle. Spain was bellicose but powerless, and only the Habsburg Emperor Leopold, with his eyes fixed on the ever-impending vacancy of the Spanish throne, was in earnest in keeping the anti-French confederacy in being. The Grand Alliance began to fall to pieces, and Louis, who had long felt the weight of a struggle upon so many fronts, was now disposed to peace. William was unable to resist the peace movement of both his friends and foes. He saw that the quarrel was still un-assuaged; his only wish was to prolong it. But he could not fight alone.

*   *   *   *   *

The Treaty of Ryswick marked the end of the first period in this world war. In fact it was but a truce. Yet there were possibilities that the truce might ripen into a lasting settlement. William and Louis interchanged expressions of the highest mutual regard. Europe was temporarily united against Turkish aggression. Many comforted themselves with the hope that Ryswick had brought the struggle against the exorbitant power of France to an equipoise. This prospect was ruined by the Tories and their allies. In order to achieve lasting peace it was vital that England should be strong and well armed, and thus enabled to confront Louis on equal terms. But the Tories were now in one of their moods of violent reaction from Continental intervention. Groaning under taxation, impatient of every restraint, the Commons plunged into a campaign of economy and disarmament. The moment the pressure of war was relaxed they had no idea but to cast away their arms. England came out of the war with an army of eighty-seven thousand regular soldiers. The King considered that thirty thousand men and a large additional number of officers was the least that would guarantee the public safety and interest. His Ministers did not dare to ask for more than ten thousand, and the House of Commons would only vote seven thousand. The Navy was cut down only less severely. Officers and men were cast upon the streets or drifted into outlawry in the countryside. England, having made every sacrifice and performed prodigies of strength and valour, now fell to the ground in weakness and improvidence when a very little more perseverance would have made her, if not supreme, at least secure.

The apparent confusion of politics throughout William's reign was largely due to the King's great reluctance to put himself at the disposal of either of the two main party groups. He wished for a national coalition to support a national effort against France, and he was constitutionally averse to committing himself. But as the months passed he was forced to realise the differing attitudes of Whigs and Tories to the Continental war, and a familiar pattern of English politics began to emerge. The Whigs were sensitive to the danger of the French aggression in Europe. They understood the deep nature of the struggle. In spite of their tactless and slighting treatment of William, they were prepared to form on many occasions an effective and efficient war Government. The Tories, on the other hand, resented the country being involved in Continental commitments and voiced the traditional isolationism of the people. The political story of the reign is thus a continuous see-saw. The Whigs managed two or three years of war, and then the Tories would return to power upon a rising tide of war weariness. The landed gentry, the class which largely financed the war through the land-tax, inevitably turns against a war Government and the fruits of warfare are incontinently thrown away. The foundation of the Bank of England strongly aroused the suspicions of this class. They foresaw the advent of a serious rival for political influence in the merchant classes, now enhanced by a formidable credit institution. The Bank had been a Whig creation. The Bank supported Government loans and drew profits from the war. Here was an admirable platform. In 1697 the Whig administration was driven from office upon such themes, and with such a programme Robert Harley, now the rising hope of Toryism, created his power and position in the House of Commons.

This singularly modern figure whom everyone nowadays can understand, born and bred in a Puritan family, originally a Whig and a Dissenter, speedily became a master of Parliamentary tactics and procedure. He understood, we are assured, the art of "lengthening out" the debates, of "perplexing" the issues, and of taking up and exploiting popular cries. In the process of opposing the Court he gradually transformed himself from Whig to Tory and from Dissenter to High Churchman, so that eventually he became a chief agent of the Tories both in Church and State. Already in 1698 he was becoming virtually their leader in the House of Commons. He it was who conducted the reckless movement for the reduction of the armed forces. He it was who sought to rival the Whig Bank of England with a Tory Land Bank. All the time however he dreamed of a day when he could step above Parliamentary manœuvrings and play a part upon the great world stage of war and diplomacy. Harley was supported by Sir Edward Seymour, the pre-eminent "sham good-fellow" of the age, who marshalled the powerful Tories of Cornwall and the West. In the Lords he was aided by Nottingham and the Earl of Rochester. Together these four men exploited those unworthy moods which from time to time have seized the Tory Party. They froze out and hunted into poverty the veteran soldiery and faithful Huguenot officers. They forced William to send away his Dutch Guards. They did all they could to belittle and undermine the strength of their country. In the name of peace, economy, and isolation they prepared the ground for a far more terrible renewal of the war. Their action has been largely imitated in our own times. No closer parallel exists in history than that presented by the Tory conduct in the years 1696 to 1699 with their similar conduct in the years 1932 to 1937. In each case short-sighted opinions, agreeable to the party spirit, pernicious to national interests, banished all purpose from the State and prepared a deadly resumption of the main struggle. These recurring fits of squalor in the Tory record are a sad counterpoise to the many great services they have rendered the nation in their nobler and more serviceable moods.[1]

*   *   *   *   *

William was so smitten by the wave of abject isolationism which swept the governing classes of the Island that he contemplated an abdication and return to Holland. He would abandon the odious and intractable people whose religion and institutions he had preserved and whose fame he had lifted to the head of Europe. He would retort their hatred of foreigners with a gesture of inexpressible scorn. It was a hard victory to master these emotions. Yet if we reflect on his many faults in tact, in conduct, and in fairness during the earlier days of his reign, the unwarrantable favours he had lavished on his Dutchmen, the injustices done to English commanders, his uncomprehending distaste for the people of his new realm, we cannot feel that all the blame was on one side. His present anguish paid his debts of former years. As for the English, they were only too soon to redeem their follies in blood and toil.

William's distresses led him to look again to Marlborough, with whom the future already seemed in a great measure to

[1] Written early in 1939.—W. S. C.

rest. The King's life and strength were ebbing, Anne would certainly succeed, and with the accession of Anne the virtual reign of Marlborough must begin. Marlborough patiently awaited this unfolding of events. William slowly divested himself of an animosity so keen that he had once said that had he been a private person Marlborough and he could only have settled their differences by personal combat. Another cause of mitigation can be discerned. The King had become deeply attached to a young Dutch courtier named Keppel. He had advanced him in a few years from being a page to a commanding position in the State. He had newly created him Earl of Albemarle. There was an affinity between them— honourable, but subtle and unusual. The lonely, childless monarch treated Keppel as if he were a well-beloved adopted son. Keppel was very friendly with Marlborough, and certainly played a part in his reconciliation with the King. Anne's sole surviving son, the Duke of Gloucester, was now nine years old, and it was thought fitting to provide the future heir apparent to the Crown with a governor of high consequence and with an establishment of his own. In the summer of 1698 William invited Marlborough to be governor of the boy prince. "Teach him, my lord," he said, "but to know what you are, and my nephew cannot want for accomplishments." At the same time Marlborough was restored to his rank in the Army and to the Privy Council.

The ice of a long frost once broken, the King felt the comfort in his many troubles of Marlborough's serene, practical, adaptive personality. In July 1698 Marlborough was nominated one of the nine Lords Justices to exercise the sovereign power in William's absence from the kingdom. From this time forth William seemed to turn increasingly towards the man of whose aid he had deprived himself during the most critical years of his reign. He used in peace the soldier he had neglected in war; and Marlborough, though stamped from his youth with the profession of arms, became in the closing years of the reign a leading and powerful politician. While helping the King in many ways, he was most careful to keep a hold upon the Tory Party, because he knew that in spite of its many vices it was the strongest force in England and representative of some of the deepest traits in the English character. He was sure that no effective foreign policy could be maintained without the support of the Tory Party. He had no desire to become a mere dependant upon the King's favour. The Princess Anne too was a bigoted Tory and Churchwoman. Thus in the last years of William's reign Marlborough stood at the same time well with the King and with the Tory Party who vexed the King so sorely. Above all, he supported William in his efforts to prevent an undue reduction of the Army, and in fact led the House of Lords in this direction. The untimely death in 1700 of the little Duke of Gloucester, who succumbed to the fatal, prevalent scourge of smallpox, deprived Marlborough of his office. He still remained in the closest association with Sidney Godolphin and at the very centre of the political system.

There was now no direct Protestant heir to the English and Scottish thrones. By an Act of Settlement the house of Hanover, descended from the gay and attractive daughter of James I who had briefly been Queen of Bohemia, was declared next in succession after William and Anne. The Act laid down that every sovereign in future must be a member of the Church of England. It also declared that no foreign-born monarch might wage Continental wars without the approval of Parliament; he must not go abroad without consent, and no foreigners should sit in Parliament or on the Privy Council. Thus were recorded in statute the English grievances against William III. Parliament had seen to it that the house of Hanover was to be more strictly circumscribed than he had been. But it had also gone far to secure the Protestant Succession.

The Spanish Succession

NO great war was ever entered upon with more reluctance on both sides than the War of the Spanish Succession. Europe was exhausted and disillusioned. The new-found contacts which had sprung up between William and Louis expressed the heartfelt wishes of the peoples both of the Maritime Powers and of France. But over them and all the rest of Europe hung the long-delayed, long-dreaded, ever-approaching demise of the Spanish Crown. William was deeply conscious of his weakness. He was convinced that nothing would make England fight again, and without England Holland could expect nothing short of subjugation. The King therefore cast himself upon the policy of partitioning the Spanish Empire, which included the southern Netherlands, much of Italy, and a large part of the New World. There were three claimants, whose pretensions are set out in the accompanying table.

The first was France, represented either by the Dauphin or, if the French and Spanish Crowns could not be joined, by his second son, the Duke of Anjou. The next was the Emperor, who claimed as much as he could, but was willing to transfer his claims to his second son by his second wife, the Archduke Charles. Thirdly, there was the Emperor's grandson by his first marriage, the Electoral Prince of Bavaria. The essence of the new Partition Treaty of September 24, 1698, was to give the bulk of the Spanish Empire to the candidate who, if not strongest in right, was at least weakest in power. Louis and William both promised to recognise the Electoral Prince as heir to Charles II of Spain. Important compensations were offered to the Dauphin. This plan concerted between Louis XIV and William III was vehemently resented by the Emperor. As it became known it also provoked a fierce reaction in Spain. Spanish society now showed that it cared above all things for the integrity of the Spanish domains and that the question of the prince who should reign over them all was secondary. At the end of the long struggle Spanish sentiment adopted exactly the opposite view, but at this moment its sole inspiration was an undivided Spanish Empire. However, it appeared that Louis and William would be able to override all resistances and enforce their solution.

But now a startling event occurred. The Treaty of Partition had been signed at William's palace at Loo in Holland in September 1698. In February 1699 the Electoral Prince of Bavaria, heir to prodigious domains, the child in whose chubby hands the greatest states had resolved to place the most splendid prize, suddenly died. Why and how he died at this moment did not fail to excite dark suspicions. But the fact glared grimly upon the world; all these elaborate, perilous conversations must be begun over again. By great exertions William and Louis arranged a second Treaty of Partition on June 11, 1699, by which the Archduke Charles was made heir-in-chief. To him were assigned Spain, the overseas colonies, and Belgium, on the condition that they should never be united with the Empire. The Dauphin was to have Naples and Sicily, the Milanese, and certain other Italian possessions.

Meanwhile the feeble life-candle of the childless Spanish King burned low in the socket. To the ravages of deformity and disease were added the most grievous afflictions of the mind. The royal victim believed himself to be possessed by

THE SPANISH SUCCESSION

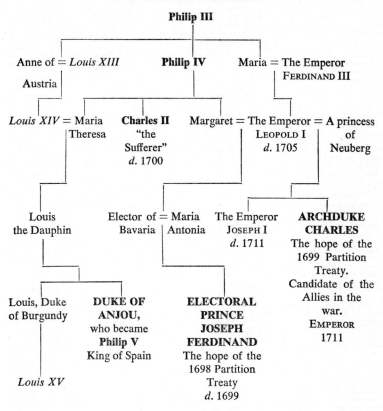

KEY

MALES

Kings of France thus: *Louis XIII*.
Emperors thus: FERDINAND III.
Kings of Spain thus: **Philip III**.
Candidates for the Spanish throne thus: **DUKE OF ANJOU.**

the Devil. His only comfort was in the morbid contemplation of the tomb. All the nations waited in suspense upon his failing pulses and deepening mania. He had however continued on the verge of death for more than thirty years, and one by one the great statesmen of Europe who had awaited this event had themselves been overtaken by the darkness of night. Charles had now reached the end of his torments. But within his diseased frame, his clouded mind, his superstitious soul, trembling on the verge of eternity, there glowed one imperial thought—the unity of the Spanish Empire. He was determined to proclaim with his last gasp that his vast dominions should pass intact and entire to one prince and to one alone. The rival interests struggled for access to his death-chamber. In the end he was persuaded to sign a will leaving his throne to the Duke of Anjou. The will was completed on October 7, and couriers galloped with the news from the Escorial to Versailles. On November 1 Charles II expired.

Louis XIV had now reached one of the great turning-points in the history of France. Should he reject the will, stand by the treaty, and join with England and Holland in enforcing it? But would England stir? On the other hand, should he repudiate the treaty, endorse the will, and defend his grandson's claims in the field against all comers? Would England oppose him? Apart from good faith and solemnly signed agreements upon which the ink was barely dry, the choice, like so many momentous choices, was nicely balanced. The Emperor had refused to subscribe to the Second Partition Treaty. Was it valid? Louis found it hard to make up his mind. A conference was held in Madame de Maintenon's room on November 8. It was decided to repudiate the treaty and stand upon the will. On November 16 a famous scene was enacted at Versailles. Louis XIV, at his levee, presented the Spanish Ambassador to the Duke of Anjou, saying, "You may salute him as your King." The Ambassador gave vent to his celebrated indiscretion, "There are no more Pyrenees."

Confronted with this event, William felt himself constrained to recognise the Duke of Anjou as Philip V of Spain. The House of Commons was still in a mood far removed from European realities. Neither party would believe that they could be forced into war against their decision—still less that their decision could change. They had just completed the disarmament of England. They eagerly accepted Louis XIV's assurance that, "content with his power, he would not seek to increase it at the expense of his grandson." A Bourbon prince would become King of Spain, but would remain wholly independent of France. Lulled by this easy promise, the Commons deemed the will of Charles II preferable to either of the Partition Treaties. It was indeed upon these superseded instruments that the Tory wrath was centred. Not only were the treaties denounced as ill-advised in themselves, and treacherous to allies, but that they should have been negotiated and signed in secret was declared a constitutional offence. The Tories even sought to impeach the Ministers responsible.

*   *   *   *   *

But now a series of ugly incidents broke from outside upon the fevered complacency of English politics. A letter from Melfort, the Jacobite Secretary of State at Saint-Germain, was discovered in the English mail-bags, disclosing a plan for the immediate French invasion of England in the Jacobite cause. William hastened to present this to Parliament as a proof of perfidy. At about the same time Parliament began to realise that the language and attitude of the French King about the separation of the Crowns of France and Spain was at the very least ambiguous. It appeared that the Spaniards had now offered to a French company the sole right of importing Negro slaves into South America. This touched English shipowners nearly, though hardly on a point of honour.

It also became apparent that the freedom of the British trade in the Mediterranean was in jeopardy. But the supreme event which roused all England to an understanding of what had actually happened in the virtual union of the Crowns of France and Spain was a tremendous military operation effected under the guise of brazen legality.

Philip V had been acclaimed in Madrid. The Spanish Netherlands rejoiced in his accession. A line of fortresses in Belgium, garrisoned under treaty rights by the Dutch, constituted the main barrier of the Netherlands against a French invasion. Louis resolved to make sure of these barrier fortresses. During the month of February 1701 strong French forces arrived before all the Belgian cities. The Spanish commanders welcomed them with open gates. They had come, it was contended, only to help protect the possessions of His Most Catholic Majesty. The Dutch garrisons, overawed by force, and no one daring to break the peace, were interned. Antwerp and Mons; Namur—King William's famous and solitary conquest—Leau, Venloo, and a dozen secondary strongholds, all passed in a few weeks, without a shot fired, by the lifting of a few cocked hats, into the hands of Louis XIV. Others, like Liége, Huy, and its neighbouring towns, fell under his control through the adhesion to France of their ruler, the Prince-Bishop of Liége. Citadels defended during all the years of general war, the loss or capture of any one of which would have been boasted as the fruits of a hard campaign, were swept away in a month. All that the Grand Alliance of 1689 had defended in the Low Countries in seven years of war melted like snow at Easter.

We have seen in our own time similar frightful losses, accepted by the English people because their mood was for the moment pacific and their interests diverted from European affairs. In 1701 the revulsion was rapid. Europe was roused, and at last England was staggered. Once more the fighting men came into their own. The armies newly dissolved, the officers so lightly dismissed and despised, became again important. Once more the drums began to beat, and smug merchants and crafty politicians turned to the martial class, whom they had lately abused and suppressed. In the early summer the Whig Party felt itself supported by the growing feeling of the nation. The freeholders of Kent presented a petition to the Commons, begging the House to grant supplies to enable the King to help his allies "before it is too late." The House committed the gentlemen who presented it to prison, an act which showed that Parliament could be as equally despotic as a king. But every day the menace from France was growing plainer. The insular structure in which England had sought to dwell cracked about her ears. In June the House of Commons authorised the King to seek allies; ten thousand men at any rate should be guaranteed to Holland. William felt the tide had set in his favour. By the middle of the year the parties in opposition to him in his two realms, the Tory majority in the House of Commons and the powerful burgesses of Amsterdam, were both begging him to do everything that he "thought needful for the preservation of the peace of Europe"—that is to say, for war.

This process united William and Marlborough. They joined forces. Nor was their partnership unequal. For while King William now saw that he could once again draw the sword of England, he felt the melancholy conviction that he himself would never more wield it. This was no time on either side for half-confidences or old grievances. Someone must carry on. In his heart the King knew there was but one man. On May 31 he proclaimed Marlborough Commander-in-Chief of the English forces assembling in Holland. In June he appointed him Ambassador Extraordinary to the United Provinces. Discretion was given him not only to frame, but, if need be, to conclude treaties without reference to

King or Parliament. Though the opportunities of the reign had been marred or missed by their quarrels and misunderstandings, the two warrior-statesmen were at last united. Though much was lost all might be retrieved. The formation of the Grand Alliance had begun.

* * * * *

It was now, in this deadly atmosphere, that the flash came which produced the British explosion. On September 16, 1701, James II died. Louis visited in state his deathbed at Saint-Germain, and announced to the shadow Court that he recognised James's son as King of England and would ever sustain his rights. He was soon astounded by the consequences of his act. All England was roused by the insult to her independence. The Act of Settlement had decreed the succession of the Crown. The Treaty of Ryswick had bound Louis, not only in formal terms, but by a gentleman's agreement, to recognise and not to molest William III as King. The domestic law of England was outraged by the arrogance and her treaty rights violated by the perfidy of the French despot. Whigs and Tories vied with one another in Parliament in resenting the affront. The whole nation became resolute for war. Marlborough's treaties, shaped and presented with much knowledge of Parliamentary susceptibilities, were acclaimed; ample supplies were tendered to the Crown. King William was able to sever diplomatic relations with France. The Emperor had already begun the war, and his famous general, Prince Eugene of Savoy, was fighting in the North of Italy.

But now William, against Marlborough's advice, made the mistake of dissolving Parliament. He could not resist the temptation of haling the Tories, so stultified by events, before the tribunal of the electorate. He hoped for an overwhelming Whig majority. But the Tories, though wrong-headed and no longer sure of themselves, nevertheless made a stout party resistance. In spite of their record they were strong enough to carry Harley back to the Speaker's chair in the new Parliament by a majority of four. They forgot their own misdeeds; they never forgave the King. He had played a party trick upon them, and the trick had failed. They longed for his death. Nevertheless they joined with the Whigs in supporting his war. In spite of the electoral changes Marlborough continued to conduct English foreign policy, and all moved forward in armaments and diplomacy towards a struggle with the might of France.

The second Grand Alliance now formed must have seemed a desperate venture to those whose minds were seared by the ill-fortune of William's seven-years war. France had gained without a shot fired all the fortresses and territory so stubbornly disputed. The widest Empire of the world was withdrawn from the Alliance and added to the resources of its antagonists. Spain had changed sides, and with Spain not only the Indies, South America, and a great part of Italy, but the cockpit of Europe—Belgium and Luxembourg. Savoy, a deserter, still rested with France, though her greatest prince was an Austrian general. The Archbishopric of Cologne was also now a French ally. Bavaria, constant to the end in the last war, was to be with France in the new struggle. The Maritime Powers had scarcely a friendly port beyond their coasts. The New World, except in the North, was barred against them. The Mediterranean had become in effect a French lake. South of Plymouth no fortified harbour lay open to British and Dutch ships. They had their superior fleets, but no bases which would carry them to the inland sea.

On land the whole Dutch barrier had passed into French hands. Instead of being the rampart of Holland, it had become the sally port of France. Louis, occupying the cities of Cologne and Treves, was master of the Meuse and of the Lower Rhine. He held all the Channel ports, and had entrenched himself from Namur through Antwerp to the sea.

His winter dispositions disclosed his intention in the spring campaign to renew the invasion of Holland along the same routes which had led almost to its subjugation in 1672. A terrible front of fortresses, bristling with cannon, crammed with troops and supplies, betokened the approaching onslaught. The Dutch sheltered behind inundations and their remaining strongholds. Finally the transference of Bavaria to the side of France laid the very heart of the Habsburg domains open to French invasion. The Hungarians were in revolt against Austrian rule and the Turks were once more afoot. In every element of strategy by sea or by land, as well as in the extent of territory and population, Louis was twice as strong at the beginning of the War of the Spanish Succession as he had been at the Peace of Ryswick. Even the Papacy had changed sides. Clement XI had abandoned the policy of Innocent XI. He espoused the cause of the Great King and his tremendous armies. Such was the prospect, as it seemed, of overwhelming adversity which had opened upon the English people largely as the result of their faction and their fickle moods.

At this moment death overtook King William. "The little gentleman in black velvet," the hero for a spell of so many enthusiastic Jacobite toasts, now intervened. On February 20, 1702, William was riding in the park round Hampton Court on Sorrel, a favourite horse. Sorrel stumbled in the new workings of a mole, and the King was thrown. The broken collarbone might well have mended, but in his failing health the accident opened the door to a troop of lurking foes. Complications set in, and after a fortnight it was evident to him and to all who saw him that death was at hand. He transacted business to the end. His interest in the world drama on which the curtain was about to rise lighted his mind as the shadows closed upon him. He grieved to quit the themes and combinations which had been the labour and the passion of his life. But he saw the approach of a reign and Government in England which would maintain the cause in which his strength had been spent. He saw the only man to whom in war or policy, in the intricate convolutions of European diplomacy, in the party turmoil of England, or amid the hazards of the battlefield, he could bequeath the awful yet inescapable task. He had made his preparations deliberately to pass his leadership to a new champion of the Protestant faith and the liberties of Europe. In his last years he had woven Marlborough into the whole texture of his combinations and policy. In his last hours he commended him to his successor as the fittest man in the realm to guide her councils and lead her armies. William died at fifty-two, worn out by his labours. Marlborough at the same age strode forward against tremendous odds upon the ten years of unbroken victory which raised the British nation to a height in the world it had never before attained.

Marlborough: Blenheim and Ramillies

THE Age of Anne is rightly regarded as the greatest manifestation of the power of England which had till then been known. The genius of Marlborough in the field and his sagacity in counsel enabled the growing strength of the nation to make its full effect on Europe. The intimate, long-developed friendships of the Cockpit circle now found their expression in the smallest and most efficient executive which has ever ruled England. Sarah managed the Queen, Marlborough managed the war, and Godolphin managed the Parliament. The Queen, for five glorious years, threw herself with happiness and confidence into these capable hands, and as in the time of Cromwell, but on a far broader, stronger foundation, the whole force of England was applied to the leadership of the then known world.

There was at that time an extraordinary wealth of capacity in the English governing class. Not only the nobility but the country gentry produced a superabundance of men of the highest qualities in mind and body. All the offices of the State, military or political, could have been filled two or three times over by able, vigorous, daring, ambitious personalities. It was also the Augustan Age of English letters. Addison, Defoe, Pope, Steele, Swift, are names which shine to-day. There was a vehement outpouring of books, poems, and pamphlets. Art and science flourished. The work of the Royal Society, founded in Charles II's reign, now bore a largesse of fruit.

Sir Isaac Newton in mathematics, physics, and astronomy completed the revolution of ideas which had begun with the Renaissance. Architecture was led to noble achievements by Wren, and to massive monuments by Vanbrugh.

All the time controversy ran to extremes. The religious passions of former years now flowed into the channels of political faction. Never was the strife of party groups so hot, so fiercely maintained, or more unscrupulous. Men and parties, conscious of their message and of the magnitude of the opportunity, strove furiously against one another for the control of the State or for a share in its governance. They carried their rivalry to all lengths; but in the earlier years of the reign there was a common purpose of beating France. This was no small undertaking, for at that time England had but five million inhabitants, while the towering French monarchy was master of near twenty millions, united under the Great King. Moreover, during the wars of King William there had been heavy cost and meagre results. Louis XIV stood triumphant, and, as it seemed, upon the threshold of unmeasured domination. He was now to be broken and humbled, and the later years of the reign of Anne were to be consumed mainly in disputes about the terms to be imposed upon him.

But all this wore a very different aspect when in March 1702 Anne ascended the throne. She presented herself to the Houses of Parliament in robes and insignia which revived memories of Queen Elizabeth. "I know my own heart," she said, "to be entirely English." She accepted Marlborough's impulse upon the whole policy of the State. In the first momentous days of her reign he was not only her chief but her sole guide. Both main parties admired him for his gifts, and for a time he stood above their warfare. It was understood in the Army that if he had the power he would pursue unswervingly the Protestant and warlike policy of King William III. The strong strain of Cromwellian and Puritan conviction which ran in the nation reinforced patriotic and national sentiments. The new reign opened in a blaze of loyalty. It was the "sunshine day" for which the Princess Anne had long waited with placid attention.

Marlborough was made Captain-General of her armies at home and abroad. He acted immediately. No sooner had the Queen met the Privy Council on March 8 than he informed the Imperial Ambassador, Wratislaw, that the Queen, like the late King, would support unswervingly the interests of the Emperor. That same night he sent a personal message of reassurance to Anton Heinsius, the Grand Pensionary or Chief Minister of Holland, offering in the name of the Queen resolute prosecution of the war and adherence to the treaties, and at the earliest moment when he could be spared he sailed for The Hague.

This was the great period of the Dutch Republic. The union of the seven provinces which had been forged in the fires of Spanish persecution and tempered by heroic war on land against France and on sea against England had now become a wonderful instrument and force in Europe. But the death of William III shook the entire structure of the Dutch oligarchy. He left no direct heir of the house of Orange whom all the United Provinces would accept as their leading Stadtholder. Who would lead their army against the gathering foes? Who would preserve the common cause of the sea-Powers? "When they had the first news of the King's death," wrote Bishop Burnet of the States-General, "they assembled together immediately; they looked to one another as men amazed; they embraced one another and promised they would stick together and adhere to the interests of their country." Hard upon the news of William's death came Marlborough's message.

Soon Marlborough was in their midst. He had already under King William negotiated the network of compacts by which the Grand Alliance had been framed. All the threads were in his hands, and there was immediately imparted to that extensive and varied body of states, great and small, and of interests often conflicting, a unity and coherence which even the royal authority of King William had not secured.

Queen Anne cherished the idea that her husband, Prince George, would become Generalissimo of the armies of the sea-Powers. There were forces in Holland which thought of a native commander for its troops. But all fell into Marlborough's hands. The office of Stadtholder and Commander-in-Chief was allowed to pass into abeyance and Marlborough was appointed Deputy Captain-General of Holland. He was thus in supreme command of the armies of the two Western Powers. Prussia, which had lately become a kingdom, and the Germanic States of the Rhine soon naturally associated themselves with this system. But although the highest title and general deference were accorded to the English General his authority could only assert itself at every stage by infinite patience and persuasiveness. He was never in a position to give indisputable orders as Napoleon was to do. He had to procure assent for almost every act from diverse and often divergent interests, and to establish his ascendancy by subtle and ever varied methods. Moreover, he was never head of the Government in London. Marlborough and the able Lord Treasurer, Godolphin, who fulfilled many of the duties of a Prime Minister, worked closely and harmoniously together. But in drawing up their plans both men had to consider the party stresses at Westminster and the powerful influence in the country of political grandees. Unquestioned authority was never granted to them; they always had to walk warily. Marlborough's reputation as a soldier was good upon the Continent, but he had never hitherto commanded a large army, and a dozen Dutch and German generals who must now work under him had seen far more service in the recent wars. The General of the

Empire, Prince Eugene, at this time carrying on his successful campaign in Italy, stood forth as the foremost soldier of the Allies.

*   *   *   *   *

For the year 1702 Louis had decided to set his strongest army against Holland. He knew the division and uncertainty into which the Republic had been thrown by the death of King William. He believed that the links which joined it to England had been at the least gravely weakened. He counted upon a period of hesitation and loss of contact which, if turned to good account by military action, might break the Dutch and scare off the English. He regarded Marlborough as a favoured Court personage, able no doubt, and busy with intrigue, but owing his influence entirely to the Queen's affection for his wife. The French High Command therefore did not hesitate to place their main army, as soon as the campaigning season began, within twenty miles of Nimwegen, at the point where the valleys of the Meuse and the Rhine divide.

In May Marlborough made for Nimwegen. He found widespread despondency among the Allied troops and jealously among the generals. But when his hand was felt upon the Army and its operations a different mood prevailed. The Dutch field-deputies, who had a veto on the movement of their troops, were induced to authorise an advance against the enemy. Although Marlborough was baulked on the heaths of Peer of the opportunity to fight what might have been a decisive battle at great advantage, the French were at once thrown on to the defensive. In a brilliant campaign the new Captain-General conquered all the fortresses of the Meuse, and thus the whole river channel was freed. The valiant but fruitless efforts of King William were replaced by the spectacle of substantial advances, and the hitherto aggressive French were seen baffled, hesitating, and in retreat. When after the storm of Liége Marlborough, narrowly escaping an ambuscade upon the Meuse, returned to The Hague he was received with intense public joy by the Dutch, and on his arrival in England he was created Duke by the Queen. In his very first year the tide of the war was set flowing in the opposite direction, and the whole Alliance, which had seemed about to collapse, was knit together by new bonds of constancy and hope.

The other English venture of 1702 was a naval expedition to Cadiz. William III had realised the importance to England of the Mediterranean and the harbours guarding its entrance. English trade with the Levant was seriously threatened by French ambition, and the French enthronement in Spain jeopardised English commercial interests. A powerful fleet and army sailed for Cadiz at the end of July under the Duke of Ormonde and Admiral Sir George Rooke. The commanders lacked the nerve to force the harbour upon the first surprise, and yielded themselves to what seemed the easier course. Troops were landed to capture the forts on the shore, and a prolonged series of desultory operations ensued, accompanied by pillage and sacrilege, tales of which spread far and wide throughout Spain. Meanwhile the defence grew continually stronger. A boom was placed across the entrance and ships were sunk in the channel by the enemy. After a month it was decided to reembark the soldiers and sail for home.

The ignominy was relieved by a lucky windfall. As Rooke and Ormonde, on the worst of terms and each blaming the other, were returning disconsolately home news was brought that the Spanish Treasure Fleet with millions from the Indies aboard had run into Vigo Bay. Excited councils of war ensued. It was decided to raid the harbour. The lure of gold and the sting of Cadiz inspired the leaders, and at last they let loose their brave men, who fought with indomitable fury. By sundown they were masters of Vigo Bay. The entire enemy fleet was sunk, burned, or captured. Not one ship escaped. The treasures of the Indies were frantically carried inland on mules before the action, but enough remained for the victors to bear home a million sterling to sustain the Treasury and appease Parliament. In spite of this a searching inquiry was ordered into the conduct of Rooke and Ormonde at Cadiz. Marlborough, who had approved the expedition, and looked upon the capture of Cadiz as a stepping-stone to the entry to the Mediterranean and the seizure of Minorca, intervened to protect the impugned commanders. Had they shown at Cadiz one-half of the spirit of Vigo Bay the sea-Powers would have been masters of the Mediterranean in 1703.

* * * * *

The beginning of Queen Anne's reign seemed to open a period of Tory prosperity. All King William's Whig Ministers were banished from power. In Godolphin's administration Rochester, the Queen's uncle, and Nottingham, King William's High Tory Minister, played substantial and grandiose parts. But from the very outset a deep division opened between Marlborough, to whom Godolphin was inseparably bound, and their Tory colleagues. The traditional Tory view was that England should not aspire to play a leading part in the Continental struggle. Her true policy was to intervene only by sea-power, and amid the conflicts of Europe to gain many territories overseas in the outer world. The Tories regarded with aversion the sending of large armies to the Continent. They looked with disparaging eyes upon victories in Europe. They groaned or affected to groan under the burden of Army expenses. They alleged that the interests which urged active intervention made great profits out of the war by subscribing to Government loans. They declared that the country gentlemen were being mulcted while the City of London, its bankers and its merchants, established an ever-growing mortgage upon the landed estates.

The Whigs, on the other hand, though banished from office,

were ardent advocates of the greatest military efforts. They supported Marlborough in all his courses. They derided the false strategy of colonial expeditions, and declared that no British interest was safe without victory in the main and decisive theatre. This clash of opinion, in which on both sides there was massive argument, governed the politics of the reign. Marlborough and Godolphin found themselves continually at variance with their other Tory colleagues upon the crucial question of how the war should be fought. If England did not join whole-heartedly in the Continental war Louis XIV would win it. The issue was radical, and much to his regret Marlborough found it necessary to use his paramount influence with the Queen against the leaders of the Tory Party.

Moreover, there was a religious complication. Queen Anne, Marlborough, and Godolphin were all Tories born and bred, and all were Anglicans. Anne had long ago abandoned the conviction that her father's son, the exiled Prince of Wales, was not her brother. The Prince lived under French protection. He is known to British history as the "Old Pretender," but more gallantly in French annals as the Chevalier of St George. Queen Anne felt herself in her inmost conscience a usurper, and she was also gnawed by the feeling that she had treated her dead father ill. Her one justification against these self-questionings was her absolute faith in the Church of England. It was her duty to guard and cherish at all costs this sacred institution, the maintenance of which was bound up with her own title and the peace of her realm. To abdicate in favour of her Papist brother would be not only to betray her religion, but to let loose the horrors of civil war upon the land she ruled, loved, and in many ways truly represented.

The Tories in the House of Commons carried on their old party warfare against Dissent. The Test Acts were still in force, but in the comradeship of the war and the loyalties of the new reign they were evaded with general acquiescence. A Puritan merchant who wished to hold office took the Sacrament on one day in the year, according to the rites of the Church of England, and thereafter kept to his Dissenting chapel. The Tories in the autumn of 1702 introduced an "Occasional Conformity Bill" with the object of disqualifying their political opponents from office by closing such means of escaping penal legislation. They declared that formal compliance was a hypocritical and blasphemous attempt to evade the law for the sake of public office, and should be stopped forthwith. The Bill, several times passed by the House of Commons, was resisted in the Lords. The Bench of Bishops, created under King William, was hostile to it. The Queen's husband, Prince George, was himself a Lutheran and was prejudicially affected. The Queen was torn between her loyalty to the Church and the wrongdoing involved in penalising loyal subjects, including her husband, who were moreover the strongest supporters of Marlborough's war policy. So powerful however was the Tory influence that Marlborough and Godolphin did not dare openly to oppose the Bill. They voted for it in public, and successfully used all their weight to compass its destruction behind the scenes.

*　　*　　*　　*　　*

For the campaign of 1703 Marlborough was able to concentrate the "Grand Army" of the Alliance around Maastricht, eighty miles south of Nimwegen, the starting-point of the previous year. He had set his heart on the capture of Ostend and of Antwerp. Ostend would give him a new communication with England; Antwerp controlled the waterways of the Scheldt, the Lys, and the canals, which, with the Meuse, formed the principal lines of advance to the French fortress zone. He deferred to Dutch opinion and began the siege of Bonn on the Rhine. When Bonn fell he made the attempt upon Antwerp, and very rapid manœuvring and hard marching followed. The "great design," as he called it, did not succeed because the Dutch were not willing to consent to the very severe offensive battle which Marlborough wished to fight. The campaign was marked by the capture of Huy on the Meuse and Limburg; and the Dutch, delighted with what they considered a year of success, struck medals with the telltale inscription "Victorious without Slaughter." But meanwhile on the Danube and the Upper Rhine the armies of the Emperor suffered constant misfortune. They were defeated in the field in Bavaria, and the loss of the famous fortified cities of Augsburg, Ratisbon, and above all Landau, gave the French control of Southern Germany and the Upper Rhine.

The Tories threw the blame of these reverses upon the Whig policy of the Continental war, and the Whigs themselves wilted under the double strain of being out of office and yet held responsible. Both at home and abroad the fortunes of the Grand Allies sank to a low ebb in the winter of 1703. Queen Anne here rose to her greatest height. "I will never forsake," she wrote to Sarah, using the private names which were current in the Cockpit circle, "your dear self, Mr Freeman [Marlborough], nor Mr Montgomery [Godolphin], but always be your constant faithful servant; and we four must never part till death mows us down with his impartial hand." With this support Marlborough during the winter months planned the supreme stroke of strategy which turned the whole fortune of the war.

But before he could proceed to the Continent it was essential to reconstitute the Government of the High Tories. Rochester was already dismissed and Nottingham was soon to go. A new figure was required to fill the void. Harley, whom we have seen so active in reducing the armed forces and opposing King William's foreign policy, had been Speaker, leader of the moderate Tories, and virtually Leader of the House of Commons. He was now invited to become a Secretary of State, and the inner circle of the Government was widened to admit him.

The combination became Marlborough, Godolphin, and Harley, with the Queen and Sarah as before. In Harley's train Henry St John, a young Member who had made himself conspicuous by his brilliant speeches in favour of the Occasional Conformity Bill and was in high favour with the Tories, became Secretary at War, a post which brought him into close contact with Marlborough. All this being arranged, and a Parliamentary majority composed of the moderate Tories and the Whigs being procured, the Duke sailed for Holland.

The Elector of Bavaria, as we have seen, had abandoned the Emperor and was now the ally of France. A French army under Marshal Marsin had been sent to his aid, and Vienna, the Emperor's capital, would evidently be exposed to mortal peril in the coming year. By subtle arts of persuasion and deceit Marlborough, with the complicity of Heinsius alone, obtained the assent of the Dutch States-General for a campaign upon the Moselle with British troops and those in British pay. Disengaging himself from the main armies left to guard Holland, he marched rapidly through Bonn to Coblenz. At this point, when friend and foe alike expected him to turn right-handed and southwards up the Moselle towards Trarbach and Treves, the first part of his true intention was revealed. The long column of redcoats passed the confluence of the rivers, crossed the Rhine upon a floating bridge, and marched day after day with extreme rapidity through Mainz and Heidelberg into the heart of Germany. Beyond the Neckar Marlborough was joined by the contingents of Prussia and other German states, and on June 11 he met the Margrave, Prince Louis of Baden, commanding the Imperial Army of the Rhine, and Prince Eugene, who, though he had no actual command, represented the supreme military control of the Empire. Here for the first time began that splendid comradeship of the Duke and Eugene which for seven years continued without jealousy or defeat.

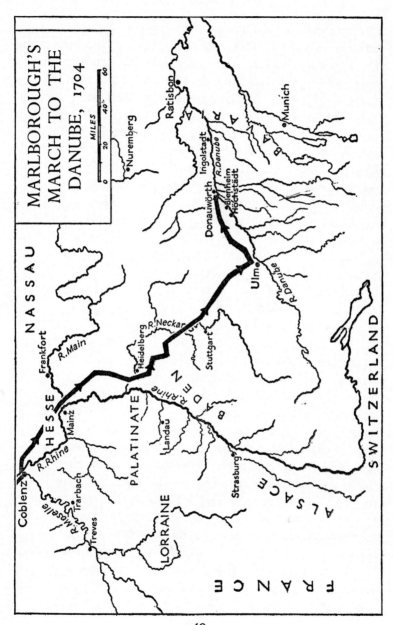

MARLBOROUGH'S MARCH TO THE DANUBE, 1704

MILES
0   20   40   60

NASSAU

HESSE

PALATINATE

LORRAINE

BADEN

ALSACE

SWITZERLAND

FRANCE

Coblenz

R.Rhine

R.Moselle

Trarbach

Treves

Mainz

Frankfort

R.Main

Heidelberg

R.Neckar

Landau

R.Rhine

Stuttgart

Strasburg

Ulm

R.Danube

Donauwörth

Blenheim

Höchstädt

Ingolstadt

R.Danube

Ratisbon

Nuremberg

Munich

The annals of the British Army contain no more heroic episode than Marlborough's march from the North Sea to the Danube. All the French plans for the campaign were held in suspense while it proceeded. As Marlborough quitted the Low Countries Marshal Villeroy moved to meet him on the Moselle. When he reached Heidelberg the French generals expected a campaign on the Upper Rhine. Only when he was already within reach of the Danube did they realise that he meant to strike at Bavaria and rescue Vienna. Marshal Tallard, with a second French army, was forthwith sent to reinforce the Elector and the French troops under Marshal Marsin. Marlborough and the Margrave, having arrived upon the Danube, in a bloody assault stormed the strong entrenchments of the Schellenberg, drove their defenders into the river, and forced an entry into Bavaria. As the Elector would not yield Marlborough delivered the country to military execution, and grievous devastation followed.

Meanwhile Eugene fell back before Tallard's superior strength and manœuvred so as to join hands with Marlborough. The two armies, French and Bavarian, now united, recrossed the Danube, and Tallard conceived himself able to force the Allies into a disastrous retreat. Marlborough persuaded the Margrave, whose counsels were obstructive, to occupy himself with the siege of Ingolstadt, and marched suddenly to join Eugene. The twin captains—"one soul in two bodies" as they were described—fell upon the French and Bavarian army at Höchstädt, on the Danube, early in the morning of August 13. The French were somewhat more numerous, and had the advantage of a far more powerful artillery and of a strong position protected by the marshy streams of the Nebel. The battle was fought with the greatest fury on both sides. Eugene commanded the right and Marlborough the left and centre. The English attack upon the village of Blindheim—or Blenheim, as it has been called in his-

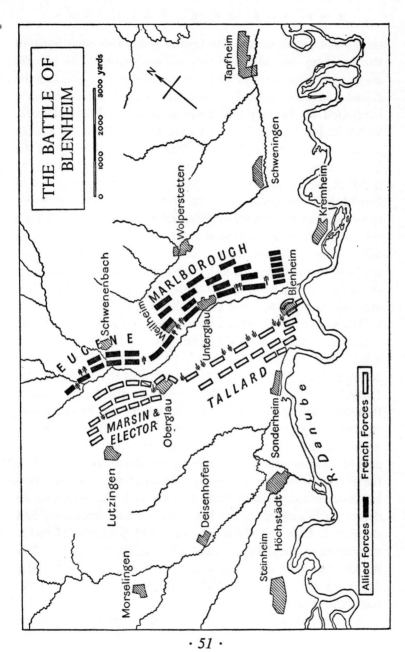

THE BATTLE OF BLENHEIM

0 1000 2000 3000 yards

Tapfheim

Schweningen

Wolperstetten

Kremheim

MARLBOROUGH

Schwenenbach

Blenheim

Weilheim

EUGENE

Unterglau

TALLARD

Oberglau

MARSIN &
ELECTOR

Sonderheim

R. Danube

Lutzingen

Deisenhofen

Morselingen

Steinheim

Höchstädt

Allied Forces ▬▬ French Forces ▭

· 51 ·

tory—was repulsed, and for several hours the issue hung in the balance; but Marlborough about half-past five in the afternoon, after a series of intricate manœuvres, crossed the Nebel and concentrated an overwhelming force of cavalry, supported by infantry and guns, against the French centre, which had gradually been denuded to withstand the attacks on either wing. At the head of eighty squadrons he broke the centre, routed the French cavalry, drove many thousands to death in the Danube, cut to pieces the remaining squares of French infantry, surrounded the great mass of French troops crowded into the village of Blenheim, and, as dusk fell on this memorable day, was able to write his famous letter to his wife: "I have not time to say more, but to beg you will give my duty to the Queen, and let her know her army has had a glorious victory. Monsieur Tallard and the two other Generals are in my coach and I am following the rest."

The victory of Blenheim almost destroyed the French and Bavarian armies on the Danube. Over forty thousand men were killed, wounded, captured, or dispersed. The remnant retreated through the Black Forest towards the Upper Rhine. One-third of both armies lay stricken on the field. Thirteen thousand unwounded prisoners, including the most famous regiments of France, passed the night of the 13th in the hands of the British infantry. Ulm surrendered after a brief siege, and Marlborough marched rapidly westward to the angle of the Rhine, where he was soon able to concentrate nearly a hundred thousand men. With Eugene and the Margrave he drove the French along the left bank towards Strasbourg and set siege to Landau, which surrendered in November. Finally, unwearied by these superb exertions, the Duke marched during October from the Rhine to the Moselle, where he closed a campaign ever a classic model of war by the capture of Trarbach and Treves.

All Europe was hushed before these prodigious events.

Louis XIV could not understand how his finest army was not merely defeated, but destroyed. From this moment he thought no more of domination, but only of an honourable exit from the war he had provoked. The whole force of the Grand Alliance was revived and consolidated. The terror of the French arms, which had weighed on Europe for a generation, was broken. Marlborough stood forth, even above his comrade, the great Eugene, as the foremost soldier of the age; and as at the same time he conducted the whole diplomacy and life of the Alliance this English General became for a while the effective head of the great league of nations united against Louis XIV. England rose with Marlborough to the summit, and the Islanders, who had never known such a triumph since Crécy and Agincourt, four centuries earlier, yielded themselves to transports of joy. The Tory Opposition, who had been scandalised at the Duke's unpardonable incursion into the midst of Europe, and who had declared their intention, should he fail, of "breaking him up like hounds upon a hare," could not entirely restrain their patriotic admiration. Queen Anne, delivered from her perils, enchanted by her glory, loaded him with wealth and honours. On New Year's Day the scores of standards and trophies of victory were borne in stately cavalcade through the streets of London to Westminster Hall. Marshal Tallard and other eminent French prisoners were distributed in honourable confinement in country houses, and for a space party spirit and even personal jealousies seemed stilled.

*　　*　　*　　*　　*

The same year had seen remarkable successes at sea. A recent treaty of alliance with Portugal made possible effective English intervention in the Mediterranean, since the harbour of Lisbon was now at the disposal of the English Navy. In May 1704 a powerful Anglo-Dutch fleet under Admiral Rooke entered the inland sea. This was the prelude to a lasting naval triumph. Reinforced by a squadron under Sir Cloudesley Shovell, Rooke turned his attention in July to the Rock of Gibraltar. This fortress was then little more than a roadstead, but the possibilities of its commanding position at the gateway of the Mediterranean were already recognised. After bombardment the Rock was taken on August 4, in the same month as Blenheim, by a combined assault, led on land by Prince George of Hesse-Darmstadt. The French and Spanish Governments were both perturbed by this eruption of a new Power into the Mediterranean. The naval balance of the war was threatened, and the whole French Fleet came out to offer battle. A long and bloody engagement, fought off Malaga, failed to give them the advantage. The French therefore decided that Gibraltar must be recovered by siege. Throughout the winter of 1704–5 the Anglo-Dutch garrison, under Darmstadt, withstood an arduous attack by heavy forces. Failure to take the Rock brought sour quarrels over strategy between France and Spain. But Gibraltar remained in English hands, and proved a sure key to maritime power.

*　　*　　*　　*　　*

In this war a curious rhythm now recurs. When the fortunes of the Allies fell all obeyed Marlborough and looked to him to find the path to safety; but when he produced, infallibly, as it seemed, a new victorious scene the bonds of fear and necessity were relaxed and he was again hampered and controlled. Just as the brilliant campaign of 1702 was succeeded by the disappointments of 1703, so the grand recovery of 1704 gave place to disunity in 1705. For this year Marlborough planned an advance up the Moselle and a march to Paris. It was for this that he had prepared the ground at the end of 1704. He arrived at The Hague in April, and took the field in May. Basing himself successively upon Coblenz, Trarbach, and Treves, he placed himself, after difficult and dangerous marches, with sixty thousand Dutch and British, opposite Saarlouis, before which Marshal Villars, with a larger army, awaited him. Marlborough had expected and minutely made ready for a concentration with the Margrave's Imperial Army and the contingents of the Princes of the Rhine. But all these forces were late at the rendezvous, and the Margrave, who had not forgiven Marlborough for leaving him out of the glories of Blenheim, showed deliberate ill-will, palliated only by serious ill-health. The Duke, unsupported, was forced to abandon his plan of fighting a decisive battle at the head of a hundred thousand men and advancing towards Paris. His position for ten days was most perilous. The difficulties of supply were formidable. "We are in a country," he wrote, "where nothing can be found, and yet should we lack bread even for one day we shall be ruined." On June 17 he extricated himself by a long night-march back to Treves, and thereafter, plunging into the wooded, mountainous region, then almost a wilderness, which lies between the Moselle and the Meuse, he reached Maastricht, and relieved Liége, upon which the French had hurled themselves.

The Dutch were overjoyed to see their Captain-General back in their home theatre. The French had constructed the famous lines of Brabant, covering the sixty miles from Antwerp to Namur, and these they now guarded with an equal army under Marshal Villeroy. Marlborough knew that he could not persuade the Dutch field deputies or their generals to contemplate a direct assault; but by a profound stratagem, which again deceived both sides, he feinted towards Namur, and then, by a long, sudden night-march, the purpose of which none but he understood, surprised the French and traversed the dreaded lines in the neighbourhood of Tirlemont without the loss of a single man. A brilliant cavalry action, in which he in person led the charge, drove back the French who were hurrying to the scene, and enabled him to establish himself amid the fortresses of Belgium. He now attempted a still more remarkable manœuvre. Filling his wagons with eight days' supplies and separating himself from his base, he marched round Villeroy's right flank, and on August 18 confronted him with superior forces on what was one day to be called the Field of Waterloo.

Like Napoleon a hundred years later, he aimed at Brussels, and also like Napoleon he sought a decisive victory over the enemy beforehand. The armies were ranged in strange posture, each facing their own country. Marlborough believed a victory was in his hands, but the Dutch generals and deputies, headed by one of Marlborough's bitter rivals, General Slangenberg, delayed and prevented the battle, and Marlborough, being nearly at the end of his wagon-borne supplies, was forced to return to his base. Thus the campaign of 1705 ended again in disappointment and recriminations between the Allies. Marlborough, who had denounced the Margrave for failing to succour him upon the Moselle, now procured the dismissal of Slangenberg from the Dutch service. But passion rose high in England, and the Tories realised that Dutch obstructiveness was a means of presenting the Continental war in an odious light. The Duke returned home to a difficult situation. The triumph of Blenheim seemed overclouded. Once again the fortunes of the Grand Alliance declined, and the central power of the French monarchy regathered its giant strength.

Wearied with the difficulties of co-operating with the Dutch and with the Princes of the Rhine, Marlborough planned through the winter an even more daring repetition of his march to the Danube in 1704. He had succeeded in procuring from the King of Prussia, with whom he had immense personal influence, a strong Prussian force to aid Prince Eugene in Northern Italy. He now schemed to march across Europe with about twenty-five thousand British and British-paid troops by Coblenz, Stuttgart, and Ulm, through the passes of the Alps, to join Eugene in Northern Italy. There amid the vineyards and the olive trees the two great captains would gain another Blenheim and strike into France from the south. The States-General showed much more imagination and confidence than they had done in 1704. Their terms were simple. If Marlborough went he must take no Dutch troops. The Queen and the English Cabinet gave full approval, and on this basis he perfected his plans, even ordering six hand-mills for every British battalion for grinding corn in this novel theatre.

But the earliest events of the campaign of 1706 destroyed the Italian project. The French forestalled the Allies in the field both on the Rhine and in Italy. At Calcinato Marshal Vendôme inflicted a severe minor defeat on the Imperial forces. In Germany Villars fell upon the Margrave and chased him over the Rhine. The key fortress of Landau was threat-ened. Marlborough's hopes were dashed. It was with melan-choly thoughts that he began his most brilliant campaign. "I cross the sea," he wrote to the Imperial Envoy, "with suffi-ciently sad reflections." "The little concern of the King of Denmark and almost all the other princes give me so dismal thoughts that I almost despair of success," he wrote to Go-dolphin. Not without pangs but certainly without the slightest hesitation he now divested himself of the troops which would have secured him a large superiority in the Low Countries and the chance of some deed "that would make a noise" and sent all possible reinforcements to Eugene. He deliberately re-signed himself to "a whole campaign" with indecisive forces among the fortresses of Brabant, at a time when personal suc-cess seemed most necessary to his position in England. But now Fortune, whom Marlborough had so ruefully but sternly dismissed, returned importunate, bearing her most dazzling gift.

Louis XIV had convinced himself, after the forcing of the

lines of Brabant and Marlborough's threat to Brussels, that a defensive war could not be maintained against such an opponent. In robust mood he authorised Marshal Villeroy to seek a battle at the beginning of the campaign, and furnished him with the best-equipped army of France, all clothed in new uniforms and in perfect order. On May 18 Marlborough's Intelligence Service reported heavy French assemblings on the left bank of the Dyle between Wavre and Louvain, and on the 19th news arrived that the French army had crossed the Dyle and advanced to within four miles of Tirlemont. The whole region was familiar to both sides, and had long been regarded as a possible ground of great battle. It was one of the most thoroughly comprehended terrains in Europe. Marlborough, summoning the Danish horse, who had hitherto been held back because they had not been paid, marched to meet Villeroy.

At dawn on May 23 the two armies were in presence near the village of Ramillies. Marlborough, having deployed, about noon began a heavy but feigned attack upon the French right with the British troops. Availing himself of the undulations of the ground, he hurled the whole mass of the Dutch, British, and Danish cavalry, over 25,000 strong, upon the French horse between the villages of Taviers and Ramillies. Here stood the finest cavalry of France, including the famous Household troops. Casting aside his veil of secrecy and manœuvre, Marlborough exclaimed, "I have five horses to two." Actually he had first four to three and finally five to three. But it was enough. After furious fighting, in which forty thousand horsemen were engaged, he broke the French line, drove their right from the field, and compromised their centre. Forgetting his duty as Commander-in-Chief, he charged into the cavalry battle, sword in hand. He was unhorsed and ridden over by the enemy. His equerry, Colonel Bingfield, while helping him to mount a second charger, had his head

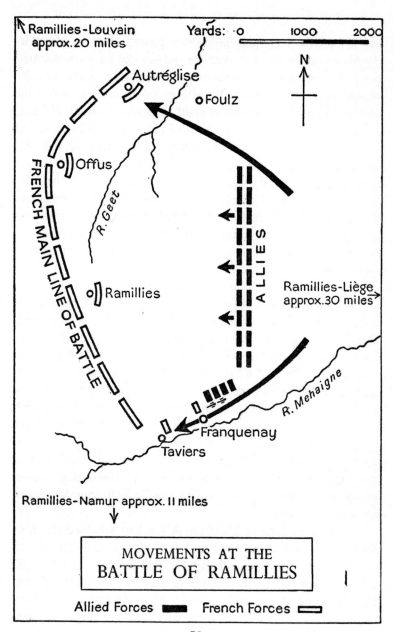

Ramillies–Louvain
approx. 20 miles

Yards: 0   1000   2000

N

Autréglise

o Foulz

o Offus

R. Geet

FRENCH MAIN LINE OF BATTLE

o Ramillies

A L L I E S

Ramillies–Liège
approx. 30 miles

R. Mehaigne

Franquenay

Taviers

Ramillies–Namur approx. 11 miles

MOVEMENTS AT THE
BATTLE OF RAMILLIES

Allied Forces ████   French Forces ▭

carried off by a cannon-ball which passed close to Marlborough's leg as he threw it over the saddle. But he soon resumed his full control of the tremendous event. His main infantry attack now broke upon the village of Ramillies, while his victorious cavalry, forming at right angles to the original front, swept along the whole rear of the French line. All the Allied troops now advanced, and the French army fled from the field in utter ruin. In this masterpiece of war, fought between armies almost exactly equal in strength and quality, the military genius of the English General, with a loss of less than five thousand men, destroyed and defeated his opponents with great slaughter and thousands of captives. Night shielded the fugitives, but less than a quarter escaped, and all their cannon were abandoned on the field.

*   *   *   *   *

The consequences of Ramillies were even more spectacular than those which had followed Blenheim. If, as was said, Blenheim had saved Vienna, Ramillies conquered Belgium. Fortresses, the capture of any one of which would have rewarded the efforts of a long campaign, fell by the dozen. Antwerp and Brussels surrendered, and the astonished Dutch saw themselves again possessors of almost the whole barrier which had been lost in the last year of King William's reign. These immense successes were enhanced by the victories of Prince Eugene in Northern Italy. Marching across the broad base of the Peninsula, he relieved Turin in a wonderful action against heavy odds, and thereafter drove the French completely out of Northern Italy.

At the same time in Spain the Allies had achieved much to their credit and come near to a striking success. The Archduke Charles, their candidate for the Spanish throne, had taken up his residence in Lisbon. It was part of the Allied plan to prosecute his claims with vigour. At first he had been supported only by a small force of about five thousand Brit-

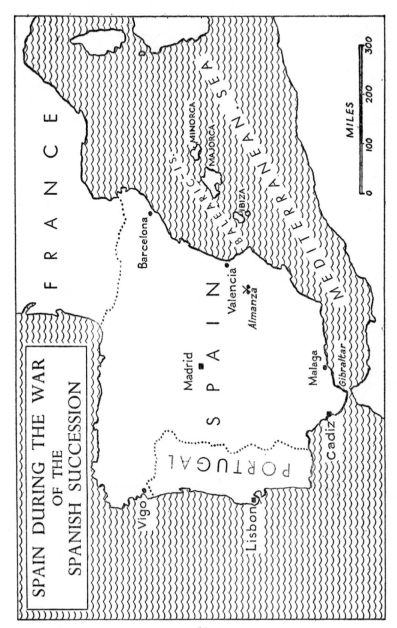

SPAIN DURING THE WAR
OF THE
SPANISH SUCCESSION

FRANCE

Barcelona

BALEARIC IS.
MINORCA
MAJORCA
IBIZA

VALENCIAN.

MEDITERRANEAN SEA

MILES
0   100   200   300

SPAIN

Madrid

Valencia
Almanza

Malaga
Gibraltar

Cadiz

PORTUGAL

Vigo

Lisbon

· 61 ·

ish and Dutch under the Earl of Galway, a Huguenot who had won a respectable reputation as a commander in King William's wars. Galway was assisted by a Portuguese army two or three times the size of his own. With these resources he could do little but make menacing gestures along the Spanish frontier. In 1705 the Allies determined on a greater effort. The Earl of Peterborough was dispatched from England with over six thousand troops and a considerable fleet under the command of Admiral Shovell. They were to pick up reinforcements at Lisbon, embark the Archduke, and sally into the Mediterranean.

There was much dispute among the commanders about their objective. Eventually however they decided upon Barcelona. Here was the populous capital of Catalonia, long restive under rule from Madrid and deeply estranged from the French-born king, Philip V. A landing was made north of the city in August and the Allies prepared to lay siege. The chief obstacle was the hill of Montjuich, which lay to the south, towering to nearly six hundred feet straight out of the sea and crowned by a bristling fortress. Peterborough was a man of mercurial mind in which daring and contentiousness vied with one another. After a period of squabbling, such as was to distract all Allied operations in Spain, Peterborough suddenly by a bold night march assaulted Montjuich. It fell to his attack the next day after a confused *mêlée* in which Darmstadt, defender of Gibraltar, was killed. Barcelona now surrendered to the Archduke. All Catalonia, Aragon, and Valencia rose in the Allied cause and proclaimed their allegiance to "King Charles III." The eastern provinces of Spain were solidly his, and there was widespread rejoicing in London.

In the spring of 1706, while Marlborough was manœuvring towards Ramillies, the Allies in Barcelona successfully withstood a siege by an imposing French army. Harried by the Catalan guerrilla, the French were uncertain of their communications. Though they in turn captured Montjuich after prolonged assault, they could not force the city. At a critical moment for the defenders providential succour arrived from an English fleet. The French gave up and retired north to the Pyrenees. Now was the time for the Allies to take advantage of French disarray and make for Madrid. Galway, already on the advance from Portugal, reached the Spanish capital in June. The "Year of Victory," as it was called in London, may close on this.

Oudenarde and Malplaquet

FOR the Dutch the fullness of success was at this time a deterrent upon further necessary efforts. Far gone were the days of 1702, when their army crouched under the ramparts of Nimwegen, and when their new English commander had invited them to take the offensive, sword in hand. The Meuse was clear to the gates of Namur. The whole course of the Rhine and all its strongholds were in Allied hands. Brussels had fallen. Antwerp, the greatest prize of all, had surrendered without a siege. Bruges, Ghent, Oudenarde, and Ostend were within their grasp, and Nieuport, Ypres, Menin, and Ath might well be gained. Behind these bristled the fortresses of the French frontier. But were these trophies essential to the preservation of the Republic? The Dutch wanted to humble the power of France. Surely it was humbled already. Were not the Great King's envoys busy enough through half a dozen channels with proposals for a separate peace, based without question upon a good barrier for Holland? If Marlborough had merely won the Battle of Ramillies, taken Louvain, and perhaps entered Brussels, the campaign of 1706 might have carried the Allied cause to victory in 1707. But he now began to experience a whole series of new resistances and withholdings by the Dutch, as well as their grabbings and graspings, all of which were destined to bring the fortunes of the Allies once again to the lowest ebb.

These Batavian reactions had their counterpart at home.

While in the field Marlborough and Eugene carried all before them, a series of English party and personal rivalries prepared a general reversal of fortune. The Whigs, who were the main prop of the war, and upon whose votes the Queen's Government depended, demanded a share of public office. They chose the Earl of Sunderland, the son of James II's erratic Minister, an orthodox, opinionated man of high ability, as the thin end of the wedge by which they would force their way into the controlling circle of the Government. According to modern ideas their majority in both Houses of Parliament gave them the right, and even at this time it gave them the power, to acquire predominance in public affairs. But Sunderland had married Marlborough's daughter. "Therefore," reasoned the chief of the Whigs, "he could not take their move as an attack upon himself." But they let Godolphin know that if he could not make the Queen accept Sunderland they would use their power in Parliament both against the Government and personally against him. Marlborough and Godolphin, confronted with the vital need of obtaining from the House of Commons supplies to carry on the war, pressed the inclusion of Sunderland upon the Queen. She resisted tenaciously. It took the Battle of Ramillies to persuade her.

Britain's military prowess and the sense of the Island being at the head of mighty Europe now bore more lasting fruit. The Union with Scotland was approaching its closing stage. It had been debated, sometimes acrimoniously, ever since the Queen's accession. At last England was prepared to show some financial generosity to the Scots, and they in turn were willing to accept the Hanoverian succession. Marlborough, who was one of the Commissioners concerned, regarded the measure as vital to the strength of the realm. Not only the two nations but their Parliaments were jointed together. If Scotland on the death of Queen Anne were to choose a different dynasty from England, all the old enmities of the Middle Ages might revive. Both sides judged it well worth some sacrifices to avoid such a breach between the two kingdoms. The Act of Union was finally passed in 1707, and in spite of some friction was generally accepted. Gradually the Scots came to benefit from the free trade with England and her colonies which was now open to them. Slowly the English accustomed themselves to the Scots playing an important part in their own politics and commerce. The union has grown in strength the longer it has lasted. In the later eighteenth century Scottish thought and letters blossomed in the figures of the philosopher David Hume, Adam Smith, the economist, and William Robertson, the historian. Robert Burns and the great Sir Walter Scott were soon to follow. This fertile growth was undoubtedly helped by the peace, prosperity, and sense of participation bestowed by the Union, all of which still endure.

*   *   *   *   *

About this time Sarah's relations with the Queen entered on a perilous phase. She had to bear the brunt of her mistress's repugnance to a Whig infusion in the Cabinet. Anne loathed the Whigs from the bottom of her heart, but her Ministers could not see how it was possible to carry on the war without the Whigs and with only half the Tory Party at their back. Sarah wore out her friendship with the Queen in her duty of urging upon her an administration in harmony with Parliament. At the same time an interloper appeared. As Sarah grew older, and as all the affairs of a great lady with much more than the power of a Cabinet Minister pressed upon her, she sought some relief from the constant strain of personal attendance upon the Queen, which had been her life for so many years. Anne's feminine friendships were exacting. She wanted her companion to be with her all day long and playing cards far into the night. Gradually Sarah sought to lighten the burden of this perpetual intercourse. In a poor relation, Abigail Hill, she found an understudy. She brought her into the

Queen's life as a "dresser" or lady's maid. The Queen, after a while, took kindly to her new attendant. Sarah experienced relief, went more to the country and lived her family life. Abigail, by the beginning of 1707, had acquired an influence of her own with the Queen destined to deflect the course of European history.

Abigail was a cousin of Sunderland's. She was at the same time a cousin of Harley's. Harley was much disconcerted by the arrival of the Whig Sunderland in the Cabinet. He saw with the eye of a skilled politician that it was the prelude to a much larger Whig incursion. He felt embarrassed in his position as leader of the moderate Tories.

One day a gardener handed him a secret letter from the Queen. She appealed for his help. No greater temptation could have been cast before an eighteenth-century statesman. Moreover, it harmonised with Harley's deep political calculations and his innate love of mystery and subterranean intrigue. Forthwith he set himself to plan an alternative Government based on the favour of the Queen, comprising Tories and moderate Whigs and sheltered by the renown and, he hoped, the services of Marlborough. This plan implied the ruin of Godolphin. Harley imagined that this would be no obstacle; but Marlborough when he became conscious of what was afoot would tolerate no severance between himself and his faithful colleague and friend. Thus Harley's intrigue became of necessity hostile to Marlborough. At the time Sarah's influence with the Queen had plainly suffered a final eclipse.

Everything went wrong in 1707. Marlborough's design was that Eugene, aided by the Prussian contingent and all the reinforcements he could send him, should debouch from Italy into France and capture Toulon. From this sure naval base the Duke purposed not only to gain the command of the Mediterranean but to invade France in great strength in the following year. He used all his power, then at its height, to further this far-reaching plan, and after innumerable objections and divergences an Imperial army under Eugene marched along the Riviera to attack Toulon. Meanwhile Marlborough faced and held the superior forces of Marshal Vendôme in the main theatre of the Low Countries. He relegated himself to a holding campaign in the North in order that his comrade might strike the decisive blow in the South. He so far denuded himself that he was not strong enough to undertake any important siege. He watched vigilantly for the change of a battle, even at a disparity in odds. But Vendôme was far too clever to give him this satisfaction. The great armies glared upon each other at close quarters for weeks at a time. Then followed swift and most critical marches; but Vendôme always managed to avoid battle except on terms of a direct assault, which Marlborough was not strong enough to make. The campaign in the north thus reduced itself to stalemate.

Great misfortunes happened in Spain. The formidable Marshal Berwick had been sent to the Peninsula by Louis XIV to rally King Philip's hopes. Berwick was steadily in receipt of fresh fighting strength from France. By the early autumn of 1706 the Earl of Galway in Central Spain with fifteen thousand men had found himself seriously outnumbered. His reception in Madrid had been cool, and he waited anxiously to be joined by the Archduke from Barcelona and Peterborough from Valencia. Weeks went by before they moved, and when they did it was with a paltry reinforcement. Castile and the other central and northern provinces had shown little desire to welcome the Austrian Archduke in place of King Philip V, who had now been in their midst for five years. Their indifference could not be forcibly overcome by the modest army at the disposal of the Allies. Galway, Peterborough, and the Archduke had to retreat towards the Mediterranean shore. The year had closed with King Philip once more propped up in Madrid, but with the Allies firmly in possession of the eastern quarter of Spain. Now in 1707 the Allied generals fatally divided their forces. They advanced with only a part of them in the direction of Madrid. They were met and engaged in battle at Almanza by a greatly superior Franco-Spanish army under the Duke of Berwick. The French commander was a Catholic Englishman, the British commander a Protestant Frenchman. In such curious ways did loyalties divide. A bloody defeat was sustained by the Allies, and the whole Spanish scene, so nearly triumphant in 1706, was now completely reversed. On the Rhine the Margrave was surprised by Marshal Villars in the celebrated Lines of Stollhofen, and all these tremendous works, which constituted the effective defence of Germany, fell in a night into the hands of the enemy. The invasion and pillage of large parts of Germany followed.

The great enterprise against Toulon, to which Marlborough had subordinated all other interests, also ended in failure. This was the only occasion in the long wars when Eugene does not seem to have maintained his high standard, and the Duke of Savoy, who nominally commanded the Army, was even less enterprising. Eugene was a land animal. He never liked a plan which depended so much upon the sea. A magnificent English armada met him on the coast. Admiral Shovell was deeply imbued with Marlborough's strategies. He helped and fed Eugene's army along the coast, turning the flank of the enemy's successive positions with the fire of the Fleet. Arrived before Toulon, he landed thousands of sailors and marines and hundreds of cannon. All the time he assured the illustrious Prince that if his communications were cut the Fleet would embark and carry all his men wherever he wanted.

The French concentrated powerful forces not only to defend but to relieve Toulon. After several costly assaults the siege failed. The Imperial army retreated upon Italy. The British Fleet, after bombarding and largely destroying the harbour of Toulon and sinking the French warships which were clustered there, sailed for home or for winter harbours. One final disaster remained. Sir Cloudesley Shovel, making the winter passage home, was wrecked in thick and violent weather upon the sharp rocks of the Scillies. Two great ships and a frigate were dashed to pieces, fifteen hundred sailors were drowned, and, worst of all, Britain's finest admiral, Marlborough's trusted naval leader, perished on the shore.

* * * * *

Marlborough returned from these tribulations to a furious party storm in England. Harley's designs were now apparent, and his strength nourished itself upon the military misfortunes. Marlborough and Godolphin together resolved to drive him from the Cabinet. An intense political crisis supervened. At this time Harley was weakened by the fact that a clerk in his office named Greg had been caught betraying the most secret dispatches into the hands of the French Government. Harley had certainly been negligent in the management of his high correspondence, and the Whigs, in their natural wrath at being excluded from rightful power, made every effort to convict him of treason. Greg however, while confessing his own guilt, died at Tyburn avowing the innocence of his chief. It was alleged he could have saved his life by incriminating him.

Upon all this Marlborough demanded Harley's dismissal from his Secretaryship of State. Anne, now completely estranged from Sarah and with Abigail at her elbow, fought a stubborn fight for her favourite Minister. When Marlborough refused to sit another day in Cabinet with Harley and tendered his resignation the Queen answered that "he might as well draw his dagger and stab her then and there as do such a thing." But a true Stuart and daughter of James II would not let Harley go. Marlborough returned to his home at St Albans. When the Cabinet met and Harley rose to read some paper one of the Ministers roughly asked the Queen how they would do business in the absence of the General and the Treasurer. Harley was unconcerned. The Queen, nearly suffocating with emotion, left the room, and the Cabinet broke up in confusion. The news spread far and wide that Marlborough and Godolphin had been dismissed. Both Houses of Parliament decided to conduct no business until they were better informed. The City was in consternation. Anne's husband, the Prince George, perturbed by what he heard and saw of the public mood, and strengthened by what he felt himself, implored his wife to bow to the storm. Even then it was Harley and not the Queen who gave way. He advised the Queen to accept his resignation. She wept, and he departed. With him went Henry St John, whom Marlborough had regarded almost as an adopted son.

This struggle gave Marlborough a final lease of power. He had to a large extent lost the Queen. He had lost the moderate Tories. He must now increasingly throw himself into the hands of the Whigs, and at every stage of this process make wider the breach with the Queen. It was on these perilous foundations that he embarked upon the campaign of 1708. The plan was in principle a renewal of the double invasion of the previous year. This time however the effort was to be in the north, and the Duke of Savoy, entering France from the south, was to play the minor but none the less essential part. Marlborough had hoped to bring Eugene's Rhine army into the Low Countries and by superior numbers to crush the French in the field and pierce the fortress barrier; but a succession of unexpected misfortunes occurred. Conditions on the Rhine compelled Eugene to leave his army behind him. The Dutch rule of the conquered Belgian cities had estranged their inhabitants. By treachery Ghent and Bruges, which together controlled the chief waterways of the Scheldt and the Lys, were delivered to the French. Marshal Vendôme, with whom were the Princes of the Blood, the Dukes of Burgundy and Berri, and the Pretender, the young Prince of Wales, commanded a field army which, after providing for all the garrisons, numbered about eighty thousand men.

For the only time in the Duke's career he bent and bowed under the convergent strains at home and in the field. Eugene, arriving with only a cavalry escort, found him near Brussels in the deepest depression. He was prostrated by fever and so ill that he had to be bled. For a few hours he seemed unable to recover from the strategic injury of the loss of the fruits of Ramillies, the Ghent and Bruges waterways which were the railways of those times. Here Eugene sustained his comrade. Marlborough rose from his sick-bed, mounted his horse, and the Army was set in motion. By a tremendous march they reached Lessines, on the Dyle. At dawn on July 11 they set out towards the fortress and bridgehead of Oudenarde, on the Scheldt, which Vendôme intended to seize. The French had not contemplated the possibility of a battle, and their great army was crossing the river in a leisurely manner at Gavre. By half-past ten General Cadogan, with the English vanguard, had reached the high ground north of Oudenarde. Including the bridges of the fortress, nine bridges in all were prepared. Behind Cadogan the whole Army, eighty thousand strong, came on in a state of extraordinary wrath and enthusiasm. Goslinga, the Dutch deputy, records, "It was not a march, but a run." The soldiers hurled all the officers' baggage-wagons from the road in their eagerness to engage. The Army had marched fifty miles in sixty-five hours before they reached the bridges of the Scheldt. Cadogan meanwhile crossed and attacked the French detachments and flank guards.

Vendôme could not at first believe that the Allies were upon the scene in force. He rode out to see for himself, and was drawn into action by degrees. As the Allies poured across the Scheldt the French army wheeled to their left to face them.

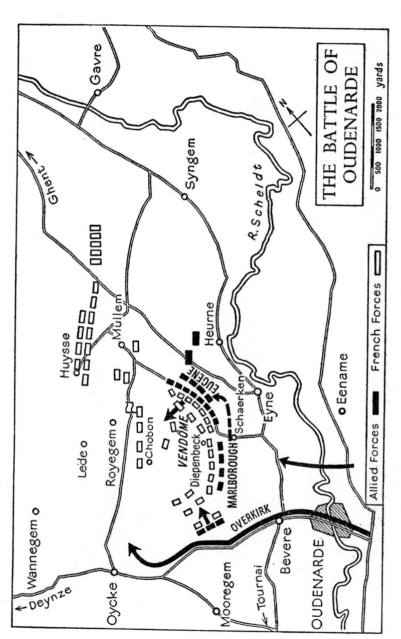

THE BATTLE OF OUDENARDE

0 500 1000 1500 2000 yards

Allied Forces ▬▬ French Forces ▭

Gavre

Syngem

R. Scheldt

Ghent

Mullem

Huysse

Heurne

Lede o

Royegem o

Chobon o

VENDÔME

EUGENE

Diepenbeck

Schaerken

Eyne

o Eename

Wannegem o

MARLBOROUGH

OVERKIRK

Oycke

Mooregem o

Bevere

Deynze

Tournai

OUDENARDE

The Battle of Oudenarde was in every aspect modern. It more nearly resembled Tannenberg in 1914 than any great action of the eighteenth century. Marlborough, giving Eugene command of the right wing, held the centre at heavy odds himself while the rest of the Army was prolonging its line to the left. This long left arm reached out continually, and the battle front flared and flamed as it grew. The operation of crossing the river corps by corps in the face of an army equal in strength was judged most hazardous by the military opinion of that age of strife. The pace of the battle and its changes prevented all set arrangement. The French fought desperately but without any concerted plan, and a large part of their army was never engaged. The shadows of evening had fallen upon a battlefield of hedges, enclosures, villages, woods, and watercourses, in which the troops were locked in close, fierce fighting, when the Dutch, under the veteran Overkirk, at length traversed the Oudenarde bridges and swung round upon the heights to the north. At the same time Eugene, with magnificent courage, broke through on the right. The opposite wings of the Allies almost met. The French army was now utterly confused and divided into two parts. More than forty thousand men were virtually surrounded by the Allies; the other forty thousand stood baffled on the ridge above the battle. It was pitch-dark when the fighting stopped. So intermingled were the combatants that orders were given to the Allies to cease firing and lie upon their arms. But the weapons of those days did not enable an encircling net to be thrown round field troops on such a scale. Most of the surrounded French escaped during the night. In furious anger and consternation Vendôme ordered a retreat on Ghent. A quarter of his army was destroyed or dispersed. Seven thousand prisoners, many high officers, and a wealth of standards and trophies were in Marlborough's hands when on the morning of July 12 he and his great companion rode their horses into the fine old square of Oudenarde.

This great victory altered the posture of the war. The Allies had recovered the initiative. Marlborough wished to march forward into France, leaving the great fortress of Lille behind him. He had already prepared in the Isle of Wight a force of seven thousand men with transports wherewith to seize Abbeville and establish a new base there behind the French barrier, from which he could march directly upon Paris. But he could not persuade Eugene. The "old Prince," as he was called, though younger than Marlborough, felt it too dangerous to leave Lille behind him, and was over-distrustful of operations dependent upon the sea. It was resolved to attack Lille, the strongest fortress of France.

The siege of Lille was not only the largest but the most complicated operation of its kind known to the eighteenth century. In many ways it is unique in military annals. Marshal Boufflers with fifteen thousand men defended the city. Eugene conducted the siege, and Marlborough with the covering army held off the largely superior forces which, both from the neighbourhood of Ghent and from France itself, sought to relieve the city or sever the communications of the besiegers. Sixteen thousand horses drew Marlborough's siege trains from Brussels to the trenches. The bringing in of these great convoys involved the movement of the whole covering army. The heavy batteries played upon the town, and a succession of bloody assaults was delivered week after week upon the breaches. At length the French cut the Allied communications with Holland. But Marlborough had meanwhile created a new line to Ostend, feeding himself from the sea. The French at Dunkirk opened the sluices; the inundations covered the coastal region, and an aquatic war developed in which the passage of every cannon-ball and sack of powder or of corn was disputed. From ship to boat, from boat to high-wheeled wagon, from these to the ordinary vehicles, the supplies of the siege were steadily conveyed.

Vendôme and the French princes, marching round to the

south side of Lille, joined an army under Berwick, who had been transferred from Spain to the Belgian front. Marlborough, keeping pace on interior lines, confronted them. Eugene joined him with every man that could be spared from the siege. The French advanced in battle array and superior force, and at the same moment Marshal Boufflers made a furious sortie upon the weakened lines. So convinced was Marlborough of the necessity of a battle that he would not allow his own front to be fortified for several days. But the position selected was already too strong by nature for the French to make the attempt. They remained the mortified spectators of the impending fall of the city.

A brilliant action pierced the gloom of the autumn months. The long line of English communications stretching to Ostend was threatened by a powerful thrust of over twenty thousand French troops. The Allied convoys moving southwards upon Lille were in peril. General Webb, a Jacobite Tory and a competent soldier, was dispatched by Marlborough to meet the danger with an inferior force. A frontal attack upon Webb's position in the woods hard by the Château of Wynendael failed with heavy loss through the magnificent fire discipline of the English soldiers. It was this action that sealed the fate of the city of Lille, which capitulated in October. To cover this loss Vendôme and Berwick attacked Brussels while the citadel of Lille still held out. But Marlborough and Eugene, marching north-east, forced the fortified line of the Scheldt and relieved the capital of Belgium. The citadel of Lille fell in December. Marlborough would not rest while Ghent and Bruges remained in hostile hands. Aided by the beginning of a memorable frost, he dragged his cannon to the assault of both these places. Bruges was recaptured at the end of December, and Ghent in the first days of January. Thus ended a campaign of struggle and hazard of which Prince Eugene said, "He who has not seen this has seen nothing."

At the same time the capture of Minorca, with its fine

harbour at Mahon, gave to the English Navy at last a secure, permanent base in the Mediterranean. Thus the year which had opened in such dismal fashion ended in complete victory for the Allies. Louis XIV made far-reaching offers of peace to the Dutch, and Marlborough himself entered into secret negotiations with his nephew Berwick for the same purpose. The war was now decisively won. The power of France was broken. The Great King was humbled. A terrible frost laid its grip upon tortured Europe. The seed froze in the ground; the cattle died in the fields, and the rabbits in their burrows. The misery of the French people reached the limit of endurance. All sought peace, and all failed to find it.

*   *   *   *   *

Meanwhile in England the Whigs had at last achieved their long purpose. They had compelled Marlborough and Godolphin to rest wholly upon them. They overbore the Queen. They drove the remaining Tories from the Cabinet, and installed a single-party administration, above which still sat the two super-Ministers, Marlborough and Godolphin. Hitherto, for all the differences upon methods, the war had had a common purpose. It was now a party policy. The Whigs, ardent, efficient masters of the Parliamentary arts, arrived in power at the very moment when their energy and war spirit were least needed. Marlborough and Godolphin, estranged from the Queen, must now conform to the decisions of a Whig Cabinet, while the Tories, sullen and revengeful in their plight, looked forward to their former leaders' downfall. Harley, by his gifts and his craft, by his injuries and his eminence, became their natural leader. To him rallied the elder statesmen, Rochester and Nottingham. Strong in the favour of the Queen, maintained up the backstairs by Abigail, Harley reached out to Shrewsbury, now back in English politics after a long retirement, and ready to play an ambitious and powerful middle part.

Marlborough's reign was ended. Henceforward he had but

to serve. His paramount position in Europe and with the armies made him indispensable to either party as long as the war continued. First he served the Whigs and afterwards the Tories. He served the Whigs as plenipotentiary and General, and later he served the Tories as General only. His great period, from 1702 to 1708, was over. There still remained three difficult campaigns, upon a scale larger than any yet seen; but he no longer had control of the policy which alone could render fruitful the sombre struggles of the Army.

When we look upon the long years of terror and spoliation to which the princes of the Grand Alliance had been subjected by Louis XIV great allowances must be made for their suspicions in the hour of victory. Nevertheless the offers now made by France were so ample as to satisfy all reasonable demands of the Allies. The Dutch barrier was settled; the claims of the Duke of Savoy were met. The German princes were reassured upon the Rhine. There remained only the question of Spain. After all, the war had been fought about the Spanish Succession, and none of the victories of Marlborough and Eugene had settled that issue. In Spain alone did French fortunes prosper. But the Spanish quarrel had developed an independent life of its own. The Spanish people from high to low had accepted the claims and espoused the cause of the Duke of Anjou. In the fierceness of the struggle they had abandoned their hopes of preserving the Spanish inheritance in its integrity. They now set their hearts only upon having a king of their own choice. All questions at issue between the Allies and Louis XIV were settled. But what was to happen in Spain? Philip V declared he would rather die than abandon the Spanish people who had rallied to his aid. He appeared ready even to defy the head of his house, the great monarch himself.

We cannot plumb the family and political relations at this juncture between Louis XIV and Philip; but there was substance in the argument of the Allies that they should not make peace with a France which they deemed at their mercy and let her recover her strength, while all the time they would have to continue a separate war in Spain. Moreover, the Dutch made it clear that they would not in any case fight in Spain. They had their barrier and all they wanted. The Whigs in England, on the contrary, were determined to drive Philip from Spain. They had committed themselves to the extravagant formula "No peace without Spain." Torcy, the French Foreign Minister and son of the great Colbert, asked what it was the Allies expected his master to do. Louis was willing to dissociate himself entirely from Philip, to withdraw all French troops from the Peninsula, even to yield important French fortresses as a guarantee. The Allied negotiators believed that he had only to give the order and Philip would abdicate. But this is by no means certain. The one thing Louis would not do was to use French troops to drive his grandson out of the kingdom he had made his own. And this was the fatal rock upon which the whole peace conference was wrecked.

Marlborough, carefully watched by the Whigs, saw the danger ahead. He thought it would be better to make peace with France, accept the proffered fortresses as hostages for its execution, and settle the war in Spain separately. He had a plan for a great Spanish campaign, in which he would invade from Lisbon and Eugene from Barcelona. This, as events ran, might well have been the quickest and most merciful course. But the forces at work were too stubborn. The Tories wanted immediate and total peace. What they got was four years' bloody and finally disastrous war. The negotiations broke on the article that Louis must himself become responsible for expelling his grandson from Spain on the pain of having the Allies renew the war against him from the bases and fortresses he was to surrender in guarantee. The Great King, old and broken, amid the ruin of his ambitions and the misery of his people, might have yielded; but the Dauphin with indignation demanded that his son should not be robbed of his kingdom by his own kin. When Torcy left the conference he passed through the headquarters of the French Army, commanded by Villars. The indomitable Marshal adjured him to tell the King that the Army could defend the honour of the monarchy. Thus driven and thus inspired, Louis XIV uttered the famous sentence, "If I must fight, it shall be with my enemies rather than with my children."

Marlborough had laboured faithfully for peace, but he had not asserted to the full the still gigantic remnants of his personal power. He had misgivings, but upon the whole he expected the French to yield. "Are there no counter-proposals?" he asked in surprise when the courier brought the rejection of the Allied ultimatum. With Eugene he made some last efforts; but nothing availed. The disappointment of the Allies found vent in a vain and furious clamour that they had once again been tricked and fooled by Louis XIV. The drums beat in the Allied camps, and the greatest armies those war-worn times had seen rolled forward to the campaign of 1709 and the carnage of Malplaquet.

*　　*　　*　　*　　*

From this time forth the character of the war was profoundly affected. Justice quite suddenly gathered up her trappings and quitted one cause for the other. What had begun as a disjointed, tardy resistance of peoples, Parliaments, and Protestantism to intolerant and aggressive military power had transformed itself gradually and now flagrantly into invasion and subjugation by a victorious coalition. From this moment France, and to a lesser degree Spain, presented national fronts against foreign inroad and overlordship. There was a strange invigoration in the patriotic spirit both of the French and Spanish peoples. A new flood of strength welling from the depths which the early years of the century had not measured

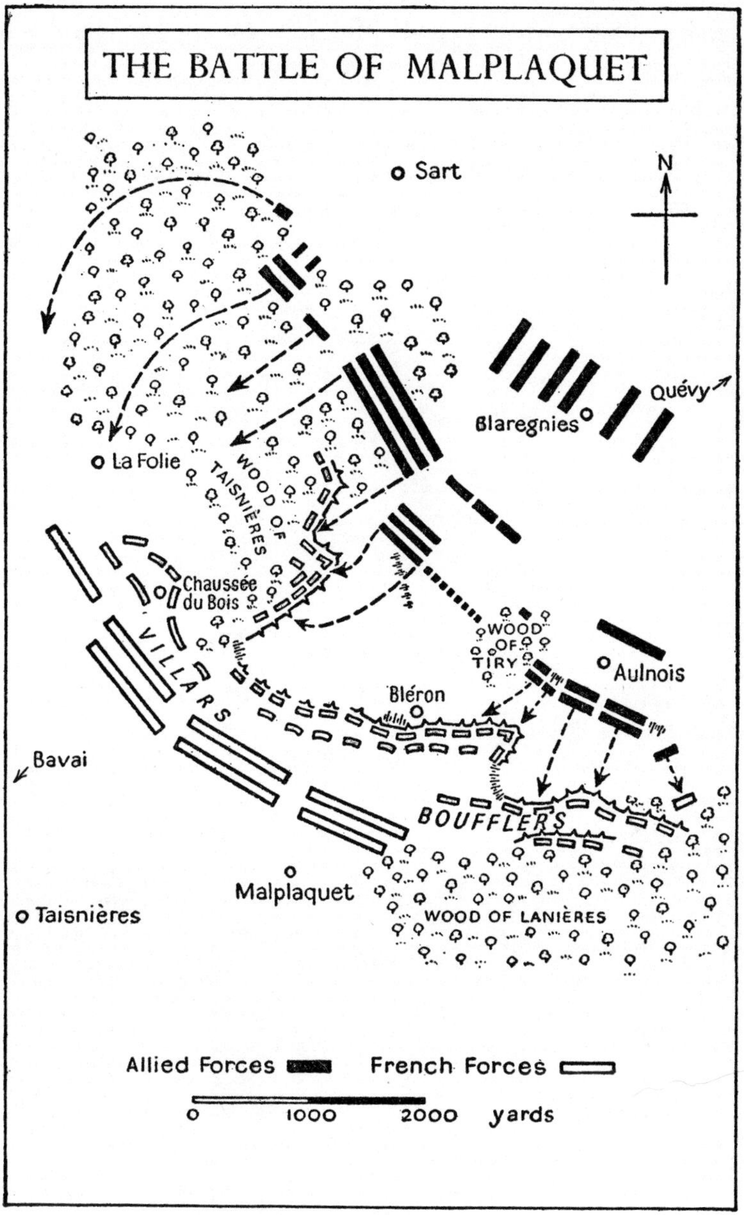

THE BATTLE OF MALPLAQUET

N

o Sart

Quévy

Blaregnies

o La Folie

WOOD OF TAISNIÈRES

Chaussée
du Bois

WOOD
OF
TIRY

o Aulnois

V I L L A R S

Bavai

Bléron

B O U F F L E R S

o Taisnières

Malplaquet

WOOD OF LANIÈRES

Allied Forces ▰▰▰   French Forces ▱▱▱

0   1000   2000   yards

revived and replenished the enfeebled nobility, the exhausted professional armies, and a ruined treasury.

The Allied army had meanwhile been raised to its highest strength, and Marlborough and Eugene, concentrating south of Ghent, began the siege of Tournai. After a large and serious operation the city and citadel surrendered at the end of August. Marlborough now looked to Mons as the next objective. All this time the negotiations had been going forward behind the scenes, and both sides still felt that the little that separated them might at any moment be removed. But suddenly an explosion of war fury, an access of mental rage, took possession of both Governments and both armies down to the private soldiers. They discarded calculation, they flung caution to the winds; the King gave Villars full freedom for battle. Marlborough and Eugene responded with equal zeal. A terrible ardour inspired all ranks. They thirsted to be at each other's throats and slay their foes, and thus bring the long war to an end.

By swift movements Marlborough and Eugene invested Mons, and, advancing south of it, found themselves confronted by Villars in the gap between the woods in which the village of Malplaquet stands, almost along the line of the present French frontier. On September 11 a hundred and ten thousand Allied troops assaulted the entrenchments, defended by about ninety thousand French. The battle was fought with extreme severity, and little quarter was asked or given. Marlborough in the main repeated the tactics of Blenheim. He first attacked both French wings. The Dutch were repelled with frightful slaughter on the left. The right wing, under Eugene, broke through the dense wood, and eventually reached the open country beyond. Under these pressures Villars and his second in command, the valiant Boufflers, were forced to thin their centre. The moment came for which Marlborough was waiting. He launched the English corps under Orkney upon the denuded redoubts, and, having seized them, brought forward his immense cavalry masses, over thirty thousand strong, which had been waiting all day close at hand. With the "Grey" Dragoons and the Scots Greys in the van, the Allied cavalry passed the entrenchments and deployed in the plain beyond. Villars had been grievously wounded, but the French cavalry came forward in magnificent spirit, and a long series of cavalry charges ensued. At length the French cavalry were mastered. Their infantry were already in retreat. "I am so tired," wrote Marlborough to Sarah a few hours later, "that I have but strength enough to tell you that we have had this day a very bloody battle; the first part of the day we beat their foot, and afterwards their horse. God Almighty be praised, it is now in our powers to have what peace we please."

Europe was appalled at the slaughter of Malplaquet. The Allies had lost over twenty thousand men, and the French two-thirds as many. There were hardly any prisoners. The victors camped upon the field, and Mons, the local object of the battle, was besieged and taken. But the event presented itself to all men as a terrible judgment upon the failure of the peace negotiations. The Dutch Republic was staggered by the slaughter of its finest troops. In England the Whigs, still for war on the most ruthless scale, proclaimed by oratory and pamphleteering that a decisive victory had been won. But the Tories accused them, and also Marlborough, of having thrown away the chance of a good peace to produce a fruitless carnage, the like of which Europe could not remember. Indeed Malplaquet, the largest and bloodiest battle of the eighteenth century, was surpassed only by Napoleon's barren victory at Borodino a hundred years later.

The Treaty
of Utrecht

ALL eyes were now turned upon the English Court. It was known throughout Europe that Marlborough's power with the Queen had vanished. Harley with infinite craft and Abigail's aid pursued his design of installing a Tory administration in power, with the object of ending a war of which all were weary.

The great armies faced one another for the campaign of 1710. Their actual numbers were larger than ever before, but Marlborough and Eugene could not or did not bring Villars to battle. Indeed it may be thought that Marlborough was so sickened by the slaughter of Malplaquet and so disheartened by the animosities crowding upon him at home that he would henceforward only wage war as if it were a game of chess. Certain it is that the twin captains looked only for battle at advantages which the skill of Villars did not concede. Douai was taken after another hot siege, and later the capture of Aire and St Venant opened the line of the Lys. These were inadequate results for a campaign so vast and costly.

While Marlborough was at these toils the political crisis of Queen Anne's reign moved steadily to its climax. The Church of England was astir, and the Tory clergy preached against the war and its leaders, especially Godolphin. Dr Sacheverell, a High Church divine, delivered a sermon in London in violent attack upon the Government, the Whigs, and the Lord Treasurer. With great unwisdom the Government ordered a State prosecution in the form of an impeachment. Not only the Tories but the London mob rallied to Sacheverell, and scenes were witnessed recalling those which had attended the trial of the Seven Bishops a quarter of a century before. By narrow majorities nominal penalties were inflicted upon Sacheverell. He became the hero of the hour.

Queen Anne, advised by Harley, now felt strong enough to take her revenge for what she considered the insult inflicted on her by the Whig intrusion into her Council. During a year by successive steps the whole character of the Government was altered. First Sunderland was dismissed; then in August Queen Anne ordered Godolphin to break his staff of office and quit her service, adding, "but I will give you a pension of four thousand a year." Godolphin spurned the pension and retired into a straitened private life. The Whig Ministers of less consequence were also relieved of office. Harley formed a predominantly Tory Government, and at his side Henry St John became Secretary of State. The new Government was largely built around the Duke of Shrewsbury, and found the support of many notables of high degree, outstanding abilities, and hungry ambition. The General Election, aptly launched, produced a substantial Tory majority in the House of Commons.

Marlborough returned from his ninth campaign to find England in the control of his political and personal foes. The Queen demanded that he should force Sarah to give up her offices at Court. He knelt before her in vain. St John, whom he had helped and cherished in the years of triumph, lectured him in insolent, patronising style. Harley bowed and scraped with stony coldness. He too had a score to pay. Yet in spite of all this Marlborough remained the most precious possession of the hostile Government and vengeful Queen. Before the Tories became responsible Ministers they thought they could have peace on victorious terms merely by intimating their willingness for it. They now realised that the downfall of Marlborough was also the revival of Louis XIV. They found themselves face to face with a very different France from the humbled monarchy of 1709. All the states of the Grand Alliance saw in bitter remorse that they had missed their chance. In their distress and returning fears they clung to Marlborough. The Dutch, the Prussians, and various Princes of the Rhine declared their troops should serve under no other commander. Harley and his lieutenant St John, who was swiftly rising to fame, now knew they had to fight another campaign. From every quarter therefore, even the most unfriendly, Marlborough was urged, implored, or conjured to serve. Defeated Whigs, exultant Tories, Harley and St John, the Queen, the States-General, the King of Prussia, the Princes of the Rhine, and, most fervent of all, the Emperor, called upon him to stand by the common cause. Although he was afterwards mocked for love of office and of war, it was his duty to comply. Terms were made between the Tory Ministers and Marlborough for the proper upkeep of the armies at the front, and the Captain-General for the tenth year in succession took the field.

Harley and St John were now in full cry. Having dispatched Marlborough to the wars, they pursued with consistency, craft, and vigour the whole policy of the Tory Party. St John sent a large, ill-managed, ill-starred expedition to take Quebec from the French. Harley, as Chancellor of the Exchequer, was deep in financial plans for the creation of a great South Sea Company, which was to take over a part of the National Debt, and add to its revenues by importing slaves and merchandise into South America. From this the South Sea Bubble was later to be blown. But above all he sought peace with France. By secret channels, unknown to the Allies, he established contact with Torcy.

Finding the French painfully stiff, he brought St John into the negotiations, which proceeded throughout 1711 without the knowledge of Parliament or of any of the confederate states. The method was treacherous, but the object reasonable.

In spite of the secret purpose they nursed in common, Harley and St John were soon estranged. Their rivalry had already become apparent when in March a French refugee, who had been discovered in treasonable correspondence with the enemy, stabbed Harley with a penknife while under examination in the Council Chamber. The Ministers, greatly excited, drew their swords and wounded the assailant, who died a week later of his injuries. Harley was not seriously hurt, but his popularity throughout the country rose with a bound. The Queen now bestowed upon him the proud titles of Earl of Oxford and Mortimer, and appointed him to the office of Lord Treasurer, which had been in commission since the fall of Godolphin. He was at the height of his career.

$$* \quad * \quad * \quad * \quad *$$

Marlborough hoped again to make the campaign of 1711 in company with Eugene, and he concentrated no fewer than a hundred and forty thousand men in the neighbourhood of Douai. But at the end of April an event occurred which affected every aspect of the war. The Emperor Joseph died of smallpox. The Archduke Charles, then maintaining himself stubbornly in Barcelona, succeeded to the hereditary domains of the house of Austria, and was certain to be elected Emperor. To interrupt the election at Frankfort Louis XIV moved a large detachment of Villars's army to the angle of the Rhine. This entailed a corresponding movement of Eugene's army, which in May quitted Marlborough's camp, leaving the Duke with ninety thousand men facing Villars, whose army was still a hundred and twenty thousand strong.

During the winter Villars had constructed an enormous system of entrenchments and inundations stretching from the sea through the fortresses of Arras and Bouchain to Maubeuge, on the Sambre. He called these lines "Ne Plus Ultra," and at the head of his mobile army courted attack. Marlborough, seeming to idle away the month of June, prepared to pierce this formidable barrier. By subtle arts and stratagems he convinced Villars that he intended to make another frontal attack on the scale of Malplaquet south of Arras.

The great armies formed against each other and the lines of battle were drawn. Everyone expected an onslaught. The Allied generals were deeply distressed. They thought that Marlborough, infuriated or deranged by his ill-treatment at home, would lead them to an appalling slaughter. On August 4 the Duke in person conducted a reconnaissance along the whole of Villars's front. He allowed large numbers of officers to accompany him. He marked the places where he would plant his batteries and pointed to the positions he would assault. Only his immense prestige prevented outspoken protests, and many observers condemned the openness with which he spoke of his plans for battle. That night Villars was filled with hope. He had summoned every single battalion and battery on which he could lay his hands from all other parts of his lines. Marlborough's soldiers had blind faith in a leader who had never led them wrong. But the high command was full of aches and fears. They did not notice that General Cadogan had silently slipped away from the great reconnaissance. They wondered at the absence of the artillery. They were not informed of the movements behind Marlborough's front. They knew nothing of his heavy concentration at Douai.

At length tattoo beat and darkness fell. Orders came to strike tents and stand to arms. Soon staff officers arrived to guide the four columns, and in less than half an hour the whole army was on the march to the left. All through the moonlit night they marched eastward. They traversed those broad undulations between the Vimy Ridge and Arras which two centuries later were to be dyed with British and Canadian blood. The march was pressed with severity; only the briefest halts were allowed. But a sense of excitement filled the troops. It was not after all to be a bloody battle. The "Old Corporal" was up to something of his own. Before five o'clock on the morning of the 5th they reached the Scarpe near Vitry. Here the Army found a series of pontoon bridges already laid, and as the light grew they saw the long columns of their artillery now marching with them.

At daybreak Marlborough, riding in the van at the head of fifty squadrons, met a horseman who galloped up from Cadogan. He bore the news that Cadogan and the Prussian general Hompesch, with twenty-two battalions and twenty squadrons, had crossed the causeway at Arleux at 3 A.M. and were in actual possession of the enemy's lines. Marlborough now sent his aides-de-camp and staff officers down the whole length of the marching columns with orders to explain to the officers and soldiers of every regiment what he was doing and what had happened, and to tell them that all now depended upon their marching qualities. "My Lord Duke wishes the infantry to step out." As the light broadened and the day advanced the troops could see upon their right, across the marshes and streams of the Sensée, that the French were moving parallel to them within half cannon-shot. But they also saw that the head of the French horse was only abreast of the Allied foot. During August 5 the bulk of the Allied army had crossed the Sensée and was drawing up inside the enemy's lines. Thousands of exhausted soldiers had fallen by the way, and large numbers died in the passion of their effort.

In the result Marlborough formed a front beyond the lines, which Villars, arriving piecemeal, was unable to attack. There was, and is, a controversy whether Marlborough should not have attacked himself. Certainly both Blenheim and Oudenarde had confronted him with graver risks. But instead of forcing a battle he moved rapidly to his left, crossed the Scheldt, and cast his siege-grip on the fortress of Bouchain. The forcing of the "Ne Plus Ultra" lines and the siege and capture of Bouchain were judged by Europe to be outstanding manifestations of the military art. Villars, with an army equal to Marlborough's whole strength, strove vehemently to interrupt the operation. Marlborough, having obtained six thousand workmen by compulsion from Flanders and Brabant, constructed lines of circumvallation around the whole of Bouchain, and also double entrenchments protecting his communications with the Scheldt. He personally conducted the siege and commanded the covering army. At all hours of the day and night he moved about the astonishing labyrinth which he had created, while he strangled Bouchain. The siege train arrived from Tournai on August 21, and the batteries began to fire on the 30th. While Marlborough bombarded Bouchain Villars bombarded him. It was a siege within a siege, with the constant possibility of a battle at adverse odds to the besiegers. There is no finer example of Marlborough's skill. Bouchain capitulated at the beginning of September. A hostile army as large as his own watched its powerful garrison marched out as prisoners of war. The Duke still wished to continue the campaign and he besieged Quesnoy. The physical forces were not lacking, but all the leaders were now morally worn out. The armies went into winter quarters and Marlborough returned home. For ten years he had led the armies of the Grand Alliance, and during all that period he never fought a battle he did not win or besieged a town he did not take. Nothing like this exists in the annals of war.

*   *   *   *   *

It was now impossible to conceal any longer the secret peace negotiations which had all this while been in progress. They came as a shock to the vehement London world. Harley—to use his former style—commanded a solid Tory majority in the Commons, but the Whigs still controlled the House of Lords. The Tory leaders were sure they could carry the peace if Marlborough would support it. To bend him to their will they had during the campaign set on foot an inquiry into the accounts of the armies, with the object of establishing a charge of peculation against him. If he would join with them in making peace and forcing it upon the Allies, or in making a separate peace, these charges would be dropped, and he would still enjoy "the protection of the Court." If not, they thought they had enough to blacken his character. The Duke, who was in close association with the Elector George of Hanover, the heir to the throne, and still enjoyed the support of the King of Prussia and the Princes of the Grand Alliance, would not agree to a separate peace in any circumstances.

Parliament opened in the winter of 1711 in intense crisis. The two great parties faced one another upon all the issues of the long war. The Whigs used their majority in the House of Lords. They carried a resolution, hostile to the Government, by a majority of twelve. But Harley, strong in the support of the House of Commons, and using to the full the favour of the Queen, met this assault with a decisive rejoinder. He loosed the charges of peculation upon Marlborough, and procured from the Queen an extraordinary creation of twelve peers to override the adverse majority in the Lords. These heavy blows succeeded. Marlborough was dismissed from all his offices and exposed to the censure of the House of Commons. The salaries and emoluments he had enjoyed as Captain-General of England, as Deputy Captain-General of Holland, and from many other posts and per-quisites had enabled him, with his thrift and acquisitiveness, to build up a large fortune. He was now charged chiefly with converting to his own use during his ten years' command the 2½ per cent. levied upon the pay of all foreign contin-gents in the Allied army.

His defence was convincing. He produced Queen Anne's signed warrant of 1702 authorising him to make this deduc-tion, which had always been customary in the Grand Al-liance from the days of King William. He declared that all the money—nearly a quarter of a million—had been ex-pended upon the Secret Service and Intelligence of the Army, which it was not denied had been the most perfect ever known. This did not prevent the Tories in the House of Commons from impugning his conduct by a majority of 276 against 165. A State prosecution was set on foot against the dismissed General for the repayment of very large sums. But all the princes of the Alliance, headed by the Elector of Hanover and the King of Prussia, solemnly affirmed in State documents "that they had freely granted 2½ per cent. to the Duke of Marlborough for the purposes of Secret Service and without expecting any rendering of account," and the Elector added: "We are fully convinced and satisfied that the Prince, Duke of Marlborough, has annually applied these sums to the Secret Services according to their destina-tion . . . and that his wise application of these amounts has forcibly contributed to the gaining of so many battles, to the passing of so many entrenchments and so many lines, successes which, after the blessing of God, are due in great part to the good intelligence and information which the said

Prince has had of the movements and condition of the enemy."

England was now riven in twain upon the issue of peace. A separate peace it must be now, for the Allies one and all repudiated the right of the British Government to abandon the Alliance and provide for themselves. In that haughty, fierce society of London and of Europe no agreement was possible. Meanwhile the French armies, haggard, but refreshed by the downfall of their grand opponent, were gathering in great force. Louis XIV found himself delivered at his last gasp, and his valiant people hastened to his aid. Harley and St John could not avoid the campaign of 1712. They appointed the Duke of Ormonde, the splendid magnifico who had failed at Cadiz, to the command. They assured the Dutch of their fidelity. Eugene was sent by the Emperor to the Low Countries. Eugene, who in a visit to England had vainly sought to rally the loyalties of the Tory Government, and had avowed his unshakeable friendship with Marlborough, found himself at the head of a sufficient strength to take the field. In exasperation at the behaviour of the London Cabinet he was betrayed into an over-audacious campaign. He laid siege to Quesnoy, and called upon Ormonde to aid him. But the British Government was now on the verge of a separate peace. St John sent secret restraining orders to Ormonde not to "partake in any siege in a way to hazard a battle"—as if such tactics were possible.

Upon a dark day the British Army, hitherto the most forward in the Allied cause and admired by all, marched away from the camp of the Allies in bitter humiliation and amid the curses of their old comrades. Only a handful of the British-paid Allies would go with them. Although deprived of their pay and arrears, the great majority declared they would fight on for the "common cause." Many of Marlborough's veterans flung themselves on the ground in shame and fury. The outraged Dutch closed the gates of their cities in the face of the deserting Ally. Villars, advancing rapidly, fell upon Eugene's magazines at Denain and inflicted upon him a cruel defeat in which many of his troops were driven into the Scheldt and drowned. Upon this collapse Villars captured all the advanced bases of the Allies and took Douai, Quesnoy, and Bouchain. Thus he obliterated the successes of the past three years, and at the end of the terrible war emerged victorious. The English Army, under Ormonde, in virtue of a military convention signed with France, retreated upon Dunkirk, which was temporarily delivered to them. After these shattering defeats all the states of the Grand Alliance were compelled to make peace on the best terms possible.

*   *   *   *   *

What is called the Treaty of Utrecht was in fact a series of separate agreements between individual Allied states with France and with Spain. The Empire continued the war alone. In the forefront stood the fact that the Duke of Anjou, recognised as Philip V, held Spain and the Indies, thus flouting the unreasonable declaration to which the English Parliament had so long adhered. With this out of the way the British Government gained their special terms; the French Court recognised the Protestant succession in Britain, and agreed to expel the Pretender from France, to demolish the fortifications of Dunkirk, and to cede various territories in North America and the West Indies, to wit, Hudson Bay, Newfoundland, Nova Scotia, which had been captured by an expedition from Massachusetts, and St Christopher. With Spain the terms were that England should hold Minorca and Gibraltar, thus securing to her, while she remained the chief sea-Power, the entry and control of the Mediterranean. Commercial advantages, one day to provoke another war, were

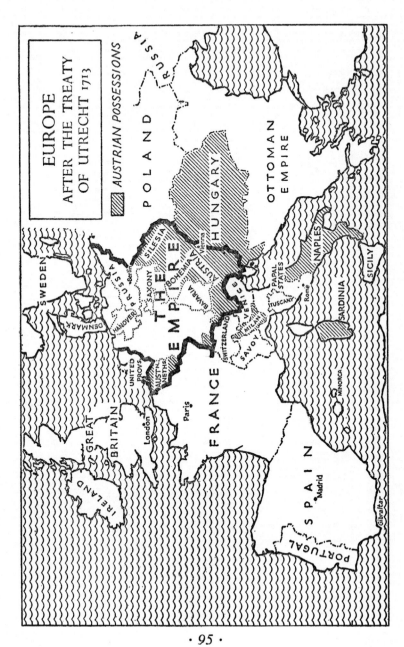

EUROPE
AFTER THE TREATY
OF UTRECHT 1713

▨ AUSTRIAN POSSESSIONS

POLAND

RUSSIA

HUNGARY

OTTOMAN
EMPIRE

SWEDEN

DENMARK

PRUSSIA

Berlin

SILESIA

SAXONY

HANOVER

BOHEMIA

THE

EMPIRE

BAVARIA

AUSTRIA

Vienna

VENICE

PAPAL
STATES

NAPLES

TUSCANY

Rome

SARDINIA

SICILY

UNITED
PROVS.

AUSTN.
NETHS.

SWITZERLAND

AUST. MILAN

SAVOY

GREAT
BRITAIN

IRELAND

London

Paris

FRANCE

MINORCA

SPAIN

Madrid

PORTUGAL

Gibraltar

obtained in Spanish South America, and in particular the
Asiento, or the sole right for thirty years to import African
Negroes as slaves into the New World. A renunciation was
made both by France and Spain of the union of their two
Crowns. This, through many strange deaths in the French
royal family, hung for its validity upon the frail child since
known to history as Louis XV. The Catalans, who had been
called into the field by the Allies, and particularly by England, and who had adhered with admirable tenacity to the
Archduke whom they called Charles III, were delivered over
under polite diplomatic phrases to the vengeance of the
victorious party in Spain.

The Dutch secured a restricted barrier, which nevertheless included, on the outer line, Furnes, Fort Knocke, Ypres,
Menin, Tournai, Mons, Charleroi, and Namur; Ghent, for
communication with Holland; and certain important forts
guarding the entrance to the Scheldt. Prussia obtained
Guelderland at the expense of Dutch claims. All other fortresses in the Low Countries beyond the barrier were restored to France, including particularly Lille. The Duke of
Savoy gained Sicily and a strong frontier on the Alps. Portugal was rewarded for feeble service with trading rights
upon the Amazon. The frontiers on the Rhine and the fate
of Bavaria and the Milanese were left to the decision of further war. Such were the settlements reached at Utrecht in
the spring of 1713, and Chatham, who inherited the consequences, was one day to declare them "an indelible blot
upon the age."

The Emperor Charles, indignant at the surrender of
Spain, fought on during the whole of 1713; but the French,
although themselves exhausted, took the key fortress of
Landau and penetrated again into Germany. In March 1714
the Emperor was forced to conclude the Peace of Rastadt.
By this treaty France regained Strasbourg and Landau and

ceded all conquests on the right bank of the Rhine. The Elector of Bavaria was reinstated in his dominions. The Milanese, Naples, and Sardinia rested with the Empire. On this basis Europe subsided into an uneasy peace, and although these terms were not comparable with what the Allies could have gained in 1706, in 1709, or 1710 they none the less ended for a while the long torment to which Christendom had been subjected.

*   *   *   *   *

Marlborough was so much pursued by the Tory Party and harassed by the State prosecutions against him for his alleged peculation that at the end of 1712 he left the country and lived in self-imposed exile in Holland and Germany till the end of the reign. He maintained his close relations with the Court of Hanover, as well as with the Whig Opposition in England, and, with Cadogan and others of his old officers, stood ready to seize the command of the British troops in the Low Countries and at Dunkirk and lead them to England to sustain the Protestant succession.

The final phase of the Tory triumph was squalid. St John, raised to the peerage as Viscount Bolingbroke, became involved in a mortal quarrel with Harley, Earl of Oxford. His scandalous life and his financial inroads upon the public exposed him to indictment at Harley's merciless hands; but, having procured the aid of Abigail by bribes, he supplanted Oxford in the Queen's favour. Anne was now broken with gout and other ailments. For many months her life hung upon a thread. She who had seen so much glory now drew towards an ignominious end. Having enjoyed in the fullest measure the love of her people for many years of splendour, she now found herself the tool of what had become a disreputable faction. Beneath this weight of hostility and reproach the poor Queen sank in sorrow to the grave. Yet her spirit burned unquenched to the end. She followed with the closest attention the bitter feuds which tore her Cabinet. No one knows whether she wished to make her half-brother, the Pretender, her heir or not. Once again the two Englands which had contended since the Great Rebellion faced each other under different guises and upon an altered scene, but with the same main antagonisms. The Whigs, strong in the Act of Succession and in the Protestant resolve of the nation, prepared openly to take arms against a Jacobite Restoration. The Elector of Hanover, supported by the Dutch and aided by Marlborough, gathered the forces to repeat the descent of William of Orange.

The closing months of 1714 were laden with forebodings of civil war. But Bolingbroke, although in the ascendant, had not the nerve or the quality to play this deadly game. The declaration of the "Pretended Prince of Wales" that he would never abandon the Roman Catholic faith made his imposition upon the British throne impracticable. All must respect his honourable scruples, more especially when they conduced so greatly to the national advantage. "Good God," exclaimed the Duke of Buckinghamshire (after he had been put out of office), "how has this poor nation been governed in my time! During the reign of King Charles the Second we were governed by a parcel of French whores, in King James the Second's time by a parcel of Popish priests, in King William's time by a parcel of Dutch footmen, and now we are governed by a dirty chambermaid, a Welsh attorney, and a profligate wretch that has neither honour nor honesty."

Many accounts converge upon the conclusion that the final scene in the long duel between Oxford and Bolingbroke at the Cabinet Council of July 27 brought about the death of Queen Anne. Already scarcely capable of standing or walking, she nevertheless followed the intense political struggles proceeding around her with absorbed attention.

She notified Oxford by gesture and utterance that he must surrender the Lord Treasurer's White Staff. The sodden, indolent, but none the less tough and crafty politician who had overthrown Marlborough and changed the history of Europe had his final fling at his triumphant rival. In savage tones across the table, both men being within six feet of the Queen, he denounced Bolingbroke to her as a rogue and a thief, and in terms of vague but none the less impressive menace made it plain that he would denounce him to Parliament. Anne was deeply smitten. She was harassed beyond endurance. She had taken all upon herself, and now she did not know which way to turn. She was assisted and carried from this violent confrontation, and two days later the afflictions which had hitherto tormented her body moved towards her brain.

Bolingbroke remained master of the field and of the day —but only for two days. On July 30, while the Queen was evidently at the point of death, the Privy Council met in the palace. They were about to transact business when the door opened and in marched the Dukes of Somerset and Argyll. Both were Privy Counsellors, but neither had received a summons. They declared that the danger to the Queen made it their duty to proffer their services. Shrewsbury, the Lord Chamberlain, who had certainly planned this stroke, thanked them for their patriotic impulse. Bolingbroke, like Oxford some years before, blenched before the challenge. The Council pressed upon the deathbed of the Queen; they urged her to give to Shrewsbury the White Staff of Lord Treasurer, which Oxford had delivered. This would make Shrewsbury virtually head of the Government. With fleeting strength Anne, guided by the Lord Chancellor, passed the symbol to him, and then sank into a coma.

The Council sat far into the night. Vigorous measures were taken to ensure the Hanoverian succession. Messengers were dispatched in all directions to rally to their duty every functionary and officer throughout the land. The Fleet was mobilised under the Whig Earl of Berkeley and ordered to patrol the Channel and watch the French ports. Ten battalions were recalled from Flanders. The garrisons were put under arms and the train-bands warned. The Dutch were reminded of their treaty obligations. Everything was prepared to secure the accession of the Elector of Hanover as George I. These orders bore the signatures not only of Shrewsbury, Somerset, and Argyll, but of Bolingbroke and his Tory colleagues. They had no other choice. All preparations were made with heralds and Household troops to proclaim King George. When Queen Anne breathed her last at half-past seven on August 1 it was certain that there would be no Popery, no disputed succession, no French bayonets, no civil war.

Thus ended one of the greatest reigns in English history. It had been rendered glorious by Marlborough's victories and guidance. The Union and the greatness of the Island had been established. The power of France to dominate Europe was broken, and only Napoleon could revive it. The last of the Stuart sovereigns had presided over a wonderful expansion of British national strength, and in spite of the moral and physical failures of her closing years she deserved to bear in history the title of "the Good Queen Anne."

BOOK EIGHT

THE FIRST BRITISH EMPIRE

The House of Hanover

DURING the late summer of 1714 all England awaited the coming of King George I. On September 18 he landed at Greenwich. This fortunate German prince, who could not speak English, viewed his new realms without enthusiasm. In accepting the throne of the United Kingdom he was conferring, as it seemed to him, a favour upon his new subjects. He was meeting the convenience of English politicians. In return he expected that British power and wealth would be made serviceable to his domains in Hanover and to his larger interests on the European scene. His royal duties would entail exile from home in an island he had only once previously visited and which he did not like. For years past, as heir presumptive, he had attentively watched the factious course of English politics. He had followed distastefully the manoeuvres of the party leaders, without understanding the stresses that gave rise to them or the principles that were at stake. Now on the banks of the Thames he looked about upon the nobles and Ministers who had come to greet him with suspicion and wariness, not unmingled with contempt. Here on English soil stood an unprepossessing figure, an obstinate and humdrum German martinet with dull brains and coarse tastes. As a commander in the late wars he had been sluggish and incompetent, and as a ruler of men he had shown no quickening ability or generosity of spirit. Yet the rigidity of his mind was relieved by a slow shrewdness and a brooding common sense. The British throne was no easy inheritance, especially for a foreign prince. King George took it up grudgingly, and it was ungraciously that he played his allotted part. He owed his crown to the luck of circumstance, but he never let it slip from his grasp.

Many holders of office under the previous reign nursed hopes of the new King. Others were filled with well-justified apprehension. Foremost among those now in acute anxiety was Bolingbroke. His fall was relentless and rapid. Upon the death of Anne he was still Secretary of State. But everyone suspected that if the Queen had lived a few weeks longer Bolingbroke would have laid the train for a Jacobite Restoration. The real designs, if he had any, of this brilliant, veering opportunist can scarcely be discerned. He had the gift of expressing in decisive language any policy that the moment required. He could hit any nail on the head, though which particular nail never seemed important to him. He had played high, and at the critical moment wavered and lost. He could expect little mercy. Nor was he left long in doubt. His name was not included among the Regents appointed to act for the King until His Majesty's arrival. Soon a curt note of dismissal arrived for him from Hanover. Retiring to the country, he hovered aimlessly between regrets and fears. The first Parliament of the new reign demanded his impeachment. In despair Bolingbroke turned for advice to Marlborough, now back from exile, whom he had once mercilessly harried and driven from office. At their interview Marlborough was all urbanity. But he contrived to suggest that Bolingbroke's life was in danger. He hinted that Bolingbroke alone of the Tory leaders would pay with his blood for their misdeeds. That night Bolingbroke fled to France disguised as a valet, his jauntiness utterly shattered. A few months later he took the plunge and became Secretary of State to the Pretender. The Court of Saint-Germain, with which he had long intrigued, was soon to disillusion him. Eight years of exile lay ahead. But this false, glittering figure has not yet passed out of our story. His great rival Robert Harley, Earl of Oxford, was meanwhile imprisoned in the Tower of London. No condign punishment was inflicted on him; but when he emerged from the Tower he was a broken man.

*   *   *   *   *

The political passions of the seventeenth century had spent themselves in the closing years of Queen Anne. The struggle of Whig against Tory had brought the country to the verge of civil war. The issue was who should succeed to the crown, the Catholic son of James II or the Protestant Elector? Now all was settled. There were no more great constitutional issues. George I had come peacefully to the throne. The Tory Party was shattered, and England settled down, grumbling but safe, under the long rule of Whiggism. A rapid change in the atmosphere marked the decades following 1714. The wrath and venom of controversy were replaced by an apathetic tolerance. Great principles were no longer dominant. Political sentiment was replaced by political interest. Public life was degraded by materialism and politics became a mere striving for office and Crown patronage by rival groups of Whigs.

The monarchy too had lost its lustre. There was no pretence that the Hanoverian kings ruled by Divine Right. They held their position by the express sanction of Parliament. Even the symbolism of royalty was curtailed. The Court was no longer the centre of beauty, rank, and fashion. A certain dowdiness creeps into the ceremonial and the persons of the courtiers. Life in the royal palaces is dominated by the panoply and surroundings of a minor German princeling. The dreary names of the German women are ever present in the memoirs of the time—the Kielmansegges and the Wallmodens, the Platens and the Schulenbergs—all soon to deck themselves out with English titles and wealth. Much is heard in political circles of the influences of the German "gang"—Bernstorff and Bothmer, advisers whom the first George brought with him, and Roberthon, his Huguenot private secretary.

The men who led the Whig Party in the days of Queen Anne were fast retiring from the scene. Wharton, long the party's great organiser, died in 1715. Charles Montagu, now Lord Halifax, who had done so much to reconstruct English finances during King William's wars, followed his colleague in the same year, and Burnet, the diligent historian and the staunchest of Whig Churchmen, was also gone. Lord Somers, the former Lord Chancellor, dragged his life out paralysed and helpless for twelve months longer. And the greatest figure of them all, John Duke of Marlborough, lived on in splendid isolation in his houses at Blenheim and St Albans, stricken with a lingering paralysis, until he was released by death in 1722. His wife Sarah was doomed to live out her life for twenty years more, a croaking reminder of the high days of the Augustan Age. But she was alone.

A new generation of statesmen—Walpole, Stanhope, Carteret, and Townshend—were to ensure the peaceful transition from the age of Anne to the age of the Georges. Among this group Stanhope gradually became the leading Minister. He had commanded in Spain during the wars and had captured Minorca. Now his main interest lay in foreign affairs. In domestic matters he was less happy, and here the Government faced no tranquil task. The country had acquiesced in the imposition by Parliament of a German royal family. But there was strong feeling in many parts of England for the house of Stuart. In London, in Oxford, and in the West Country there were riots and shouting. The houses and meeting-places of the Dissenters were once more looted and wrecked as symbols of the new Whig régime. Portraits of King William were burnt in ceremony at Smithfield. The ablest supporter of the Jacobite Pretender, Marshal Berwick, the illegitimate son of

James II and Marlborough's sister, estimated that in 1715 five out of six persons in England were Jacobite. This was certainly an exaggeration; yet, although the Government had very successfully managed the elections of the previous year, they had every reason to fear the feelings of the people. They had achieved their greatest victory by cooler leadership and better organisation, but they had no illusion about commanding the general sentiment of the country. In the dual task of humouring a German king and a peevish nation their patience was sorely tried. Their first actions involved England in Northern Europe on behalf of the house of Hanover. The English Fleet was sent to acquire Swedish ports on the North German coast which had long been coveted by Hanoverian Electors. There were angry mutterings that England's resources were being used for German interests. But the Whig Ministers, though nervous, took good precautions. The British Ambassador in Paris kept them closely informed of the Jacobite movements in France. Plans were being hatched for a general rising not only in England but also in Scotland, restless and as yet disappointed at the results of the Act of Union. When the blow came the Government was ready. Moreover the Jacobites suffered a severe stroke by the death of Louis XIV on September 1. The Great King had been their protector and encourager. The Regent Orleans, now at the head of French affairs, was cool to their projects.

On September 6 the Earl of Mar raised the Jacobite standard at Perth. Within a few weeks ten thousand men were in arms against Hanoverian rule in Scotland. But they had no proper plans and no solid link with the exiles in France. The Government in London acted at once. Parliament passed the Riot Act to curb disturbances in the English towns. Oxford was occupied by a body of cavalry. Sellers of seditious pamphlets, talkers of seditious opinions, were swiftly arrested. Habeas corpus was suspended. A reward of £100,000 was posted for the apprehension of the Pretender, dead or alive. Dutch troops were demanded from Holland under the terms of the Barrier Treaty guaranteeing the Protestant succession in England, and the regular forces moved quietly northwards against the rebels.

In the North of England a small band of gentry, led by Lord Derwentwater, rose in support of the Stuarts. They were unable to form effective contact with Mar; but, reinforced with four thousand Scots, they made a rash and forlorn attempt to raise help from the towns and countryside to the south of them. The Duke of Marlborough was consulted by the military authorities. "You will beat them," he said, marking Preston with his thumbnail on the map, "there." And on November 13 beaten there they were.

The Government forces in Scotland, led by the Whig Duke of Argyll, met the Jacobite army at Sheriffmuir on the same day. The battle was indecisive, but was followed by desertion and discouragement in the Jacobite ranks. With all hope of success gone, the Pretender landed in bad December weather upon the Scottish coast. He brought neither money nor ammunition. Assembling the leaders, he evacuated them in a French vessel and returned to France. The collapse was followed by a batch of treason trials and about thirty executions. Despite the incompetence of the rising, the Government perceived and feared the unorganised opposition throughout the country to the new régime. They felt they must strengthen their grip on the administration. A Septennial Act prolonged the life of the existing House of Commons for another four years and decreed septennial Parliaments henceforth. This was the boldest and most complete assertion of Parliamentary sovereignty that England had yet seen. Later the Lords took a further step. They tried to perpetuate the Whig monopoly in their House by a Bill to stop the Crown's creating more than six fresh peerages. But this was too blatant. Loud protests were heard in the Commons, led by Walpole, who had left the Ministry and was now its chief critic. It was not the curtailment of royal power which they opposed, but their own eternal banishment from the ranks of the peerage. They rejected the Bill by a large majority.

Political power was henceforth founded on influence: in the dispensation of Crown patronage; stars, sinecures, pensions; the agile use of the Secret Service fund; jobs in the Customs for humble dependants; commissions or Church livings for younger sons. Thus the Whigs established control of the Parliamentary machine. Though they had split among themselves, there was no hope of an organised opposition to the Whig oligarchy. The first two Georges were preoccupied with European affairs and showed little interest in the home politics of their adopted country. The Tory Party had no focus in Parliament after the flight of Bolingbroke. The 1715 rebellion made it even more easy for the Government to brand all Tories as Jacobites and disturbers of the peace. With political power and influence barred except to the favoured few, men turned to other pursuits and new adventures.

*　　*　　*　　*　　*

Financial speculation was encouraged. The Government was burdened with a war debt of nearly fifty millions, and the idea of benefiting from the commercial prosperity of the world was not unattractive. In 1710 a Tory Ministry had granted a charter to a company trading with the South Seas, and had arranged for it to take over part of the National Debt. This connection had rapidly expanded the wealth of the South Sea Company, and in 1720 a group of Directors approached the Government with a plan to absorb the whole National Debt, then standing at about £30,000,000. The scheme soon came to stink of dishonesty, but the politicians were too greedy to reject it. There was a chance of wiping out the whole debt in twenty-five years. £1,250,000 is said to have been spent in bribes to Ministers, Members of Parliament, and courtiers. The Whig Chancellor of the Exchequer, John Aislabie, purchased £27,000 worth of South Sea stock before introducing the project to the House of Commons. The Bank of England, nervous of a growing financial rival, competed for the privilege of undertaking this gigantic transaction. But the South Sea Company outbid the Bank. In April 1720 the Bill sanctioning these proposals was brought before the House. It received a sober and savage attack at the hands of Robert Walpole, whose reputation was rising. "The scheme countenanced the pernicious practice of stock-jobbing, by diverting the genius of the nation from trade and industry; it held out a dangerous lure for decoying the unwary to their ruin by a false prospect of gain, and to part with the gradual profits of their labour for imaginary wealth." Success, he argued, depended on the rise of the South Sea stock. "The great principle of the project was an evil of the first magnitude; it was to raise artificially the value of the stock, by exciting and keeping up a general infatuation and by promising dividends out of funds which would not be adequate to the purpose." But the Members were dazzled at the prospect of private gain. The House sleepily emptied even as Walpole spoke. The Bill was carried on April 2 by 172 votes to 55, and five days later an equally large majority secured its passage through the Lords, where Lord Cowper compared it to the wooden horse of Troy.

The mania for speculation broke loose. Stock soared in three months from 128 to 300, and within a few months more to 500. Amid the resounding cries of jobbers and speculators a multitude of companies, some genuine and some bogus, was hatched. By June 1721 the South Sea stock stood at 1050. Robert Walpole himself had the luck to make a handsome profit on his quiet investments. At every coffee-house in London men and women were investing their savings in any enterprise that would take their money. There was no limit to the credulity of the public. One promoter floated a company to manufacture an invention known as Puckle's Machine Gun, "which was to discharge round and square cannon-balls and bullets and make a total revolution in the art of war," the round missiles being intended for use against Christians and the square against the Turk. Other promoters invited subscriptions for making salt water fresh, for constructing a wheel of perpetual motion, for importing large jackasses from Spain to improve the breed of English mules, and the boldest of all was the advertisement for "a company for carrying on an undertaking of Great Advantage, but no one to know what it is." This amiable swindler set up a shop in Cornhill to receive subscriptions. His office was besieged by eager investors, and after collecting £2,000 in cash he prudently absconded.

The Government took alarm, and the process of suppressing these minor companies began. The South Sea Company was only too anxious to exterminate its rivals, but the pricking of the minor bubbles quickened and precipitated a slump. An orgy of selling began, and by October the South Sea stock stood at 150. Thousands were ruined. The porters and ladies' maids who had bought carriages and fineries found themselves reduced to their former station. Clergy, bishops, poets, and gentry found their life savings vanish overnight. There were suicides daily. The gullible mob whose innate greed had lain behind this mass hysteria and mania for wealth called for vengeance. The Postmaster-General took poison. His son, a Secretary of State, was snatched from his accusers by opportune smallpox. Stanhope, the chief Minister, died of strain. The Directors of the Company were arrested and their estates forfeited for the benefit of the huge army of creditors.

A secret committee was appointed by the House of Commons to inquire into the nature and origins of these astonishing transactions. The books of the company were mutilated and incomplete. Nevertheless it was discovered that 462 members of the Commons and 122 peers were involved. Groups of frantic bankrupts thronged the Parliamentary lobbies. The Riot Act was read. There was a general outcry against the cupidity of the German ladies. "We are ruined by Trulls—nay, what is more, by old, ugly Trulls, such as could not find entertainment in the most hospitable hundreds of Old Drury." Walpole came to the rescue with a scheme for grafting a large section of the South Sea capital on to the Bank of England's stock and for reconstructing the National Debt. Apart from the estates of the Directors there were few assets for the mass of creditors. The brief hour of dreamed-of riches closed in wide-eyed misery. Bringing order to the chaos that remained was the first task of Britain's first Prime Minister.

Sir Robert Walpole

THE scandal of the South Sea Bubble roused the hopes of the Tories. Their revival as a political force seemed imminent. The Government had been thoroughly discredited, and the exiled Bolingbroke was hopefully intriguing with his supporters in England. A brilliant and vitriolic bishop, Francis Atterbury, of Rochester, was spinning a new web of secret contacts with the Jacobites in France. The Hanoverian régime had been hit in its most delicate spot, the financial credit of the Government.

One man only amid the crash and panic of 1721 could preserve the Whig monopoly. He was Robert Walpole, now established as the greatest master of figures of his generation. Soon he was to become a Knight of the Garter, one of the few Commoners to hold the honour. This Norfolk squire, who hunted five days a week, had risen to prominence as Secretary at War in the days of Marlborough. He had been imprisoned in the Tower after the Whig defeat of 1710, and since his release had been a leading figure of the Whig Party in the House of Commons. He had already been Chancellor of the Exchequer for three years, but he and his brother-in-law, Townshend, had resigned in 1717 in protest at the excessive pliancy of certain Whigs to the Hanoverian foreign policy of the King. Walpole had witnessed the disastrous effect on the Whig Party of the public impeachment of Sacheverell. He had no intention of repeating the mistake. The political crisis was quickly ended. A Jacobite plot was swiftly and silently supressed. Atterbury was convicted of treason by a Bill of Pains and Penalties, and quietly pushed into exile without the chance of using his brilliant gifts as an orator and pamphleteer. At the same time Walpole did not prevent the pardon and return of Bolingbroke. There is a story that at Dover Atterbury met Bolingbroke returning from France and remarked, "My lord, we are exchanged."

Walpole, on becoming head of the Government, immediately turned to financial reconstruction. He was First Lord, or Commissioner, of the Treasury, for the great office of Lord Treasurer had been abolished and its powers placed in the hands of a commission. The last sections of the National Debt taken over by the South Sea Company were portioned out between the Bank of England and the Treasury. The Sinking Fund he had instituted in 1717, whereby a sum of money was set aside from the revenue each year to pay off the National Debt, was put into operation. Within a few months the situation improved and England settled down again under another edition of Whig rule.

*   *   *   *   *

With a business man at the head of affairs the atmosphere of national politics became increasingly materialistic. Walpole realised that the life of his Government depended on avoiding great issues that might divide the country. He knew that a mass of hostile opinion smouldered in the manor-houses and parsonages of England, and he was determined not to provoke it.

By careful attention to episcopal appointments, delicately handled by his friend Edmund Gibson, the Whig Bishop of London, Walpole increased the preponderance of his party in the House of Lords. He refused a comprehensive measure of toleration for the Dissenters, for this might have introduced religious strife into the world of politics. But while unwilling to legislate broadly on grounds of principle he took care that his Dissenting supporters who accepted office in local government in defiance of the Test Acts were quietly protected by annual Acts of Indemnity. Any sign of Tory activity was greeted by Walpole with the deadly accusation of Jacobitism. But he was by nature kindly, and though he had the lives of some of his Tory opponents in his hands he never used his power to the shedding of blood.

"The charge of systematic corruption," Burke wrote, "is less applicable to Sir Robert Walpole than to any other Minister who ever served the Crown for such a length of time." He had no illusions about the virtue of his supporters; but he knew there was a point beyond which corruption would not work. There was a limit to the mercenary nature of the men with whom he dealt, and it was plain that in the last resort they would be moved to vote by fear or anger rather than according to their interests. Anything tending to crisis must be avoided as the plague. For the rest, by pensions to the German mistresses and by a liberal Civil List he could be assured of the continued enjoyment of the royal confidence.

Walpole's object was to stabilise the Hanoverian régime and the power of the Whig Party within a generation. Taxation was low; the land tax, which was anxiously watched by the Tory squires, was reduced by economy to one shilling. The National Debt decreased steadily, and an overhaul of the tariff and the reduction of many irksome duties stimulated and expanded trade. By an *entente* with France and by rigid non-intervention in European politics Walpole avoided another war. He was the careful nurse of England's recovery after the national effort under Queen Anne. But men remembered the great age that had passed and scorned the drab days of George I. A policy of security, prosperity, and peace made small appeal to their hearts, and many were ready to attack the degeneration of politics at home and the futility of England abroad.

A high-poised if not sagacious or successful opposition to

Walpole persisted throughout the twenty-one years of his administration. It drew its force from the association of those Whigs who either disliked his policy or were estranged by exclusion from office with the Tories in the shades. Very attractive, these Tories in the shades! Romantic, enveloped in lost causes, based upon the land, its past and its fullness, "the gentlemen of England," as Bolingbroke had extolled them in the days when he was sapping Marlborough's strength, were still the core of the nation. Dignity, morale, passion in subjection, the sense of tradition, the Old World—and then, in a fancy perhaps growing fainter every year, the rightful King!

Bolingbroke had offered an alliance, but Walpole had refused to allow him to regain his place in the House of Lords. The younger Whigs, like William Pulteney and John Carteret, were too clever to be allowed to shine in Walpole's orbit. Nor could they weaken his hold on the House of Commons while he exercised the patronage of the Crown. There was no hope except to undermine his position with the King. A series of appeals to the German ladies by flattery and cash followed. Walpole was always quicker in satisfying their cupidity than his opponents. The Parliamentary Opposition gathered round the Prince of Wales. It was the Hanoverian family tradition that father and son should be on the worst of terms, and the future George II was no exception. The Government depended on the King; the Opposition looked to his son. All had an interest in the dynasty. But for the strong support of Caroline, Princess of Wales, Walpole would have been in serious danger. Indeed, on the accession of George II in 1727 he suffered a brief eclipse. The new King dismissed him. But the Opposition leaders failed to form an alternative Government. The titular head of their stop-gap administration had to get Walpole to write the royal speech at the opening of George II's first Parliament. Secure in the confidence of Queen Caroline, Walpole returned to office and entrenched himself more firmly than before.

There had always been a danger that discontented, ambitious members of his Government would play on the King's interest in Hanoverian affairs. They would espouse the causes dear to the royal heart—the ancestral home, the great Continental scene, the Grand Alliance, the wars of Marlborough. This lure of European politics was too much for several of the men around Walpole. He meant to do as little as possible: to keep the peace, to stay in office, to juggle with men, to see the years roll by. But others responded to more lively themes. Walpole was forced to quarrel. His own brother-in-law, Charles Townshend, was dismissed at the end of 1729. He then entered into close co-operation with a man of limited intelligence and fussy nature, but of vast territorial and electoral wealth—Thomas Pelham Holles, Duke of Newcastle. Newcastle became Secretary of State because, as Walpole said, he himself "had experienced the trouble that a man of parts gave in that office." By his enemies Walpole was now mockingly called the "Prime Minister"—for this honourable title originated as a term of abuse. The chances of a successful Opposition seemed to be gone for ever. With every weapon of wit and satire at their command, the brilliant young men who gathered round Bolingbroke and the surviving mistress of George I, the Duchess of Kendal, herself a subscriber to Bolingbroke's newspaper *The Craftsman*, could make no dint on the dull, corrupt, reasonable solidity of the administration.

However, in 1733 a storm broke. Walpole proposed an excise on wines and tobacco, to be gathered by Revenue officers in place of a duty at the ports. The measure was aimed at the vast smuggling that rotted this source of the revenue. Every weapon at their command was used by the Opposition. Members of Parliament were deluged with letters. Popular ballads and pamphlets were thrust under the doors.

National petitions and public meetings were organised throughout the land. Doleful images were raised of the tyranny of the Excisemen. The Englishman's castle was his home; but this citadel would be invaded night and day by Revenue officers to see whether the duty had been paid. Such was the tale—then novel. It was spread among the regiments of the Army that their tobacco would cost them more, and one officer reported that he could be sure of his troops against the Pretender, but not against Excise. The storm swamped the country and alarmed the Government majority in the House of Commons. The force of bribes was overridden by fear of expulsion from the enclosure in which they were distributed. Walpole's majority dwindled; his supporters deserted him like sheep straying through an open gate. Defeated by one of the most unscrupulous campaigns in English history, Walpole withdrew his Excise reform. After a near division in the House of Commons he uttered the famous saying, "This dance can no longer go." He crawled out of the mess successfully, and confined his revenge to cashiering some of the Army officers who had helped his opponents. The violence of his critics recoiled upon themselves, and the Opposition snatched no permanent advantage.

Bolingbroke now despaired of ever achieving political power, and in 1735 he retired once more to France. Those Whigs who were out of office grouped themselves round Frederick, the new Prince of Wales. He in his turn became the hope of the Opposition, but all they could produce was an increased Civil List for this ungifted creature. Their arrogance showed Walpole that people were growing tired of his colourless rule. One of his sharpest critics was a young Cornet of Horse named William Pitt. He was deprived of his commission for his part in the attack. In 1737 Walpole's staunch ally, Queen Caroline, died. There was steadily growing a reaction, both in the country and in the House of Commons, to the

interminable monopoly of political power by this tough, un-
sentimental Norfolk squire, with his head for figures and
his horror of talent, keeping the country quiet, and, though
it was only an incident, feathering his own nest.

At long last the Opposition discerned the foundation of
Walpole's ascendancy, namely, the avoidance of any contro-
versy which might stir the country as a whole. Their campaign
against the Excise, which appealed to popular forces outside
Walpole's command, pointed the path to his final overthrow.
Supreme in the narrow circle of the Commons and the Court,
Walpole's name angered many and inspired no one. The
country was bored. It rejected a squalid, peaceful prosperity.
Commercial wealth advanced rapidly. Trade figures swelled.
Still the nation was dissatisfied. There was something lacking;
something which was certainly not Jacobite, but was certainly
deeper than the discontent of ambitious, unemployed Whig
politicians. All that was keen and adventurous in the English
character writhed under this sordid, sleepy Government.
Sometimes whole sessions of the House of Commons rolled
by without a division.

All that was needed to destroy the mechanism of Wal-
pole's rule was an issue that would stir the country, and
which would in its turn stampede the quiescent, half-squared
Members of Parliament into a hostile vote against the
Minister. The crack came from a series of incidents in
Spanish America.

*   *   *   *   *

In 1713 the Treaty of Utrecht had granted the English the
right to send one shipful of Negro slaves a year to the Spanish
plantations in the New World. Such was the inefficiency of
Spanish administration that it was easy to run contraband
cargoes of Negroes in defiance of what was called the
"Asiento contract," and the illicit trade grew steadily in the
years of peace. But when the Spanish Government at last

began to reorganise and extend its colonial government English ships trading unlawfully in the Spanish seas were stopped and searched by the Spanish coastguards. Having in vain struggled for many years with inadequate weapons to put down, not slaving, but the smuggling of slaves along the coasts of the Spanish colonies, the guards were far from gentle when they managed to intercept an English vessel in the wide ocean. Profits were high, and merchants in London forced Walpole to challenge the right of search. A series of negotiations followed with Madrid.

The Directors of the South Sea Company were interested in these regions. Suppressing English interlopers was not in itself to their disadvantage, but they were themselves involved in dispute with Spain over payments due to the Spanish king under the Asiento contract for the annual ship. Driven to the verge of bankruptcy, they hoped to use the anti-Spanish feeling in London to avoid their obligations. They claimed they had suffered losses at the hands of the Spanish Fleet during the brief wars in 1719 and 1727. Other issues were involved. The ships that suffered most from seizure and molestation came usually from the English West Indian colonies, which had long traded for log-wood in Campeachy Bay and the Gulf of Honduras. Walpole and Newcastle hoped for a peaceful settlement. The preliminary Convention of Prado was settled and negotiated at Madrid in January 1739. Spain, also nearly bankrupt, was just as anxious to avoid war. She offered many concessions, and Walpole drastically reduced the claims of English merchants. But the Opposition would have none of it. The South Sea Company had been excluded from the preliminary Convention, and continued its quarrel with the Spanish Government independently of official negotiations. In May Spain suspended the Asiento and refused to pay any of the compensations agreed by the Prado Convention.

Meanwhile the Opposition in Parliament had opened a broad attack on the Government's negotiations with Spain. Much was heard of the honour of England and the great traditions of Elizabeth and Cromwell, and there was vehement appeal to national prejudices and sentiments. A captain trading with the Spanish possessions, one Jenkins, was brought before the House of Commons to produce his ear in a bottle, and to maintain that it had been cut off by Spanish coastguards when his ship was searched. "What did you do?" he was asked. "I commended my soul to God and my cause to my country," was the answer put in his mouth by the Opposition. Jenkins's ear caught the popular imagination and became the symbol of agitation. Whether it was in fact his own ear or whether he had lost it in a seaport brawl remains uncertain, but the power of this shrivelled object was immense. A vociferous group of orators led by Pulteney became known ironically as the "Patriots." Without troubling to study the terms of the preliminary agreement with Spain, the Opposition drove their attack home. As one of Walpole's supporters wrote, "The Patriots were resolved to damn it before they knew a word of it, and to influence the people against it, which they have done with great success." And, as the British envoy in Madrid, Benjamin Keene, put it to Walpole months later, "The Opposers make the war."

The Spaniards might have ignored the bellicose Opposition in the British Parliament. Walpole and Newcastle were not strong enough to do so. If the country demanded war with Spain the Ministers were prepared to ride with them rather than resign. Spain had disarmed her Fleet after signing the Convention of Prado as proof of her sincerity. English ships in the Mediterranean had been ordered home, but after the storm at Westminster the orders were revoked in March. Walpole was further alarmed by the hostile attitude of France; but none the less he yielded ground slowly and steadily. On

October 19, 1739, war was declared. The bells rang out from the London churches and the crowds thronged the streets shouting. Looking down upon the jubilant mob, the Prime Minister remarked sourly, "They are ringing their bells now, but soon they will be wringing their hands." Now opened a mighty struggle, at first with Spain only, but later by the family compact between the Bourbon monarchs involving France. Thus began that final duel between Britain and her nearest neighbour which in less than a century was to see the glories of Chatham, the follies of Lord North, the terrors of the French Revolution and the rise and fall of Napoleon.

By sure degrees, in the confusion and mismanagement which followed, Walpole's power, as he had foreseen, slipped from him. The operations of the ill-manned Fleet failed. The one success, the capture of Portobello, on the isthmus of Panama, was achieved by Admiral Vernon, the hero of the Opposition. Captain Anson's squadron, filled up with Chelsea pensioners, disappeared into the Pacific. It inflicted little damage on the Spaniards. But in a voyage lasting nearly four years Anson circumnavigated the globe, charting as he went. In the course of it he schooled a new generation of naval officers. Meanwhile the tide of national feeling ran high. There were riots in London. The Prince of Wales appeared everywhere, to be cheered by opponents of the Government. A new tune was on their lips, with Thomson's resounding words, "Rule, Britannia."

In February 1741 an Opposition Member, Samuel Sandys, proposed an address to the King for the dismissal of Walpole. For the last time the old Minister outwitted his foes. He had made overtures to the Jacobite group in the Commons, even letting it be supposed that he would countenance a Jacobite Restoration. To the amazement of all, the Jacobites voted for him. The Opposition, in the words of Lord Chesterfield, "broke in pieces." But under the Septennial Act elections were due. The Prince of Wales spent lavishly in buying up seats, and his campaign, managed by Thomas Pitt, brother of William, brought twenty-seven Cornish seats over to the Opposition. The electoral influence of the Scottish earls counted against Walpole, and when the Members returned to Wesminster his Government was defeated on an election petition (contested returns were in those days decided by the House on purely party lines) and resigned. It was February 1742. Sir Robert had governed England for twenty-one years. During the last days before his fall he sat for hours on end, alone and silent, brooding over the past in Downing Street. He was the first Chief Minister to reside at Number Ten. He had accomplished the work of his life, the peaceful establishment of the Protestant succession in England. He had soothed and coaxed a grumbling, irritated country into acquiescence in the new régime. He had built up a powerful organisation, fed and fattened on Government patronage. He had supervised the day-to-day administration of the country, unhampered by royal interference. The sovereign had ceased after 1714 to preside in person over the Cabinet, save on exceptional occasions—a most significant event, though it was only the result of an accident. Queen Anne had always, when in good health, presided on Sunday evenings over her Cabinet meetings at Kensington Palace. The Ministers regarded themselves as individually responsible to her and under faint obligations to each other. But George I could not speak English and had to converse with his Ministers in French or such dog-Latin as they remembered from Eton. Walpole had created for himself a dominating position in this vital executive committee, now deprived of its titular chairman. He tried to make himself supreme over his Ministers and establish in practice that rebellious colleagues were dismissed by the King. But he founded no convention of collective Ministerial responsibility. One of the charges against him after his fall was that he had sought to become "sole and Prime Minister."

He had kept England at peace for nearly twenty years. Now he went to the House of Lords as Earl of Orford. His obstinate monopoly of political power in the Commons had put all men of talent against him, and in the end his policy enabled the Opposition to arouse the public opinion he had so assiduously lulled. He was the first great House of Commons man in British history, and if he had resigned before the war with Spain he might have been called the most successful.

The Austrian Succession and the "Forty-Five"

THE war between Britain and Spain, which the Opposition
had forced upon Walpole, was soon merged in a general
European struggle. Britain had expected to fight naval and
colonial campaigns in Spanish waters and on the Spanish
Main. Instead she found herself engaged in a Continental
war. Two royal deaths in 1740 set the conflict in motion.
East of the Elbe the rising kingdom of Prussia acquired a
new ruler. Frederick II, later called the Great, ascended his
father's throne. He inherited a formidable army which he
fretted to use. It was his ambition to expand his scattered
territories and weld them into the strongest state in Germany.
Military gifts and powers of leadership, a calculating spirit
and utter ruthlessness, were his in equal portion. Almost immediately he had the chance to put them to the test. In
October the Habsburg Emperor Charles VI died, leaving his
broad domains, though not his Imperial title, to his daughter
Maria Theresa. The Emperor had extracted solemn guarantees from all the Powers of Europe that they would recognise
her accession in Austria, Hungary, Bohemia, and the Southern Netherlands. But these meant nothing to Frederick. He
attacked and seized the Austrian province of Silesia, which
lay to the south of his own territories. France, ever jealous
of the Habsburgs, encouraged and supported him. Thus

Europe was plunged into what is termed the War of the Austrian Succession.

In England King George II was much beset by the problems that arose. His hereditary Electorate of Hanover was dearer to his heart than the Kingdom of Great Britain. He correctly measured the ambitions of his nephew, Frederick of Prussia. He was fearful that the next Prussian onslaught might engulf his own estates in Germany. In London, after Walpole's fall, King George's Government was managed by Henry Pelham, First Lord of the Treasury, and his brother, the Duke of Newcastle, long a Secretary of State. Their great territorial wealth and electoral influence enabled them to maintain Whig dominion over the House of Commons. They were skilled in party manœuvre, but inexpert in the handling of foreign or military affairs. Newcastle knew much of Europe. By nature however he was cautious, and inconsequential. The exercise of patronage at home meant more to him than the conduct of war. George II turned for help and advice to the Pelhams' rival, Lord Carteret. Under Walpole Carteret had shared the fate of all men who were clever enough to be dangerous, and was dismissed to the Lord-Lieutenancy of Ireland. Sir Robert's fall restored him to public life at Westminster. By supporting the King's German interests he was now able to outbid the Pelhams for the royal favour. Carteret wanted Hanover and England to preserve and promote a balance of power in Europe. He thought he held the clue to the Continental maze. He spoke German and was an intimate of the sovereign. He discerned the growing Prussian menace, and realised that a Franco-Prussian alliance could create measureless dangers for Britain. In 1742 he was appointed a Secretary of State. To meet the combination of France, Spain, and Frederick the Great he negotiated a treaty with Maria Theresa and renewed the traditional agreements with the Dutch. Financial help was promised to Austria, and preparations were made for raising an army to aid the Queen of Hungary, as Maria Theresa was proudly called. Forty years earlier Britain had supported her father, when he was the Archduke Charles, in his attempt to win the throne of Spain. Now the Island was again allied with the House of Austria against France. It was not for the last time.

Carteret, to his misfortune, lacked both the personal position and the political following to put his decisions to good effect. He was an individualist, with no gift for party organisation, depending essentially and only upon the favour of the Crown. Hostility soon gathered against him in Parliament. Foremost among his critics was William Pitt, Member for the ancient but uninhabited borough of Old Sarum. His grandfather had been Governor of Madras and owner of the famous Pitt diamond. From Eton Pitt had gone into the Army. His commanding officer, Lord Cobham, had been deprived of his regiment by Walpole for agitating against the Excise scheme. This had soon put an end to the young cornet's military career, and he followed his patron and colonel into Opposition politics. Lord Cobham was head of the Temple family and related to the Grenvilles and Lytteltons. In close political association with this group of disaffected Whigs Pitt began his political career. He played a noisy part in the Opposition campaign for war against Spain, and was a relentless critic of Newcastle's conduct of the operations.

This was indeed lamentable, but the main attack fell upon the extension of the war to Europe. The Opposition proclaimed it a disgraceful and irresponsible subservience to Hanoverian influences. Pitt made a withering speech against the subsidies proposed for raising Hanoverian troops, which gained him the lasting displeasure of the King. In another speech he declared that if Walpole had "betrayed the interest of his country by his pusillanimity, our present Minister sacrifices it by his quixotism." These attacks on Carteret were not unwelcome to Pelham and Newcastle. Intensely jealous of their brilliant colleague, they were only waiting for an occasion to remove him, and when that time came Pitt's eloquence would be remembered, and rewarded.

Thirty thousand British troops, under the command of one of Marlborough's old officers, the Earl of Stair, fought on the Continent. In the spring of 1743 the King himself, accompanied by his younger son, the Duke of Cumberland, left England to take part in the campaign. The Allied forces were concentrated upon the river Main, in the hope of separating the French from their German allies. Bavaria too had taken advantage of the turmoil to attack Queen Maria Theresa, and the Bavarian Elector, with French backing, had been declared Holy Roman Emperor. In the Empire this was the first departure from the Habsburg line in three hundred years. It proved to be a brief interlude. A superior French army under Marshal Noailles lay in the neighbourhood, with the object of cutting off his enemy from their bases in Holland and destroying them in open battle. At the village of Dettingen, near Aschaffenburg, the forces came into conflict. The French cavalry, impatient at delays, charged the Allied left wing. King George's horse bolted, but, dismounting, and sword in hand, he led the Hanoverian and British infantry into action against the French dragoons. They broke and fled, and many were drowned in trying to cross the Main. The French foot failed to retrieve the day, and after four hours' fighting the Allies were in possession of the field. They had lost barely two thousand men, the French twice as many. For the last time an English king had fought at the head of his troops. His son, the Duke of Cumberland, had also shown marked bravery in this sharp action. The witness was a young officer named James Wolfe. But though the house of Hanover had proved their gallantry on the field, they lacked the higher arts of generalship. No decisive results were achieved by their victory at Dettingen.

The campaign subsided. There was bickering between the English and the Hanoverians and much inactivity. The battle of Dettingen raised a brief enthusiasm in London, but opinion slowly hardened against the continuance of a major European war. England was again the head and the paymaster of another Grand Alliance. A new Bourbon Family Compact had been signed between France and Spain, and Secret Service agents reported Jacobite intrigues in Paris. There was talk in London of a French invasion. Dutch troops were hastily brought over to Sheerness. At the end of 1744 Carteret, now Lord Granville, was driven from office. Newcastle again dominated the Government, but he could hardly repudiate the commitments which Carteret and George II had forced upon him, and he was not yet strong enough to oblige the King to accept Pitt. As he complained to his brother, "We must not, because we seem to be in, forget all we said to keep Lord Granville out."

For the campaign of 1745 the King made Cumberland Captain-General of the Forces on the Continent. This young martinet had created the illusion of military capacity by his bravery at Dettingen. His conduct at the head of the Army was, said one of his officers, "outrageously and shockingly military." He had to face the most celebrated soldier of the day, Marshal Saxe. The French Army concentrated against the barrier fortress line, the familiar battleground of Marlborough's wars, now held by the Dutch. Having masked Tournai, Saxe took up a strong position centring upon the village of Fontenoy, near the Mons road. Cumberland drew up his army in battle order, and marched it under fire to within fifty paces of the French army. He was outnumbered by nearly two to one. Lieutenant-Colonel Lord Charles Hay, of the

1st (Grenadier) Guards, stepped from the front ranks, took out a flask, raised it in salute to the French Household troops, and declared, "We are the English Guards, and hope you will stand till we come up to you, and not swim the Scheldt as you did the Main at Dettingen." Cheers rang out from both sides. The English advanced, and at thirty paces the French fired. The murderous fusillade did not halt the Allied infantry, and they drove the enemy from their positions. For hours the French cavalry tried to break the Allied columns, and, watching the Irish Brigade of the French Army sweeping into action, Cumberland exclaimed, "God's curse on the laws that made those men our enemies." It is a more generous remark than is usually recorded of him. At the fall of darkness he withdrew in perfect order down the road to Brussels.

The set battle-pieces of Dettingen and Fontenoy were perhaps useless, but certainly the most creditable engagements in which English troops took part in the middle eighteenth century. At any rate England played no further part in the War of the Austrian Succession. In October 1745 Cumberland withdrew his men to meet the Young Pretender's invasion of England, and our Continental allies were beaten on every front. The only good news came from across the Atlantic. English colonists, supported by a naval squadron, captured the strongest French fortress in the New World, Louisburg, on Cape Breton. This "Dunkirk of North America," commanding the mouth of the St Lawrence and protecting communications between Canada and France, had cost the French over a million pounds. London recognised the significance of the achievement. "Our new acquisition of Cape Breton," wrote Chesterfield, "is become the darling object of the whole nation; it is ten times more so than ever Gibraltar was."

Newcastle, "the impertinent fool" as King George called him, was in confusion. He had no war policy, and having ousted Carteret from the Government had now to "broaden the bottom of the administration," as they said in the terms of those days. The Pelham régime, built up upon the support of Whig family groups, was artificial, but it had its merits. Henry Pelham was a good administrator, economical and efficient, but he was a lesser Walpole faced with a major European war. Newcastle, in his own whimsical way, looked upon the work of government as the duty of his class, but he had no clear ideas on how to discharge it. Lord Shelburne, later Prime Minister, describes these brothers: "They had every talent for obtaining Ministry, and none for governing the kingdom except decency, integrity, and Whig principles. . . . Their forte was cunning, plausibility, and the cultivation of mankind; they knew all the allures of the Court; they were in the habits of administration; they had long been keeping a party together. . . . Mr Pelham had a still more plausible manner than his brother, who rather cajoled than imposed upon mankind, passing for a man of less understanding than he was."

But the war dominated everything. For ten years the Pelham brothers made constant and frantic efforts to create a stable Government. The ghost of King William hovered over them. Their foreign policy was a faint and distorted shadow of the previous generation's. Austria and Holland were no longer Great Powers on the Continent. The Grand Alliance was dead. Fumbling and out of date in Europe, and unmindful of the great future overseas, the Broad-bottomed Administration of the 1740's was a painful affair. One man saw the need for a new policy—William Pitt. And what likelihood was there that the King would admit him to his councils?

*　　*　　*　　*　　*

There had been much discontent in Scotland since the Union of 1707. In the inaccessible Highlands, where the writ of English government hardly ran, there was a persistent loyalty to the house of Stuart and the Jacobite cause. Living in their mountain villages like hill tribesmen, a law unto themselves, the immemorial zest for plunder and forays was still unslaked among the clans. The Union had not alleviated their poverty. "Not infrequently," writes Lecky, "the chiefs increased their scanty incomes by kidnapping boys or men, whom they sold as slaves to the American planters. Generations of an idle and predatory life had produced throughout the Highlands the vices of barbarians. The slightest provocation was avenged with blood. Fierce contests between chiefs and clans were perpetuated from age to age, and the pile of stones which marked the spot where a Highlander had fallen preserved for many generations the memory of the feud. In war the Highlanders usually gave no quarter. Their savage, merciless ferocity long made them the terror of their neighbours."[1]

While the rest of Scotland was gripped by the discipline of the Presbyterian Kirk, the Highlands were ruled by chiefs incapable of combining among themselves or of keeping the peace, but still preserving the tatters of warlike and romantic honour.

After the failure of the rising in 1715 the Jacobites had stayed quiet, but once England was involved in war upon the Continent their activities revived. The Old Pretender was now living in retirement, and his son, Prince Charles Edward, was the darling of the impecunious exiles who clustered round him in Rome and Paris. His handsome presence and gay demeanour fortified the popularity of his cause. In 1744 he sought the help of the French Government and established a base at Gravelines. His hopes of invading England in that year with French assistance were frustrated. Nothing daunted,

[1] W. E. H. Lecky, *History of England in the Eighteenth Century* (1878), vol. ii.

he sailed from Nantes in June 1745 with a handful of followers and landed in the Western Isles of Scotland. Thus began one of the most audacious and irresponsible enterprises in British history. Charles had made scarcely any preparations. He could command support only in the Highlands, which contained but a small proportion of the whole population of Scotland. The clans were always ready to fight, but never to be led. Arms and money were short, the Lowlands hostile, and the Highland troops were hated. The commercial classes regarded them as bandits. The cities had long accepted Hanoverian rule.

Twelve hundred men under Lord George Murray raised the Jacobite standard at Glenfinnan. About three thousand Government troops gathered in the Lowlands under Sir John Cope. The rebels marched southwards; Prince Charles entered the palace at Holyrood, and Cope was met and routed on the battlefield of Prestonpans. By the end of September Charles was ruler of most of Scotland in the name of his father, "King James VIII"; but his triumph was fleeting. The castle of Edinburgh held out for King George, and from time to time discharged a sullen shot. The mass of the Scottish people were apathetic. In London however there was panic; a run on the Bank was only met by paying out in sixpences. Most of the Army was still in Flanders.

With five thousand men the Young Pretender crossed the Border. Three forces were assembled against him. General Wade stood at Newcastle; Cumberland marched to block the London road at Lichfield and strike westwards if he tried to join the Jacobites in the Welsh mountains. A third, encamped on Finchley Common to protect London, still lives in Hogarth's satirical print. This the King did not like. He fancied himself as a warrior and thought it unbecoming to make fun of soldiers.

The Highlanders were quick on the move. Plundering as

they went, they marched due south, occupying Carlisle, Penrith, Lancaster, and Preston. The number of English adherents that came in was depressingly small. They had hopes of getting reinforcements in Manchester. A drummer boy and a whore preceded them into the town as an inducement for recruits. Their combined efforts brought in two hundred men. Many Highlanders deserted and returned home during the southward march. Liverpool was staunchly Hanoverian, and equipped a regiment at its own expense.

The chieftains demanded to return to Scotland. Charles knew of the panic in London, and hoped to profit by it, but he had no control over his followers. By brilliant tactics Lord George Murray had manœuvred Cumberland away from the London road and the path to the capital was open. But it was December. The English commanded the sea; there was no hope from France; the Dutch and Hessians were sending troops to England. There was feverish recruitment in London. A six-pound bonus was paid to everyone who enlisted in the Guards.

At Derby Charles gave the signal to retreat. Two days later news came that the Jacobites in Wales were ready to rise. A winter march began to the fastnesses of Northern Scotland. The English forces followed like vultures, hanging upon the rear and wings of the rebel army. Murray showed great skill in the withdrawal, and in rearguard actions his troops were invariably successful. They turned and mauled their pursuers at Falkirk. But with Teutonic thoroughness the Duke of Cumberland concentrated the English armies for a decision, and in April 1746 on Culloden Moor the last chances of a Stuart Restoration were swept into the past for ever. The Stuarts were to linger in men's memories as a sentimental, though ill-founded, legend of gracious and kindly kings. No quarter was given on the battlefield, where Cumberland earned his long-lived title of "Butcher." Charles Edward escaped over the moors with a few faithful servants. Disguised as a woman, he was smuggled across to the island of Skye by that heroine of romance, Flora Macdonald. Thence he sailed for the Continent, to drink out his life in perpetual exile. Flora Macdonald, for her gallant and virtuous part in this episode, was imprisoned for a time in the Tower of London.

Ruthless repression measured the fears of the Hanoverian Government for their régime. The Highlanders were disarmed and the remnants of feudalism abolished. Jacobitism vanished from the political life of Great Britain. Wade, now a Field-Marshal, drove military roads far into the Highlands, garrisons were established at Inverness and elsewhere, and finally, when the Seven Years' War broke out, Pitt canalised the martial ardour of the Highlanders into the service of his Imperial dreams. Highland regiments brought glory to Scotland under Wolfe at Quebec, and ever since have stood in the forefront of the British Army. Highland traditions and Jacobite legends survived in the romances of Sir Walter Scott. There is still a White Rose League.

*   *   *   *   *

In the crisis of the rebellion the Pelhams delivered their ultimatum. They must have Pitt or they would resign. In April 1746 Pitt became Paymaster of the Forces, an office of immense emolument in time of war. By a custom, openly avowed, the Paymaster was permitted to carry his balances to his private account and draw the interest on them. Further, he received commission on the subsidies paid to foreign allies for the maintenance of their troops in the field. Pitt refused to accept a penny beyond his official salary. The effect on public opinion was electric. By instinct rather than calculation he gained the admiration and confidence of the middle classes, the City, the rising mercantile towns, and the country freeholders. A born actor, by this gesture he caught the eye of the people, and held it as no statesman had held it before him. For nine years Pitt learnt the day-to-day work of administration. The dismal war on the Continent ended with the Treaty of Aix-la-Chapelle in 1748. Nothing was settled between Britain and France by this peace. The only gainer was Frederick the Great, who had stepped in and out of the war as it suited him. He kept Silesia.

Pitt now spent many hours in earnest discussion with Newcastle on the need for a new foreign policy. He pointed out the danger of ignoring Prussia. "This country and Europe," he declared, "are undone without a secure and lasting peace; the alliance as it now stands has not the force ever to obtain it without the interposition of Prussia." The French menace obsessed his mind. His ideas were forming and clarifying during this period of subordinate office. Pelham was delighted with the new recruit. "I think him the most able and useful man we have among us; truly honourable and strictly honest." But Pitt fretted, impotent to control or to criticise the policy of the administration of which he was a member. By acid and frequent attacks he had forced his way into the Government, only to find himself paralysed by the displeasure of the sovereign. He could not achieve supreme political power by traditional means. He must gain it by appealing to the imagination of the country. But in the interlude of peace between 1748 and 1754 the issues were too confused and the intrigues too virulent for a dramatic move. In 1751 Frederick, Prince of Wales, the nominal head of the Opposition, died. Pitt and other young politicians had once entertained great hopes of achieving power when this nonentity should succeed to the throne. His death weakened the unity of a potential Ministry. In 1754 Henry Pelham expired and the flimsy administration tottered. Pitt was enveloped in the toils of group politics. He was now a powerful candidate for high office, backed by his political allies, the Cobhams and the Grenvilles, and what was left of the Prince of Wales's circle who met at Leicester House. But the King was relentless in his dislike of Pitt, and Cumberland, who had a political following of his own, succeeded in pushing into the Cabinet Pitt's most dangerous rival, Henry Fox.

Hope of a great political career seemed at an end for William Pitt. He could gain little from the smiles of the Princess of Wales, the garrulous promises of Newcastle, or the narrow backing of his own political group. As he himself wrote to Lyttelton, "Consideration and weight in the House of Commons generally arises but from one or two causes— the protection of the Crown or from weight in the country, generally from opposition to public measures." To this latter he was now forced. Breaking away from the constricted field of politics, which Newcastle managed by the methods of Walpole, Pitt was to revive and rekindle the national senti- ment of the English which had been inspired by Marlborough's wars. Appealing over the heads of petty groups to the nation at large, he was eventually to knock down the fragile struc- tures of contemporary politicians and bring a driving wind of reality into politics. But the arrival of Fox in the Govern- ment, an avaricious expert in contemporary political method, made Pitt despair. After a great speech in the Commons he was dismissed from the Pay Office in November 1755.

Two months later a diplomatic revolution took place to- wards which the four main Powers of Europe had for some time been groping. A convention was signed between Britain and Prussia, shortly followed by a treaty between the French and the Austrians. Thus there was a complete reversal of alliances. A third war with France began with a new and vigorous ally on England's side, the Prussia of Frederick the Great, but with a fumbling Government at Westminster. The mismanagement of the early years of the struggle, which had been precipitated by the bellicose Cumberland, gave Pitt his chance. The loss of the island of Minorca raised a national outcry. The Government, faced with this national disgrace, lost its nerve. Cumberland's favourite, Henry Fox, bolted into retirement. The Government shifted the blame on to Admiral Byng, whose ill-equipped fleet had failed to relieve the Minorca garrison. By one of the most scandalous evasions of responsibility that an English Government has ever perpetrated Byng was shot for cowardice upon the quarterdeck of his flagship. Pitt pleaded for him with the King. "The House of Commons, Sir, is inclined to mercy." "You have taught me," the King replied, "to look for the sense of my people elsewhere than in the House of Commons." Pitt's hour had almost come. "Walpole," Dr Johnson once remarked, "was a Minister given by the Crown to the people. Pitt was a Minister given by the people to the Crown." But he had learnt by experience that "weight in the country" was not enough without Parliamentary influence, such as the Duke of Newcastle commanded. The Duke, thoroughly frightened by the general outcry, knew that all his connections, all his patronage, would not save him if the nation was determined to call him to account. The two men drew together. Pitt was ready to leave the jobbing to the Duke. And the Duke showed himself ready to lead a quiet life behind the glory of Pitt's achievements and the splendour of his eloquence.

The American Colonies

PITT'S rise to power and his victorious conduct of a world-wide war were to have a profound effect on the history of North America. We must now survey the scene presented by the American colonies, which had been quietly and steadily growing for the past hundred and fifty years. Throughout the first half of the seventeenth century Englishmen had poured into the American continent. Legally the colonies in which they settled were chartered bodies subordinate to the Crown, but there was little interference from home, and they soon learned to govern themselves. While distracted by the Civil War the Mother Country left them alone, and although Cromwell's Commonwealth asserted that Parliament was supreme over the whole of the English world its decree was never put into practice, and was swept away by the Restoration. But after 1660 the home Government had new and definite ideas. For the next fifty years successive English administrations tried to enforce the supremacy of the Crown in the American colonies and to strengthen royal power and patronage in the overseas possessions. Thus they hoped to gain credit and advantage. Committees were formed to deal with America. New colonies were founded in Carolina and Pennsylvania, and New Netherland was conquered from the Dutch. Precautions were taken to assure the Crown's authority in these acquisitions. There were efforts to rescind or modify the charters of the older colonies. All this led to unceasing conflict with the colonial assemblies, who resented the threat to royalise and unify colonial administration. Most of these assemblies were representative bodies of freeholders who claimed and exercised the same rights, procedure, and privileges as the Parliament at Westminster. The men who sat in them were many of them bred in a tradition hostile to the Crown. Their fathers had preferred exile to tyranny, and they regarded themselves as fighting for the same issues as had divided the English Parliament from Strafford and Charles I. They resisted the royal encroachments of the Board of Trade and Plantations. These were reckoned overseas to be a direct attack on rights and privileges guaranteed by the original colonial charters, and a tyrannical menace to vested rights.

For a long time the English Parliament played no part in the conflict. The struggle lay between the colonies and the King's Ministers in the Privy Council. These officials were determined to call a halt to self-government in America. In 1682 they were asked to grant a charter for settling vacant lands on the borders of the Spanish possession of Florida. The Council refused, saying it was the policy of the Crown "not to constitute any new propriety in America nor to grant any further powers that might render the plantations less dependent on the Crown." Under James II these royalist tendencies were sharpened. New York became a royal province in 1685. The New England colonies were united into a "dominion of New England" on the French model in Canada. The main argument was the need for union against French expansion, but the move was fiercely resisted and the English Revolution of 1688 was a signal for the overthrow and collapse of the "dominion of New England."

England's motives were not entirely selfish. Slowly the menace of French imperialism loomed upon the frontiers of her possessions. The reforms of Colbert, the chief Minister of Louis XIV, had greatly strengthened the power and wealth

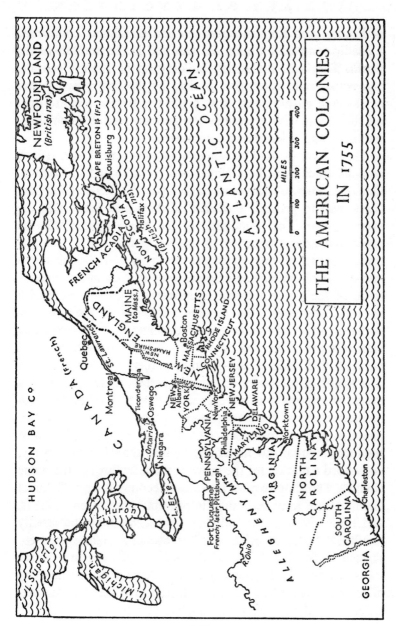

THE AMERICAN COLONIES
IN 1755

MILES
0   100   200   300   400

HUDSON BAY C°

NEWFOUNDLAND
(British 1713)

CAPE BRETON IS (Fr.)
Louisburg

CANADA (French)

FRENCH ACADIA

NOVA SCOTIA (British)
Halifax
1713

Quebec

St. Lawrence R.

Montreal

Ticonderoga

L. Ontario   Oswego

Niagara

L. Erie

L. Huron

L. Michigan

L. Superior

MAINE
(to Mass.)

NEW HAMPSHIRE

MASSACHUSETTS

Boston

R.I.
RHODE ISLAND

CONNECTICUT

NEW YORK

Albany

ATLANTIC OCEAN

PENNSYLVANIA

Fort Duquesne
(French; later Pittsburgh)

Mts.

ALLEGHENY

R. Ohio

VIRGINIA

NEW JERSEY

Philadelphia

New York

DELAWARE

MARYLAND

Yorktown

NORTH CAROLINA

SOUTH CAROLINA

Charleston

GEORGIA

· 141 ·

of France, and English statesmen and merchants confronted a deadly competition upon the seas and in the markets of the world. They saw the steady building up of French colonial and commercial enterprise, backed by the centralised power of absolute government. How could the British Empire fight off the threat with a factious Parliament, fretful colonial assemblies, and a swarm of committees?

The answer devised was an eminently practical one. British colonial trade must be planned and co-ordinated in London. One of its main objects must be to foster the British Merchant Navy, and to provide a reserve of ships and seamen in the event of war. The foundation of the whole system was the series of enactments known as the Navigation Laws. Colonial trade must travel only in British bottoms, with British crews and to British ports. The colonies were forbidden any outside trade of their own that might hinder the growth of British shipping. Moreover, the economic theories of the age supported these checks on colonial independence. The prevailing view of trade was based on the desire for self-sufficiency and on economic nationalism—or mercantilism as it was called. The wealth of a country depended upon its trade balance. An excess of imports over exports meant loss of bullion and economic weakness. National prosperity required the control of plentiful natural resources. Colonies were vital. They must produce essential raw materials, such as timber for the Navy, and afford a market for the growing manufactures of the home country. The Empire must be a closed economic unit. Colonial manufactures must be limited to prevent competition inside it, and trade between the colonies themselves must be strictly regulated. Such, in brief, was the economic conception enshrined in the legislation of the seventeenth century. There was no room in this scheme for the independent development of the colonies. They must remain the providers of raw materials, and the recipients of English manufactures.

The system was more irksome on paper than in practice. No seventeenth-century Government could enforce such a code over thousands of miles. American assemblies grumbled but went their own way, ingeniously evading the Westminster restrictions.

The English Revolution of 1688 changed the whole position. Hitherto the colonies had regarded the Parliament in England as their ally against the Crown. But the time was to come when Parliament, victorious over the Crown in the constitutional struggles at home, would attempt to enforce its own sovereignty over America. The clash was delayed by the War of the Spanish Succession. The long European struggle with France compelled the avoidance of fundamental issues elsewhere; and in the hope of marshalling the resources of the English-speaking peoples for the supreme conflict all efforts to impose the authority of the English Government in the New World were dropped. The Board of Trade and Plantations was allowed to subside and the colonies were largely left to themselves.

The spirit of amity which it was thus hoped to secure fell far short of expectation. There were ample reasons for this. Both in outlook and tradition the colonies had been steadily growing apart from the Mother Country. A colonial-born generation now inhabited the American plantations, trained in the harsh struggle with nature, expanding rapidly in the limitless lands stretching westwards from the seaboard, and determined to protect their individuality and their privileges. The doctrines of the English Revolution and the ideas of the seventeenth-century Whigs struck an even deeper echo in the New World than at home. The youthful energies of the Americans found paper obstacles at every turn to the development of their resources. All these causes indisposed them to any great effort on behalf of England. On the other hand, though quick to realise their potential strength and wealth, the colonists were slow to organise; and being still instinctively loyal to their race and conscious of the French menace beyond their own frontiers they were as anxious as Britain to avoid a serious quarrel. They even took an active but ill-organised part in the attempts to conquer French Canada which culminated in the futile expedition of 1711. But, jealous as they were not only of the home Government but of each other, they soon lapsed into quarrelsome isolation.

*   *   *   *   *

These conditions persisted throughout the administration of Walpole, who perceived the necessity for avoiding friction at all costs. But in the course of time the colonists grew more and more resolved to press their advantage, and the middle years of the eighteenth century witnessed a vehement assault by the colonial Assemblies upon the authority of the Imperial Government. They were bent on making themselves into sovereign Parliaments, supreme in the internal government of the several colonies, and free of all restrictions or interference from London. Innumerable struggles took place between the Governors and the legislatures of the colonies. There were many complaints on both sides. The Crown looked upon posts overseas as valuable patronage for its servants, the Government for their supporters. Thus the whole colonial administration was tainted with the prevailing corruption of English public life. Governors, counsellors, judges, and many other officials were all appointed by the Crown, and they were seldom chosen with due regard to the interests of the colonists. "America," said one of her historians, "is the hospital of Great Britain for its decayed M.P.s and abandoned courtiers." By no means all the British officials were of such a type. Particularly in the North, the Governors often came from the leading colonial families, and the ablest men in colonial administration were of this class. But there were inevitable contests within the colonies themselves. The Governors were particularly vulnerable in matters of finance. Their salaries were fixed by the assemblies, and frequently the assemblies withheld their votes. Irritation between the officials and the assemblies grew and mounted as the years passed by.

Behind the squabbling of day-to-day administration lay vital developments. The Royal Prerogative, so drastically modified in England after the Revolution of 1688, still flourished in the New World. Though the colonial Assemblies persistently tried to copy the English pattern, they were hampered at every turn. Not only were they bound by written charters or constitutions, but special customs, organisations, and Admiralty courts exercised their jurisdiction upon colonial soil, and although the English Government tried to avoid any open meddling, matters went from bad to worse. America was still regarded as existing for the economic benefit of England. The mainland colonies supplied naval stores and tobacco, and the West Indies sent cargoes of sugar to English ports. But the energy and population of America were growing. There were signs that the colonies would produce their own manufactured goods and close their markets to the United Kingdom. As early as 1699 Parliament had legislated against the setting up of industries in the New World. The economic position, particularly in New England, was becoming more and more strained. The Americans could only pay for the increasing volume of English imports by selling their produce to their immediate neighbours and to the English and foreign possessions in the West Indies. This violated the provisions of the Navigation Acts. The economic pressure from England grew stronger with the years. The balance of trade turned steadily against the colonies, and by the middle of the century their annual deficit was over three million pounds. The colonial merchants could only scrape together enough cash by illegal methods. This drift of money from America was to help keep England solvent in the coming first world war. The City knew it; Pitt knew it, and on his monument in Guildhall we may still read how under his administration commerce had been unified and made to flourish by war. But the effect upon the New World was serious. The Americans had no mints, no regularised currency. Their unco-ordinated issues of paper money, which rapidly depreciated, made matters worse, and English merchants loudly complained of the instability of colonial credit.

* * * * *

The early eighteenth century saw the foundation of the last of the Thirteen Colonies. The philanthropist James Oglethorpe had been painfully moved by the horrible condition of the small debtors in English prisons. After much thought he conceived the idea of allowing these people to emigrate to a new colony. The Government was approached, and in 1732 a board of trustees was created to administer a large tract of territory lying below South Carolina. The following year the first settlement was founded at Savannah. Small estates were created, and religious toleration was proclaimed for all except Catholics. The first settlers were English debtors, but the foundation promised a new life for the oppressed in many parts of Europe. Bands of Jews quickly arrived, followed by Protestants from Salzburg, Moravians from Germany, and Highlanders from Skye. The polyglot community, named Georgia, soon attracted ardent missionaries, and it was here that John Wesley began his ministering work.

The high moral atmosphere of these beginnings was soon polluted by mundane quarrels. The settlers, like their brethren in the other colonies, coveted both rum and slaves. The trustees of the community wearied of their task of government; and their prolonged bickering with the rising merchants of Savannah ended in the cancellation of the charter. In 1752 Georgia came under royal control. This colony was the last foundation of the Mother Country in the territories that were later to become the United States. Emigration from England had now dwindled to a trickle, but new settlers arrived from other parts. Towards the end of the seventeenth century there had been an influx of Scottish-Irish refugees, whose industrial and commercial endeavours at home had been stifled by the legislation of the English Parliament. They formed a strong English-hating element in their new homes. Pennsylvania received a steady flow of immigrants from Germany, soon to number over two hundred thousand souls. Hard-working and prosperous Huguenots arrived from France in flight from religious persecution. People were also moving from colony to colony. The oases of provincial life were linked up. The population was rapidly doubling itself. Limitless land to the West offered homes for the sons of the first generation. The abundance of territory to be occupied encouraged large families. Contact with primeval conditions created a new and daring outlook. A sturdy independent society was producing its own life and culture, influenced and coloured by surrounding conditions. The Westward march had begun, headed by the Germans and the Ulster Irish in Pennsylvania. The slow trail over the mountains in search of new lands was opening. There was a teeming diversity of human types. On the Western farms which bordered the Indian country were rugged pioneers and sturdy yeomen farmers, and in the New England colonies assertive merchants, lawyers, and squires, and the sons of traders. This varied society was supported in the North by the forced labour of indentured servants and men smuggled away from the press-gangs in English towns, in the South by a mass of slaves multiplied by yearly shiploads from Africa. Events in Europe, of which most Americans were probably scarcely conscious, now came to bear upon the destiny of the Thirteen Colonies.

The First World War

WHEN Pitt first joined the Ministry as Secretary of State in November 1756 Frederick the Great declared, "England has long been in labour, but at last she has brought forth a man."

Nothing like it had been seen since Marlborough. From his office in Cleveland Row Pitt designed and won a war which extended from India in the East to America in the West. The whole struggle depended upon the energies of this one man. He gathered all power, financial, administrative, and military, into his own hands. He could work with no one as an equal. His position depended entirely on success in the field. His political enemies were numerous. He would tolerate no interference or even advice from his colleagues in the Cabinet; he made no attempt either to consult or to conciliate, and he irritated Newcastle and the Chancellor of the Exchequer by interfering in finance. But in the execution of his military plans Pitt had a sure eye for choosing the right man. He broke incompetent generals and admirals and replaced them with younger men upon whom he could rely: Wolfe, Amherst, Conway, Howe, Keppel, and Rodney. Thus he achieved victory.

But Pitt's success was not immediate. He had opposed the popular clamour for Admiral Byng's court-martial. He was at odds with his colleagues, and the Duke of Cumberland used his powerful and malevolent influence against him. The City merchants were still suspicious of the alliance with Prussia. In April 1757 Pitt was dismissed by the King. Nevertheless he had already made his mark with the nation. He received from the towns and corporations of England a manifestation of their deep feeling—"a shower of gold boxes." For three months there was no effective Government, though Pitt gave all the orders and did the day-to-day work. A stable war Ministry was not formed until June, but for the next four years Pitt was supreme.

Pitt did not confine himself to a single field of operations. By taking the initiative in every quarter of the globe Britain prevented the French from concentrating their forces, confused their plan of campaign, and forced them to dissipate their strength. Pitt had fiercely attacked Carteret for fighting in Europe, but he now realised that a purely naval and colonial war, such as he had advocated in the 1740's, could yield no final decision. Unless France were beaten in Europe as well as in the New World and in the East she would rise again. Both in North America and in Europe she was in the ascendant. At sea she was a formidable enemy. In India it seemed that if ever a European Power established itself on the ruins of the Mogul Empire its banner would be the lilies and not the cross of St George. War with France would be a world war— the first in history; and the prize would be something more than a rearrangement of frontiers and a redistribution of fortresses and sugar islands.

Whether Pitt possessed the strategic eye, whether the expeditions he launched were part of a considered combination, may be questioned. Now, as at all times, his policy was a projection on to a vast screen of his own aggressive, dominating personality. In the teeth of disfavour and obstruction he had made his way to the foremost place in Parliament, and now at last fortune, courage, and the confidence of his countrymen had given him a stage on which his gifts could be displayed and his foibles indulged. To call into life and action the depressed and languid spirit of England; to weld all her resources of wealth and manhood into a single instrument of war which should be felt from the Danube to the Mississippi; to humble the house of Bourbon, to make the Union Jack supreme in every ocean, to conquer, to command, and never to count the cost, whether in blood or gold—this was the spirit of Pitt, and this spirit he infused into every rank of his countrymen, admirals and powder-monkeys, great merchants and little shopkeepers; into the youngest officer of the line, who felt that with Pitt in command failure might be forgiven but hesitation never; into the very Highlanders who had charged at Prestonpans and now were sailing across the Atlantic to win an empire for the sovereign who had butchered their brethren at Culloden.

On the Continent Britain had one ally, Frederick of Prussia, facing the combined power of Austria, Russia, and France. Sweden too had old grudges to avenge, old claims to assert against him. Frederick, by a rapid march through Saxony into Bohemia, sought to break through the closing circle. But in 1757 he was driven back into his own dominions; Cumberland, sent to protect Hanover and Brunswick, was defeated by the French and surrendered both. Russia was on the march; Swedish troops were again seen in Pomerania. Minorca had already fallen. From Canada Montcalm was pressing against the American frontier forts. Never did a war open with darker prospects. Pitt's hour had come. "I know," he had told the Duke of Devonshire, "that I can save this country and that no one else can." He sent back the foreign troops paid to protect England from invasion. He disavowed Cumberland's surrender. Life began to tingle in the torpid frame of English administration. Before the year was out it seemed as if Fortune, recognising her masters, was changing sides. Frederick, supported by the subsidies which Pitt had spent the eloquence of his youth in denouncing, routed the French at Rossbach and the Austrians at Leuthen.

So the great years opened, years for Pitt and his country of almost intoxicating glory. The French were swept out of Hanover; the Dutch, fishing in the murky waters of Oriental intrigue, were stopped by Clive and made to surrender their ships at Chinsura; Cape Breton was again taken, and the name of the "Great Commoner" stamped on the map at Pittsburgh, Pennsylvania. France's two main fleets, in the Mediterranean and in the Channel, were separately defeated. Combined they might have covered an invasion of England. Admiral Boscawen, fresh from the capture of Louisburg, was detailed to watch the Toulon squadron. He caught it slipping through the Straits of Gibraltar, destroyed five ships and drove the rest into Cadiz Bay, blockaded and out of action. Three months later, in the short light of a November day, in a high gale and among uncharted rocks and shoals, Admiral Hawke annihilated the Brest fleet. For the rest of the war Quiberon was an English naval station, where the sailors occupied their leisure and maintained their health by growing cabbages on French soil. Between these victories Wolfe had fallen at Quebec, leaving Amherst to complete the conquest of Canada, while Clive and Eyre Coote were uprooting the remnants of French power in India. Even more dazzling prizes seemed to be falling into British hands. Pitt proposed to conquer the Spanish Indies, West and East, and to seize the annual Treasure Fleet. But at this supreme moment in his career, when world peace and world security seemed within his grasp, the Cabinet declined to support him and he resigned.

*　　*　　*　　*　　*

It is necessary to examine these triumphs and disasters at closer hand. In America Pitt faced a difficult and complex task. The governors of the English colonies had long been aware of the threat beyond their frontiers. The French were moving along the waterways beyond the mountain barrier of the Alleghenies and extending their alliances with the Red Indians in an attempt to link their colony of Louisiana in the

South with Canada in the North. Thus the English settlements would be confined to the seaboard and their Westward expansion would stop. Warfare had broken out in 1754. General Braddock was sent from England to re-establish British authority west of the Alleghenies, but his forces were cut to pieces by the French and Indians in Pennsylvania. In this campaign a young Virginian officer named George Washington learnt his first military lessons. The New England colonies lay open to attack down the easy path of invasion, the Hudson valley. A struggle began for a foothold at the valley head. There was little organisation. Each of the colonies attempted to repel Red Indian raids and French settlers with their own militias. They were united in distrusting the home Government, but in little else. Although there were now over a million British Americans, vastly outnumbering the French, their quarrels and disunion extinguished this advantage. Only the tactful handling of Pitt secured their co-operation, and even so throughout the war colonial traders continued to supply the French with all their needs in defiance of the Government and the common interest.

The year 1756 was disastrous for England in America, and indeed upon all fronts. Oswego, the only English fort on the Great Lakes, was lost. The campaign of 1757 was hardly more successful. The fortress of Louisburg, which commanded the Gulf of St Lawrence, had been taken by an Anglo-Colonial force in the 1740's and returned to France at the peace treaty of 1748 at Aix-la-Chapelle. English troops were now sent to recapture it. They were commanded by an ineffectual and unenterprising officer, Lord Loudon. Loudon prepared to attack by concentrating at Halifax such colonial troops from New England as the colonies would release. This left the Hudson valley open to the French. At the head of the valley were three small forts: Crown Point, Edward, and William Henry. The French, under the Governor of Canada,

Montcalm, and his Red Indian allies, swept over the frontier through the wooded mountains and besieged Fort William Henry. The small colonial garrison held out for five days, but was forced to surrender. Montcalm was unable to restrain his Indians and the prisoners were massacred. The tragedy bit into the minds of the New Englanders. It was Loudon who was to blame. The British were not defending them; while New England was left exposed to the French, the troops which might have protected them were wasting time at Halifax. Indeed, by the end of July Loudon decided that Louisburg was impregnable and had given up the attempt.

Pitt now bent his mind to the American war. Throughout the winter he studied the maps and wrote dispatches to the officers and governors. A threefold strategic plan was framed for 1758. Loudon was recalled. His successor, Amherst, with Brigadier Wolfe, and naval support from Halifax, was to sail up the St Lawrence and strike at Quebec. Another army, under Abercromby, was to seize Lake George at the head of the Hudson valley and try to join Amherst and Wolfe before Quebec. A third force, under Brigadier Forbes, would advance up the Ohio valley from Pennsylvania and capture Fort Duquesne, one of a line of French posts along the Ohio and the Mississippi. The Fleet was so disposed as to stop reinforcements leaving France.

A mind capable of conceiving and directing these efforts was now in power at Whitehall, but supervision at a distance of three thousand miles was almost impossible in the days of sail. Amherst and Wolfe hammered at the northern borders of Canada. In July Louisburg was captured. But Abercromby, advancing from Ticonderoga, became entangled in the dense woods; his army was badly beaten and his advance was halted. The Pennsylvanian venture was more successful. Fort Duquesne was taken and destroyed and the place renamed Pittsburgh; but lack of numbers and organisation compelled the

British force to retire at the end of the campaign. In a dispatch to Pitt Forbes gave a bitter description of the affair: "I vainly at the beginning flattered myself that some very good Service might be drawn from the Virginia & Pennsylvania Forces, but am sorry to find that, a few of their principal Officers excepted, all the rest are an extream bad Collection of broken Innkeepers, Horse Jockeys, & Indian traders, and that the Men under them are a direct Copy of their Officers, nor can it well be otherwise, as they are a gathering from the scum of the worst people, in every Country. . . ." These remarks reflect the worsening relations and woeful lack of understanding between British officers and American colonists.

There was little enough to show for such efforts, but Pitt was undaunted. He realised the need for a combined offensive along the whole frontier from Nova Scotia to the Ohio. Isolated inroads into French territory would bring no decision. On December 29, 1758, further instructions were accordingly sent to Amherst. The necessity for cutting across the French line of expansion was again emphasised. "It were much to be wished," the instructions continue, "that any Operations on the side of Lake Ontario could be pushed as far as Niagara, and that you may find it practicable to set on foot some Enterprize against the Fort there, the Success of which would so greatly contribute to establish the uninterrupted Dominion of that Lake, and at the same time effectually cut off the Communication between Canada and the French Settlements to the South."

There was also much talk about the need of acquiring Red Indian allies. Amherst thought little of this. Several months earlier he had written to Pitt that a large number of Indians were promised him: "They are a pack of lazy, rum-drinking people and little good, but if ever they are of use it will be when we can act offensively. The French are much more afraid of them than they need be; numbers will increase their

Terror and may have a good Effect." Nevertheless it was fortunate for the British that the Six Nations of the Iroquois, who occupied a key position between the British and French settlements near the Great Lakes, were generally friendly; they, like the American colonists, were alarmed at French designs on the Ohio and the Mississippi.

According to the new plan, in the coming year the Navy would attack the French West Indies, and the invasion of Canada up the St Lawrence would be pushed harder than ever in spite of the bitter experience of the past. Since the campaign of 1711 there had been several attempts to ascend the mighty river. Wolfe reported the Navy's "thorough aversion" to the task. It was indeed hazardous. But it was to be backed by a renewed advance up the Hudson against the French fort of Niagara on the Great Lakes, the importance of which Pitt had emphasised in his instructions.

The plan succeeded. The year 1759 brought fame to British arms throughout the world. In May the Navy captured Guadeloupe, the richest sugar island of the West Indies. In July Amherst took Ticonderoga and Fort Niagara, thus gaining for the American colonies a frontier upon the Great Lakes. In September the expedition up the St Lawrence attacked Quebec. Wolfe conducted a personal reconnaissance of the river at night, and beguiled the officers by reciting Gray's "Elegy": "The paths of glory lead but to the grave." By brilliant co-operation between Army and Navy Wolfe landed his men, and led them by the unsuspected path, under cover of darkness, up the steep cliffs of the Heights of Abraham. In the battle that followed Montcalm was defeated and killed and the key fortress of Canada was secured. Wolfe, mortally wounded, lived until victory was certain, and died murmuring, "Now God be praised, I will die in peace."

But it needed another year's fighting to gain Canada for the English-speaking world. In May 1760 the British garrison in

Quebec was relieved after a winter siege. With cautious and dogged organisation Amherst converged on Montreal. In September the city fell and the huge province of French Canada changed hands. These were indeed the years of victory.

The inactivity of the French Fleet is a remarkable feature of the war. If they had blockaded New York in 1759 while the English ships were gathered at Halifax they could have ruined Amherst's advance on Montreal. If they had attacked Halifax after Wolfe and the English ships had left for the St Lawrence they could have wrecked the whole campaign for Quebec. But now it was too late. Further English naval reinforcements were sent to the New World. In 1761 Amherst dispatched an expedition to Martinique. The capture of yet another great commercial prize was received with jubilation in London. In one of his letters Horace Walpole wrote, "I tell you [the eloquence of Pitt] has conquered Martinico. . . . The Romans were three hundred years in conquering the world. We subdued the globe in three campaigns—and a globe as big again."

North America was thus made safe for the English-speaking peoples. Pitt had not only won Canada, with its rich fisheries and Indian trade, but had banished for ever the dream and danger of a French colonial empire stretching from Montreal to New Orleans. Little could he know that the extinction of the French menace would lead to the final secession of the English colonies from the British Empire.

*   *   *   *   *

Pitt's very success contributed to his fall. Just as Marlborough and Godolphin had been faced by a growing war-weariness after Malplaquet, so now Pitt, an isolated figure in his own Government, confronted an increasing dislike of the war after the great victories of 1759. To the people at large he was the "Great Commoner." This lonely, dictatorial man had caught their imagination. He had broken through the narrow circle of aristocratic politics, and his force and eloquence gained him their support. Contrary to the conventions of the age, he had used the House of Commons as a platform from which to address the country. His studied orations in severe classical style were intended for a wider audience than the place-holders of the Duke of Newcastle. Pitt had a contempt for party and party organisations. His career was an appeal to the individual in politics. His vast powers of work and concentration tired all who came in contact with him. Afflicted early in life with severe gout, he had to struggle with ill-health through the worst anxieties of war government. He hardly troubled to see his colleagues. All business was conducted from his office, except for weekly meetings with Newcastle and the Treasury Secretary to arrange the finances of his strategy, money and troops for Wolfe and Clive, subsidies for Frederick the Great. But his power was transient. There were not only enemies within the Government, stung by his arrogance and his secrecy, but also among his former political allies, the Princess of Wales and her circle at Leicester House. Here the young heir to the throne was being brought up amid the Opposition views of his mother and her confidant, the Earl of Bute. Pitt had been their chosen candidate for the sunshine days when the old King should die. They now deemed him a deserter. They branded his acceptance of office in 1746 as a betrayal. Bute, with his close position at this future Court, was the most dangerous of Pitt's opponents, and it was he who stimulated opinion and the Press against the war policy of the Minister.

Pitt's position was indeed perilous. He had destroyed France's power in India and North America and had captured her possessions in the West Indies. It seemed as if Britain had achieved everything she desired. All that was left was the unpopular commitment to Prussia, and Bute found it only too easy to convert the feelings of weariness into an effective opposition to Pitt. Among his colleagues there were some who honestly and patriotically doubted the wisdom of continuing the war, from which Britain had gained more than perhaps she could keep; a war which had raised her once more to the height at which she had stood after Ramillies. The war had to be paid for. It was already producing the inevitable consequences of even the most glorious war. Heavy taxation on the industrial and landed classes was matched by huge fortunes for the stock-jobber and the contractor. It was in vain that Pitt attempted to show that no lasting or satisfactory peace could be secured till France was defeated in Europe. Making terms before France was exhausted would repeat the Tory mistakes at Utrecht and only snatch a breathing-space for the next conflict. It was with bitterness that Pitt realised his position. His Imperial war policy had succeeded only too well, leaving him with the detested and costly subsidies to Prussia which he knew were essential to the final destruction of French power.

In October 1760 George II died. He had never liked Pitt, but had learnt to respect his abilities. The Minister's comment was pointed: "Serving the King may be a duty, but it is the most disagreeable thing imaginable to those who have that honour." The temper of the new ruler was adverse. George III had very clear ideas of what he wanted and where he was going. He meant to be King, such a King as all his countrymen would follow and revere. Under the long Whig régime the House of Commons had become an irresponsible autocracy. Would not the liberties of the country be safer in the hands of a monarch, young, honourable, virtuous, and appearing thoroughly English, than in a faction governing the land through a packed and corrupt House of Commons? Let him make an end of government by families, choose his own Ministers and stand by them, and end once and for all the corruption of political life. But in such a monarchy what was the place of a man like Pitt, who owed nothing to corruption, nothing to the Crown, and everything to the people and to his personal domination of the House of Commons? So long as he was in power he would divide the kingdom with Cæsar. He could not help it. His profound reverence for the person and office of George III could not conceal from either of them the fact that Pitt was a very great man and the King a very limited man. Bute, "the Minister behind the curtain," was now all-powerful at Court. Newcastle, who had long chafed under the harsh, domineering ways of his colleague, was only too ready to intrigue against him. There was talk of peace. Negotiations were opened at The Hague, but broke down when Pitt refused to desert Prussia. The French War Minister, Choiseul, like Torcy fifty years before, saw his chance. He realised that Pitt's power was slipping. In 1761 he made a close alliance with Spain, and in September the negotiations with England collapsed. With the power of Spain behind her in the Americas, France might now regain her dominance in the New World.

Pitt hoped that war with Spain would rouse the same popular upsurge as in 1739. The chance of capturing more Spanish colonies might appeal to the City. His proposal for the declaration of war was put to the Cabinet. He found himself isolated. He made a passionate speech to his colleagues: "Being responsible I will direct, and will be responsible for nothing I do not direct." He met with a savage rebuke from the old enemy whose career he had broken, Carteret, now Lord Granville. "When the gentleman talks of being responsible to the people, he talks the language of the House of Commons, and forgets that at this board he is only responsible to the King." He had no choice but resignation.

William Pitt ranks with Marlborough as the greatest Englishman in the century between 1689 and 1789. "It is a considerable fact in the history of the world," wrote Carlyle, "that he was for four years King of England." He was not the first English statesman to think in terms of a world policy and to broaden on to a world scale the political conceptions of William III. But he is the first great figure of British Imperialism. Pitt too had brought the force of public opinion to bear upon politics, weakening the narrow monopoly of the great Whig houses. His heroic period was now over. "Be one people," he commanded the factions. Five years later he was to hold high office once more amid tragic circumstances of failing health. In the meantime his magnificent oratory blasted the policies of his successors.

*   *   *   *   *

Unsupported by the fame of Pitt, the Duke of Newcastle was an easy victim, and the administration slid easily into the hands of Lord Bute. His sole qualification for office, apart from great wealth and his command of the Scottish vote, was that he had been Groom of the Stole to the King's mother. For the first time since the assassination of the Duke of Buckingham the government of England was committed to a man with no political experience, and whose only connection with Parliament was that he had sat as a representative peer of Scotland for a short time twenty years before. The London mob delivered their verdict on the King's choice in the image of a Jack Boot and a Petticoat.

Within three months of Pitt's resignation the Government were compelled to declare war on Spain. This led to further successes in the West Indies and elsewhere. The British Fleet seized the port of Havana, which commanded the trade routes of the Spanish Main and the movement of the Treasure Fleets. In the Pacific Ocean an expedition from Madras descended upon the Philippines and captured Manila. At sea and on land England was mistress of the outer world. These achievements were largely cast away.

Fifty years after the Treaty of Utrecht Britain signed a new peace with France. Bute sent the Duke of Bedford to Paris to negotiate its terms. The Duke thought his country

· 160 ·

was taking too much of the globe and would be in perpetual danger from European coalitions and attacks by dissatisfied nations. He believed in the appeasement of France and Spain and the generous return of conquests. Pitt, on the other hand, demanded the decisive weakening of the enemy. To his mind there would be no secure or permanent peace until France and Spain were placed at a lasting disadvantage. He could take no part in the negotiations, and he vehemently denounced the treaty as undermining the safety of the realm.

Britain's acquisitions under the terms of the Peace of Paris in 1763 were nevertheless considerable. In America she secured Canada, Nova Scotia, Cape Breton, and the adjoining islands, and the right to navigate the Mississippi, important for Red Indian trade. In the West Indies Grenada, St Vincent, Dominica, and Tobago were acquired. From Spain she received Florida. In Africa she kept Senegal. In India, as will be related, the East India Company preserved its extensive conquests, and although their trading posts were returned the political ambitions of the French in the sub-continent were finally extinguished. In Europe Minorca was restored to England, and the fortifications of Dunkirk were at long last demolished.

Historians have taken a flattering view of a treaty which established Britain as an Imperial Power, but its strategic weakness has been smoothly overlooked. It was a perfect exposition of the principles of the Duke of Bedford. The naval power of France had been left untouched. In America she received back the islands of St Pierre and Miquelon, in the Gulf of the St Lawrence, with the right to fish upon the shores of Newfoundland. These were the nursery of the French Navy, in which about fourteen thousand men were permanently employed. Their commercial value was nearly half a million pounds a year. They might form naval bases or centres for smuggling French goods into the lost province of Canada. In the West Indies the richest prize of the war, the sugar island of Guadeloupe, was also handed back, together with Martinique, Belle Isle, and St Lucia. Guadeloupe was so rich that the English Government even considered keeping it and in exchange returning Canada to the French. These islands were also excellent naval bases for future use against England.

Spain regained the West Indian port of Havana, which controlled the maritime strategy of the Caribbean. She also received back Manila, an important centre for the China trade. If the English had retained them the fleets of France and Spain would have been permanently at their mercy. In Africa, in spite of Pitt's protests, France got back Goree—a base for privateers on the flank of the East Indian trade routes. Moreover, the treaty took no account of the interests of Frederick the Great. This ally was left to shift for himself. He never forgave Britain for what he regarded as a betrayal, which rankled long afterwards in the minds of Prussian leaders.

These terms fell so short of what the country expected that, in spite of the general desire for peace, it seemed doubtful if Parliament would ratify them. By some means or other a majority had to be ensured, and the means were only too familiar. All the arts of Parliamentary management were employed. Lords and Commoners known to be hostile to the Government were dismissed from any office they had been fortunate enough to acquire. Vain was it that Pitt denounced the treaty and prophesied war. It was approved by 319 votes to 65. Appeasement and conciliation won the day. But the sombre verdict of the man who endured the deliberate maiming of his work contained the historic truth. He saw in its terms the seeds of a future war. "The peace was insecure, because it restored the enemy to her former greatness. The peace was inadequate, because the places gained were no equivalent for the places surrendered."

The Quarrel with America

T HE accession of George III caused a profound change in
English politics. In theory and in law the monarchy still
retained a decisive influence and power in the making of
policy, the choice of Ministers, the filling of offices, and the
spending of money. In these and in many other fields the
personal action of the King had for many centuries been far-
reaching, and generally accepted, and only since the instal-
lation of the Hanoverian dynasty had the royal influence been
largely exercised by the Whig Ministers in Parliament. Walpole and Newcastle had been much more than Ministers;
they were almost Regents. There had been many reasons
why they and their supporters had achieved and held such
power for nearly half a century. Both George I and George II
were aliens in language, outlook, upbringing, and sympathy;
their Court was predominantly German; their interests and
ambitions had centred on Hanover and on the Continent of
Europe, and they owed their throne to the Whigs. Now all
was changed. George III was, or thought he was, an Englishman born and bred. At any rate he tried to be. He had
received a careful education in England from his mother
and from the Earl of Bute, who was a Scotsman and in his
opponents' eyes a Tory. George's earliest recorded literary
achievement is a boyhood essay on Alfred the Great. "George,
be King," his mother had said, according to tradition, and
George did his best to obey. That he failed in the central

problems of his reign may, in the long run of events, have been fortunate for the ultimate liberty of England. Out of the disasters that ensued rose the Parliamentary system of government as we now know it, but the disasters were nevertheless both formidable and far-reaching. By the time that George died America had separated herself from the United Kingdom, the first British Empire had collapsed, and the King himself had gone mad.

But at first all promised well. The times were opportune for a revival of the royal influence. So long as the Hanoverian right to the Crown was challenged the Whigs could exclude the Tories from office by denouncing them as Jacobites, but by 1760 the cause of the Stuart Pretenders was dead, the succession was undisputed, and George III ascended the throne on the crest of a loyalist and patriotic reaction against the Whig monopoly of power. The large Tory-minded section of the "Country Party" was at last reconciled to the monarchy, and they rallied to him and to themselves all those elements in the nation which hated the narrow aristocratic domination of the Whig families. George III was thus supported by many "King's Friends," loyal, hungry for power, and eager to help him "turn out the old gang." This he and Bute proceeded to do. In 1761 elections were held throughout England, in which Newcastle was not allowed to control all the royal patronage and many offices in the gift of the Crown were bestowed on supporters of the new monarch. In March Bute was appointed Secretary of State, and Newcastle was shuffled querulously out of office in the following spring. Within two years of his accession the "King's Friends" predominated in the House of Commons. They were not a political party in the modern sense, but they were generally prepared to support almost any administration appointed by the King. The Crown was once more a factor in politics, and young George had beaten the Whigs at their own game. It was not however till 1770 that he was in firm control of the political machine, and for a long time he was unfortunate in his search for trustworthy Ministers.

* * * * *

The first decade of his reign passed in continual and confused manœuvring between the different Parliamentary groups, some of them accepting the new situation, some making passive resistance to the new tactics of the Crown. George was angry and puzzled at the wrangling of the political leaders. Pitt sat moodily in Parliament, "unconnected and unconsulted." Many people shared Dr Johnson's opinion of the Scots, and Bute, who was much disliked, fell from power early in 1763. His successor, George Grenville, was a mulish lawyer, backed by the enormous electoral power of the Duke of Bedford, of whom "Junius" wrote in his anonymous letters, "I daresay he has bought and sold more than half the representative integrity of the nation." Grenville refused to play the part of "the Minister behind the curtain"; but for two years he clung to office, and must bear a heavy share of responsibility for the alienation of the American colonies.

There were other conflicts. On April 23, 1763, a newspaper called *The North Briton* attacked Ministers as "tools of despotism and corruption. . . . They have sent the spirit of discord through the land, and I will prophesy it will never be extinguished but by the extinction of their power." Grenville's Ministry was denounced as a mere reflection of the unpopular Lord Bute. The writer hinted that the peace treaty with France was not only dishonourably but also dishonestly negotiated, and that the King was a party to it. George was incensed. A week later his Secretary of State issued a warrant commanding that the authors, printers, and publishers of *"The North Briton,* No. 45," none of whom was named, should be found and arrested. Searches were made, houses were entered, papers were seized, and nearly fifty suspects were put in prison. Among them was John Wilkes, a rake and a Member of Parliament. He was sent to the Tower. He refused to answer questions. He protested that the warrant was illegal and claimed Parliamentary privilege against the arrest. There was a storm in the country. The legality of "general" warrants which named no actual offender became a constitutional question of the first importance. Wilkes was charged with seditious libel and outlawed. But his case became a national issue when he returned to fight for his Parliamentary seat. The radical-minded Londoners welcomed this rebuff to the Government, and in March 1768 he was elected for Middlesex. The next February he was expelled from the House of Commons and there was a by-election. Wilkes stood again, and obtained 1,143 votes against his Government opponent, who polled 296. There were bonfires in London. The election was declared void by Parliament, and Wilkes, now once more in prison for printing an obscene parody of Pope's "Essay on Man," entitled "Essay on Woman," became the idol of the City. Finally his opponent in Middlesex was declared duly elected. When Wilkes was released from gaol in April 1770 London was illuminated to greet him. After a long struggle he was elected Lord Mayor, and again a Member of Parliament.

The whole machinery of eighteenth-century corruption was thus exposed to the public eye. By refusing to accept Wilkes the Commons had denied the right of electors to choose their Members and held themselves out as a closed corporation of privileged beings. Wilkes's cause now found the most powerful champion in England. Pitt himself, now Earl of Chatham, in blistering tones attacked the legality of general warrants and the corruption of politics, claiming that more seats in the counties would increase the electorate and diminish the opportunities for corruption, so easy in the small boroughs. His speeches were indeed the first demands for Parliamentary reform in the eighteenth century. It was not however for many years that anything was accomplished in this field.

Nevertheless the outcry against general warrants led directly to important pronouncements by the judges on the liberty of the individual, the powers of the Government, and freedom of speech. Wilkes and the other victims sued the officials who had executed the warrants. The judges ruled that the warrants were illegal. The officials pleaded that they were immune because they were acting under Government orders. This large and sinister defence was rejected by the Chief Justice in words which remain a classic statement on the rule of law. "With respect to the argument of State necessity," declared Lord Camden, "or a distinction which has been aimed at between State offences and others, the Common Law does not understand that kind of reasoning, nor do our books take notice of any such distinction." If a Minister of the Crown ordered something to be done which was unlawful, then both he and his servants must answer for it in the ordinary courts of law in exactly the same way as a private person. The Under-Secretary who entered Wilkes's house and took away his papers and the King's Messengers who arrested the printer were mere trespassers and were liable as such. They were guilty of false imprisonment, and the judges refused to interfere when juries awarded large sums by way of compensation. Wilkes obtained £4,000 damages from the Secretary of State himself. Another suitor, who had been detained only for a few hours and fed with steak and beer, recovered £300. "The small injury done to the plantiff," said the Chief Justice, "or the inconsiderableness of his station and rank in life did not appear to the jury in that striking light in which the great point of law touching the liberty of the subject appeared to them at the trial."

Here indeed was a potent weapon against overbearing ministers and zealous officials. Habeas Corpus might, and did,

protect the subject from unlawful arrest, or at any rate ensure
his speedy release from gaol, but a civil action for false imprisonment hit the authorities where it hurt most, in their
private pockets, and the unfettered right of juries to assess the
damages at whatever figure they thought fit was a formidable
deterrent to such as might be tempted to offend public opinion by relying on "reasons of State." The lesson bit deep. Even
in the dark times to come, when the struggle with Napoleon
forced the Government to take all sorts of repressive measures
against real or imagined traitors, the powers of the executive
to infringe the liberty of the subject were narrowly circumscribed and vigilantly watched by Parliament. Not until the
world wars of the twentieth century was the mere word of a
Minister of the Crown enough to legalise the imprisonment
of an Englishman.

Freedom of the Press and freedom of speech developed
by much the same unspectacular, technical, but effective steps.
Long before George I had mounted the throne Parliament
declined to renew the Licensing Act. The last relics of the
censorship once exercised by the Court of Star Chamber
thereby disappeared, and ever since Englishmen have been
generally free to say what they like in print without prior
leave of the Government or of anyone else. Parliament's decision was taken, not on any high ground of principle, but
because the detailed working of the Act was causing vexation.
The freedom of the Press was thus never deliberately established in Britain; it was allowed to begin for quite inconsider-
able reasons. That a man can speak without prior permission
however does not mean that he may say what he likes. If he
is libellous or seditious or blasphemous or obscene, or com-
mits any other legal wrong, he can afterwards be made liable for it; and this is the limitation on freedom of expression
which still exists to-day. The boundaries of this freedom are
fixed by the definitions of a large number of criminal and

civil wrongs; and these definitions, expanded to meet the requirements of succeeding generations and confirmed in their expanded form by the doctrine of precedent, have come to hedge freedom rather closely in certain directions. The common remedy for this strictness of the law has been the good sense of prosecutors, who do not enforce it to the letter. But this is not enough if feelings run high, as they did in eighteenth-century politics, when critics of the Government were apt to be put in the dock for seditious libel, and a better safeguard was finally established in the powers of the jury. Through many years and in many trials it was hotly argued that the jury should decide not only whether or not the defendant had published the matter complained of, but also whether or not it was a libel, and Fox's Libel Act eventually established this opinion as law. The letter of the law was thus subjected in each case to the discretion of a jury, and in the last year of the eighteenth century it could be said that "a man may publish anything which twelve of his countrymen think is not blameable." History will not deny some share in the credit for this achievement to Alderman John Wilkes.

*   *   *   *   *

The contest with America had meanwhile begun to dominate the British political scene. Vast territories had fallen to the Crown on the conclusion of the Seven Years' War. From the Canadian border to the Gulf of Mexico the entire hinterland of the American colonies became British soil, and the parcelling out of these new lands led to further trouble with the colonists. Many of them, like George Washington, had formed companies to buy these frontier tracts from the Indians, but a royal proclamation restrained any purchasing and prohibited their settlement. Washington, among others, ignored the ban and wrote to his land agent ordering him "to secure some of the most valuable lands in the King's part [on the Ohio], which I think may be accomplished after a while, notwithstanding the proclamation that restrains it at present, and prohibits the settling of them at all; *for I can never look upon that proclamation in any other light (but this I say between ourselves) than as a temporary expedient to quiet the minds of the Indians."* [1] This attempt by the British Government to regulate the new lands caused much discontent among the planters, particularly in the Middle and Southern colonies.

George III was also determined that the colonies should pay their share in the expenses of the Empire and in garrisoning the New World. For this there were strong arguments. England had supplied most of the men and the money in the struggle with France for their protection, and indeed their survival; but the methods used by the British Government were ineffective and imprudent. It was resolved to impose a tax on the colonies' imports, and in 1764 Parliament strengthened the Molasses Act. This measure was originally passed in 1733 to protect the West Indian sugar-growers. It created a West Indian monopoly of the sugar trade within the Empire and imposed a heavy duty on foreign imports. It had long been evaded by the colonists, whose only means of acquiring hard cash to pay their English creditors was by selling their goods for molasses in the French and Spanish West Indies. The new regulations were a serious blow. As one merchant put it, "The restrictions which we are laid under by the Parliament put us at a stand how to employ our vessels to any advantage, as we have no prospect of markets at our own islands and cannot send elsewhere to have anything that will answer in return."

The results were unsatisfactory on both sides of the Atlantic. The British Government found that the taxes brought in very little money, and the English merchants, already con-

[1] Author's italics.—W.S.C.

cerned at the plight of their American debtors, had no desire to make colonial finance any more unstable. Indirect taxation of trade being so unfruitful, Grenville and his lieutenant Charles Townshend consulted the Law Officers about levying a direct tax on the colonies. Their opinion was favourable and Grenville proposed that all colonial legal documents should be stamped, for a fee. The colonial agents in London were informed, and discussed the plan by post with the Assemblies in America. There were few protests, although the colonists had always objected to direct taxation, and in 1765 Parliament passed the Stamp Act.

With two exceptions it imposed no heavy burden. The stamps on legal documents would not in any case produce a large revenue. The English stamp duty brought in £300,000 a year. Its extension to America was only expected to raise another £50,000. But the Act included a tax on newspapers, many of whose journalists were vehement partisans of the extremist party in America, and the colonial merchants were dismayed because the duty had to be paid in bullion already needed for meeting the adverse trade balance with England. The dispute exposed and fortified the more violent elements in America, and gave them a chance to experiment in organised resistance. The future revolutionary leaders appeared from obscurity—Patrick Henry in Virginia, Samuel Adams in Massachusetts, and Christopher Gadsden in South Carolina—and attacked both the legality of the Government's policy and the meekness of most American merchants. A small but well-organised Radical element began to emerge. But although there was an outcry and protesting delegates convened a Stamp Act Congress there was no unity of opinion in America. The stamp-distributors were attacked and their offices and houses wrecked, but all this was the work of a few merchants and young lawyers who were trying their hand at rousing the unenfranchised mobs. The most effective opposition came from English merchants, who realised that the Act imperilled the recovery of their commercial debts and denounced it as contrary to the true commercial interests of the Empire and a danger to colonial resources.

*   *   *   *   *

The personality of George III was now exercising a preponderant influence upon events. He was one of the most conscientious sovereigns who ever sat upon the English throne. Simple in his tastes and unpretentious in manner, he had the superficial appearance of a typical yeoman. But his mind was Hanoverian, with an infinite capacity for mastering detail, and limited success in dealing with large issues and main principles. He possessed great moral courage and an inveterate obstinacy, and his stubbornness lent weight to the stiffening attitude of his Government. His responsibility for the final breach is a high one. He could not understand those who feared the consequences of a policy of coercion. He expressed himself in blunt terms. "It is with the utmost astonishment that I find any of my subjects capable of encouraging the rebellious disposition which unhappily exists in some of my colonies in America. Having entire confidence in the wisdom of my Parliament, the Great Council of the Nation, I will steadily pursue those measures which they have recommended for the support of the constitutional rights of Great Britain and the protection of the commercial interests of my kingdom."

But now, writhing under the domination of Grenville and his friends, alarmed at the growing disorder and disaffection of the country, aware at last of his folly in alienating the Whig families, the King sought a reconciliation. In July 1765 the Marquis of Rockingham, a shy, well-meaning Whig who was disturbed at George's conduct, undertook to form a Government, and brought with him as private secretary a young Irishman named Edmund Burke, already known in literary circles as a clever writer and a brilliant talker. He was much more. He was a great political thinker. Viewing English politics and the English character with something of the detachment of an alien, he was able to diagnose the situation with an imaginative insight beyond the range of those immersed in the business of the day and bound by traditional habits of mind.

The political history of the years following 1714 had led to a degeneration and dissolution of parties. The personal activity of the sovereign after 1760 and the emergence of great issues of principle found the Whigs helpless and divided into rival clans. The King's tactics had paralysed them. Burke's aim was to create out of the Rockingham group, high-principled but small in numbers and with no original ideas of its own, an effective political party. He could supply the ideas, but first he had to convince the Whigs that a party could be formed and held together on a ground of common principles. He had to overcome the notion, widely prevalent, that party was in itself a rather disreputable thing, a notion which had been strengthened by Pitt's haughty disdain for party business and organisation. It was an old tradition that politicians not in power need not bother to attend Parliament, but should retire to their country estates and there await the return to royal favour and a redistribution of the sweets of office. Individualists of different schools, such as Shelburne and Henry Fox, consistently opposed Burke's efforts to organise them into a party. "You think," Henry Fox had written to Rockingham, "you can but serve the country by continuing a fruitless Opposition. I think it impossible to serve it at all except by coming into office."

A consistent programme, to be advocated in Opposition and realised in office, was Burke's conception of party policy, and the new issues arising plainly required a programme. On Ireland, on America, on India, Burke's attitude was definite.

He stood, and he brought his party to stand, for conciliation of the colonies, relaxation of the restraints on Irish trade, and the government of India on the same moral basis as the government of England. At home he proposed to deliver Parliament from its subservience to the Crown by the abolition of numerous sinecures and the limitation of corruption. What he lacked was, in his own words, "the power and purchase" which a strong and well-organised party could supply. For years Burke was a voice crying in the wilderness, and too often rising to tones of frenzy. An orator to be named with the ancients, an incomparable political reasoner, he lacked both judgment and self-control. He was perhaps the greatest man that Ireland has produced. The same gifts, with a dash of English indolence and irony—he could have borrowed them from Charles James Fox, Henry Fox's famous son, who had plenty of both to spare—might have made him Britain's greatest statesman.

Rockingham's Government, which lasted thirteen months, passed three measures that went far to soothe the animosities raised by Grenville on both sides of the Atlantic. They repealed the Stamp Act, and induced the House of Commons to declare general warrants and the seizure of private papers unlawful. At the same time they reaffirmed the powers of Parliament to tax the colonies in a so-called Declaratory Act. But the King was determined to be rid of them, and Pitt, whose mind was clouded by sickness, was seduced by royal flattery and by his own dislike of party into lending his name to a new administration formed on no political principle whatever. His arrogance remained; his powers were failing; his popularity as the "Great Commoner" had been dimmed by his sudden acceptance of the Earldom of Chatham. The conduct of affairs slipped into other hands: Charles Townshend, the Duke of Grafton, and Lord Shelburne. In 1767 Townshend, against the opposition of Shelburne, introduced a Bill imposing duties on American imports of paper, glass, lead, and tea. There was rage in America. The supply of coin in the colonies would be still more depleted, and any surplus from the new revenue was not, as originally stated, to be used for the upkeep of the British garrisons but to pay British colonial officials. This threatened to make them independent of the colonial assemblies, whose chief weapon against truculent governors had been to withhold their salaries. Even so, revolt was still far from their minds.

Intelligent men, like Governor Hutchinson of Massachusetts, preferred not to impose taxes at all if they could not be enforced, and declared that another repeal would only "facilitate the designs of those persons who appear to be aiming at independency." John Dickinson, of Pennsylvania, in his *Letters from a Farmer,* voiced the opposition in the most widely read pamphlet of the time. It was studiously cautious in tone, and at this stage there were few people who desired secession. The authority of Parliament over the colonies was formally denied, but there was a general loyalty to King and Empire. Most of the opposition still came from respectable merchants, who believed that organised but limited resistance on the commercial plane would bring the British Government to reason.

The Massachusetts Assembly accordingly proposed a joint petition with the other colonial bodies against the new duties. Colonial resistance was now being organised on a continental scale and the barriers of provincialism and jealousy were being lowered. Non-importation agreements were concluded and there was a systematic and most successful boycott of English goods. But tempers began to rise. In May 1768 the sloop *Liberty,* belonging to John Hancock, the most prominent Boston merchant, was stopped and searched near the coast by Royal Customs officers. The colonists rescued it by force. By 1769 British exports to America had fallen by one-half.

The Cabinet was not seriously apprehensive, but perturbed. It agreed to drop the duties, except on tea. By a majority of one this was carried. Parliament proclaimed its sovereignty over the colonies by retaining a tax on tea of threepence a pound.

Suddenly by some mysterious operation of Nature the clouds which had gathered round Chatham's intellect cleared. Ill-health had forced him to resign in 1768, and he had been succeeded in office by Grafton. The scene on which he re-opened his eyes was lurid enough to dismay any man. In England, as we have seen, a senseless craving for revenge had driven the King and his friends in Parliament to an attempt to expel John Wilkes from the House, which was in fact an attack on the rights of electors throughout the country. The unknown "Junius" was flaying every Minister who provoked his lash. In America blood had not yet flowed, but all the signs of a dissolution of the Empire were there for those who could read them. But George III, after twelve years' intrigue, had at last got a docile, biddable Prime Minister. Lord North became First Lord of the Treasury in 1770. A charming man, of good abilities and faultless temper, he presided over the loss of the American colonies.

At first all seemed quiet. The American merchants were delighted at the repeal of the import duties, and by the middle of 1770 reconciliation seemed complete, except in Boston. Here Samuel Adams, fertile organiser of resistance and advocate of separation, saw that the struggle was now reaching a crucial stage. Hitherto the quarrel had been at bottom a commercial dispute, and neither the American merchants nor the English Ministers had any sympathy for his ideas. Adams feared that the resistance of the colonies would crumble and the British would reassert their authority unless more trouble was stirred up. This he and other Radical leaders proceeded to do.

News that the duties were withdrawn had hardly reached America when the first blood was shed. Most of the British garrison was stationed in Boston. The troops were unpopular with the townsfolk, and Adams spread evil rumours of their conduct. The "lobsters" in their scarlet coats were insulted and jeered at wherever they appeared. In March 1770 the persistent snowballing by Boston urchins of an English sentry outside the custom-house caused a riot. In the confusion and shouting some of the troops opened fire and there were casualties. This "massacre" was just the sort of incident that Adams had hoped for. But moderate men of property were nervous, and opinion in the colonies remained disunited and uncertain. The Radicals persisted. In June 1772 rioters burned the British Revenue cutter H.M.S. *Gaspee,* off Rhode Island.

"Committees of Correspondence" were set up throughout Massachusetts, and by the end of the year had spread to seventy-five towns. The Virginian agitators, led by the young Patrick Henry, created a standing committee of their Assembly to keep in touch with the other colonies, and a chain of such bodies was quickly formed. Thus the machinery of revolt was quietly and efficiently created.

Nevertheless the Radicals were still in a minority and there was much opposition to an abrupt break with England. Benjamin Franklin, one of the leading colonial representatives in London, wrote as late as 1773: ". . . There seem to be among us some violent spirits who are for an immediate rupture; but I trust that the general prudence of our country will see that by our growing strength we advance fast to a situation in which our claims must be allowed, that by a premature struggle we may be crippled and kept down, . . . that between governed and governing every mistake in government, every encroachment on right, is not worth a rebellion, . . . remembering withal that this Protestant country (our mother, though lately an unkind one) is worth preserving, and that her weight in the scales of Europe and her safety in a great degree may depend on our union with her." In spite of the Boston "massacre," the violence on the high seas, and the commercial squabbles, the agitations of Adams and his friends were beginning to peter out, when Lord North committed a fatal blunder.

The East India Company was nearly bankrupt, and the Government had been forced to come to its rescue. An Act was passed through Parliament, attracting little notice among the Members, authorising the company to ship tea, of which it had an enormous surplus, direct to the colonies, without paying import duties, and to sell it through its own agents in America. Thus in effect the company was granted a monopoly. The outcry across the Atlantic was instantaneous. The extremists denounced it as an invasion of their liberties, and the merchants were threatened with ruin. American shippers who brought tea from the British customs-houses and their middle-men who sold it would all be thrown out of business. The Act succeeded where Adams had failed: it united colonial opinion against the British.

The Radicals, who began to call themselves "Patriots," seized their opportunity to force a crisis. In December 1773 the first cargoes were lying in Boston. Rioters disguised as Red Indians boarded the ships and destroyed the cases. "Last night," wrote John Adams, Samuel's cousin, and later the second President of the United States, "three cargoes of Bohea tea were emptied into the sea. . . . This is the most magnificent movement of all. There is a dignity, a majesty and sublimity in this last effort of the Patriots that I greatly admire. . . . This destruction of the tea is so bold, so daring, so firm, intrepid, and inflexible, and it must have so important consequences, and so lasting, that I cannot but consider it as an epoch in history. This however is but an attack upon property. Another similar exertion of popular power may produce the destruction of lives. Many persons wish that as many dead carcases were floating in the harbour as there are chests of tea. A much less number of lives however would remove the causes of all our calamities."

When the news reached London the cry went up for coercion and the reactionaries in the British Government became supreme. In vain Burke and Chatham pleaded for conciliation. Parliament passed a series of "Coercion Acts" which suspended the Massachusetts Assembly, declared the colony to be under Crown control, closed the port of Boston, and decreed that all judges in the colony were henceforth to be appointed by the Crown. These measures were confined to Massachusetts; only one of them, the Quartering Act, applied to the rest of the colonies, and this declared that troops were to be quartered throughout all of them to preserve order. Thus it was hoped to isolate the resistance. It had the opposite effect.

In September 1774 the colonial assemblies held a congress at Philadelphia. The extremists were not yet out of hand, and the delegates still concentrated on commercial boycotts. An association was formed to stop all trade with England unless the Coercion Acts were repealed, and the Committees of Correspondence were charged with carrying out the plan. A Declaration of Rights demanded the rescinding of some thirteen commercial Acts passed by the British Parliament since 1763. The tone of this document, which was dispatched to London, was one of respectful moderation. But in London all moderation was cast aside. The "sugar interest" in the House of Commons, jealous of colonial competition in the West Indies; Army officers who despised the colonial troops; the Government, pressed for money and blinded by the doctrine that colonies only existed for the benefit of the Mother Country: all combined to extinguish the last hope of peace. The petition was rejected with contempt.

Events now moved swiftly. The Massachusetts Military Governor, General Thomas Gage, tried to enforce martial law, but the task was beyond him. Gage was an able soldier, but he had only four thousand troops and could hold no place outside Boston. The Patriots had about ten thousand men in the colonial militia. In October they set up a "Committee of Safety," and most of the colonies started drilling and arming. Collection of military equipment and powder began. Cannon were seized from Government establishments. Agents were sent abroad to buy weapons. Both France and Spain refused the British Government's request to prohibit the sale of gunpowder to the Americans, and Dutch merchants shipped it in large glass bottles labelled "Spirits."

The Patriots began accumulating these warlike stores at Concord, a village twenty miles from Boston, where the Massachusetts Assembly, which Parliament had declared illegal, was now in session. Gage decided to seize their ammunition and arrest Samuel Adams and his colleague John Hancock. But the colonists were on the alert. Every night they patrolled the streets of Boston watching for any move by the English troops. As Gage gathered his men messengers warned the assembly at Concord. The military supplies were scattered among towns farther north and Adams and Hancock moved to Lexington. On April 18, 1775, eight hundred British troops set off in darkness along the Concord road. But the secret was out. From the steeple of the North Church, messengers were warned with lantern signals. One of the patrols, Paul Revere, mounted his horse and rode hard to Lexington, rousing Adams and Hancock from their beds and urging them to flight.

At five o'clock in the morning the local militia of Lexington, seventy strong, formed up on the village green. As the sun rose the head of the British column, with three officers riding in front, came into view. The leading officer, brandishing his sword, shouted, "Disperse, you rebels, immediately!" The militia commander ordered his men to disperse. The colonial committees were very anxious not to fire the first shot, and there were strict orders not to provoke open conflict with the British regulars. But in the confusion someone fired. A volley was returned. The ranks of the militia were thinned and there was a general *mêlée*. Brushing aside the survivors, the British column marched on to Concord. But now the countryside was up in arms and the bulk of the stores had been moved to safety. It was with difficulty that the British straggled back to Boston, with the enemy close at their heels. The town was cut off from the mainland. The news of Lexington and Concord spread to the other colonies, and Governors and British officials were expelled. With strategic insight the forts at the head of the Hudson valley were seized by Patriot troops under Ethan Allen, leader of the "Green Mountain Boys" from the region that became Vermont, and of Benedict Arnold, a merchant from Connecticut. The British were thus denied any help from Canada, and the War of Independence had begun.

The War of
Independence

IN May 1775 a congress of delegates from the American
colonies met in the Carpenters' Hall of the quiet Pennsylvanian town of Philadelphia. They were respectable lawyers,
doctors, merchants, and landowners, nervous at the onrush of
events, and seemingly unfitted to form a revolutionary committee. The first shots had been fired and blood had been shed,
but all hope of compromise had not yet vanished, and they
were fearful of raising a military Power which might, like
Cromwell's Ironsides, overwhelm its creators. They had no
common national tradition except that against which they
were revolting, no organisation, no industries, no treasury, no
supplies, no army. Many of them still hoped for peace with
England. Yet British troops under General Sir William Howe
were on their way across the Atlantic, and armed, violent,
fratricidal conflict stared them in the face.

The centre of resistance and the scene of action was Boston,
where Gage and the only British force on the continent were
hemmed in by sixteen thousand New England merchants and
farmers. There was continual friction within the town, not
only between Patriots and soldiery, but between Patriots and
Loyalists. Derisive placards were hung outside the quarters
of the troops and all was in ferment. On May 25 Howe, accompanied by Generals Clinton and Burgoyne, sailed into the
harbour with reinforcements which brought the total English
troops to about six thousand men.

Thus strengthened Gage took the offensive. To the north, across a short tract of water, lay a small peninsula connected by a narrow neck with the mainland. Here Breed's Hill and Bunker Hill dominated the town. If the colonists could occupy and hold these eminences they could cannonade the English out of Boston. On the evening of June 16 Gage determined to forestall them, but next morning a line of entrenchments had appeared upon the heights across the water. Patriot troops, warned by messages from Boston, had dug themselves in during the night. Their position nevertheless seemed perilous. The English ships could bombard them from the harbour or put landing-parties on the neck of the peninsula and cut them off from their base. But neither course was attempted. Gage was resolved on a display of force. He had under his command some of the best regiments in the British Army, and he and his fellow-countrymen had acquired a hard contempt for the colonials in earlier wars. He decided to make a frontal attack on the hill, so that all Boston, crowded in its windows and upon its roofs, should witness the spectacle of British soldiers marching steadily in line to storm the rebel entrenchments.

On the hot afternoon of the 17th Howe, under Gage's orders, supervised the landing of about three thousand British regulars. He drew up his men and made them a speech. "You must drive these farmers from the hill or it will be impossible for us to remain in Boston. But I shall not desire any of you to advance a single step beyond where I am at the head of your line." In three lines the redcoats moved slowly towards the summit of Breed's Hill. There was silence. The whole of Boston was looking on. At a hundred yards from the trenches there was still not a sound in front. But at fifty yards a hail of buck-shot and bullets from ancient hunting guns smote the attackers. There was shouting and curses. "Are the Yankees cowards?" was hurled from the breastworks of the trenches. Howe, his white silk breeches splashed with blood, rallied his men, but they were scattered by another volley and driven to their boats. Howe's reputation was at stake and he realised that ammunition was running short on the hill-top. At the third rush, this time in column, the regulars drove the farmers from their line. It was now evening. The village of Charlestown, on the Boston side of the peninsula, was in flames. Over a thousand Englishmen had fallen on the slopes. Of the three thousand farmers who had held the crest a sixth were killed or wounded. Throughout the night carriages and chaises bore the English casualties into Boston.

This sharp and bloody action sent a stir throughout the colonies, and has been compared in its effects with Bull Run, eighty-six years later. The rebels had become heroes. They had stood up to trained troops, destroyed a third of their opponents, and wiped out in blood the legend of Yankee cowardice. The British had captured the hill, but the Americans had won the glory. Gage made no further attack and in October he was recalled to England in disgrace. Howe succeeded to the command. On both sides of the Atlantic men perceived that a mortal struggle impended.

It was now imperative for the Patriots to raise an army. Massachusetts had already appealed to Congress at Philadelphia for help against the British and for the appointment of a Commander-in-Chief. Two days before the action at Breed's Hill Congress had agreed. There had been much talk of whom they were to choose. There was jealousy and dislike of the New Englanders, who were bearing the brunt of the fighting, and largely for political reasons it was decided to appoint a Southerner. Adams's eye centred upon a figure in uniform, among the dark brown clothes of the delegates. He was Colonel George Washington, of Mount Vernon, Virginia. This prosperous planter had fought in the campaigns of the 1750's and had helped extricate the remnants of Braddock's force from their disastrous advance. He was the only man of any military experience at the Congress, and this was limited to a few minor campaigns on the frontier. He was now given command of all the forces that America could raise. Great calls were to be made on the spirit of resolution that was his by nature.

The colonies contained about 280,000 men capable of bearing arms, but at no time during the war did Washington succeed in gathering together more than twenty-five thousand. Jealousy between the colonies and lack of equipment and organisation hampered his efforts. His immediate task was to provide the ragged band at Boston with discipline and munitions, and to this he devoted the autumn and winter months of 1775. Congress nevertheless resolved on an offensive. An expedition was dispatched to Canada under Benedict Arnold, who was to be for ever infamous in American history, and Richard Montgomery, who had once served under Wolfe. They marched along the same routes which the British troops had taken in the campaign of 1759, and they had only eleven hundred men between them. Montgomery captured and occupied Montreal, which was undefended. He then joined Arnold, who after desperate hardships had arrived with the ghost of an army before the fortifications of Quebec. In the depth of winter, in driving snow, they flung themselves at the Heights of Abraham, defended by Sir Guy Carleton with a few hundred men. Montgomery was killed and Arnold's leg was shattered. The survivors, even after this repulse, hung on in their wind-swept camp across the river. But in the spring, when the ice melted in the St Lawrence, the first reinforcements arrived from England. Having lost more than half their men, the Patriots thereupon trudged back to Maine and Fort Ticonderoga. Canada thus escaped the revolutionary upsurge. French Canadians were on the whole content with life under the British Crown. Soon Canada was to harbour many refugees from the United States who were unable to forswear their loyalty to George III.

Meanwhile Howe was still confined to Boston. He shrank from taking reprisals, and for at least the first two years of the war he hoped for conciliation. Both he and his generals were Whig Members of Parliament, and they shared the party view that a successful war against the colonists was impossible. He was a gallant and capable commander in the field, but always slow to take the initiative. He now set himself the task of overawing the Americans. This however needed extensive help from England, and as none arrived, and Boston itself was of no strategic importance, he evacuated the town in the spring of 1776 and moved to the only British base on the Atlantic seaboard, Halifax, in Nova Scotia. At the same time a small expedition under General Clinton was sent southwards to the Loyalists in Charleston in the hope of rallying the Middle and Southern colonies. But the Patriot resistance was stiffening, and although the moderate elements in Congress had hitherto opposed any formal Declaration of Independence the evacuation of Boston roused them to a sterner effort. Until they acquired what would nowadays be called belligerent status they could get no military supplies from abroad, except by smuggling, and supplies were essential. The Conservative politicians were gradually yielding to the Radicals. The publication of a pamphlet called *Common Sense,* by Tom Paine, an English extremist lately arrived in America, put the case for revolution with enormous success and with far greater effect than the writings of intellectuals like Adams.

But it was the British Government which took the next step towards dissolving the tie of allegiance between England and America. Early in 1776 it put in force a Prohibitory Act forbidding all intercourse with the rebellious colonies and declaring a blockade of the American coast. At the same time,

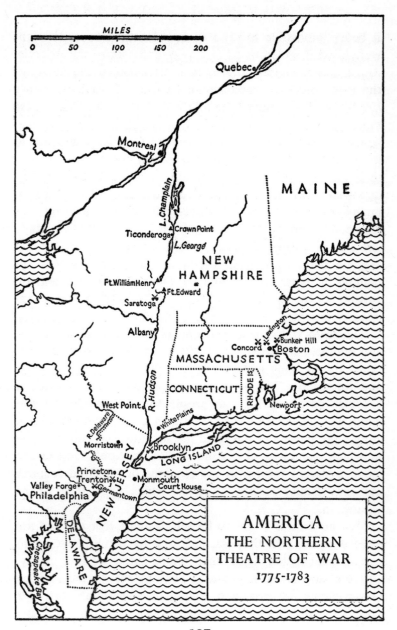

MILES

0   50   100   150   200

Quebec

Montreal

L. Champlain

Crown Point
Ticonderoga
L. George

MAINE

NEW
HAMPSHIRE

Ft. William Henry
Ft. Edward
Saratoga

Albany

Lexington
Concord   Bunker Hill
Boston

MASSACHUSETTS

R. Hudson

CONNECTICUT   RHODE IS.

West Point   Newport

White Plains

R. Delaware
Morristown

NEW JERSEY

Brooklyn
LONG ISLAND

Princeton
Trenton   Monmouth
Valley Forge   Court House
Philadelphia   Germantown

DELAWARE

Chesapeake Bay

AMERICA
THE NORTHERN
THEATRE OF WAR
1775-1783

it being impossible to raise enough British troops, Hessians were hired from Germany and dispatched across the Atlantic. The resulting outcry in America strengthened the hands of the extremists. At Philadelphia on June 7 Richard Henry Lee, of Virginia, moved the following resolution: "That these united colonies are and of right ought to be free and independent states; that they are absolved from all allegiance to the British Crown, and that all political connection between them and the state of Great Britain is and ought to be totally dissolved." But six of the thirteen colonies still opposed an immediate Declaration. A large-scale British invasion was feared. No foreign alliances had yet been concluded. Many felt that a formal defiance would wreck their cause and alienate their supporters. But at last a committee was appointed, a paper was drafted by Thomas Jefferson, and on July 4, 1776, the Declaration of Independence was unanimously accepted by the Congress of the American colonies.

This historic document proclaimed the causes of the revolt, and enumerated twenty-eight "repeated injuries and usurpations" by the King of Great Britain. The opening is familiar and immortal: "When, in the course of human events, it becomes necessary for one people to dissolve the political bands which have connected them with another, and to assume among the powers of the earth the separate and equal station to which the Laws of Nature and of Nature's God entitle them, a decent respect to the opinions of mankind requires that they should declare the causes which impel them to the separation.

"We hold these truths to be self-evident: that all men are created equal, that they are endowed by their Creator with certain unalienable rights, that among these are life, liberty, and the pursuit of happiness. That to secure these rights Governments are instituted among men, deriving their just powers from the consent of the governed. That whenever any form of government becomes destructive of these ends it is the right of the people to alter or to abolish it, and to institute new government, laying its foundation on such principles and organising its powers in such form as to them shall seem most likely to effect their safety and happiness."

The Declaration was in the main a restatement of the principles which had animated the Whig struggle against the later Stuarts and the English Revolution of 1688, and it now became the symbol and rallying centre of the Patriot cause. Its immediate result was to increase the number of Loyalists, frightened by this splendid defiance. But the purpose of the colonies was proclaimed. The waverers were forced to a decision. There was now no turning back.

*   *   *   *   *

All this time the British had remained at Halifax awaiting reinforcements from England and meditating their strategy. Military success hinged on control of the Hudson valley. If they could seize and hold the waterway, and the forts which guarded it, New England would be sundered from the Middle and Southern colonies, which contained two-thirds of the population and most of the food and wealth. The first step was to capture New York, at the river-mouth. Howe could then move northwards, subdue the forts, and join hands with a force from Canada. Thereafter the South, where the settlements lay largely upon the rivers, could be crushed with the help of the Fleet. The plan seemed promising, for the colonists possessed no Navy and Great Britain should have been able to blockade the Atlantic seaboard. But the Fleet was no longer in the high efficiency to which it had been raised by Chatham's admirals. It was able to bring reinforcements across the Atlantic, but in the event New England privateers did much damage to military operations on the coast and harassed transport vessels and supplies. In June 1776 Howe moved to New York, and began to invest the city, and in July his brother, Admiral Howe, arrived from England with a fleet of over five hundred sail and reinforcements. Howe was now in command of some twenty-five thousand men. This was the largest armed force that had yet been seen in the New World. But Washington was ready. He concentrated his army, now reduced by desertions and smallpox to about twenty thousand men, around the city. From the British camp on Staten Island the American lines could be seen across the bay on the spurs of Long Island, and on the heights of Brooklyn above the East River. In August Howe attacked. The slaughter of Bunker Hill, for thus the action at Breed's Hill is known, had taught him caution and this time he abstained from a frontal assault. He made a feint against the Long Island entrenchments, and then flung his main force to the left of the Americans and descended upon their rear. The stroke succeeded and Washington was compelled to retreat into New York City. Adverse winds impeded the British fleet and he and his army escaped safely across the East River.

In this disaster Washington appealed to Congress. It seemed impossible to make a stand in New York, yet to abandon it would dismay the Patriots. But Congress agreed that he should evacuate the city without fighting, and after skirmishing on the Harlem heights he withdrew slowly northwards. At this juncture victory lay at Howe's finger-tips. He was master of New York and of the Hudson River for forty miles above it. If he had pursued Washington with the same skill and vigour as Grant was to pursue Lee eighty-eight years later he might have captured the whole colonial army. But for nearly a month Washington was unmolested. At the end of October he was again defeated in a sharp fight at White Plains; but once more the English made no attempt to pursue, and Washington waited desperately to see whether Howe would attack up the Hudson or strike through New Jersey at Philadelphia. Howe resolved to move on Philadelphia. He turned south, capturing as he went the forts in the neighbourhood of New York, and the delegates at Philadelphia fled. Thousands of Americans flocked to the British camp to declare their loyalty. The only hope for the Patriots seemed a mass trek across the Alleghenies into new lands, a migration away from British rule like that of the Boers in the nineteenth century. Even Washington considered such a course. "We must then [*i.e.*, if defeated] retire to Augusta County, in Virginia. Numbers will repair to us for safety and we will try a predatory war. If overpowered we must cross the Alleghany Mountains." [1] Meanwhile he traversed the Hudson and fell back southwards to cover Philadelphia.

The British were hard on his heels and began a rapid occupation of New Jersey. The Patriot cause seemed lost. But Washington remained alert and undaunted and fortune rewarded him. With an imprudence which is difficult to understand, and was soon to be punished, outposts from the British Army were flung about in careless fashion through the New Jersey towns. Washington determined to strike at these isolated bodies before Howe could cross the Delaware River. He selected the village of Trenton, held by a force of Hessians. On Christmas Night the Patriot troops fought their way into the lightly guarded village. At the cost of two officers and two privates they killed or wounded a hundred and six Hessians. The survivors were captured and sent to parade the streets of Philadelphia. The effect of the stroke was out of all proportion to its military importance. It was the most critical moment in the war. At Princeton Lord Cornwallis, a subordinate of Howe's of whom more was to be heard later, tried to avenge the defeat, but was foiled. Washington marched behind him and threatened his line of communications. The year thus ended with the British in winter quarters in New Jersey, but confined by these two actions to the east

[1] J. Fisher, *The Writings of John Fisher* (1902), vol. i.

of the Delaware. Their officers spent a cheerful season in the society of New York. Meanwhile Benjamin Franklin and Silas Deane, first of American diplomats, crossed the Atlantic to seek help from France.

*   *   *   *   *

Posterity should not be misled into thinking that war on the American colonies received the unanimous support of the British people. Burke for one had no illusions. "No man," he had written after Bunker Hill, "commends the measures which have been pursued, or expects any good from those which are in preparation, but it is a cold, languid opinion, like what men discover in affairs that do not concern them. . . . The merchants are gone from us and from themselves. . . . The leading men among them are kept full fed with contracts and remittances and jobs of all descriptions, and are indefatigable in their endeavours to keep the others quiet. . . . They all, or the greatest number of them, begin to snuff the cadaverous *haut goût* of lucrative war. War is indeed become a sort of substitute for commerce. The freighting business never was so lively, on account of the prodigious taking up for transport service. Great orders for provisions and stores of all kinds . . . keep up the spirits of the mercantile world, and induce them to consider the American war not so much their calamity as their resource in an inevitable distress." Powerful English politicians denounced not only the military and naval mismanagement, but the use of force against the colonists at all.

There was gloating over every setback and disaster to the British cause. "The parricide joy of some in the losses of their country makes me mad," wrote a Government supporter. "They do not disguise it. A patriotic duke told me some weeks ago that some ships had been lost off the coast of North America in a storm. He said a thousand British sailors were drowned—not one escaped—with joy sparkling in his

· 192 ·

eyes. . . . In the House of Commons it is not unusual to speak of the provincials as 'our Army.' " Such antics only made things worse. Indeed, but for the violence of the Opposition, which far outran the country's true feelings, it is probable that Lord North's administration would have fallen much sooner. As it was, he commanded large majorities in the House of Commons throughout the war. Not all the Opposition Members were so foolish or so extreme, but in the King's mind all were traitors. George III grew stubborn and even more intent. He closed his ears to moderate counsel and refused to admit into his Government those men of both parties who, like many American Loyalists, foresaw and condemned the disasters into which his policy was tottering and were horrified at the civil war between the Mother Country and her colonies. Even Lord North was half-hearted, and only his loyalty to the King and his sincere old-fashioned belief, shared by many politicians of his day, that a Minister's duty was to carry out the personal wishes of the sovereign stopped him resigning much sooner than he did. Though technically responsible as First Lord of the Treasury and Chancellor of the Exchequer, he had no grip on the conduct of affairs and allowed the King and the departmental Ministers to control the day-to-day work of government. George III tirelessly struggled to superintend the details of the war organisation, but he was incapable of co-ordinating the activities of his Ministers. These were of poor quality. The Admiralty was headed by Wilkes's comrade in debauch, the Earl of Sandwich. His reputation has been mauled, but recent research has shown that at least the Fleet was in much better condition than the Army.

Rarely has British strategy fallen into such a multitude of errors. Every maxim and principle of war was either violated or disregarded. "Seek out and destroy the enemy" is a sound rule. "Concentrate your force" is a sound method. "Maintain your objective" is common sense. The enemy was Washington's army. The force consisted of Howe's troops in New York and Burgoyne's columns now assembled in Montreal. The objective was to destroy Washington's army and kill or capture Washington. If he could be brought to battle and every man and gun turned against him, a British victory was almost certain. But these obvious truths were befogged and bedevilled by multiplicity of counsel. Howe was still determined to capture Philadelphia, the seat of the revolutionary Congress and the fountain-head of political resistance. Burgoyne, on the other hand, was hot for a descent from Canada into the upper reaches of the Hudson valley, and a seizure, with the aid of a trust from New York, of the forts which dominated the waterway. Once in control of the Hudson, New England could be isolated and speedily subdued. Burgoyne had obtained leave of absence and journeyed to England late in the autumn of 1776. He offered his advice to the London Government. George III approved his plan and endorsed it in his own hand. Burgoyne was to advance from Montreal through the wooded borders of the frontier and seize the fort at Ticonderoga near the valley-head. At the same time a force from New York would strike north, capture the citadel of West Point, which had recently been strengthened with the help of French engineers, and join him at Albany.

Thus the London planners. The ultimate responsibility for co-ordinating these movements lay with the War Minister, Lord George Germain. Germain's career in the army had ended in disgrace, though his military experience may not have been a fair guide to his capacities. Twenty years before he had refused to charge with his cavalry at the Battle of Minden, and been declared unfit to serve by a court-martial. But, secure in the favour of the young King, he had made himself into a politician. The Government were well aware that Howe intended to move in the opposite direction to

Burgoyne, namely, southwards against Philadelphia, but did nothing to dissuade him. They gave him no orders to join forces at Albany and they stinted him of reinforcements. "The extraordinary spectacle was thus presented," writes an American historian, "of a subordinate general going to London and getting the King's approval to one plan of campaign; of the King's Minister sending full instructions to one general and none to the other who was to co-operate with him; and of this other general making his own independent plan. . . ."[1] On his return to Canada Burgoyne nevertheless sent Howe no fewer than three letters about the plan to meet at Albany, but in the absence of precise directions from England Howe saw no reason to abandon his project against Philadelphia. He held to his course. Having tried and failed to bring Washington to battle, he left a garrison of eight thousand men in New York under Sir Henry Clinton and sailed in July 1777 with the main part of his army to Chesapeake Bay. Instead of concentrating their strength, the British forces were now dispersed over five hundred miles of country, and divided between Burgoyne in Canada, Howe on the Chesapeake, and Clinton in New York.

* * * * *

Washington, from his winter quarters at Morristown, on the borders of New Jersey, moved hastily south-westwards to screen Philadelphia. Having abandoned New York without a serious fight, he could hardly do the same at the capital of the Congress, but with his ill-disciplined force, fluctuating in numbers, he could only hope to delay the British advance. At the beginning of September Howe advanced with about fourteen thousand men. Washington, with a similar force, drew up his lines on the north bank of the river Brandywine, barring the road to the capital. Howe perceived and exploited the faulty equipment of the army in front of him, its lack of an

[1] F. V. Greene, *The Revolutionary War* (1911).

efficient staff and its inability to get quick information. He made the same feinting movements which had served so well at Long Island. On the morning of the 11th he divided his army, and, leaving a powerful body to make a frontal attack, marched up-river with Cornwallis, crossed it, and descended on Washington's right flank. His tactics went like clockwork. The attack was successful, disorder spread, and the British troops on the far bank crossed the river and drove the whole American force before them. By sunset Washington was in full retreat. As the Marquis de Lafayette, a young French volunteer in the American army, described it, "Fugitives, cannon, and baggage crowded without order into the road." But here, as at Long Island, Howe refused to pursue and capture the enemy. He was content. On September 26 his advance-guards entered Philadelphia. There was a confused fight to the north of the city at Germantown, but the British pressed on, and soon afterwards the capital fell.

By now however the London plans for the northern theatre were beginning to miscarry. Burgoyne, with a few hundred Indians and seven thousand regulars, of whom half were German, was moving through the Canadian forests expecting to join with the British forces from New York. After an arduous journey he reached Fort Ticonderoga, from which the Americans promptly retired, leaving their artillery behind them. He pushed eagerly southwards. If only Howe was moving up to West Point nothing could prevent an overwhelming success. But where was Howe? On the day that Burgoyne moved upon the next American fort Howe had sailed southwards from New York. All concerned were confident that after capturing Philadelphia Howe could quickly return to New York and reach out to the expedition from Canada. He failed to do so, and Burgoyne paid the price.

As Burgoyne advanced the New England militia gathered against him. He was a popular and dashing commander, but the country was difficult, he was harassed by raids, and his troops began to falter and to dwindle. He could still succeed if help came from New York. Clinton's garrison there had been halved, since Howe had called upon him for reinforcements. Nevertheless Clinton marched north and captured two forts below West Point, but as the autumn rains descended Burgoyne was cornered at Saratoga, and the New Englanders, their strength daily increasing, closed in. He was only thirty miles from Albany, where he should have met the column from New York, but he could make no headway. Days of hard fighting in the woodlands followed. His supplies ran low, and he was heavily outnumbered. The Americans were operating in their own country by their own methods. Each man fighting mostly on his own initiative, hiding behind bushes and in the tops of trees, they inflicted severe casualties upon some of the best regiments that Europe could muster. The precise drill and formations of Burgoyne's men had no effect. An American deserter brought news that Clinton was moving northwards. It was too late. The Germans refused to fight any longer, and on October 17, 1777, Burgoyne surrendered to the American commander, Horatio Gates. The surrender terms were violated by Congress and the main body of his army were kept prisoners until the signing of the peace. Burgoyne returned to England to attack and be attacked by the Ministry.

*   *   *   *   *

At this point in the struggle the Old World stepped in to aid and comfort the New. Although militarily indecisive in America, Saratoga had an immediate effect in France. The French, though technically at peace with Britain, had been supplying the Patriots with arms, and French volunteers were serving in the colonial army. At Versailles Benjamin Franklin and Silas Deane had been urging an open alliance, but for a year both sides had wavered. The French Ministers hesitated to support the cause of liberty overseas while suppressing it at home, and many Americans feared that France would exact a heavy price for declaring war on England. Now all doubts were swept away. The colonists could not survive without French supplies, and the mass of Frenchmen were vehement to avenge the defeats of the Seven Years' War. The French Navy had been strengthened; the British Fleet was disintegrating; and when the news arrived of Saratoga Louis XVI resolved on an official alliance. There was consternation in London, where the Whig Opposition had long warned the Government against harsh dealings with the colonists, and the British Ministry formulated a generous compromise. It was too late. On February 6, 1778, before the Congress could be appraised of the new offer, Benjamin Franklin signed an alliance with France.

Thus began another world war, and Britain was now without a single ally. She had lost one army as prisoners in America. There were no more troops to be hired in Germany. Old fears of invasion spread panic through the country. The Ministry was discredited. In the agony all minds except the King's turned to Chatham. On April 7 Chatham dragged himself upon crutches to make his last speech against an Opposition address for recalling the Army in America. He had always stood for conciliation and not for surrender. The corpse-like figure, swathed in flannel bandages, tottered to its feet. The House was hushed with the anticipation of death. In whispering sentences, shot through with a sudden gleam of fierce anger, he made his attack "against the dismemberment of this ancient and most noble monarchy." He warned the nation of the dangers of French intervention and the use of German mercenaries. He scourged his countrymen for their inhumanity. "My lords, if I were an American as I am an Englishman, while a foreign troop was landed in my country I never would lay down my arms—never, never, never." He dismissed the threat of invasion with contemptuous sarcasm. He struggled to speak again after the reply of the Opposition leader, the Duke of Richmond, but collapsed senseless in an apoplectic fit. On May 11 he died as his son William was reading to him from Homer the solemn scene of Hector's funeral and the deep despair of Troy. George III displayed his smallness of mind by opposing the plan to erect a monument, which would be, he said, "an offensive measure to me personally"; but the City of London defied him, and Burke's inscription was a fitting memorial: "The means by which Providence raises a nation to greatness are the virtues infused into great men." Such men were very few in the England of Lord North.

The United States

WASHINGTON in 1777 took up his winter quarters at Valley Forge, to the north of Philadelphia. At the end of every campaign there were many desertions, and he was now reduced to about nine thousand men, of whom another third were to melt away by the spring. Short of clothing and shelter, they shivered and grumbled through the winter months, while in Philadelphia, a score of miles away, nearly twenty thousand well-equipped English troops were quartered in comfort. The social season was at its height, and the numerous Loyalists in the capital made the stay of Howe and his officers pleasing and cheerful. The British made no move to attack the Patriot army. While Washington could not count on provisions for his men even a day in advance, Howe danced and gambled in Philadelphia. As at Long Island, as at White Plains, as at the Brandywine River, he refused to follow up his victory in the field and annihilate his enemy. Unnerved perhaps by the carnage at Bunker Hill, and still hoping for conciliation, he did nothing. Some inkling of his reluctance may have reached the ears of the Government; at any rate, when news of the French alliance with the rebels reached England at the beginning of the New Year his resignation was accepted.

Howe's successor was Sir Henry Clinton, the former commander of New York, who held very different views on the conduct of hostilities. He perceived that European tactics of march and counter-march and the siege and capture of towns and cities would never prevail against an armed and scattered population. The solution, he thought, was to occupy and settle the whole country. He also made a momentous change of strategy. He resolved to abandon the offensive in the North and begin the process of reduction by subduing the South. Here was the bulk of the population and the wealth, and the main repository of such supplies as the Continent could furnish. Here also were many Loyalists. They must be heartened and organised. A new base would be needed, for New York was too far away, and Clinton's eye rested on Charleston and Savannah. Much could be said for all this, and much might have been achieved if he had been allowed to try it out, but there now appeared a new force which abruptly checked and in time proved deadly to the realisation of these large plans. Savannah was eight hundred miles and fifty days' march from New York. Hitherto Britain had held command of the sea and could shift her troops by salt water far more speedily than the Patriots could move by land, but all was now changed by the intervention of France and the French Fleet. Sea-power was henceforth to dominate and decide the American struggle for independence, and Clinton soon received a sharp reminder that this was now in dispute.

In April 1778 twelve French ships of the line, mounting, with their attendant frigates, over eight hundred guns, set sail from Toulon. Four thousand soldiers were on board. News of their approach reached Clinton and it became his immediate and vital task to stop them seizing his main base at New York. If they captured the port, or even blockaded the mouth of the Hudson, his whole position on the Continent would be imperilled. On June 18 he accordingly abandoned Philadelphia and marched rapidly across New Jersey with ten thousand troops. Washington, his army swollen by spring recruiting to about equal strength, set off in parallel line of pursuit. At Monmouth Court House there was a confused fight. Clinton beat off the Americans, not without heavy loss, and did not reach New York till the beginning of July. He was only just in time. Shortly after his arrival a French fleet under d'Estaing appeared off the city. They were confronted by a British squadron under Admiral Howe, brother of the superseded military commander, and for ten days the two forces manœuvred outside the harbour. The French attempted to seize Rhode Island, but were frustrated, and Howe in a series of operations which has drawn high praise from American naval historians defeated all efforts by his opponent to intervene. In the autumn d'Estaing abandoned the struggle and sailed for the West Indies. Here also Clinton managed to forestall the French by sending troops forthwith to St Lucia. D'Estaing arrived too late to intercept them, and this strategic island became a British base.

Nevertheless these successes could not disguise the root facts that Clinton's campaign against the South had been delayed for a year and that Britain was no longer in undisputed command of the sea. The French Fleet dominated the Channel and hindered the transport to New York of men and supplies from Britain, while New England privateers waged a lively and profitable warfare against English commerce. Military operations in America came slowly to a standstill, and although three thousand of Clinton's troops occupied Savannah in Georgia on December 29 his plans for subduing the rebels from a Loyalist base in the South were hampered and curtailed. A furious civil war between Loyalists and Patriots had erupted in these regions, but he could do little to help. Stalemate continued throughout 1779, and for a time the main seat of war shifted from the New World. Both armies in America were crippled, the American from the financial chaos and weak credit of the Congress Government, and the British for want of reinforcements. Fear of invasion gripped the British Government and troops intended for Clinton were kept in the British Isles. The French, for their part, realised that they could get all they wanted in America by fighting Britain on the high seas, and this was anyway much more to the taste of the autocratic Government at Versailles than helping republican rebels. Except for a few volunteers, they did not at this stage send any military or naval help to their allies across the Atlantic; but stores of munitions and clothing preserved the Patriot cause from collapse. In June the world conflict spread and deepened and another European Power entered the struggle. French diplomacy brought Spain into the war. Britain was still further weakened, her naval communications in the Mediterranean were imperilled, and within a few months Gibraltar was besieged. In the New World she was forced to keep watch against a Spanish incursion into Florida, and American privateers based on the port of New Orleans harassed English commerce in the Caribbean.

In European waters one of these privateers provided a colourful episode. An American captain of Scottish birth named John Paul Jones was supplied by the French with an ancient East India merchantman, which he converted in French dockyards into a man-of-war. It was named the *Bonhomme Richard,* and in September Captain Jones, with a polyglot crew and in company with three smaller vessels, sailed his memorable craft into the North Sea. Off Flamborough Head he intercepted a convoy of merchantmen from the Baltic, and straightway attacked the English escorts, the men-of-war *Serapis* and *Scarborough.* The merchant ships escaped, and on the evening of the 23rd battle commenced between the *Serapis* and the *Bonhomme Richard.* The English vessel was superior in construction, equipment, and guns, but Jones manœuvred his vessel alongside and lashed himself to his adversary. Throughout the night the two vessels rocked together, the muzzles of their guns almost touching, mauling each other with broadsides, musketry volleys, and hand-grenades. At times both ships were on fire. Jones's three smaller vessels circled the inferno, firing broadsides into both ships. The English and American captains fought grimly on. At last towards dawn there was a violent explosion in the powder magazine of the *Serapis*. Her guns were wrecked and all abaft the mainmast were killed. The English were forced to surrender; but the *Bonhomme Richard* was so shattered that she sank two days later. The encounter made a lively stir in French and American society and Jones became a hero.

*   *   *   *   *

All this time Washington's army had remained incapable of action. They could do little except keep watch on Clinton. Simply to have kept his army in existence during these years was probably Washington's greatest contribution to the Patriot cause. No other American leader could have done as much. In December Clinton decided to try his hand once more at subduing the South. He resolved to capture Charleston, and on the 26th sailed for South Carolina with eight thousand men. For a time he prospered, heartened by news that the French fleet in the West Indies had been beaten by Admiral Rodney. Bad weather delayed him and the main siege did not begin till the end of March, but in May 1780 the town fell and five thousand Patriot troops surrendered in the biggest disaster yet sustained by American arms. Then fortune began to turn against Clinton. He had gained a valuable base, but he was confronted with civil war. He found himself faced, not with a regular army in the field, but with innumerable guerrilla bands which harassed his communications and murdered Loyalists. It became evident that a huge army would be needed to occupy and subdue the country. But again sea-power intervened. Rumours that French troops were once more crossing the Atlantic made Clinton hasten back to New York, leaving Cornwallis, his second-in-command, to do the best he could in the South. This was little enough. Washington sent a small force against him under Gates, the victor of Saratoga. Cornwallis defeated Gates at the Battle of Camden and marched into North Carolina, routing the guerrillas as he went, but the countryside rose in arms behind him. There was no crucial point he could strike at, and the only effect of his exertions was the destruction of a quantity of crops which the rebels might have traded to Europe for munitions.

In the North Clinton for the second time found himself in great peril. Another fleet had indeed arrived from France, and this time he was too late to forestall a landing. Over five thousand French troops under the Comte de Rochambeau had disembarked in July at Newport, in Rhode Island. Washington, vigilant and alert, was encamped at White Plains in the Hudson valley; Benedict Arnold, who had led the expedition to Canada in 1776 and fought with distinction at Saratoga, commanded the fort at West Point; at any moment the French might advance inland from the coast and join him. New York, Clinton's base and harbour, seemed lost. But events, in the form of treachery, ran for a time with the British. Arnold had long been dissatisfied with the conduct of the Patriots, and he had recently married a Loyalist lady. He was in debt and he had recently been reprimanded by court martial for misappropriating Government property. His discontent and his doubts were deepened by the news of Gates's defeat at Camden, and he now offered to surrender West Point to Clinton for the sum of twenty thousand pounds. Its loss would not only destroy Washington's grip on the Hudson valley, but might ruin the whole Patriot power. Clinton seized on the conspiracy as the one chance of retrieving his position in the North, and sent a young major named André in disguise to arrange the details of the capitulation.

On September 21, 1780, André sailed up the Hudson in a sloop, and met Arnold late at night on the west shore not far from Stony Point. Here Arnold gave him written descriptions of the forts, their armaments and stores, the strength of the garrisons, copies of their orders in case of attack, and copies of the proceedings of a council of war recently held at West Point. On his way back across the No Man's Land between the two armies André fell into the hands of some irregular scouts, and was delivered to the nearest American commander. The documents were found in his boots. The commander could not believe in Arnold's treachery, and a request for an explanation was sent to West Point. Arnold escaped, followed by his wife, and was rewarded with a general's commission in King George's service and the command of a British force. He died in disgrace and poverty twenty years after. André was executed as a spy. He wrote a graceful and dignified letter to Washington asking to be shot instead of hanged —in vain. He was a young man of great personal beauty, and in his scarlet uniform, standing upon the gallows, and himself arranging the noose round his neck, he made an appealing sight. His courage reduced to tears the rough crowd that had gathered to see him die. In all the anger of the struggle, with the exasperation of Arnold's desertion hardening every Patriot heart, no one could be found to perform the task of executioner, and in the end a nameless figure, with his face blackened as a disguise, did the work. Forty years later André was re-buried in Westminster Abbey.

Arnold's act of betrayal, though discovered in time, had a marked, if temporary, effect on the sentiment and cohesion of the Patriots. They had been very near disaster. Many Americans were strongly opposed to the war, and Loyalists throughout the country either openly or secretly supported the British. The South was already smitten with hideous civil strife in which American slew American and each man suspected his neighbour. Was the same frightful process to engulf the North, hitherto steadfast in the Patriot cause? If the commander of West Point was a traitor, then who could be trusted? These anxieties and fears were deepened by a reversal of the Patriot fortunes at sea. Admiral Rodney arrived before New

York with a substantial fleet and blockaded the French in Newport till the end of the campaigning season. Then he struck again, this time in the West Indies, where the Dutch had been making large fortunes by shipping arms and powder to the Patriots. The centre of their trade was St Eustatius, in the Leeward Islands. In the autumn news came that Holland had joined the coalition against Great Britain, and Rodney was ordered to seize the island. This he did early in 1781, and a large store of munitions and merchandise consigned to General Washington fell into the hands of the British Fleet.

*   *   *   *   *

Strategic divergences between Clinton and Cornwallis now brought disaster to the British and Loyalist cause. Cornwallis had long chafed under Clinton's instructions, which tethered him to his base at Charleston. Clinton judged that the holding of South Carolina was the main object of the war in the South, and that any inland excursion depended on naval control of the coast. Cornwallis on the other hand was eager to press forward. He maintained that the American guerrillas in North Carolina prevented any effective occupation of the South, and until and unless they were subdued the British would have to retire within the walls of Charleston. He held that Virginia was the heart and centre of the Patriot cause and that all efforts should be concentrated on its conquest and occupation. The first step therefore was to overrun North Carolina. There is no doubt he was wrong. Charleston, not Virginia, was the military key to the South. It was the only Southern port of any consequence, and the only place from which he could receive supplies for himself and deny them to the rebels. From here he could not only dominate the state of Georgia to the South, but by establishing small posts in North Carolina, and at Chesapeake Bay, "keep up the appearance," as Washington wrote at the time, "of possessing four hundred miles upon the coast, and of consequence have a pretext for setting up claims

which may be very detrimental to the interest of America in
European councils." [1] But Cornwallis's military reputation
had been in the ascendant since the Battle of Camden, and he
was encouraged by the British Government to proceed with
his plans, which largely depended for their success on the
Southern Loyalists. In spite of their unpromising behaviour in
the previous campaign, and in spite of the nomination of
Washington's ablest general, Nathanael Greene, to command
the Patriot forces in the South, Cornwallis resolved to advance.
Thus he marched to destruction.

In January 1781 he moved towards the borders of North
Carolina. His forward detachments clashed with the Americans at Cowpens on the morning of the 17th. The British
tactics were simple and costly. Cornwallis had experienced
the marksmanship of the American frontiersmen, and knew
the inefficiency in musketry of his own troops. He therefore
relied on sabre and bayonet charges. The American commander had placed his ill-organised and ill-disciplined militia
with the Broad River behind them to stop their dispersing.
Washington always doubted the value of these troops, and
had declared that no militia would "ever acquire the habits
necessary to resist a regular force." But this time, stiffened by
Continental troops, they mauled the British.

Cornwallis nevertheless pressed on. He was now far from
his base, and Greene's army was still in the field. His only
hope was to bring Greene to battle and destroy him. They
met at Guilford Court House on March 15. The American
militia proved useless, but the trained nucleus of Greene's
troops drawn up behind a rail fence wrought havoc among
the British regulars. Again and again, headed by their officers,
the regiments assaulted the American line. An English sergeant who kept a journal of the campaign thus describes the
scene: "Instantly the movement was made, in excellent order,

[1] *The Writings of George Washington*, ed. W. C. Ford (1891), vol. ix.

MARYLAND

DELAWARE

Baltimore

VIRGINIA

R.James

Yorktown

Guilford
Court House

NORTH CAROLINA

Cowpens

R.Broad

Camden

SOUTH CAROLINA

R.Santee

GEORGIA

Charleston

Savannah

ALLEGHENY MTS.

AMERICA
THE SOUTHERN
THEATRE OF WAR
1775-1783

MILES

0.   50   100   150

in a smart run with arms charged; when arrived within forty yards of the enemy's line it was perceived that this whole force had their weapons presented and resting on a rail fence, the common partitions in America. They were taking aim with nicest precision." [1] In the end this devoted and disciplined bravery drove the Americans from the field, but the slaughter was indecisive. The Patriot force was still active while the British were far from home and had lost nearly a third of their men. Cornwallis had no choice but to make for the coast and seek reinforcements from the Navy. Greene let him go. His army had done enough. In just under eight months they had marched and fought over nine hundred miles of swampy and desolate country. Outnumbered by three to one, he had reconquered the whole of Georgia except Savannah, and all but a small portion of South Carolina. He lost the battles, but he won the campaign. Abandoning the wide spaces of North Carolina, he now moved swiftly southwards to raise the country against the British.

Here the fierce civil war in progress between Patriots and Loyalists—or Whigs and Tories as they were locally called— was darkened by midnight raids, seizure of cattle, murders, ambushes, and atrocities such as we have known in our own day in Ireland. Greene himself wrote: "The animosities between the Whigs and Tories of this state [South Carolina] renders their situation truly deplorable. There is not a day passes but there are more or less who fall a sacrifice to this savage disposition. The Whigs seem determined to extirpate the Tories and the Tories the Whigs. Some thousands have fallen in this way in this quarter, and the evil rages with more violence than ever. If a stop cannot be put to these massacres the country will be depopulated in a few months more, as neither Whig nor Tory can live." While Greene began to subdue the isolated British posts in South Carolina, Cornwallis

[1] *The Journal of Sergeant Lamb* (Dublin, 1809).

continued his advance to Virginia. He devastated the countryside in his march, but was fiercely and skilfully harried by
Lafayette and a meagre Patriot band.

Throughout these months Clinton lay in New York, and as
Cornwallis drew nearer it seemed possible that Clinton might
evacuate the Northern base and concentrate the whole British
effort on preserving the hold on the Southern colonies. This, if
it had succeeded, might have wrecked the Patriot cause, for
the Congress was bankrupt and Washington could scarcely
keep his army together. But once again the French Fleet
turned the scales, this time for ever.

The desperate situation of the Americans was revealed to
the French naval commander in the West Indies, De Grasse.
In July he sent word to Washington, who had now been joined
at White Plains by Rochambeau from Newport, that he would
attack the Virginian coast. He called for a supreme effort to
concentrate the whole Patriot force in this region. Washington
seized the opportunity. Taking elaborate precautions to deceive Clinton, he withdrew his troops from the Hudson and,
united with Rochambeau, marched quickly southwards.

Cornwallis in the meantime, starved of supplies, and with
ever-lengthening lines of communication, marched to the
coast, where he hoped to make direct contact with Clinton by
sea. In August he arrived at Yorktown, on Chesapeake Bay,
and began to dig himself in. His conduct in the following
months has been much criticised. He had no natural defence
on the land side of the town, and he made little effort to strike
at the enemies gathering round him. The Franco-American
strategy was a feat of timing, and the convergence of force
was carried out over vast distances. Nearly nine thousand
Americans and eight thousand French assembled before
Yorktown, while De Grasse blockaded the coast with thirty
ships of the line. For nearly two months Cornwallis sat and
waited. At the end of September the investment of Yorktown

began, and the bombardment of the French siege artillery shattered his earth redoubts. Cornwallis planned a desperate sortie as the defences crumbled. At the end one British cannon remained in action. On October 19, 1781, the whole army, about seven thousand strong, surrendered. On the very same day Clinton and the British squadron sailed from New York, but on hearing of the disaster they turned back.

Thus ended the main struggle. Sea-power had once more decided the issue, and but for the French blockade the British war of attrition might well have succeeded.

In November, his task accomplished, De Grasse returned to the West Indies and Washington was left unaided to face Clinton in New York and the menace of invasion from Canada. Two years were to pass before peace came to America, but no further military operations of any consequence took place.

*   *   *   *   *

The surrender at Yorktown had immediate and decisive effects in England. When the news was brought to Lord North his amiable composure slid from him. He paced his room, exclaiming in agonised tones, "Oh, God, it is all over!"

The Opposition gathered strongly in the Commons. There were riotous meetings in London. The Government majority collapsed on a motion censuring the administration of the Navy. An address to stop the American war was rejected by a single vote. In March North informed the Commons that he would resign. "At last the fatal day has come," wrote the King. North maintained his dignity to the last. After twelve years of service he left the House of Commons a beaten man. As the Members stood waiting in the rain for their carriages on that March evening in 1782 they saw North come down the steps and get into his own vehicle, which had been forewarned and was waiting at the head of the line. With a courtly bow to the drenched and hostile Members crowding round him he said, "That, gentlemen, is the advantage of being in the secret," and drove quickly away.

King George, in the agony of personal defeat, showed greater passion. He talked of abdication and retiring to Hanover. The violent feeling in the country denied him all hope of holding a successful election. He was forced to come to terms with the Opposition. Through the long years of the American war Rockingham and Burke had waited in patience for the collapse of North's administration. Now their chance had come. Rockingham made his terms with the King: independence for the colonies and some lessening of the Crown's influence in politics. George III was forced to accept, and Rockingham took office. It fell to him and his colleague, Lord Shelburne, to save what they could from the wreckage of the First British Empire.

BOOK EIGHT · CHAPTER FIFTEEN

The Indian Empire

THE eighteenth century saw a revolutionary change in the
British position in India. The English East India Company, founded simply as a trading venture, grew with increasing speed into a vast territorial Empire. About the
year 1700 probably no more than fifteen hundred English
people dwelt in India, including wives, children, and transient seamen. They lived apart in a handful of factories, as
their trading stations were called, little concerned with Indian politics. A hundred years later British officials and soldiers in their thousands, under a British Governor-General,
were in control of extensive provinces. This remarkable development was in part a result of the struggle between Britain
and France, which filled the age and was fought out all over
the globe. In America the French had the satisfaction of helping the United States to independence. In that field Britain
was worsted. It was otherwise in India, where often the fight
went on when in Europe Britain and France were at peace.
But the Anglo-French conflict would never have spread violently across India if the times had not been ripe for European intervention. The great Empire of the Moguls was disintegrating. For two centuries these Moslem descendants of
Tamburlaine had gripped and pacified a portion of the world
half as large as the present United States. Centred in Delhi
and supported by able proconsuls, they had kept the peace
in Oriental fashion and conferred on the eighty million inhabitants of the sub-continent an orderly existence which
they were not to know again for another hundred years. Early
in the eighteenth century this formidable dynasty was shaken

· *214* ·

by a disputed succession. Invaders from the North soon poured across the frontiers. Delhi was sacked by the Shah of Persia. The Viceroys of the Moguls revolted and laid claim to the sovereignty of the Imperial provinces. Pretenders rose up to challenge the usurpers. In Central India the fierce fighting tribes of the Mahrattas, bound in a loose confederacy, saw and seized their chance to loot and to raid. The country was swept by anarchy and bloodshed.

Hitherto European traders in India, English, French, Portuguese, and Dutch, had plied their wares in rivalry, but so long as "the Great Mogul" ruled in Delhi they had competed in comparative peace and safety. The English East India Company had grown into a solid affair, with a capital of over a million and a quarter pounds and an annual dividend of 9 per cent. The population of Bombay, which Charles II had leased to the Company for ten pounds a year in 1668, had multiplied more than sixfold and exceeded sixty thousand souls. Madras, founded and fortified by the British in 1639, was the chief trading centre on the eastern coast. Calcutta, uninhabited till the servants of the corporation built a factory at the mouth of the Hoogli River in 1686, had become a flourishing and peaceful emporium. The French *Compagnie des Indes,* centred at Pondicherry, had also prospered, though, unlike its British rival, it was in effect a Department of State and not a private concern. Both organisations had the same object, the promotion of commerce and the gaining of financial profit. The acquisition of territory played little part in the thoughts and plans of either nation, and indeed the English Directors had long been reluctant to own any land or assume any responsibilities beyond the confines of their trading stations. About 1740 events forced them to change their tune. The Mahrattas slaughtered the Nawab, or Imperial Governor, of the Carnatic, the five-hundred-mile-long province on the south-eastern coast. They threatened Madras and Bombay, and raided the depths of Bengal. It was becoming impossible for the European traders to stand aside. They must either fight on their own or in alliance with Indian rulers or quit. Most of the Dutch had already withdrawn to the rich archipelago of the East Indies; the Portuguese had long since fallen behind in the race; the French and English resolved to stay. Thus these two European Powers were left alone in the field.

As has so often happened in the great crises of her history, France produced a man. Joseph Dupleix, Governor of Pondicherry since 1741, had long foreseen the coming struggle with Britain. He perceived that India awaited a new ruler. The Mogul Empire was at an end, and a Mahratta Empire seemed unlikely to replace it. Why then should not France seize this glittering, fertile prize? When the War of the Austrian Succession broke out in Europe Dupleix acted with decision. He appealed to the Nawab of the Carnatic to forbid hostilities within his jurisdiction, where most of the French stations lay. This granted, he proceeded to attack Madras. Its English Governor asked the new Nawab to enforce a similar neutrality on the French, but omitted to accompany his request with a suitable bribe. Dupleix, on the other hand, promised to hand over the city once it was captured. Thus reassured, the Nawab stood aside, and after a five-day bombardment the town surrendered on September 10, 1746. Some of its British defenders escaped to the near-by Fort St David. Among them was a young clerk of twenty-one, named Robert Clive.

Dupleix, victorious, refused to surrender Madras to the Nawab and spent the rest of the year repelling his attacks. He then assaulted Fort St David, but news arrived that the war in Europe had ceased and that the peace treaty of Aix-la-Chapelle prescribed that Madras was to be returned to the British in return for the cession of Louisburg, in Nova Scotia, to France. Thus ended a dismal and inglorious opening to the great struggle in India.

*   *   *   *   *

Clive had watched these events with anger and alarm, but hitherto there had been few signs in his career to mark him as the man who would reverse his country's fortunes and found the rule of the British in India. He was the son of a small squire, and his boyhood had been variegated and unpromising. Clive had attended no fewer than four schools, and been unsuccessful at all. In his Shropshire market town he had organised and led a gang of adolescent ruffians who extorted pennies and apples from tradesmen in return for not breaking their windows. At the age of eighteen he was sent abroad as a junior clerk in the East India Company at a salary of five pounds a year and forty pounds expenses. He was a difficult and unpromising subordinate. He detested the routine and the atmosphere of the counting-house. Twice, it is said, he attempted suicide, and twice the pistol misfired. Not until he had obtained a military commission and served some years in the armed forces of the Company did he reveal a military genius unequalled in the British history of India. The siege of Madras and the defence of Fort St David had given him a taste for fighting. In 1748 a new upheaval gave him the chance of leadership.

Indian pretenders seized the Mogul viceroyalty of the Deccan and conquered the Carnatic. With a few French soldiers and a couple of thousand Indian troops Dupleix expelled them and placed his own puppets on the throne. The British candidate, Mahomet Ali, was chased into Trichinopoly and fiercely besieged. At a stroke France had become master of Southern India. The next blow would obviously be against the English. Here was the end of any hope of peaceful trading, or of what would nowadays be called non-intervention in Indian affairs, and it became evident that the

East India Company must either fight or die. Clive obtained a commission. He made his way to Trichinopoly, and saw for himself that Mahomet Ali was in desperate peril. If he could be rescued and placed on the throne all might be well. But how to do it? Trichinopoly was beset by a combined French and Indian army of vast numbers. The English had very few soldiers, and were so ill-prepared and so short of officers that Clive, still only twenty-five, was given the chief military command. The direct relief of Trichinopoly was impossible, and Clive at once perceived that his blow must be struck elsewhere. Arcot, capital of the Carnatic, had been stripped of troops; most of them were at Trichinopoly besieging Mahomet Ali. Capture Arcot and they would be forced to come back. With two hundred Europeans, six hundred Indians, and eight officers, of whom half were former clerks like himself, Clive set forth. The town fell easily to his assault, and he and his small handful prepared desperately for the vengeance which was to come. Everything turned out as Clive had foreseen. The Indian potentate, dismayed by the loss of his capital, detached a large portion of his troops from Trichinopoly and attacked Clive in Arcot. The struggle lasted for fifty days. Twenty times outnumbered, and close to starvation, Clive's puny force broke the onslaught in a night attack in which he served a gun himself, and the siege was lifted by the threat of an admiring Mahratta chieftain to come to the aid of the British. This was the end of Dupleix, and of much else besides. By 1752 Clive, in combination with Stringer Lawrence, a regular soldier from England, had defeated the French and the French-sponsored usurpers and placed Mahomet Ali on the throne. The Carnatic was safe. Next year Clive, newly wed, but in bad health, sailed to England. He was much enriched by the "presents," as they were politely called, which he had received from Indian rulers. Dupleix struggled on, but was recalled to

INDIA
IN THE TIME OF
CLIVE AND HASTINGS

BRITISH
TERRITORY IN 1785

AFGHAN
SUPREMACY

RAJPUTANA

Delhi

NEPAL

OUDH

LANDS OF THE
MAHRATTAS

BENGAL

Plassey

Chandernagore

Calcutta

ORISSA

Bombay
(British)

Assaye

Poona

NIZAM'S
DOMINIONS

Hyderabad

MYSORE

Seringapatam

Arcot

Madras

CARNATIC

Pondicherry
Porto Novo

Trichinopoly

CEYLON

France in 1754, and died nine years later in poverty and disgrace. The contrast is striking between the wealth and power won by the English leaders in India and the sad fate that befell most of the French.

In England Clive used a part of his fortune in an attempt to enter Parliament for a "rotten borough" in Cornwall. He was unsuccessful, and in 1755 he returned to India. He was only just in time, for a new struggle was about to open in the North-East. Hitherto French, Dutch, and English had traded peacefully side by side in the fertile province of Bengal, and its docile, intelligent, and industrious inhabitants had largely escaped the slaughter and anarchy of the South. Calcutta, at the mouth of the Ganges, was earning good dividends. Peace had been kept by a Moslem adventurer from the North-West who had seized and held power for fourteen years. But he died in 1756, and the throne passed to his nephew, Surajah Dowlah, young, vicious, violent, and greedy. Fearing, with some justice, that what came to be called the Seven Years' War between Britain and France, lately broken out, would engulf his dominions and reduce him to a puppet like his fellow-princes in the Deccan, he called on both the European communities to dismantle their fortifications. The French at Chandernagore, up-river from Calcutta, returned a soothing answer. The English, aware that war with France was imminent, had extended their fortifications on the river-bank, where the French attack was expected, and ignored his demands. Other frictions increased his anger. In May Surajah Dowlah struck.

Gathering a large army, including guns and Europeans trained to use them, he marched on Calcutta. Modern research has cleared the Governor and the English authorities from the graver charges of cowardice and incompetence denounced by Macaulay, but the landward approach to the city was unfortified, there was mismanagement and confusion, and the evacuation by ships developed into a panic scramble. The small garrison and most of the English civilians fought bravely, but in three days it was all over. They had lived in peace too long. A terrible fate now overtook them. A hundred and forty-six Europeans surrendered after the enemy had penetrated the defences under a flag of truce. They were thrust for the night into a prison cell twenty feet square. By the morning all except twenty-three were dead. The victors departed, having looted the Company's possessions. "Little though he guessed it," says Lord Elton, "the dealings of Surajah Dowlah with the British had ensured they would become the next rulers of India. For the tragedy of the Black Hole had dispelled their last wishful illusion that it might still be possible for them to remain in India as traders and no more. There was an outrage to avenge, and at last they were more than ready to fight." [1]

The news reached Madras in August. The Directors had not yet learnt that war with France had already broken out in Europe, but there were rumours, as in Calcutta, of a French attack, both by sea and from the Deccan. They nevertheless gave Clive all their naval power and nearly all their troops. In January 1757, with nine hundred European and fifteen hundred Indian soldiers, he recaptured Calcutta and repulsed Surajah Dowlah's army of forty thousand men. The war with France now compelled him to retreat, but only long enough for him to attack Chandernagore, which he dared not leave in French hands, before hastening back to Madras. In March Chandernagore fell; its garrison, fighting very bravely, withdrew. Then fortune came to Clive's aid. Surajah Dowlah's cruelty was too much, even for his own people. A group of courtiers resolved to depose him and place a new ruler, Mir Jafar, on the throne. Clive agreed to help. On June 23, his army having grown to three thousand men, of whom less than

[1] Lord Elton, *Imperial Commonwealth* (1945).

a third were British, he met Surajah Dowlah at Plassey. He was outnumbered seventeen to one. The Hoogli River, now in flood behind him, forbade retreat; the enemy gathered in a semicircle on the open plain. Clive disposed his force along the edge of a mango grove and awaited the onslaught. Battle there was none. Nevertheless it was a trial of strength, on which the fortunes of India turned. For four hours there was a cannonade. Then Surajah Dowlah, sensing treachery in his own camp, and listening to the counsel of those plotting to betray him, ordered a withdrawal. Clive had resolved to let him go and make a night attack later on, but a junior officer advanced against orders. It became impossible to check the pursuit. The enemy dispersed in panic, and a few days later Surajah Dowlah was murdered by Mir Jafar's son. For the loss of thirty-six men Clive had become the master of Bengal and the victor of Plassey.

Much however still remained to be accomplished. Mir Jafar, who had taken no part in the so-called battle, was placed on the throne, but the province swarmed with Moslem fighting men from the North and was fertile in pretenders. The neighbouring state of Oudh was hostile; the French were still active; and even the Dutch showed signs of interfering. Clive beat the lot. If the English would not rule the country themselves, they must ensure that a friendly local potentate did so. Indirect control was the order of the day. The alternative was more anarchy and more bloodshed. When Clive sailed once more to England in February 1760 Britain was the only European Power left in India. In little more than four years he had brought about a great change upon the Indian scene. The French were still allowed to keep their trading posts, but their influence was destroyed, and nine years later the *Compagnie des Indes* was abolished. Clive had now accumulated a fortune of a quarter of a million pounds. He bought his way into Parliament, as was the custom of the time, and was created an Irish peer. His services in India were not yet over.

*   *   *   *   *

Modern generations should not mistake the character of the British expansion in India. The Government was never involved as a principal in the Indian conflict, and while Pitt, who justly appreciated the ability of Clive, supported him with all the resources at his command his influence on events was small. In any case he already had a world war on his hands. Faced with the difficulties of communication, the distance, and the complexities of the scene, Pitt left Clive with a free hand, contenting himself with advice and support. The East India Company was a trading organisation. Its Directors were men of business. They wanted dividends, not wars, and grudged every penny spent on troops and annexations. But the turmoil in the great sub-continent compelled them against their will and their judgment to take control of more and more territory, till in the end, and almost by accident, they established an empire no less solid and certainly more peaceful than that of their Mogul predecessors. To call this process "Imperialist expansion" is nonsense, if by that is meant the deliberate acquisition of political power. Of India it has been well said that the British Empire was acquired in a fit of absence of mind.

Clive's triumph created as many problems as it solved, and the years which followed his departure contain some of the most squalid pages in the history of the British in India. The object of the East India Company was to make profits. How the country was ruled they neither knew nor cared so long as peace was maintained and trade prospered. They deposed the ageing Mir Jafar, and, when his puppet-successor became restless, defeated him in a bloody battle and sold the throne of Bengal by auction. The ill-paid servants of the Company were both forced and encouraged to take bribes, presents, and every kind of shameful perquisite from the inhabitants. Tales of corruption and the gaining of vast and illicit private fortunes crept back to England. The Directors of the Company suddenly found that they had lost both their dividends and their good name. They appealed to Clive, made him Governor-General of all their Indian territories, and in June 1764 he sailed to India for the last time. His reforms were drastic, high-handed, and in effect more far-reaching than the victory at Plassey. Their success prompted the Mogul Emperor to invite him to extend a British protectorate to Delhi and all Northern India. Clive refused. He had long doubted the ability of the Company to undertake the larger responsibilities of Empire, and five years earlier he had suggested in a letter to Pitt that the Crown should assume the sovereignty of the Company's possessions in India. This advice was disregarded for nearly a century. Meanwhile, in return for a subsidy the Great Mogul ceded to the Company the right to administer the revenues. Administration of justice remained with the Indian rulers. Such division of responsibilities could not last, and was soon to create formidable problems, but at least it was a step forward. The British held the purse-strings, and "the power," wrote Clive, "is now lodged where it can only be lodged in safety." In January 1767 he returned to England. The British public were critical and ill-informed. Clive was assailed in the House of Commons. He defended himself in an eloquent speech. He pointed out that by his exertions the Directors of the East India Company "had acquired an Empire more extensive than any kingdom in Europe. They had acquired a revenue of four millions sterling and trade in proportion." About the gains which he himself had made he exclaimed in a celebrated passage, "Am I not rather deserving of praise for the moderation which marked my proceedings? Consider the situation in which the victory at Plassey had placed me. A great prince was dependent on my pleasure; an opulent city lay at my mercy; its richest bankers bid against each other for my smiles; I walked through vaults which were thrown open to me alone, piled on either hand with gold and jewels. Mr Chairman, at this moment I stand astonished at my own moderation." The House of Commons unanimously passed a resolution that "Robert Lord Clive rendered great and meritorious services to this country." The vehement, tormented spirit who was the subject of this motion was not appeased. A few years later he died by his own hand.

*   *   *   *   *

Clive was soon followed in India by as great a man as himself, but with a somewhat different background. Warren Hastings was poor, but his ancestors had once owned large estates in Worcestershire. The wars of Oliver Cromwell had compelled his great-grandfather to sell the family home at Daylesford, and from early boyhood Hastings dreamed of winning it back. His mother died when he was very young, and an uncle brought him up and sent him to school at Westminster. There he became the senior classical scholar, and the masters wanted him to go to a university. His uncle refused, and sent him to India instead. He was then sixteen years of age.

He served the East India Company as a subordinate through the great period of Clive's triumphs, and a year after Clive's final departure he became a member of the Council in Calcutta. From this position of limited but definite responsibility he witnessed the squalor and confusion which prevailed. The Company's servants continued to build their fortunes at the expense of their employers and of the inhabitants. The Mahrattas seized Delhi and menaced Oudh. Madras was threatened, and even Bombay, hitherto so peaceful, was involved in the civil wars. Between 1769 and 1770 a third of the population of Bengal died of famine. Throughout these ordeals Warren Hastings held fast to an austere way of life. He desired fame and power, and enough money to buy back Daylesford. The gathering of private fortunes he left to others. Rapacity was not in his nature. In 1772 he became Governor of the stricken, preyed-upon, but still wealthy province of Bengal. He made two resolutions: to keep up the Company's dividends and to make the British collect the taxes. By now however the whispers and worse on which Clive had been nearly censured by Parliament had taken hold of public opinion in England. Rich adventurers from the East were making and marring the repute of the new Empire in India. Too wealthy and too arrogant to subside into the levels of society from which they had emerged, and too upsprung to mix with the aristocracy, the "Nabobs", as they were called—it is the same word as Nawab, but in different spelling—were disliked or envied by all classes in Great Britain. The courage and discipline which had won the day at Arcot and at Plassey and had avenged the Black Hole were overlooked. Nor was this wholly unjust, since many of the Nabobs had been too busily engaged in amassing wealth to lend much help to Clive. "India," declared the ageing Chatham, "teems with iniquities so rank as to smell to heaven and earth." Jealousy, ignorance, and sentimentality combined in a cry for reform. There were also solid grounds for complaint. Within nine years nearly three million pounds had been collected as personal rewards by the Company's servants from the inhabitants of Bengal. The instrument for reform happened to be Lord North.

North did his best within his lights. His motto was "Shackle the great," and the year after Hastings became Governor of Bengal he induced Parliament to pass a Regulating Act. The measure was not totally lacking in merit. The administration of British-held territory in India was unified. Bombay and Madras were subjected to a "Governor-General" established at Calcutta, and Warren Hastings was made the first Governor-General, with a salary of twenty-five thousand pounds a year. But in trying to make sure that power was not abused it was made impotent. On paper it was divided between the Nawab of Bengal, the Board of Directors, the Governor-General, and a Council appointed to veto and control him. For years Hastings fought against his shackles. His principal opponent was his new colleague, Philip Francis, the reputed author of the savage *Letters of Junius* which had attacked the Government at home during the agitations over Wilkes. Francis never ceased to intrigue against him, openly and behind his back. But Hastings knew what needed to be done, and he was determined to do it. Though naturally a man of quick temper, he learned the virtues of patience and cool persistence. At one moment the Government tried to recall him. Then two of the most ignorant and hostile members of his Council died, and soon afterwards France, roused by the revolt in America and seeking to regain her power in India, once again delared war on Britain. Hastings at last was free to act. His liberation came only just in time.

By 1778 a French fleet was approaching the southern coast, Hyder Ali of Mysore was overrunning the Carnatic, the British Governor of Madras had been imprisoned by his own corrupt officials, and Bombay was at war with the Mahrattas. In the space of six years Hastings retrieved everything. His naval forces were weaker than the French, and although they fought no fewer than five engagements they were unable to prevent the French landing on the Madras coast. The Government of Madras was purged and reanimated. Sir Eyre Coote, who had served at Plassey, and was still the ablest British soldier in India, was sent hurriedly southwards. He defeated Hyder Ali at Porto Novo in 1781, and his son Tipu Sultan a year later. Peace was negotiated with the Mahrattas. By 1783 the only active enemies who remained were the French, and their hopes of progress were stopped by the conclusion of the Treaty of Versailles. England had lost one Empire in America and gained another in India.

All this train of action had cost a lot of money. Hastings could get very little help, financial or material, from England, exhausted and overstrained by the conflict in America, Europe and on the seas. His only course was to raise it on the spot. The inhabitants of Bengal were wealthy. They were also, thanks to British arms and leadership, comparatively safe. They should pay for their protection, and Hastings had been quite ruthless in making them do so. Thus he gathered the funds to rescue Bombay and the Carnatic and to stop the bloodshed once more engulfing Bengal. His critics, and those of the East India Company, were not slow to point out that only a third of the two million pounds he raised was spent on the war. The rest leaked away in familiar directions. But Hastings himself was careless of money and came home with no great fortune. He left India in 1785, not without the gratitude of the inhabitants. Unlike many Englishmen in India at this time, he spoke the local languages well. He enjoyed the society of Indians, and had once been rebuked on this account by the formidable Clive. Though proud of his birth and ancestry, consciousness of race, colour, or religion never influenced or distracted him.

In the beginning Hastings was welcomed and honoured in England. His achievements and victories were some compensation for the humiliations and disasters in America, and the Company had much to thank him for. A year before his return the younger Pitt had passed an India Act making the Board of Control subject to the Cabinet and assuming the political powers of the East India Company. Hastings had disapproved of this. Though the Governor-General was thus freed from the fetters of the Council at Calcutta imposed by North's ill-conceived measure, patronage passed into the hands of Pitt's friend and adviser, Henry Dundas, appointed President of the Board of Control. In fact, a flow of ambitious, earnest, and incorrupt young Scotsmen started to fill and fortify the British administrative posts in India, where, thanks to Clive and to Hastings, most of them could now gain a living without taking bribes and pickings. All this was very good. But not so easily did Parliament forget the "rank iniquities" which Chatham had denounced. The "Nabobs" in England were still obtrusive, vulgar, and ostentatiously wealthy. Soon after Hastings's return a Parliamentary inquiry into his conduct had been set on foot. No personal charge of corruption could be proved against him, but he was arrogant and tactless in his dealings with the politicians of all parties. Headed by Burke, Fox, and Sheridan, Parliament resolved to have his blood. Philip Francis, whom he had wounded in a duel in Calcutta, malignly urged his enemies on. The ancient weapon of impeachment was resurrected and turned against him. The trial opened in Westminster Hall on February 13, 1788. It lasted over seven years. Every aspect and detail of Hastings's administration was scrutinised, denounced, upheld, misunderstood, or applauded. At the end he was acquitted. Though much of the uproar was unfair and uncomprehending the proceedings proclaimed to the public and the world the support of the British peoples for Burke's declaration that India should be governed "by those laws which are to be found in Europe, Africa, and Asia, that are found amongst all mankind—those principles of equity and humanity implanted in our hearts, which have their existence in the feelings of mankind that are capable of judging."

Hastings was nearly bankrupt by the cost of defending himself. The Company however had given him enough money to buy back Daylesford, and many years later, when testifying in the Commons on Indian affairs, the House uncovered in his honour. He never held office again. But at any rate he was more fortunate than his old opponents from France, several of whom had long before been beheaded or made penniless. Posterity has redeemed his name from the slurs of the Whigs.

*   *   *   *   *

It is convenient at this point to look ahead in the story of British India. The Napoleonic wars were accompanied by a vast extension of British power. On the eve of the Revolution in France the rule of the East India Company was confined to the province of Bengal and to a few coastal strips around the ports of Madras and Bombay. By the morrow of Waterloo it embraced all except the north-westerly portions of the subcontinent.

The impeachment of Warren Hastings was a turning-point in the history of the British in India. The chief power was no longer to be grasped by obscure, brilliant servants of the Company who could seize and merit it, and the post of Governor-General was henceforward occupied by personages distinguished on their own account and drawn from the leading families in England: the Marquess Cornwallis, uncowed by the surrender at Yorktown, the Marquess Wellesley, Lord Minto, the Marquess of Hastings, Lord Amherst, and Lord Dalhousie. In effect, though not in name, these men were Viceroys, untempted by the hope of financial gain, impatient of restraint by ill-informed Governments in London, and sufficiently intimate with the ruling circles in Britain to do what they thought right and without fear of the consequences. And indeed there had been much for them to do. The Carnatic, hinterland of Madras, was presided over in 1785 by an Indian Nawab, supported by British arms and British money. The state of Mysore, stretching to the western coast, had been seized from the Moguls by Hyder Ali, and was heartily misgoverned by his son, Tipu Sultan, who coveted the domination of all Southern India. In the south-central portion of the peninsula the Nizam of Hyderabad ruled feebly over the Deccan, unreliable for keeping order and in theory a vassal of the puppet Emperor in Delhi. Beyond all these swarmed the Mahrattas, a confederacy of military families, fierce Hindu fighting-men, lightly armed and mounted on swift horses, who could disperse as speedily as they attacked, ancient opponents of the Mahometan Moguls, and avid to found an Indian Empire of their own. Bengal alone lay peacefully in the British grip, precariously shielded from the turmoil by the weak buffer-state of Oudh.

Cornwallis was soon compelled to deal with Tipu. In the last decade of the eighteenth century he marched against him, captured most of Mysore, and made him surrender half his territory. Cornwallis's successor, a nonentity who came to power in the same year as Louis XVI was beheaded, tried to call a halt, but Indian rulers were now taking French officers into their pay and training their armies on the European pattern. The Marquess Wellesley was left in 1798 to extinguish the threat. Napoleon, victorious in Egypt, and himself seeking an empire in the East, offered help to Tipu, who began to assemble a French-trained army. The struggle between France and England once again loomed over India. There was a danger of naval attack from the French-held island of Mauritius, in the Indian Ocean. Wellesley acted with speed and resolution. He offered Tipu what was termed a "subsidiary treaty," whereby Tipu was to dismiss all Frenchmen, disband his troops, and pay for the Company's protection of his dominions. Tipu preferred to fight, and in 1799 he was driven back to his capital at Seringapatam and killed. Wellesley then annexed the outlying portions of Mysore, and returned the rest to the Hindu potentates whom Hyder Ali had dispossessed. They did not survive for long. When the French Oriental ambitions foundered in the Battle of the Nile Wellesley turned his attention to the Carnatic. Its Government was bankrupt

and oppressive, and in 1801 he pensioned off the Nawab and
made it into the Madras Presidency. In the same year he
dealt with Oudh. Here all was far from well. The Nawab,
though under British protection, had surrendered his dominions to pillage and exploitation, by his own mutinous troops
and by greedy adventurers from Europe. On him also Wellesley
imposed a subsidiary treaty. In return for a guarantee of protection, he ceded most of his territories to the British, except
for a small portion round Lucknow, dismissed all Europeans
from his service except those approved by the Company, and
promised to govern according to the Company's advice.

Lastly Wellesley dealt with the Mahrattas. Some years previously they had captured Delhi, seized the person of the
Mogul Emperor, and demanded tribute on his behalf from
Bengal. Now they started fighting among themselves. Their
chief escaped and appealed to Wellesley, who restored him
to his capital at Poona. The rest of them thereupon declared
war on the British, and after heavy fighting were defeated at
Assaye and elsewhere by Wellesley's younger brother, the future Duke of Wellington. On them also Wellesley imposed a
subsidiary treaty, and Orissa and most of the province of
Delhi were surrendered to the British. "In seven years," writes
a distinguished historian, "he had transformed the map of India and launched his countrymen on a career of expansion
which only stopped at the Afghan mountains half a century
later. . . . These proceedings appear, superficially, ambitious and high-handed in the extreme. For their justification
they must plead that in every case they operated to the advantage of the populations concerned. Eighteenth-century India resembled fifth-century Europe. Wellesley knew that British rule was the only alternative to bloodshed, tyranny, and
anarchy, and he had no false delicacy in translating his conviction into fact. Europe after the fall of Rome took many weary
centuries to settle down into a land where the common man

might live his life in security; in India British authority accomplished a settlement in the space of fifty years." [1] The East India Company however took a different view. The Directors still wanted trade, not conquests, and were so hostile and critical that Wellesley resigned in 1805.

His successor, Lord Minto, was expressly forbidden to take on any new territorial responsibilities, and for a brief period he succeeded in marking time. But it was impossible to do this for long. The pacification which Wellesley had begun must either be completed or perish. The disbanding of local armies which he had imposed on so many Indian rulers let loose a horde of unemployed and discontented soldiery, who formed themselves into robber gangs. Helped by the Mahrattas, who mistook British neutrality for weakness, these gangs began the pillage of Central India. The Marquess Hastings, appointed Governor-General in 1814, was compelled to subdue them with a large force. The Mahrattas, seeing their last chance vanish of succeeding to the Empire of the Moguls, promptly revolted. They too were defeated, their chief was deposed, and his Principality of Poona added to the Presidency of Bombay. Against its wishes and almost in spite of itself, the Company was now overlord of three-quarters of India.

[1] J. A. Williamson, *A Short History of British Expansion* (1922), p. 578.

BOOK NINE

NAPOLEON

The Younger Pitt

THE Marquis of Rockingham had waited long for his opportunity to form a Government, and when at last it came in March 1782 he had but four months to live. The surrender of Cornwallis at Yorktown in Virginia had a decisive effect on British opinion. Dark was the scene which spread around the ambitious Island and its stubborn King. Britain was without a single ally; she stood alone amid a world war in which all had gone amiss. A French squadron was threatening her communications in the Indian Ocean and French money was nourishing the hopes of the Mahrattas on the Indian subcontinent; the combined Fleets of France and Spain were active in the Channel and had blockaded Gibraltar; Minorca had fallen; Washington's army lay poised before New York, and the American Congress had incontinently pledged itself not to make a separate peace. Admiral Rodney indeed regained command of West Indian waters in a great victory off the Saintes, and in September Howe was to relieve Gibraltar from a three-year siege. Elsewhere over the globe England's power and repute were very low. Such was the plight to which the obstinacy of George III had reduced the Empire.

Rockingham died in July, and Lord Shelburne was entrusted with the new administration. He had no intention of following the design which Rockingham and Burke had long cherished of composing a Cabinet, united on the main issues of the day, which would dictate its policy to the King in accordance with its collective decisions. This plan was cast aside. Shelburne sought to form a Government by enlisting politicians of the most diverse views and connection. But the entire structure of British politics was ruptured in its personal loyalties by the years of defeat to which King George III had led them. Now, by enlisting the help of the many, the new Prime Minister incurred the suspicion of all. Of great ability, a brilliant orator, and with the most liberal ideas, he was nevertheless, like Carteret before him, distrusted on all sides. The King found him personally agreeable and gave him full support. But politics were now implacably bitter between three main groups, and none of them was strong enough alone to sustain a Government. Shelburne himself had the support of those who had followed Chatham, including his son, the young William Pitt, who was appointed Chancellor of the Exchequer. But North still commanded a considerable faction, and, smarting at his sovereign's cold treatment after twelve years of faithful service, coveted a renewal of office. The third group was headed by Charles James Fox, vehement critic of North's régime, brilliant, generous-hearted, and inconsistent. Burke, for his part, lacked family connections; he had no great gift for practical politics, and since the death of his patron, Rockingham, was without influence.

Hostility to Shelburne grew and spread. Nevertheless, by negotiations in which he displayed great skill, the Prime Minister succeeded in bringing the world war to an end on the basis of American independence. The French Government were now close to bankruptcy. They had only aided the American Patriots in the hope of dismembering the British Empire, and, apart from a few romantic enthusiasts like Lafayette, had no wish to help to create a republic in the New World. His own Ministers had long warned Louis XVI that this might shake his absolute monarchy. Spain was directly hostile to American independence. She had entered the war mainly because France had promised to help her to recapture Gibraltar in return for the use of her Fleet against England. But the revolt of the Thirteen Colonies had bred trouble among her own overseas possessions, Gibraltar had not fallen, and she now demanded extensive compensation in North America. Although Congress had promised to let France take the lead in peace negotiations, the American Commissioners in Europe realised their danger, and without French knowledge and in direct violation of the Congressional undertaking they signed secret peace preliminaries with England. Shelburne, like Chatham, dreamt of preserving the Empire by making generous concessions, and he realised that freedom was the only practical policy. In any case Fox had already committed Britain to this step by making a public announcement in the House of Commons.

The most important issue was the future of the Western lands lying between the Allegheny Mountains and the Mississippi. Speculators from Virginia and the Middle Colonies had long been active in these regions, and their influence in Congress was backed by powerful men such as Franklin, Patrick Henry, the Lee family, and Washington himself. The Radical New Englanders, led by Samuel and John Adams, had no direct interest in these Western territories, but agreed to press for their complete cession provided the British were made to recognise the rights of the Northern colonies to fish off Newfoundland.

Shelburne was by no means hostile to the American desire for the West. The difficulty was the Canadian frontier. Franklin and others went so far as to demand the whole province of Canada, but Shelburne knew that to yield to this would bring down his Government. After months of negotiation a frontier was agreed upon which ran from the borders of Maine to the St Lawrence, up the river, and through the Great Lakes to their head. Everything south of this line, east of the Mississippi and north of the borders of Florida, became American territory. This was by far the most important result of the treaty. Shelburne had shown great statesmanship, and frontier wars between Britain and America were, with one exception, prevented by his concessions. The only sufferers were the Canadian fur companies, whose activities had till now extended from the province of Quebec to the Ohio; but this was a small price. The granting of fishery rights to New England satisfied the Northern states.

In return the British Government attempted to settle two disputes, namely, over the unpaid debts of the American merchants to England accumulated before the war and the security of about a hundred thousand American Loyalists. Shelburne fought hard, but the Americans showed little generosity. They knew only too well that the game was already theirs and that the British Government dared not break off negotiations on these comparatively minor points. It was merely provided that "creditors on either side shall meet with no lawful impediment in the recovery of their debts" and that Congress should "earnestly recommend the several states to restore Loyalist property." South Carolina alone showed an understanding spirit about Loyalist property, and between forty and fifty thousand "United Empire Loyalists" had to make new homes in Canada.

France now made her terms with England. An armistice was declared in January 1783, and the final peace treaty was signed at Versailles later in the year. The French kept their possessions in India and the West Indies. They were guaranteed the right to fish off Newfoundland, and they reoccupied the slave-trade settlements of Senegal on the African coast. The important cotton island of Tobago was ceded to them, but apart from this they gained little that was material. Their main object however was achieved. The Thirteen Colonies had been wrested from the United Kingdom, and England's position in the world seemed to have been gravely weakened.

Spain was forced to join in the general settlement. Her American ambitions had melted away, her one gain in this theatre being the two English colonies in East Florida; but this was at the expense of the English retention of Gibraltar, the main Spanish objective. She had conquered Minorca, the English naval station in the Mediterranean during the war, and she kept this at the peace. Holland too was compelled by the defection of her allies to come to terms.

Thus ended what some then called the World War. A new state had come into being across the Atlantic, a great future force in the councils of the nations. The first British Empire had fallen. England had been heavily battered, but remained undaunted.

Her emergence from her ordeal was the work of Shelburne. In less than a year he had brought peace to the world and had negotiated the terms on which it stood. That he received small thanks for his services is a remarkable fact. He resigned after eight months, in February 1783. Later he was created Marquis of Lansdowne, and descendants of his under that name have since played a notable part in British politics. Shelburne's Government was followed by a machine-made coalition between North and Fox. It was said that this combination was too much even for the agile consciences of the age. Fox had made his name by savage personal assaults on North's administration. Only five years before he had publicly declared that any alliance with North was too monstrous to be admitted for a moment. Yet this was what was now presented to an astonished public. Shelburne had lived upon his task. The Fox-North Government had nothing on which to rest their feet. Within nine months this Ministry also collapsed. The immediate cause of its fall was a Bill which Fox drafted with the laudable intention of reforming the Government of India. His design was to subject the East India Company, now the rulers of vast territories in Asia, to some degree of control by a political board in London. His critics were quick to point out that extensive patronage would be vested in the hands of this political board and opportunities for corruption immeasurably increased. Only close supporters of the Government could hope to benefit. All party groups, except Fox's personal followers, were therefore hostile to the proposal.

The King now seized his chance of regaining popularity by destroying a monstrous administration. Party and personal issues alike being exhausted by the weight of the disaster, George III saw his opportunity if he could find the man. Only one figure stood in the House of Commons not committed to the past. If he lacked the traditional elements on which Parliamentary strength had been built in former times, he was at least free from a wholly discredited process. In William Pitt, the son of the great Chatham, the King found the man. He had already held the Chancellorship of the Exchequer during the Shelburne administration. His reputation was honourable and clear. By what was certainly the most outstanding domestic action of his long reign, in December 1783, the King asked Pitt to form a Government. The old Parliamentary machine had failed, and as it broke down a new combination took its place whose efforts were vindicated by the events of the next twenty years.

* * * * *

The revolt of the American colonies had shattered the complacency of eighteenth-century England. Men began to study the root causes of the disaster and the word "reform" was in the air. The defects of the political system had plainly contributed to the secession, and the arguments used by the American colonists against the Mother Country lingered in the minds of all Englishmen who questioned the perfection of the Constitution. Demand for some reform of the representation in Parliament began to stir; but the agitation was now mild and respectable. The main aim of the reformers was to increase the number of boroughs which elected Members of Parliament, and thus reduce the possibilities of Government corruption. There was even talk of universal suffrage and other novel theories of democratic representation. But the chief advocates of reform were substantial landowners or country clergymen like Christopher Wyvill, from Yorkshire, or mature, well-established politicians like Edmund Burke. They would all have agreed that Parliament did not and need not precisely represent the English people. To them Parliament represented, not individuals, but "interests"—the landed interest, the mercantile interest, even the labouring interest, but with a strong leaning to the land as the solid and indispensable basis of the national life. These well-to-do theorists were distressed at the rapid spread of political corruption. This was due partly to the Whig system of controlling the Government through the patronage of the Crown, and partly to the purchase of seats in Parliament by the new commercial and industrial classes. The "Nabobs" of the East India interest, as we have seen, appeared at Westminster, and the incursion of the money power into politics both widened the field of corruption and threatened the political monopoly of the landowning classes. Thus the movement in governing circles was neither radical nor comprehensive. It found expression in Burke's Economic Reform Act of 1782, disfranchising certain classes of Government officials who had hitherto played some part in managing elections. This was a tepid version of the scheme Burke had meant to introduce. No general reform of the franchise was attempted, and when people talked about the rights of Englishmen they meant the sturdy class of yeomen vaunted as the backbone of the country, whose weight in the counties it was desired to increase. Many of the early reform schemes were academic attempts to preserve the political power and balance of the rural interest. The individualism of eighteenth-century England assumed no doctrinaire form. The enunciation of first principles has always been obnoxious to the English mind. John Wilkes had made a bold and successful stand for the liberty of the subject before the law, but the whole controversy had turned on the narrow if practical issue of the legality of general warrants. Tom Paine's inflammatory pamphlets had a considerable circulation among certain classes, but in Parliament little was heard about the abstract rights of man. In England the revolutionary current ran underground and was caught up in provincial eddies.

Nevertheless the dream of founding a balanced political system on a landed society was becoming more and more unreal. In the last forty years of the eighteenth century exports and imports more than doubled in value and the population increased by over two millions. England was silently undergoing a revolution in industry and agriculture, which was to have more far-reaching effects than the political tumults of the times. Steam-engines provided a new source of power in factories and foundries, which rapidly multiplied. A network of canals was constructed which carried coal cheaply to new centres of industry. New methods of smelting brought a tenfold increase in the output of iron. New roads, with a hard and durable surface, reached out over the country and bound it more closely together. An ever-expanding and assertive industrial community was coming into being. The rapid growth of an urban working class, the gradual extinction of small freeholders by enclosures and improved farming methods, the sudden development of manufactures, the appearance of a prosperous middle class for whom a place must be found in the political structure of the realm, made the demands of reformers seem inadequate. A great upheaval was taking place in society, and the monopoly which the landowners had gained in 1688 could not remain.

There was also a profound change in the emotional and intellectual life of the people. The American Revolution had thrown the English back upon themselves, and a mental stock-taking exposed complacencies and anomalies which could ill stand the public gaze. The religious revival of John Wesley had broken the stony surface of the Age of Reason. The enthusiasm generated by the Methodist movement and its mission to the poor and humble accelerated the general dissolution of the eighteenth-century world. The Dissenters, who had long supported the Whig Party, increased in wealth and importance and renewed their attack on the religious monopoly of the Established Church. Barred from Parliament and from the franchise, fertile in mind, they formed an intelligent, thrustful, and unsatisfied body of men. Such, in brief, were the turmoils and problems which confronted William Pitt when he became Prime Minister of Britain at the age of twenty-four.

* * * * *

The elections which carried Pitt into power were the most carefully planned of the century. There has been a legend that a great wave of popular reaction against the personal government of George III brought him into office. In fact it was George himself who turned to Pitt, and the whole electoral machinery built up by the King's agents, headed by the backstairs figure of John Robinson, the Secretary of the Treasury, was put at the disposal of the young politician. In December 1783 Robinson and Pitt met to discuss their plan at a house in Leicester Square belonging to one of Pitt's close associates, Henry Dundas. Robinson drew up a detailed report on the constituencies, and convinced Pitt that a majority in the Commons could be obtained. Three days later Fox and North were dismissed by the King, and the ensuing elections created a majority which William Pitt preserved into the next century. The plan had been justified, and the nation at large accepted the result as the true verdict of the country.

This majority rested on a number of elements—Pitt's personal following; the "Party of the Crown," put at his disposal by George III; the independent country gentlemen; the

East India interest, alienated by Fox's attempt to curb their political power; and the Scottish Members, marshalled by Dundas. Here was a rank and file which represented a broad basis of popular favour. Pitt had no intention of being a second Lord North. The Tories supported him because he appeared to be rescuing the King from an unscrupulous Government. The Whigs remembered that he had refused office under North, and that he had advocated a reform of the Parliamentary system. The "old gang," with whom he had no connections, had failed, disgraced the nation, and wrecked its finances. With all the renown of his father's name behind him, this grave, precocious young man, eloquent, incorruptible, and hard-working, stood upon the uplands of power.

Even at this age he had few close acquaintances. But two men were to play a decisive part in his life, Henry Dundas and William Wilberforce. Dundas, a good-humoured, easygoing materialist, embodied the spirit of eighteenth-century politics, with its buying up of seats, its full-blooded enjoyment of office, its secret influences, and its polished scepticism. He was an indispensable ally, for he commanded both the electoral power of Scotland and the political allegiance of the East India Company, and it was he who kept the new majority together. For Pitt, although personally incorruptible, leant heavily upon the eighteenth-century machinery of government for support.

William Wilberforce, on the other hand, was the friend of Pitt's Cambridge days, and the only person who enjoyed his confidence. Deeply religious and sustained by a high idealism, Wilberforce became the keeper of the young Minister's conscience. He belonged to the new generation which questioned the cheerful complacency of the eighteenth century. The group who gathered round him were known not unkindly as "the Saints." They formed a compact body in the House of Commons, and their prime political aim was the abolition of the slave trade. They drew towards them the religious fervour of the new Evangelical, or "Low Church," movement. Between these contrary characters stood Chatham's son.

The greatest orators of the age, Fox and Burke, were Pitt's opponents. They dwelt eloquently on the broad themes of reform. Yet it was Pitt, aided by Dundas, who in a quiet, businesslike way reconstructed the practical policies of the nation. The variety of his following however limited the scope of his work. A multitude of interests stifled his early hopes. He failed to legislate against the slave trade. Wilberforce and his "Saints" were consistently thwarted by the Bristol and Liverpool merchants, who were political supporters of the Ministry and whom Pitt refused to alienate. Such was the meagreness of Pitt's efforts that many doubted his sincerity as a reformer: abolition of the slave trade had to wait until Fox again came into office. But Wilberforce never permitted a syllable of doubt to be spoken unchallenged against his friend, and trusted to the end in Pitt's Parliamentary judgment.

Pitt was to need great patience in the coming years. His supporters were stubborn, jealous, and at times rebellious. They frustrated his attempts to reform the Irish Government, now imperative since the loss of the American colonies. It was only after a hard fight that Pitt and Dundas persuaded the House of Commons to pass an India Bill establishing a Board of Control not unlike that which Fox had proposed, though less effective. The system endured until after the Indian Mutiny sixty years later. Since Dundas immediately acquired the management of this Board, the patronage thus placed in his hands greatly enhanced his own political position. In April 1785 the King and the borough Members extinguished another of Pitt's hopes, a measure of Parliamentary Reform.

Thus from the outset Pitt was overcome by the dead hand

of eighteenth-century politics. He failed to abolish the slave trade. He failed to make a settlement in Ireland. He failed to make Parliament more representative of the nation, and the one achievement in these early months was his India Act, which increased rather than limited the opportunities for political corruption. He saw quite clearly the need and justification for reform, but preferred always to compromise with the forces of resistance.

*   *   *   *   *

It was in the most practical and most urgent problem, the ordering and reconstruction of the finances of the nation, that Pitt achieved his best work, and created that Treasury tradition of wise, incorruptible management which still prevails. His Ministry coincided with a revolution in economic and commercial thought. In 1776 Adam Smith had published *The Wealth of Nations,* which quickly became famous throughout educated circles. Pitt was deeply influenced by his book. The first British Empire was discredited and had almost vanished from the map. Another was gradually growing in Canada, in India, and in the Antipodes, where Cook had just charted the scarce-known Southern Continent. But the conception of a close economic Imperial unit, with the colonies eternally subject in matters of trade to the Mother Country and fettered by comprehensive restrictions upon their commercial intercourse with other nations, had proved disastrous. The times were ripe for an exposition of the principles of Free Trade. In steady, caustic prose Adam Smith destroyed the case for Mercantilism. Pitt was convinced. He was the first English statesman to believe in Free Trade, and for a while his Tory followers accepted it. The antiquated and involved system of customs barriers was now for the first time systematically revised. There were sixty-eight different kinds of customs duties, and some articles were subject to many separate and cumulative imposts. A pound of nutmegs paid, or ought to have paid, nine different duties. In 1784 and 1785

Pitt was able to bring a degree of order into this chaos, and the first visible effect of his wide-ranging revision of tariffs was a considerable drop in smuggling.

Further reform consolidated the revenue. It is to Pitt that we owe the modern machinery of the "Budget." By gathering around him able officials he reorganized the collection and disbursement of the revenue. The Audit Office was established, and numerous sinecures at the Treasury were abolished. The state of the national finances was lamentable. At the end of 1783 over forty million pounds which had been voted by Parliament for war purposes had not been accounted for. Government credit was low, the Ministry was distrusted. The National Debt stood at two hundred and fifty million pounds, more than two and a half times as great as in the days of Walpole. Pitt resolved to acquire a surplus in the revenue and apply it to the reduction of this swollen burden.

In 1786 he brought in a Bill for this purpose. Each year a million pounds would be set aside to buy stock, and the interest would be used to reduce the National Debt. Here was the famous oft-criticised Sinking Fund. The scheme depended on having an annual Budget surplus of revenue over expenditure, and Pitt was often forced in later years, when there was no such surplus, to feed the Sinking Fund with money borrowed at a high rate of interest. His reasons for so costly a procedure were psychological. The soundness of the national finances was judged by the amount in the Sinking Fund, which gave an impression of stability to the moneyed classes of the City. Trade revived, prosperity increased, and what then seemed the handsome sum of ten millions was paid off in ten years.

In this same year, 1786, the Customs and Excise were amalgamated, and a reconstituted Board of Trade established in its modern form. But perhaps the most striking achievement of Pitt's management was the negotiation of the Eden treaty with France—the first Free Trade treaty according to the new economic principles. William Eden, one of Pitt's able young officials, was sent to Paris to get French tariffs against English cotton goods lowered in return for a reduction of English duties on French wines and silks. These did not of course compete with any English product, but the export of Lancashire cotton goods damaged the textile manufacturers in North-Eastern France and increased the discontent among the French industrial classes affected by this enlightened measure.

The hope of further reconstruction and improvement was shattered by war and revolution upon the European scene. For Pitt it was a personal tragedy. His genius lay essentially in business management; his greatest memorials are his financial statements. He was most at home in the world of figures. His mind had set and developed at an unduly early age, without, as Coleridge said, "the ungainliness or the promise of a growing intellect." He found human contacts difficult, and his accession to power cut him off from other men. From 1784 until 1800 he moved exclusively between the narrow world of political London and his house at Putney. He knew nothing of the lives of his countrymen outside the limited area of the Metropolis. Even amid the fellowship of the House of Commons and the political clubs he stood aloof.

Fully aware of the economic changes in eighteenth-century England, Pitt was less sensitive to signs of political disturbance abroad. He believed firmly in non-intervention, and the break-up of the Old Régime in France left him unimpressed. He watched with quiet malice the quarrel on this issue of his leading Parliamentary opponents, Fox and Burke. His interests lay elsewhere. If the French chose to revolt against their rulers it was their own affair. It might be flattering that they should want a constitutional monarchy like the British, but it was no concern of his. The First Minister was deaf to the zealous campaign of the Whig Opposition in favour of the

French revolutionaries, and ignored the warnings of Burke and others who believed that the principles of monarchy, and indeed of civilised society, were endangered by the roar of events across the Channel.

It is remarkable to witness the peaceful triteness of English politics, operating almost as if in a vacuum, during the years 1789 to 1793, when the terrible and world-shaking upheavals in Paris and in the provinces of France convulsed men's minds. The Budget speech; the dismissal of Lord Chancellor Thurlow for intriguing against Pitt, an event which pointed towards the convention of mutual loyalty and singleness of view between all the members of the Cabinet; motions against the slave trade—such was the news from London. Pitt was determined to stand clear of the impending European conflict. He was convinced that if the French revolutionaries were left alone to put their house in order as they chose England could avoid being dragged into war. He steadily avoided any manifestation which could be interpreted as provocative or as demonstrative of sympathy. He watched unmoved the passion of the Opposition for an armed crusade against unenlightened despotism. They were possessed with the fear that the Austrian and Prussian monarchs would intervene to quell the revolution. Led by Fox, they saw in war a hope of breaking Pitt's monopoly of political power. But Burke was closer to the general feeling of the country when he remarked that "the effect of liberty to individuals is that they may do as they please: we ought to see what it will please them to do before we risk congratulations." The sympathies of the Court were not unmoved by the plight of the French monarchy, and if intervention became inevitable the Court was naturally in favour of supporting Louis XVI. Pitt maintained an even course of neutrality, and with characteristic obstinacy held to it for over three tumultuous years.

The American Constitution

THE War of Independence was over and the Thirteen Colonies were free to make their own lives. The struggle had told heavily upon their primitive political organisation. The Articles of Confederation to which they had subscribed in 1777 set up a weak central Government enjoying only such authority as the Americans might have allowed to the British Crown. Their Congress had neither the power nor the opportunity in so vast a land of creating an ordered society out of the wreckage of revolution and war.

The strongest element behind the American effort had been the small farmers from the inland frontier districts. It was they who had supplied the men for the Army and who had in most of the states refashioned the several constitutions on democratic lines. They now dominated the legislatures, and jealously guarded the privileges of their own states. With the close of hostilities it seemed that the Union embodied in an unwieldy Congress might snap or wither under the strain of post-war problems. American society was rent by strong conflicting interests. The farmers were heavily in debt to the city classes. The issue of too much paper money by Congress had bred inflation. By 1780 one gold dollar was worth forty paper ones. Every state was burdened with enormous debts, and the taxes imposed to meet the interest fell heavily upon the land. Small impoverished farmers were everywhere being sold up. War profiteers had emerged. A gulf was widening in American society between debtor and creditor, between farmer and merchant-financier. Agitation and unrest marched with a deepening economic crisis. There were widespread movements for postponing the collection of debts. In Massachusetts farmers and disbanded soldiers, fearing foreclosure on their mortgages, rose in rebellion. In the autumn of 1786 Captain Daniel Shays, with a mob of armed farmers, attempted to storm the county courts. There was sharp fear that such incidents would multiply. Washington, himself as strong an upholder of property as Cromwell, wrote, "There are combustibles in every state which a spark might set fire to. I feel infinitely more than I can express for the disorders which have arisen."

It was not only internal conditions that clamoured for action. Some awkward points in the peace treaty were still unresolved. Debts to the British merchants, compensation for Loyalists, British evacuation of trading posts and forts on the Canadian boundary, all pressed for settlement. The British Government was legislating against American shipping. Spain was re-embedded in Florida and hostile to American expansion in the South-West. America was entangled in an official alliance with France, where the stir of great changes to come was already felt. Far-seeing men perceived the imminence of another world conflict. Distracted by internal disorder, without national unity or organisation, the American states seemed an easy prey to foreign ambitions.

Demand for revision of the Articles of Confederation grew among the people of the towns. Shays' Rebellion was the spur to action, and in May 1787 a convention of delegates from twelve of the states met at Philadelphia to consider the matter. The partisans of a strong national Government were in a large majority. Of the possible leaders of the farmers, or agrarian democrats as they were now called, Patrick Henry of Virginia refused to attend, and the greatest figure of them all,

Thomas Jefferson, was absent as envoy in Paris. One of the leading personalities of the assembly was Alexander Hamilton, who represented the powerful commercial interests of New York City. This handsome, brilliant man, the illegitimate son of a West Indian merchant, had risen rapidly on Washington's staff during the war. He had entered New York society and married well. He was determined that the ruling class, into which he had made his way by his own abilities, should continue to rule, and he now became the recognised leader of those who demanded a capable central Government and limitation of states' powers. A sense of the overhanging crisis in Europe and of the perils of democracy guided these men in their labours, and the debates in the Convention were on a high level. Most of the delegates were in favour of a Federal Government, but methods and details were bitterly contested. Many divisions cut across the discussions. The small states were anxious to preserve their equality in the great community of the Thirteen, and vehemently opposed any scheme for representation in a Federal Government on a simple basis of numbers.

All the delegates came from long-established centres on the Atlantic seaboard, but they realised with uneasiness that their power and influence would soon be threatened by the growing populace of the West. Here, beyond the Ohio and the Alleghenies, lay vast territories which Congress had ordained should be admitted to the Union on an equal footing with the original states as soon as any of them contained sixty thousand free inhabitants. Their population was already expanding, and it was only a question of time before they claimed their rights. Then what would happen to the famous Thirteen States? It was they who had expelled the British, and they felt with some justification that they knew more about politics and the true interests of the Union than the denizens of these remote, half-settled regions. As Gouverneur

Morris of Pennsylvania put it—he owed his unusual Christian name to his mother, who had been a Miss Gouverneur—"The busy haunts of men, not the remote wilderness, is the proper school of political talents. If the Western people get the power in their hands they will ruin the Atlantic interests." Both principles were right. The Atlantic communities had the wealth and the experience, but the new lands were fully entitled to join the Union, and to the lasting credit of the Philadelphia delegates no step was taken to prevent them doing so. But one day the clash would come. The power and the future lay with the West, and it was with misgiving and anxiety that the Convention addressed itself to framing the Constitution of the United States.

This was a concise document defining the powers of the new central Government. It established a single executive: a President, appointed indirectly by electors chosen as the state legislatures might decide, and serving for four years, with the right of veto over the acts of Congress, but subject to impeachment; head of the Army and administration, responsible only to the people, completely independent of the legislative power. The Lower House, or the House of Representatives as it was now called, was to be elected for two years, upon a population basis. But this concession to the democratic principle was tempered by the erection of a Senate, elected for six years by the state legislatures. The Senate was to restrain any demagogy of the Lower House, to defend the interests of property against the weight of a Lower House chosen upon the numerical principle, and by its share in the appointing and treaty-making powers of the President to control this powerful functionary. At the summit of the constitutional edifice stood a Supreme Court, composed of judges nominated for life by the President, subject to the ratification of the Senate. It assumed the task of judicial review—namely, a coercive supervision of the Acts not only of Congress, but also of the state legislatures, to ensure their conformity with the Constitution.

Such was the federal machinery devised at Philadelphia in September 1787. A national authority had been created, supreme within its sphere. But this sphere was strictly defined and soon further limited; all powers not delegated under the Constitution to the Federal Government were to rest with the states. There was to be no central "tyranny" of the kind that King George's Ministers at Westminster had tried to exercise. The new nation that had with difficulty struggled into being was henceforth fortified with something unheard of in the existing world—a written Constitution. At first sight this authoritative document presents a sharp contrast with the store of traditions and precedents that make up the unwritten Constitution of Britain. Yet behind it lay no revolutionary theory. It was based not upon the challenging writings of the French philosophers which were soon to set Europe ablaze, but an Old English doctrine, freshly formulated to meet an urgent American need. The Constitution was a reaffirmation of faith in the principles painfully evolved over the centuries by the English-speaking peoples. It enshrined long-standing English ideas of justice and liberty, henceforth to be regarded on the other side of the Atlantic as basically American.

Of course, a written constitution carries with it the danger of a cramping rigidity. What body of men, however farsighted, can lay down precepts in advance for settling the problems of future generations? The delegates at Philadelphia were well aware of this. They made provision for amendment, and the document drawn up by them was adaptable enough in practice to permit changes in the Constitution. But it had to be proved in argument and debate and generally accepted throughout the land that any changes proposed would follow the guiding ideas of the Founding Fathers. A prime object of the Constitution was to be conservative; it was to guard the principles and machinery of State from capricious and ill-considered alteration. In its fundamental doctrine the American people acquired an institution which was to command the same respect and loyalty as in England are given to Parliament and Crown.

*   *   *   *   *

It now remained to place the scheme before the people. The delegates foresaw that the democratic, isolationist state legislatures would probably reject it, and they accordingly advised that local conventions should be elected to vote upon the new project of government. Hamilton and Robert Morris, whose strong and well-organised group had become known as the Federalist Party, hoped that all men with a stake in the country, who had probably not wanted to sit on the revolutionary bodies formed during the war for the administration of the different states, would see the value and reason in the new Constitution and limit the influence of the more extreme elements.

To the leaders of agrarian democracy, the backwoodsmen, the small farmers, the project seemed a betrayal of the Revolution. They had thrown off the English executive. They had gained their local freedom. They were now asked to create another instrument no less powerful and coercive. They had been told they were fighting for the Rights of Man and the equality of the individual. They saw in the Constitution an engine for the defence of property against equality. They felt in their daily life the heavy hand of powerful interests behind the contracts and debts which oppressed them. But they were without leaders. Even so in Virginia, New York, and elsewhere there was a fierce and close contest upon the passing of the Constitution. Jefferson in his diplomatic exile in Paris brooded with misgiving on the new régime. But the party of Hamilton and Morris, with its brilliant propaganda, in a series of public letters called *The Federalist,* carried the day.

The Federalist letters are among the classics of American literature. Their practical wisdom stands pre-eminent amid the stream of controversial writing at the time. Their authors were concerned, not with abstract arguments about political theory, but with the real dangers threatening America, the evident weakness of the existing Confederation, and the debatable advantages of the various provisions in the new Constitution. Hamilton, Jay, and Madison were the principal contributors. The first two were New Yorkers, Madison a Virginian; none came from New England, which was losing its former predominance in the life of the nation. They differed widely in personality and outlook, but they all agreed upon one point, the importance of creating a collective faith in the Constitution as the embodiment of the American ideal. Only thus could the many discordant voices of the Thirteen States be harmonised. How well they succeeded and how enduring has been their success is testified by the century and three-quarters that have elapsed since they wrote. The faith generated by *The Federalist* has held and sustained the allegiance of the American people down to our own day.

Liberty, *The Federalist* argued, might degenerate into licence. Order, security, and efficient government must be established before disaster overtook America. In an article in this great political series one of the Federalists stated the eternal problem with breadth and power.

> The diversity in the faculties of men, from which the rights of property originate, is . . . an insuperable obstacle to a uniformity of interests. The protection of these faculties is the first object of government. From the protection of different and unequal faculties of acquiring property the possession of different degrees and kinds of property immediately results; and from the influence of these on the sentiments and views of the respective proprietors ensues a division of the society into different interests and parties.

The latent causes of faction are thus sown in the nature of man; and we see them everywhere brought into different degrees of activity, according to the different circumstances of civil society. A zeal for different opinions . . . [has] divided mankind into parties, inflamed them with mutual animosity, and rendered them much more disposed to vex and oppress each other than to co-operate for their common good. . . . But the most common and durable source of factions has been the various and unequal distribution of property. Those who hold and those who are without property have ever formed distinct interests of society. Those who are creditors and those who are debtors fall under a like discrimination. A landed interest, a manufacturing interest, a mercantile interest, a moneyed interest, with many lesser interests, grow up of necessity in civilised nations, and divide them into different classes actuated by different sentiments and views. The regulation of these various and interfering interests forms the principal task of modern legislation, and involves the spirit of party and faction in the necessary and ordinary operations of the Government.

It was in vain that their opponents counter-attacked in print. "Because we have sometimes abused democracy I am not among those who think a democratic branch a nuisance," wrote Richard Henry Lee of Virginia. "Every man of reflection must see that the change now proposed is a transference of power from the many to the few." In the midst of faction fights and the collisions of Federalist and Radical mobs the Constitution was within a year ratified by eleven of the states. Rhode Island and North Carolina stood aside for a little longer. Distrust of social revolution had bitten deep into the New World, and the gulf between the two elements that composed its society remained unbridged. The men who believed in the Rights of Man were forced to bide their time. Those, like Hamilton, who feared the mob in politics, and realised the urgent need for settlement, order, and protection for the propertied interests of the seaboard states, had triumphed.

In March 1789 the new Federal bodies were convened. Opponents of the Constitution exulted in the difficulties of gathering a quorum in the Upper and Lower House. There seemed little vigour and enthusiasm in the new régime. But by the end of the month sufficient people had arrived in New York, where the Government was to meet. The first step was to elect a President, and General Washington, the commander of the Revolution, was the obvious choice. Disinterested and courageous, far-sighted and patient, aloof yet direct in manner, inflexible once his mind was made up, Washington possessed the gifts of character for which the situation called. He was reluctant to accept office. Nothing would have pleased him more than to remain in equable but active retirement at Mount Vernon, improving the husbandry of his estate. But, as always, he answered the summons of duty. Gouverneur Morris was right when he emphatically wrote to him, "The exercise of authority depends on personal character. Your cool, steady temper is *indispensably necessary* to give firm and manly tone to the new Government."

There was much confusion and discussion on titles and precedence, which aroused the mocking laughter of critics. But the prestige of Washington lent dignity to the new, untried office. On April 30, 1789, in the recently opened Federal Hall in New York, he was solemnly inaugurated as the first President of the United States. A week later the French States-General met at Versailles. Another great revolution was about to burst upon a bewildered world. The flimsy, untested fabric of American unity and order had been erected only just in time.

* * * * *

Many details had yet to be worked out. The first step was the passing of a Bill of Rights. The lack of such fundamental assertions in the Constitution had been a chief complaint of its critics. They were now incorporated in ten Amendments. Next the Judiciary Act of 1789 made the Supreme Court the most formidable part of the Federal machinery. "With elaborate detail," wrote the historians Charles and Mary Beard,

> the law provided for a Supreme Court composed of a Chief Justice and five associates, and a Federal District Court for each state, with its own Attorney, Marshal, and appropriate number of deputies. Such were the agencies of power created to make the will of the national Government a living force in every community from New Hampshire to Georgia, from the seaboard to the frontier. . . . After contriving an ingenious system of appeal for carrying cases up to the Supreme Court, the framers of the Judiciary Act devised a process by which the measures of the local Governments could be nullified whenever they came into conflict with the Federal Constitution. . . . In a word, something like the old British Imperial control over provincial legislatures was re-established, under judicial bodies chosen indirectly and for life, within the borders of the United States.[1]

As yet there were no administrative departments. These were quickly set up: Treasury, State, and War. The success of the new Federal Government depended largely upon the men chosen to fill these key offices: Alexander Hamilton, the great Federalist from New York; Thomas Jefferson, the Virginian democrat, now returned from Paris; and, to a lesser extent, General Knox of Massachusetts.

From 1789 to his resignation six years later Hamilton used his brilliant abilities to nourish the Constitution and bind the economic interests of the great merchants of America to the new system. A governing class must be created, and Hamilton proposed to demonstrate that Federal government meant

[1] Charles A. Beard and Mary R. Beard, *The Rise of American Civilization* (1930), vol. i.

a strong national economy. At his inspiration a series of great measures followed. In January 1790 his *First Report on Public Credit* was laid before the House of Representatives. State debts were to be assumed by Congress; public credit must depend on the assumption of past obligations. The war debts of the states were to be taken over by the Federal Government in order to woo the large class of creditors to the national interest. The whole debt was to be funded; all the old bonds and certificates which had been rotted by speculation were to be called in and new securities issued. A sinking fund was to be created and a national bank set up.

The moneyed interest was overjoyed by this programme, but there was bitter opposition from those who realised that the new Government was using its taxing powers to pay interest to the speculative holders of state debts now assumed by Congress. The clash between capitalist and agrarian again glared forth. The New England merchants had invested most of their war-time profits in paper bonds, which now gained enormously in value. Massachusetts, which had the largest state debt, profited most. The mass of public debt was concentrated in the hands of small groups in Philadelphia, New York, and Boston. The nation was taxed to pay them at par for what they had purchased at a tremendous discount. In Virginia there was a fierce revolt against Hamilton's scheme. The planters distrusted the whole idea of public finance. They foresaw the worst elements of Whig plutocracy dominating the new Government. "They discern," wrote Patrick Henry,

a striking resemblance between this system and that which was introduced into England at the Revolution [of 1688], a system which has perpetuated upon that nation an enormous debt, and has, moreover, insinuated into the hands of the executive an unbounded influence, which, pervading every branch of the Government, bears down all opposition, and daily threatens the destruction of everything that appertains to English liberty. The same causes produce the same effects. In an agricultural country like this, therefore, to erect and concentrate and perpetuate a large moneyed interest is a measure which . . . must in the course of human events produce one or other of two evils, the prostration of agriculture at the feet of commerce, or a change in the present form of Federal Government, fatal to the existence of American liberty. . . . Your memorialists can find no clause in the Constitution authorising Congress to assume the debts of the states.

This cleavage is of durable importance in American history. The beginnings of the great political parties can be discerned, and they soon found their first leaders. Hamilton was quickly recognised as head of the financial and mercantile interest centring in the North, and his opponent was none other than Jefferson, Secretary of State. The two men had worked together during the first months of the new Government. Hamilton indeed had only secured enough votes for the passage of his proposals on state debts by winning Jefferson's support. This he did by agreeing that the new capital city which would house Congress and Government should be sited on the Potomac River, across the border from Virginia. In the meantime Philadelphia was to succeed New York as the temporary capital. But a wave of speculation which followed the financial measures of Hamilton now aroused the Secretary's opposition. The two leaders misunderstood each other fundamentally. Washington, impressed by the need to stabilise the new Constitution, exerted his weighty influence to prevent an open rupture. But by 1791 Jefferson and his Virginian planters were seeking alliance with the malcontents of Hamilton's party in New York and the North.

Before the break came Hamilton presented his *Report on Manufactures,* which was to be the basis of future American Protectionist theory. Protective duties and bounties were to be introduced to encourage home industries. A vision of a prosperous and industrial society in the New World, such as was rapidly growing up in England, was held before the eyes of the Americans.

The outward unity of the Federal administration was preserved for a few months by the re-election of Washington as President. But the conflict between Jefferson and Hamilton was not confined to economics. A profoundly antagonistic view of politics separated them. They held radically opposed views of human nature. Hamilton, the superbly successful financier, believed that men were guided by their passions and their interests, and that their motives, unless rigidly controlled, were evil. "The people!" he is supposed to have said. "The people is a great beast." Majority rule and government by the counting of heads were abhorrent to him. There must be a strong central Government and a powerful governing circle, and he saw in Federal institutions, backed by a ruling business class, the hope and future of America. The developing society of England was the ideal for the New World, and such he hoped to create across the Atlantic by his efforts at the Treasury Department. He represents and symbolises one aspect of American development, the successful, self-reliant business world, with its distrust of the collective common man, of what Hamilton himself in another mood called "the majesty of the multitude." But in this gospel of material success there was little trace of that political idealism which characterises and uplifts the American people. "A very great man," President Woodrow Wilson was to call him, adding with evident bias, "but not a great American."

Thomas Jefferson was the product of wholly different conditions and the prophet of a rival political idea. He came from the Virginian frontier, the home of dour individualism and faith in common humanity, the nucleus of resistance to the centralising hierarchy of British rule. Jefferson had been the principal author of the Declaration of Independence and leader of the agrarian democrats in the American Revolution. He was well read; he nourished many scientific interests, and he was a gifted amateur architect. His graceful classical house, Monticello, was built according to his own designs. He was in touch with fashionable Left-Wing circles of political philosophy in England and Europe, and, like the French school of economists who went by the name of Physiocrats, he believed in a yeoman-farmer society. He feared an industrial proletariat as much as he disliked the principle of aristocracy. Industrial and capitalist development appalled him. He despised and distrusted the whole machinery of banks, tariffs, credit manipulation, and all the agencies of capitalism which the New Yorker Hamilton was skilfully introducing into the United States. He perceived the dangers to individual liberty that might spring from the centralising powers of a Federal Government. With reluctance he came home from Paris to serve the new system. The passage of time and the stress of the Napoleonic wars were to modify his dislike of industrialism, but he believed in his heart that democratic government was only possible among free yeomen. It was not given to him to foresee that the United States would eventually become the greatest industrial democracy in the world.

"The political economists of Europe have established it as a principle," Jefferson declared,

that every state should endeavour to manufacture for itself; and this principle, like many others, we transfer to America. . . . But we have an immensity of land courting the industry of the husbandman. Is it best then that all our citizens should be employed in its improvement, or that one half should be called off from that to exercise manufactures and handicraft arts for the other? . . . Corruption of morals in the mass of cultivators is a phenomenon of which no age nor nation has furnished an example. It is the mark set on those who, not looking up to heaven, to their own soil and industry, as does the husbandman, for their subsistence, depend for it on casualties and caprice of customers. Dependence begets subservience and venality, suffocates the germ of virtue, and prepares fit tools for the designs of ambition. . . . While we have land to labour, then, let us never wish to see our citizens occupied at a work-bench or twirling a distaff. . . . *For the general operations of manufacture let our workshops remain in Europe. It is better to carry provisions and materials to workmen there than bring them to the provisions and materials and with them their manners and principles.*[1] . . . The mobs of great cities add just so much to the support of pure government as sores do to the strength of the human body. It is the manners and spirit of a people which preserve a republic in vigour. A degeneracy in these is a canker which soon eats to the heart of its laws and constitution.

Jefferson held to the Virginian conception of society, simple and unassailed by the complexity, the perils, and the challenge of industrialism. In France he saw, or thought he saw, the realisation of his political ideas—the destruction of a worn-out aristocracy and a revolutionary assertion of the rights of soil-tilling man. Hamilton, on the other hand, looked to the England of the Younger Pitt as the embodiment of his hopes for America. The outbreak of war between England and France was to bring to a head the fundamental rivalry and conflict between Hamilton and Jefferson and to signalise the birth of the great American parties, Federalist and Republican. Both were to split and founder and change their names, but from them the Republican and Democratic parties of to-day can trace their lineage.

[1] Author's italics.—W.S.C.

The French Revolution

THE convulsion which shook France in 1789 was totally different from the revolutions that the world had seen before. England in the seventeenth century had witnessed a violent shift in power between the Crown and the People; but the basic institutions of State had been left untouched, or at any rate had soon been restored. Nor as yet had there been in England any broadening of popular sovereignty in the direction of universal suffrage. The liberties of the ordinary Englishman were well understood and had often been asserted. He could not lay claim to equality. The lack was not felt to be a very serious grievance, since the classes mingled together and transition from one class to another was, if not easy, at least possible, and quite often achieved. America in her Revolution had proclaimed the wider rights of mankind. Across the Atlantic shone a noble example of freedom which in the end was to exercise a formidable influence upon the world. But in the late eighteenth century America's commanding future was scarcely foreseen, even by her own statesmen. In Europe the impulse towards liberty, equality, and popular sovereignty had to come from elsewhere. It came from France. The English Revolution had been entirely a domestic affair. So in the main had the American. But the French Revolution was to spread out from Paris across the whole Continent. It gave rise to a generation of warfare, and its echoes reverberated long into the nineteenth century and afterwards. Every great popular and national movement, until the Bolsheviks gave a fresh turn to events in 1917, was to invoke the principles set forth at Versailles in 1789.

France in the reign of Louis XVI was by no means the most oppressively governed of countries, though this is often alleged. She was rich and many of her people prospered. Why then did revolution break out? Volumes have been written on this subject, but one fact is clear. French political machinery in no way expressed the people's will. It did not match the times and could not move with them. It had been given its form and shape by Louis XIV. Under his majestic hands the machine had worked, almost to the end. His successors inherited all his panoply of power but none of his capacity. They could neither work the machine nor would they alter it. At the same time the growing middle classes in France were reaching out for the power that was withheld from them. They felt they should have a say in how they were governed. An intellectual ferment filled the land which was denied a political outlet. An explosion was inevitable and had long been expected by all inquiring minds. As a British official reported from Paris, the French people had been "infused by a spirit of discussion of public matters which did not exist before." At some moment the widespread frustrations of Frenchmen were bound to seek active expression. They merely needed an igniting spark. This was supplied by the royal Government's incorrigible system of faulty finance.

The Government of France had long been bankrupt. Louis XIV had exhausted the nation in a procession of wars which had lasted for thirty years, and when he died in 1715 the public debt was more than sixteen times the annual revenue. From this burden the French never contrived to escape. Many men had laboured, but without success, to make France solvent. The obstacles were formidable. A substantial section of the population, which included the most prominent if not always the most powerful of French citizens, were largely exempt from taxation. Of these the nobility numbered about four hundred thousand. Their privileges might once have been justified by the services they had formerly rendered to the community as landlords and military leaders; but this was no longer true. In England the armed aristocracy had destroyed itself in the dynastic civil wars of the fifteenth century. France had been less well served by her history, and the French monarchy had long endured the assaults and insurrections, both real and threatened, of a warlike, virile, and ambitious nobility. Successive French kings and their Ministers had been driven to policies that in the long run proved harmful. If the nobles were allowed to live on their estates they would rebel, but if they were made to live at Court they could be supervised. Idleness and luxury were effective methods of disarmament. Both could be provided at Versailles, largely at the expense of the victims, and at Versailles most of the nobles had been compelled or persuaded to live. In the glitter of the great Court, which at one time numbered about two hundred thousand people, they could squander their time and money, and the most formidable weapon they needed was the duelling sword. Thus arose a class of absentee landlords forbidden to meddle in politics, far from their estates, unbeloved by their tenantry, yielding no services either to the soil or to the State, and drawing large and mainly untaxed profits from the lands they no longer tended.

The privileges of the clergy were no less remarkable. The Church owned about one-fifth of the land of France, with many valuable buildings upon it. From these sources the ecclesiastical authorities received an annual income of perhaps £45 millions sterling. This was augmented by as much again in tithes. Yet for three generations about 140,000 priests, monks, and nuns had paid no taxes on their properties or their fortunes. Their sanctity was as uneven as their share of the national wealth. Most of the rank and file were devout, self-denying, and upright, but a crust of politically covetous, worldly, and cynical prelates had weakened and degraded the dignity and influence of organised Christianity. The Catholic Church in France was powerless against the forces of anarchy and atheism, which, in the most cultured state in Europe, were seething and fomenting.

The heaviest fiscal burden lay upon the peasants. Their plight must not be exaggerated. Since the beginning of the century they had been buying land, and on the eve of the explosion which was to shatter the stability of Europe and engage its peoples in a generation of mortal struggle they owned a third of the soil of France. Nevertheless their grievances were substantial. The tax on "peasant" land was nearly five times as much as on "noble" land. They and they alone paid the most hated tax of all, the *taille,* fifty-three livres in every hundred, and much abused and perverted by the tax-farming to which the parched Government had been compelled. A multitude of indirect taxes and impositions added their weight of misery. The winter of 1788 was very severe. Many died of starvation. Yet it has been well said that revolutions are not made by starving people. The peasants were no worse off and probably slightly more comfortable than a century before. Most of them were uninterested in politics. They desired only freedom from oppressive landlords and antiquated taxes. The revolutionary impulse came from elsewhere. The nobles had lost their energy and their faith in themselves. The clergy were divided. The Army was unreliable. The King and his Court lacked both the will and the ability to govern. Only the *bourgeois* possessed the appetite for power and the determination and self-confidence to seize it.

The *bourgeois* were not democratic as we understand the

word to-day. They distrusted the masses, the crowd, the mob, and with some reason, but they were nevertheless prepared to incite and use it against the "privileged" nobility, and, if necessary, in the assertion of their own status, against the monarchy itself. Rousseau in his famous *Social Contract* and other essays had preached the theme of equality. Every man, however humble, was born with a right to play his part in the government of State. This is doctrine long since acknowledged by all democracies, but Rousseau was the first to formulate it in broad and piercing terms. Voltaire and the group of scholars and publicists who contributed to Diderot's *Encyclopedia* had long been casting doubt on all accepted values, religious and social. The rule of reason and the quest of knowledge for its own sake were the aims that the Encyclopedists held up before Frenchmen. In the cramped political world of the Old Régime these ideas worked as a powerful leaven. No one could tell in the reign of Louis XVI how far they would lead the middle classes in their pursuit of power.

Unfortunately it was not easy to capture or even discover the seat of power in eighteen-century France. The country was administered by a multitude of civil servants, some paid by the Government, some subsisting on the commissions and profits of their posts, some privately hired. The system had long floundered in decay and inefficiency. Files and complications flourished. A French historian, writing soon after the event, relates how it took forty years of correspondence to mend a broken tile on a church roof. Confusion, not despotism, oppressed and exasperated the nation, and on the eve of the Revolution a Minister reported to the King that the country was "impossible to govern."

* * * * *

There had been many attempts at reforming this expensive muddle, and even more to find money to pay for it. During the long reign of Louis XV the public debt had been much reduced. When Louis XVI ascended the throne in 1774, dimly imbued with good intentions, he appointed the able and upright Turgot as Controller-General of Finance. Turgot's plans were simple, and might well have been effective if he had been permitted to carry them out. He proposed to meet the national deficit by fierce economies in the civil service and at Court. The *corvée*, or compulsory peasant labour on the roads, was to be abolished, together with sine-cures and local customs duties. Wealth and enterprise were to be stimulated by the suppression of craft-guilds or *corporations* and by the promotion of internal free trade in corn. But free trade in corn led to speculation, sudden rises in the price of bread, and riots. The nobility were affronted by Turgot's attack on their privileges. Headed by the Queen, Marie Antoinette, the Court denounced him as a revolution-ary, and in four years he was dismissed. Nearly all his reforms were swept away. Their necessity was obvious. It was also obvious to the nation that their new King was incapable of carrying them out.

Turgot fell in 1778, and in the same year France allied her-self with the embattled American colonies. His disappearance solved nothing. More money was needed for war with Britain. The national deficit was five hundred million livres, or about twenty-five millions sterling. Even in those days this was not a staggering sum. A reasonable system of taxation could have dealt with it. But where at Versailles was reason to be found? In desperation Louis XVI made Necker, a Swiss Protestant, "Director-General of Finance." Necker com-prehended the significance of Turgot's fate. He realised that it was impossible to touch the privileges of the nobility. He accordingly turned his energies to the reform of prisons and hospitals and the abolition of torture for extracting confes-sions from suspected criminals. He did more. He set up provincial Assemblies to discharge and animate the work of local government; but they were gorged with new and impractical ideas and blind hatred of the central Government. They sank amid uproar and few survived. Thwarted and disappointed, Necker resigned in May 1781.

The birth of the American republic had none the less inspired the mass of Frenchmen with a new taste for liberty. If the United States could achieve it why not they? French volunteers under Lafayette and a royal army under Rochambeau had played their part in the struggle. Why must the *Ancien Régime* stifle the pride and energy of France? But the Court remained extravagant, the administration chaotic, the treasury empty. Louis XVI, without Turgot, without Necker, and with no taste for rule and no passions beyond hunting, clockmaking, and gluttony, was left with but one expedient, to borrow. By 1785 the credit of the Government was exhausted. In the following year an Assembly of Notables was asked to agree to a tax on all properties alike and the abolition of fiscal privilege. The Assembly refused. The Notables declined to pay taxes till they knew the causes of the disaster. The clergy were adverse. They all went home. Collapse of the public administration was imminent. Paris was in riot. The Queen and the chief Minister were burned in effigy. The Government could raise no loans except on the promise of calling together the States-General. Louis bowed to the storm. In 1788 Necker was recalled amid acclamation. He faced the urgent financial predicament, and the States-General was summoned. A British Member of Parliament, visiting France at this time, prophetically wrote, "So much perturbation and heat will not easily subside. . . . The whole kingdom seems ripe for a Revolution."

*   *   *   *   *

The States-General was the Parliament of France. It had been convoked to lead the nation and support the Crown at every great crisis in French history. But it had not met for a hundred and seventy-five years. There was no living tradition to guide its conduct of business. What it might now accomplish and where its powers stopped were matters for conjecture. The King's Ministers had drawn up no policy on which its deliberations could be centred. Before the deputies assembling at Versailles there lay unlimited opportunities of decision, whether for wisdom or folly. They could set themselves to reform and regenerate France, or through factious struggles for power plunge the country into anarchy and war. As it happened, in less than three years the States-General and its successors had carried out a sweeping revolution and started a momentous European conflict. But there was no foretelling on the spring day of May 5, 1789, how far and how quickly political passions were to drive the hearts of men. There seemed every prospect that the ancient representative body of France would make its terms with the monarchy, which at this stage hardly even a fanatic had dreamt of overthrowing. The hope was that each institution would sustain the other in common purpose and that France would soon take her place among the growing number of the world's constitutional states. When the deputies went to Mass at Notre Dame on May 4 none dreamed that their work would lead to the first of the ruthless dictatorships of modern Europe, which would earn without cavil the name of "the Terror." Nor did they imagine that their incapacities would prepare the way for the rule of the greatest man of action born in Europe since Julius Cæsar.

About fifteen hundred deputies had been elected by five million voters under the broadest franchise yet enjoyed by any European country. The clergy and the nobles made their choice separately. The Third Estate, who numbered half the total Assembly, included landed proprietors, men of business, numerous lawyers, doctors, administrators, and members of the other professions. They came to Versailles armed with the complaints of their constituents. Their feelings may be summed up in familiar English terms: redress of grievances before they would vote supplies to the Crown. They represented the middle class; their property, education, and natural talents gave them a stake in the realm for which they now claimed to exercise a voice. They were disciples of the Enlightenment; some of them had read Voltaire, Rousseau, and the writings of the Encyclopedists. They were well acquainted with abstract reasonings about liberty and equality; now within their own practical spheres they were determined to apply them. A few drew inspiration from the great experiment in democracy taking shape across the Atlantic Ocean. All were intent to assert their rights, not only to be heard but to take the due part in government so long denied them. The views of the Third Estate were shared by many of the humbler clergy and a minority of liberal-minded nobles.

The opening question for the States-General was how it should vote. The Third Estate saw at once that if all three houses met and voted together there would be a substantial majority for reform. But the Court had now awakened to the dangers it had evoked. By compelling the Estates to vote separately it could retain the power to play off the two privileged ones against the Third. Urged on by his exigent Queen, Louis XVI took action. He called up troops, closed the doors of the Parliament House against the Third Estate and threatened to dissolve them. By these steps he brought about the first turning-point in the Revolution. The Commons were undaunted. They had already changed their name and proclaimed themselves the National Assembly. Faced with locked doors, they now withdrew to an adjoining tennis court, and there on June 20 took the famous oath never to suspend their deliberations and "to go on meeting wherever circumstances may dictate until the constitution of the realm is set up and consolidated on firm foundations." Thus came into being a single Constituent Assembly, soon reinforced by its sympathisers among nobles and clergy. Henceforth the other two Estates ceased to exist.

At this crisis the King wavered. He would have liked to use force, but he hesitated to shed blood. His irresolution was compounded of natural lethargy and genuine goodwill. He tried delivering a stern lecture to the deputies. It was of no avail. "No one," he was firmly told by their President, "can give orders to the assembled nation." Not for the last time Louis gave way. An English commentator on these events has aptly expressed the opinion formed by the world. He was Author Young, farmer and student of agriculture, then on a tour of France. "They have at one stroke," he wrote of the Assembly, "converted themselves into the Long Parliament of Charles I." It was a prophetic remark. But in France history was to march faster than it had done in seventeenth-century England. King Louis had only three years to live.

The scene now shifts to Paris. This great metropolis, with six hundred thousand inhabitants, had for half a century been the buzzing intellectual capital of the nation. Here, and not amid the stiff ceremonies of Versailles, were focused the hopes, ideas, and ambitions of the French people. Paris was alarmed by the concentration around it of royal troops. Spontaneously in all its sixty districts a citizens' militia began to enrol. *"Aux armes!"* was the cry. There were volunteers in plenty, but few arms. A remedy was quickly found. Early in the morning of July 14 a mob forced its way into the Invalides and seized a large stock of muskets and some guns. These were distributed. Now for powder and shot. The capital's main store of powder was lodged in the Bastille, a grim medieval fortress, long used as a royal prison. All the morning till past noon parleys took place with its Governor, de Launey. No one knows how fighting started. By treachery or mistake de Launey fired on the crowd outside, whose leaders bore white flags. His action gave the signal for general assault. Guns were brought up; there was a cannonade; the citizen militia fought with reckless valour, and after two hours' struggle the fortress surrendered. It was immediately sacked, and stone by stone its demolition began. De Launey was murdered, and his bleeding head raised aloft on a pike, a portent of atrocities to come.

Thus fell a prime symbol of royal authority. The Bastille held only seven prisoners, one of them a lunatic. But their release from the cells was hailed throughout France. Louis XVI, the most benevolent of the Bourbons, had hitherto issued no fewer than fourteen thousand *lettres de cachet,* consigning his subjects to prison often with good reason but always without trial. The fall of the Bastille marked the end of such royal absolutism. It was a triumph for the cause of liberty, and for the Parisian mob. With this victory for violence the Revolution had taken a bloody step forward.

*   *   *   *   *

To the world outside in the summer of 1789, and to foreigners in France, the Revolution seemed to have fulfilled its aims. All was over, it was thought: privilege had been overthrown; the people's rights had been asserted; King and National Assembly would settle down to draft a new future for their country. The British Ambassador in Paris put a common view when he reported that "the greatest revolution that we know anything of has been effected with the loss of very few lives; from this moment we may consider France a free country." Burke, meditating in England, was more farsighted. In his *Reflections on the French Revolution,* soon to be published, he discerned the shape of things to come. The convulsion in France, as he eloquently pointed out, was not a dignified, orderly change, carried out with due regard for tradition, like the English Revolution of 1688. A complete break with the past had been made. For two years further the monarchy was to survive while the Assembly deliberated upon the ideal constitution under which twenty-five million French men and women might freely pursue their affairs. But in the name of reason irrational forces had been let loose. These were not easily to be assuaged. France was fated to undergo every form of revolutionary experience. The pattern has been repeated in other countries, at later times, but with not very different results. France was the crucible in which all the modern elements of Revolution were first put to the test.

The King at Versailles was not unduly perturbed by the fall of the Bastille. But its significance was plain to his youngest brother, the Count d'Artois, much later, as King Charles X, to be the victim of another Revolution. Artois and a following of recalcitrant nobles fled the country. The first emigration of reactionaries then ensued. Some two hundred thousand members of the nobility and their dependants are said to have asked for their passports during the next three months. These *émigrés,* as they were called, took refuge in Germany and Italy, many at Coblenz and Turin. From beyond the frontiers they busily intrigued against the new order in France. With them the King, the Queen, and the Court were in clandestine correspondence. The National Assembly and the mobs of Paris stood in constant fear that their newly made constitutional King would betray them by joining with the *émigrés* and, supported by foreign aid, reimpose the Old Régime. Nor were their fears groundless. Like Charles I of England, the King counted duplicity as a royal prerogative. He saw nothing wrong in outwardly accepting many distasteful reforms while secretly at the instigation of the Queen working for their overturn.

Paris was not slow to realise this. Its municipal leaders were now setting the pace. In October they resolved to recall the

King from Versailles and to keep him and the Assembly under surveillance and in their midst. In the meantime the citizens' militia had become the National Guard. Its commander was Lafayette, the hero of the American War of Independence. He was a soldier of high ideals who now cast himself for the rôle of referee of the Revolution. But it was not a game in which there were rules to be observed. On the 5th a procession of Parisian women set out for Versailles in protest against the high prices of bread. The National Guard, comprising many of their husbands, decided to accompany them. Why should they not? It made for a family outing. Lafayette was reluctantly at their head. At midnight they reached the palace. There disorderly scenes took place and the King and Queen were obliged to confront the mob. They bore themselves with dignity. Lafayette gave his personal word that if Louis came to Paris he would guarantee his safety. The King complied, and on the next day was joyfully received in his capital. Paris had won another victory, and at Versailles the shutters were put up and the blinds drawn for the first time since the reign of Louis XIV.

*   *   *   *   *

The Assembly followed the King back to Paris. But not before some three hundred members had resigned or begged leave of absence. Alarmed by the speed of events and fearful for their safety in the capital, they retired to the provinces or went into exile. Already the Assembly had decreed the end of feudalism and drawn up a Declaration of the Rights of Man, proclaiming equal citizenship for all. It proceeded to abolish hereditary titles and to nationalise the lands immemorially belonging to the Church. These lands were now freely sold and distributed. There came into existence a solid new class of peasant proprietors who owed their all to the Revolution. They were to form the backbone of its armies and of those of Napoleon's Empire.

The zeal of the deputies did not stop at this. They reformed the administration of justice; they turned the clergy, or such of them as would accept the change, into paid servants of State; they wiped off the map the proud old French provinces and parcelled out the country into the eighty-six departments that still exist. The Old Régime was torn up by the roots and a new order planted. Compromise was unknown to the men of '89; they would permit no interplay of fruitful assimilation. Europe was amazed and increasingly alarmed by the headlong courses pursued in Paris. Shortly the principles of the Revolution were to reach out from France and be forcibly imposed upon the most ancient states of the Continent. The French Revolutionary leaders began to dream of spreading the gospel of the brotherhood of man by resort to arms.

One figure might perhaps have controlled the swell of events, had he been granted the power. The Count de Mirabeau was an ugly, loose-living man, who yet possessed within him a true grasp of affairs. Macaulay has well described him thus: "Resembling Wilkes in the lower and grosser parts of his character, he had in his higher qualities some affinity to Chatham." Mirabeau towered above his fellow deputies in ability, eloquence, and judgment. For that reason he aroused widespread jealousy and distrust. Nor would the Court listen to him or take his frequently proffered advice. In April 1791 he died, his prodigious ambitions unfulfilled. In him a man almost of Cromwell's calibre was lost to France.

Leadership in the Assembly now passed to demagogues and extremists: first to the Girondins, called after the department round Bordeaux from which their chief men came; next to the Jacobins, who took their name from a former monastery near the Tuileries which now supplied them with the amenities of a political club.

To all the actions of these zealots the King had so far assented. He feigned to put up with the position thrust upon him. But though he said "Yes" in public "No" was the word in his heart. At his side stood his masterful Habsburg Queen, ever convinced that she could and would reverse the march of history. For long the King had been secretly advised to quit Paris and in some provincial centre rally around himself the conservative elements of the nation. Kings of France had successfully done so before when Paris became too hot for them. Louis resolved upon a desperate venture. He would escape from his bondage to the north-eastern frontier; he would place himself at the head of the *émigrés* and with the support of Austrian arms re-establish royal authority. Disguised as a valet, he slipped out of the palace at midnight on June 20. He was joined by the Queen, dressed as a governess, and by the royal children. Together in a fast four-horse coach they drove through the night and throughout the following hot summer day. It was the longest day in the year. Late that evening, at the town of Varennes, a hundred and forty miles from Paris, and only thirty from the frontier, they missed by a series of accidents the loyal escorts awaiting them. While the horses were being changed Louis showed himself at the window of the coach to get some air. He was recognised by a fervid revolutionary posting-master, who identified him from the royal head on the slips of paper money with which he was paid. King, Queen, and children were forced to alight, placed under guard, and next day ignominiously conducted back to Paris. The flight had failed, and its failure doomed the monarchy. The Chief of State in the eyes of the revolutionaries had tried to betray his trust. Nothing now could save him. Eighteen months of uneasy life lay before Louis. His every action was closely watched. Mobs broke into the Tuileries and insulted him to his face. Soon he was imprisoned; formally deposed; brought to trial as Citizen Capet;

and on January 21, 1793, executed by the machine of death recently invented by Dr Guillotin. Courage and dignity walked with him to the last; but as his severed head fell the Republic triumphed.

By now Europe was at war. A conflict had begun in the previous April which terminated twenty-three years later on the field of Waterloo. The anxious Girondin Ministers, perpetually looking over their shoulders in dread at the fanatical Jacobins who were to supplant them, had declared war upon Austria. They hoped to buttress their tottering Government by a crusade of liberation. Across the Rhine Austrian, Prussian, and *émigré* armies had for some time been gathering. Their resounding proclamations threatened the extinction of Revolutionary France. Some idle months passed by while the Austrian and Prussian monarchs dismembered Poland and swallowed more of that unhappy republic's territories than they could quickly digest. In the autumn the invasion of France began. To the world it seemed plain that the hastily assembled French citizen armies would never withstand the professional might of Prussia and Austria. But France was rapidly becoming a nation in arms. The whole country was inspired when General Dumouriez unexpectedly repulsed the Prussians by the cannonade of Valmy. He went on to invade and occupy the Austrian provinces of the Netherlands. At one stroke the revolutionary republic had overrun the lands for which Louis XIV had for forty years struggled in vain. For the first time in history the entire man-power and resources of a state were being marshalled for total war. New figures came forward to lead and direct the forces of France. Among them was Danton, a figure of tumultuous power and dedicated energy; Robespierre, a ruthless, incorruptible tyrant; Marat, a venomous rabble-rouser of genius; and Carnot, who survived them all, the War Minister and organiser of victory. In Dumouriez's army were to be found young enthusiastic officers and sergeants whose names were to be legends: Ney, Soult, Murat, Lannes, Davout, Marmont, Masséna, Victor, Junot, and Bernadotte. For France the epoch of her greatest military glory was opening. Before the rest of Europe lay a long ordeal.

France Confronted

IN England the Whigs, and especially the reformers and
Radicals, had at first welcomed the French Revolution.
They were soon repelled by its excesses. Eighteenth-century
London was not without experience of popular upheavals.
But in the Wilkes agitations and the riots of 1780 led by
Lord George Gordon the law had always gained the upper
hand over the mob. Now France gave a frightful demonstra-
tion of what happens when the social forces unleashed by
reformers break free from all control. Most Englishmen recoiled in horror. In the House of Commons Fox alone, in the
broad optimism of his mind, spoke out for the Revolution
as long as he conscientiously could. For this he was vehemently attacked by his former friend and ally, Burke, and the
number of his faithful followers among the Opposition diminished. In the country similar feelings prevailed. Liberty-
loving young men had enthusiastically applauded the events
of 1789. "Bliss was it in that dawn to be alive," Wordsworth
wrote. Other poets and writers of the fertile new Romantic
Movement shared his views. A few years later most of them
were disillusioned. Some groups of scientists and political
thinkers with progressive opinions also gave their allegiance,
as they have done in our own day, to foreign revolutionary
ideas. At the meetings of their societies they toasted the
Fourteenth of July and the French Constitution. But they
were only a small leaven amid the solid English Conservative
mass. More dangerous were the Radical working-men's clubs
which were springing up in the principal towns, generally
under middle-class leadership. They kept up a close corre-

spondence with the Jacobins in Paris, and fraternal delegates were sent to the National Assembly and its successor, the Convention. These agitators formed a small but vociferous minority of the British public, and eventually the Government took drastic action against them.

Such was the scene in Britain as the idea of world revolution gathered force in Paris. The unprovoked massacre of political prisoners by the new rulers of France in 1792 was a further shock to the faith of many would-be revolutionaries in the United Kingdom. The execution of the French King in January 1793 was a supreme act of defiance. In his celebrated speech Danton summarised the French Revolutionary attitude: "Allied kings threaten us, and we hurl at their feet as a gage of battle the head of a king." Marat cried, "We must establish the despotism of liberty to crush the despotism of kings." The French Republican armies were a threat not only to the Austrian and Prussian enemy, but also to their own Government. It was essential that they should be kept in the field. As a Girondin Minister put it frankly, "Peace is out of the question. We have three hundred thousand men in arms. We must make them march as far as their legs will carry them, or they will return and cut our throats."

In his Budget speech of 1792 Pitt had announced that he believed in fifteen years of peace for Europe. Non-intervention was his policy. Something more vital to Britain than a massacre of aristocrats or a speech in the Convention, something more concrete than a threat of world revolution, had to happen before he would face the issue of war. The spark, as so often in England's history, came from the Netherlands. By November the French decree instructing their generals to pursue the retreating Austrians into any country in which they might take refuge was a clear threat to the neutrality of Holland. A second pronouncement declared the navigation of the Scheldt open between Antwerp and the sea. A week later French men-of-war were bombarding the citadel of Antwerp, and on November 28 the city fell into French hands. The whole delicate balance of eighteenth-century international politics was deranged.

In a note to the French Ambassador on December 31 Lord Grenville, the Foreign Secretary, stated the position of His Majesty's Government in words which have ever since been accepted as a classic exposition of English foreign policy:

> England will never consent that France shall arrogate the power of annulling at her pleasure, and under the pretence of a pretended natural right, of which she makes herself the only judge, the political system, established by solemn treaties, and guaranteed by the consent of all the Powers. This Government, adhering to the maxims which it has followed for more than a century, will also never see with indifference that France shall make herself, either directly or indirectly, sovereign of the Low Countries, or general arbiter of the rights and liberties of Europe. If France is really desirous of maintaining friendship and peace with England she must show herself disposed to renounce her views of aggression and aggrandisement, and to confine herself within her own territory, without insulting other Governments, without disturbing their tranquillity, without violating their rights.

On the last day of January 1793 the French Convention, with Danton's defiant speech in their ears, decreed the annexation of the Austrian Netherlands to the French Republic. The next day France declared war on Great Britain and Holland, firm in the belief that an internal revolution in England was imminent. Pitt now had no choice. English security was imperilled by French occupation of the Flemish coast, and particularly the Scheldt estuary. Trade with the Continent would be endangered, and the English Channel was no longer safe. But for this deliberate provocation from Paris, Pitt might

have avoided the issue a little longer. But now, with the
Southern Netherlands in French hands and with world revolution in view, the threat was direct and inescapable.

In a speech in the House of Commons in March Pitt in
sorrow produced his first proposals for war finance and outlined the causes of the conflict.

Many are the motives which have induced us to enter into
war. I have heard of wars of honour; and such too have been
deemed wars of prudence and policy. On the present occasion
whatever can raise the feelings or animate the exertions of a
people concurs to prompt us to the contest. The contempt
which the French have shown for a neutrality on our part most
strictly observed; the violations of their solemn and plighted
faith; their presumptuous attempts to interfere in the government of this country and to arm our subjects against ourselves;
to vilify a monarch, the object of our gratitude, reverence, and
affection; and to separate the Court from the people, by representing them as influenced by different motives and acting
from different interests. After provocation so wanton, so often
repeated, and so highly aggravated, does not this become, on
our part, a war of honour; a war necessary to assert the spirit
of the nation and the dignity of the British name? I have heard
of wars undertaken for the general security of Europe; was it
ever so threatened as by the progress of the French arms and
the system of ambition and aggrandisement which they have
discovered? I have heard of wars for the defence of the Protestant religion: our enemies in this instance are equally enemies of all religion—of Lutheranism, of Calvinism; and
desirous to propagate everywhere, by the force of their arms,
that system of infidelity which they avow in their principles.
I have heard of wars undertaken in defence of the lawful succession; but now we fight in defence of our hereditary monarchy. We are at war with those who would destroy the whole
fabric of our Constitution. When I look at these things they
afford me encouragement and consolation, and support me in

discharging the painful task to which I am now called by my duty. The retrospect to that flourishing state in which we were placed previous to this war ought to teach us to know the value of the present order of things and to resist the malignant and envious attempts of those who would deprive us of that happiness which they despair themselves to attain. We ought to remember that that very prosperous situation at the present crisis supplies us with the exertions and furnishes us with the means which our exigencies demand. In such a cause as that in which we are now engaged I trust that our exertions will terminate only with our lives. On this ground I have brought forward the resolutions which I am now to propose; and on this ground I now trust for your support.

Britain was to be at war for over twenty years, and was now confronted with the task of making a major war effort, with her armed forces more crippled, perhaps, than at any time before by lack of equipment, leaders, and men. The conditions of service and the administration of the Army and Navy were so appalling that it is wonderful that anything was achieved at all. Pitt himself knew nothing of war or strategy, and the conduct of military affairs fell largely upon Henry Dundas, who was first and foremost a business man. In the old tradition of the eighteenth century he advocated a colonial and trade war, which would be popular among the mercantile classes and produce some commercial returns. For several years British resources were dissipated in ill-manned and ill-planned expeditions to the West Indies. It was with the greatest difficulty that any men could be raised for these mistaken enterprises.

If Britain had possessed even a small effective army it would not have been difficult, in concert with allies moving from the Rhine, to strike from the French coast at Paris and overthrow the Government responsible for provoking the conflict. But Pitt was barely able to send five thousand men to help his Dutch allies protect their frontiers from invasion. The campaigning which followed was no credit to British arms. An attempt to take Dunkirk ended lamentably. By 1795 the British forces on the Continent were driven back upon the mouth of the Ems on the German border, whence they were evacuated home. Great hopes had been founded in London upon the French Royalists, who launched daring schemes to arrest the Revolution by civil war in France. In 1793 they seized Toulon, and but for the fact that Dundas had already assigned all available troops to the West Indies a vital base for future invasion might have been secured.

*　　*　　*　　*　　*

Something else happened at Toulon. A young lieutenant of the French Army, sprung from a leading Corsican family, well versed in artillery and other military matters, happening to be on leave from his regiment, looked in on the camp of General Dugommier, who commanded the Jacobin besieging army. He walked along the line of batteries, and pointed out that their shot would not reach half-way. This error was adjusted, and the expert lieutenant began to have a say at that incompetent headquarters. Presently orders arrived from Paris prescribing the method of siege according to customary forms, for which however the necessary material resources were lacking. None dared dispute the instructions of the terrible Committee of Public Safety which was now at the head of French affairs. Nevertheless, at the council of war, held in daylight, on bare ground, the expert lieutenant raised his voice. The orders, he said—or so he claimed later—were foolish, and all knew it. There was however a way of taking Toulon. He placed his finger on the map where Fort l'Aiguillette on its promontory commanded the entrance to the harbour. "There is Toulon," he said, and all, taking their lives in their hands, obeyed him. He organised and led the assault upon Fort l'Aiguillette. After a hot fight it fell.

The whole wide front of the Toulon defences, manned by thousands of Royalists, remained intact, and the feeble lines of the besiegers gazed upon it from a safe distance. But on the morning after Fort l'Aiguillette fell the British Fleet was seen to be leaving the harbour. The lieutenant had understood not only the military significance of the captured fort, but the whole set of moral and political forces upon which the Royalist defence of Toulon hung. Once the British Fleet had departed all resisting power perished. There was a stampede to escape upon such vessels as remained. The city surrendered, and horrible vengeance was wreaked upon thousands of helpless captives, who might have been the vanguard of Counter-Revolution. When these matters were reported to Robespierre and his brother and the Committee in Paris they thought they would like to know more about this competent and apparently well-disposed lieutenant. His name was Napoleon Bonaparte; and, after all, he had taken Toulon.

Meanwhile the Terror rose to its height, and in the political frenzy of Paris no one knew when his hour would come. Men and women went by forties and fifties every day to the guillotine. In self-preservation politicians and people combined against Robespierre. It was July 27, 1794, or by the new French reckoning the 9th Thermidor of the year II, for the Revolutionaries had decided to tear up the calendar of Julius Cæsar and Pope Gregory and start afresh. On that day, in a furious convulsion, Robespierre was dragged down and sent where he would have sent the rest. Our lieutenant of Toulon fame was cast back by this event. He was associated with the Robespierres. He was their "maker of plans." By a spin of the coin he might have followed them into the shades. But the extremity of the Terror had died with Robespierre, and the Directorate which succeeded soon had need of him. In 1795 a strong movement to set up a respectable Government led to an armed rising in the well-to-do quarters of

Paris. One of the members of the Directorate, Barras, all being in dire peril, remembered the lieutenant who had taken Toulon. Placed in command of the military forces, Bonaparte planted his cannon around the legislature, and scattered the citizens who declared they were seeking a free and fair election in accordance with the public will. This cannonade of the 13th Vendémiaire (October 4) was the second leap upward of Bonaparte. On its morrow he claimed command of the French army against the Austrians in Northern Italy. He animated his ragged and famishing troops by the hopes of glory and of booty. He led them in 1796 through the passes of the Alps into a smiling, fertile, and as yet unravaged land. In a series of most hazardous minor battles, gained at heavy odds, he routed the Austrian commanders and conquered the broad base of the Italian peninsula. By these victories he outstripped all rivals in the military field and became the sword of the Revolution, which he was determined to exploit and to destroy. This was the third phase. Corsican, Jacobin, General, were milestones he had left behind him. He now saw as his next step nothing less than a conquest of the Orient after the fashion of Alexander the Great. He planned the invasion of Egypt as a preliminary to the capture of Constantinople, and all that lay in Asia.

*   *   *   *   *

In England the Government had been forced to take repressive measures of a sternness unknown for generations. Republican lecturers were swept into prison. The Habeas Corpus Act was suspended. Distinguished writers were put on their trial for treason; but juries could not be prevailed on to convict. The mildest criticism of the Constitution brought the speaker under danger from a new Treason Act. Ireland, governed since 1782 by a Protestant Parliament independent of Westminster, was now on the verge of open rebellion, which, as Pitt saw, could only be averted by liberal concessions to the Irish Catholics. Henry Grattan, the eloquent Irish leader, who had done so much to win more freedom for his country, urged that Catholics should be given both the vote and the right to sit in Parliament and hold office. They got the vote, but seats in Parliament were still denied them.

Few victories came to brighten these dark years. In 1794 the French Channel Fleet, ill-equipped and under-officered, was half-heartedly engaged by Admiral Howe. Three years later, off Cape St Vincent, the Spanish Fleet—Spain being now in alliance with France—was soundly beaten by Jervis and Nelson. But such had been the neglect of conditions of service in the Navy that the ships at Spithead refused to put to sea. The movement spread to the Nore, and for some weeks London was in effect blockaded by the British Fleet, while a French squadron was on the high seas making for Ireland on a vain quest. The men were entirely loyal; indeed, on the King's birthday the salute which they fired was so hearty and the guns so well charged that the fortifications of Sheerness tumbled down. Some slight concessions satisfied the mutineers, and they retrieved their honour in a handsome victory off Camperdown over the Dutch, who were now satellites of France. Meanwhile the Bank of England had suspended cash payments.

On the Continent the French were everywhere triumphant. Bonaparte, having reduced Northern Italy, was preparing to strike at Austria through the Alpine passes. In April 1797 he signed with her the preliminaries of Leoben, converted some months later into the Treaty of Campo Formio. Belgium was annexed to France; the Republic of Venice, with a glorious history reaching into the Dark Ages, became an Austrian province. Milan, Piedmont, and the little principalities of Northern Italy were welded into a new Cisalpine Republic. France, dominant in Western Europe, firmly

planted in the Mediterranean, safeguarded against attack
from Germany by a secret understanding with Austria, had
only to consider what she would conquer next. A sober judge-
ment might have said England, by way of Ireland. Bonaparte
thought he saw his destiny in a larger field. In the spring of
1798 he sailed for Egypt. Nelson sailed after him.

During the afternoon of August 1 a scouting vessel from
Nelson's fleet signalled that a number of French battleships
were anchored in Aboukir Bay, to the east of Alexandria. In a
line nearly two miles long the thirteen French "seventy-fours"
lay close in to the shallow water, headed west, with dangerous
shoals to port. The French Admiral Brueys was convinced
that not even an English admiral would risk sailing his ship
between the shoals and the French line. But Nelson knew his
captains. As evening drew near, the *Goliath,* followed by the
Zealous, cautiously crept to landward of the French van,
and came into action a few minutes before sundown. Five
British ships passed in succession on the land side of the
enemy, while Nelson, in the *Vanguard,* led the rest of his
fleet to lie to on the starboard of the French line.

The French sailors were many of them on shore and the
decks of their vessels were encumbered with gear. They had
not thought it necessary to clear the gun ports on their landward side. In the rapidly falling darkness confusion seized
their fleet. Relentlessly the English ships, distinguished by
four lanterns hoisted in a horizontal pattern, battered the
enemy van, passing from one disabled foe to the next down
the line. At ten o'clock Brueys's flagship, the *Orient,* blew up.
The five ships ahead of her had already surrendered; the
rest, their cables cut by shot, or frantically attempting to
avoid the inferno of the burning *Orient,* drifted helplessly.
In the morning hours three ran ashore and surrendered, and
a fourth was burned by her officers. Of the great fleet that

had convoyed Napoleon's army to the adventure in Egypt only two ships of the line and two frigates escaped.

Nelson's victory of the Nile cut Napoleon's communications with France and ended his hopes of vast Eastern conquests. He campaigned against the Turks in Syria, but was checked at Acre, where the defence was conducted by Sir Sydney Smith and a force of English seamen. In 1799 he escaped back to France, leaving his army behind him. The British Fleet was once again supreme in the Mediterranean Sea. This was a turning-point. With the capture of Malta in 1800 after a prolonged siege Britain had secured a strong naval base in the Mediterranean, and there was no further need to bring the squadrons home for the winter as in the early part of the war.

But still the British Government could conceive no co-ordinated military plan upon the scale demanded by European strategy. Their own resources were few and their allies seldom dependable. Minor expeditions were dispatched to points around the circumference of the Continent. Descents were made upon Brittany, in Spain, and later in Southern Italy. These harassed the local enemy commanders, but scarcely affected the larger conduct of the war. Meanwhile Napoleon again took charge of the French armies in Italy. In June 1800 he beat the Austrians at Marengo, in Piedmont, and France was once more mistress of Europe. The main contribution of the Island to the war at this time was the vigilance of her fleets and the payment of subsidies to allies. Napoleon's taunt of "a nation of shopkeepers" had some foundation. The time had not yet come when British troops were to distinguish themselves except by pin-pricks and gadfly tactics. General Sir Ralph Abercromby sourly remarked that "There are risks in a British warfare unknown to any other army." He was soon to disprove the slur he thus cast on his troops by landing in Egypt and forcing the capitulation of the

French. His victory at Alexandria in 1801, in which he was mortally wounded, offered the first light of dawn. The French were cleared from the Orient.

* * * * *

In 1800 the political situation in Britain was dominated by the passing of the Act of Union with Ireland. The shocks and alarums of the previous years determined Pitt to attempt some final settlement in that troubled island. The concessions already won by the Irish from British Governments in difficulty had whetted their appetite for more. At the same time Irish Catholics and Protestants were at each other's throats. In Ulster the Protestants founded the Orange Society for the defence of their religion. In the South the party of United Irishmen under Wolfe Tone had come more and more in their desperation to look to France. Rebellion, French attempts at invasion, and brutal civil war darkened the scene. The hopes that had once been pinned in the independent Parliament at Dublin faded away. Even by eighteen-century standards this body was shockingly corrupt. Pitt decided that the complete union of the two kingdoms was the only solution. Union with Scotland had been a success. Why not with Ireland too? But the prime requisite for any agreement must be the emancipation of Irish Catholics from the disabilities of the penal laws. Here Pitt was to stumble upon the rock of the conscience of a monarch now half-crazy. Unscrupulous backstairs influences, false colleagues within the Cabinet Council, pressed George III to stand by his coronation oath, which he was assured was involved. Pitt had committed himself to the cause of Catholic freedom without extracting a written agreement from the King. When George refused his assent, on March 14, 1801, Pitt felt bound to resign. Catholic emancipation was delayed for nearly thirty years. The Act of Union had meanwhile been carried through the Irish Parliament by wholesale patronage and bribery against vehement opposition. Grattan made the greatest speech of his career against the Union, but in vain. Westminster absorbed the Irish Members. Bitter fruits were to follow from this in the later nineteenth century.

Pitt was worn and weary, and perplexed by the uncongenial task of organising England for war. He has been blamed by later historians for his incapacity in directing an extensive war, and for his methods of finance, in which he preferred loans to increased taxation, thereby burdening posterity, as others have done since. He chose to incur gigantic debts, and to struggle haphazardly through each year until the dismal close of the campaigning season, living from day to day and hoping for the best. But if Pitt was an indifferent War Minister his successors were no improvement.

Indeed, with all his defects William Pitt stood high above his contemporaries. Certainly he held more popular confidence than any other man. He possessed perseverance and courage and never flinched from criticism. In ringing tones and well-turned oratory he retorted upon his opponents:

> He [Mr Fox] defies me to state, in one sentence, what is the object of the war. I know not whether I can do it in one sentence, but in one word I can tell him that it is "security"; security against a danger, the greatest that ever threatened the world. It is security against a danger which never existed in any past period of society. It is security against a danger which in degree and extent was never equalled; against a danger which threatened all the nations of the earth; against a danger which has been resisted by all the nations of Europe, and resisted by none with so much success as by this nation, because by none has it been resisted so uniformly and with so much energy.

Pitt was succeeded by a pinchbeck coalition of King's Friends and rebels from his own party. Masquerading as a

Government of National Union, they blundered on for over three years. Their leader was Henry Addington, an amiable former Speaker of the House of Commons whom no one regarded as a statesman. As the young George Canning, a rising hope of the Tories, put it in jesting rhyme,

> As London is to Paddington
> So is Pitt to Addington.

War-time conditions demanded some form of Coalition Government. The Whig Opposition, if only for their lack of administrative experience, were deemed unfit. In 1800 they had been reduced to impotence by the transformation of the war from one against world revolution to one against world Cæsarism. Until the rise of Bonaparte they had steadfastly pleaded for peace and understanding with the revolutionaries. Now they were reduced to points of strategy and military detail upon which they carried no authority. The sense of being the only possible national leader seems to have affected Pitt's actions remarkably little. Young men like Canning and Lord Castlereagh were trained in office under him. And they remained loyal to their chief. As Canning wrote, "Whether Pitt *will* save us I do not know, but surely he is the only man that *can*."

In March 1802 Addington's Government made terms with Napoleon by the Treaty of Amiens, and for a time there was a pause in the fighting. Pitt supported the Government over the peace in spite of the arguments of some of his own followers. English tourists flocked to France, Fox among them, all eager to gaze upon the scenes of Revolution and to see at first hand the formidable First Consul, as he now was. But the tourist season was short. In May of the following year war was renewed, and once more mismanaged. The administration had failed entirely to use the breathing-space for improving the defences. Napoleon was now assembling his forces at Boulogne, intent upon the invasion of England. Pitt was in retirement at Walmer, in Kent. The strain of the past years had broken his health. He was prematurely aged. He had lived a lonely, artificial life, cheered by few friendships. The only time that he ever came in contact with the people was during this brief interval from office, when as Warden of the Cinque Ports he organised the local militia against the threat of invasion. Few things in England's history are more remarkable than this picture of an ex-Prime Minister, riding his horse at the head of a motley company of yokels, drilling on the fields of the South Coast, while a bare twenty miles away across the Channel the Grand Army of Napoleon waited only for a fair wind and a clear passage.

Trafalgar

IN 1804 Pitt was recalled to power. Feverishly he flung himself into the work of reorganising England's war effort. Since the renewal of war Britain had found herself alone against Napoleon, and for two years she maintained the struggle single-handed during one of the most critical periods in her history. Pitt's exertions eventually resulted in the creation of another coalition with Austria and Russia. But this took time. The French had for the moment cowed the Continent into a passive acceptance of their mastery. The opportunity was now at hand to concentrate the whole weight of the armed forces of France against the stubborn Islanders. Elaborate plans went forward to bring about their subjugation. An enormous army was organised and concentrated at the Channel ports for the invasion of England. A fleet of flat-bottomed boats was built to bring two hundred thousand men across the Channel to what seemed inevitable success. At the crest of his hopes Napoleon had himself crowned by the Pope as Emperor of the French. One thing alone was lacking to his designs—command of the sea. It was essential to obtain naval control of the Channel before embarking upon such an enterprise. As before and since in her history, the Royal Navy alone seemed to stand between the Island and national destruction. Its tasks were manifold. Day in, day out, winter and summer, British fleets kept blockade of the French naval bases of Brest and Rochefort on the Atlantic coast and Toulon in the Mediterranean. At all costs a junction of the main French fleets must be prevented. The seas must be kept free for the trade and commerce upon which

Britain's strength depended. Such French squadrons as oc-
casionally escaped must be hunted down and sunk, or driven
back to port. The Western Approaches to the English Channel must infallibly be guarded against French intrusion. Here
was the rallying point for the far-flung British fleets when
danger of invasion threatened the Island, and here lay the
main naval force under Admiral Cornwallis. As the American
historian Admiral Mahan has said, "It was these distant
storm-beaten ships upon which the Grand Army never looked
which stood between it and the dominion of the world."

In May 1803 Nelson had returned to the Mediterranean
to resume command of his fleet. Here the fate of his
country might be decided. It was his task to contain the
French fleet in Toulon and stop it from raiding Sicily and the
Eastern Mediterranean, or sailing into the Atlantic, whence
it might lift the blockade of Rochefort and Brest, force the
Channel, and co-operate with the armada from Boulogne.
Nelson was well aware of the grim significance of the moment,
and all his brilliance as a commander was employed on
creating a first-class machine. The crews were reorganised,
the ships refitted under dangerous and difficult circumstances.
He had no secure base from which to watch Toulon.
Gibraltar and Malta were both too far away, and Minorca
had been given back to Spain at the Treaty of Amiens.
Provisions had to be brought from the coast towns of Sardinia
and Spain, and when water ran out he was forced each time
to raise the blockade and move his whole force into Sardinian
harbours. He was not even superior in numbers to the main
French fleet in Toulon harbour. Under such circumstances a
literal hemming in of the French was impossible. Nelson's
burning desire was to lure them out and fight them. An-
nihilation was his policy. He kept a screen of frigates watching Toulon, and himself with his battleships lay off Sardinia,
alert for interception. Twice in the course of two years the
French attempted a sortie, but retired. Throughout this time

Nelson never set foot on shore. The constant nightmare in his mind revolved round the direction in which the French would make. For Sicily and Egypt? Or Spain and the Atlantic? He had to cover all escape routes.

In the centre of the web sat Napoleon, and the elaborate scheme for the final blow against England was slowly woven. But the vital instrument in his hand was brittle. The French Navy had suffered a crushing blow in the days of the Revolution. With the breakdown of the finances the existing ships had fallen into disrepair and for some time no further additions were made to the Fleet. The officer class had been almost wiped out on the guillotine. Discipline was bad and the French Navy in no state to play a decisive rôle. But strenuous efforts at recovery were made by Napoleon's Minister of Marine. New French commanders distinguished themselves in commerce-raiding upon the oceans. In May 1804 the Emperor had confided the Toulon fleet to Admiral Villeneuve, an excellent seaman, who realised that his ships, except for the luck of circumstance, could only play a defensive part. Napoleon would brook no obstacles, and a complicated series of feints was worked out to deceive the British agents who swarmed into France to gather such information as they could. Spain was dragged into his schemes, her Fleet being a necessary adjunct to the main plan. In the early months of 1805 Napoleon made his final arrangements. Over ninety thousand assault troops, picked and trained, lay in the camps round Boulogne. The French Channel ports were not constructed to take battleships, and the French fleets in the Atlantic and Mediterranean harbours must be concentrated elsewhere to gain command of the Channel. The Emperor fixed upon the West Indies. Here, after breaking the Mediterranean and Atlantic blockades, and drawing off the British Fleet, as he thought, into the waters of the Western Atlantic, his ships were ordered to gather. The combined French and Spanish fleets would then unite with Ganteaume, the admiral of the Brest squadron, double back to Europe, sail up the Channel, and assure the crossing from Boulogne. The scheme was brilliant on paper, but it took no account of the state of the French ships, and it ignored the vital strategy of concentration always pursued by British admirals when the enemy was at large.

Nelson was lying in wait off the Sardinian coastline in April 1805 when news reached him that Villeneuve was at sea, having slipped out of Toulon on the dark night of March 30, sailing, as Nelson did not yet know, in a westerly direction with eleven ships of the line and eight frigates. The fox was out and the chase began. Fortune seemed against Nelson. His frigates lost touch with Villeneuve, and he had first to make sure that the French were not running for Sicily and the Near East. This done, he headed for Gibraltar. Fierce westerly gales prevented him reaching the Straits until May 4, when he learnt that Villeneuve had passed through to Cadiz more than three weeks before. Six Spanish battle-ships had come out to join him, and the long voyage across the Atlantic began. Nelson, picking up scattered reports from frigates and merchantmen, pieced together the French design. All his qualities were now displayed to the full. Out of perplexing, obscure, and conflicting reports he had fathomed the French plan. There was no evidence to show that Villeneuve had gone to the north, and there could hardly be any reason for his sailing south along the West African coast. Therefore on May 11 Nelson made the momentous decision to sail westwards himself. He had ten ships of the line to follow seventeen of the enemy. The passage was uneventful. In stately procession at an average rate of five and a half knots the English pursued their quarry, and a game of hide-and-seek followed among the West Indian islands. Villeneuve and his Spanish allies reached Martinique on May 14. Nelson made landfall at Barbados on June 4. False intelligence led

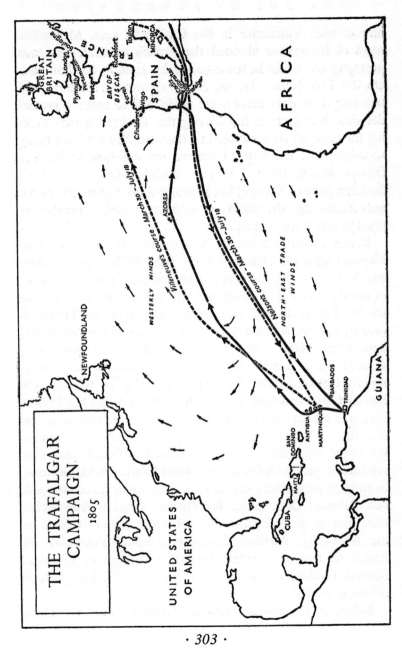

THE TRAFALGAR CAMPAIGN
1805

GREAT BRITAIN
London
Plymouth
Portsmouth
Brest
BAY OF BISCAY
FRANCE
Boulogne
Rochefort
Ferrol
C.Finisterre
Vigo
SPAIN
MINORCA
Toulon
Cadiz
Trafalgar
AFRICA

AZORES

WESTERLY WINDS

Villeneuve's course - March 30 - July 18
Nelson's course - March 30 - July 18

NORTH · EAST TRADE WINDS

NEWFOUNDLAND

UNITED STATES
OF AMERICA

CUBA
HAITI
SAN DOMINGO

ANTIGUA
MARTINIQUE
BARBADOS
TRINIDAD
GUIANA

him to miss Villeneuve in the Caribbean seas. Meanwhile news of his arrival alarmed the French admiral, who was promptly out again in the Atlantic by June 8, heading east. On the 12th Nelson lay off Antigua, where Villeneuve had lain only four days earlier. He again had to make a crucial decision. Was he right in believing that the French were making for Europe? As he wrote in a dispatch, "So far from being infallible, like the Pope, I believe my opinions to be very fallible, and therefore I may be mistaken that the enemy's fleet has gone to Europe; but I cannot think myself otherwise, notwithstanding the variety of opinions which a number of good people have formed."

Before leaving the islands Nelson sent a fast sloop back to England with dispatches, and on June 19 it passed Villeneuve's fleet, noting his course and position. The commander of the sloop saw that Villeneuve was heading north-eastwards for the Bay of Biscay, and raced home, reaching Plymouth on July 8. Lord Barham, the new First Lord of the Admiralty, aged seventy-eight and with a lifetime's naval experience, at once realised what was happening. Nelson was sailing rapidly eastwards after Villeneuve, believing he would catch him at Cadiz and head him off the Straits, while the French fleet was making steadily on a more northerly course in the direction of Cape Finisterre. Villeneuve intended to release the Franco-Spanish squadron blockaded at Ferrol, and, thus reinforced, join with Ganteaume from Brest. But Ganteaume, in spite of peremptory orders from Napoleon, failed to break out. Admiral Cornwallis's fleet in the Western Approaches kept him in port. Meanwhile, on orders from Barham at the Admiralty, Admiral Calder intercepted Villeneuve off Finisterre, and here in late July the campaign of Trafalgar opened. Calder's action was indecisive, and the French took refuge in Ferrol.

Nelson meanwhile had reached Cadiz on July 18. There

he found Collingwood on guard, but no sign of the enemy. Realising that Villeneuve must have gone north, Nelson replenished his fleet in Morocco and sailed for home waters on the 23rd. On the same day Napoleon arrived at Boulogne. The crisis was at hand and the outlying squadrons of the Royal Navy instinctively gathered at the mouth of the Channel for the defence of the Island. Calder joined Cornwallis off Brest on August 14, and on the next day Nelson arrived with twelve more ships, bringing the main fleet up to a total of nearly forty ships of the line. Thus was the sea-barrier concentrated against the French. Nelson went on alone with his flagship, the *Victory,* to Portsmouth. In the following days the campaign reached its climax. Villeneuve sailed again from Ferrol on August 13 in an attempt to join Ganteaume and enter the English Channel, for Napoleon still believed that the British fleets were dispersed and that the moment had come for invasion. On August 21 Ganteaume was observed to be leaving harbour, but Cornwallis closed in with his whole force and the French turned back. Meanwhile Villeneuve, having edged out into the Atlantic, had changed his mind. Well aware of the shortcomings of his ill-trained fleet, desperately short of supplies, and with many sick on board, he had abandoned the great venture on August 15 and was already speeding south to Cadiz. The threat of invasion was over.

Early in September dispatches reached London telling that Villeneuve had gone south. Nelson, summoned from his home at Merton, was at once ordered to resume his command. "I hold myself ready to go forth whenever I am desired," he wrote, "although God knows I want rest." Amid scenes of enthusiasm he rejoined the *Victory* at Portsmouth and sailed on September 15. All England realised that her fate now lay in the hands of this frail man. A fortnight later he joined the fleet off Cadiz, now numbering twenty-seven ships of the line. "We have only one great object in view," he wrote to Collingwood, "that of annihilating our enemies." His object was to starve the enemy fleet, now concentrated in Cadiz harbour, and force it out into the open sea and to battle. This involved patrolling the whole adjacent coast. He organised his own ships into blockading squadrons. His energy and inspiration roused the spirit of his captains to the highest pitch. To them he outlined a new and daring plan of battle. He intended to ignore the Admiralty's "Fighting Instructions." To gain a decisive victory, he was resolved to abandon the old formal line of battle, running parallel to the enemy's fleet. He would break Villeneuve's line, when it came out of port, by sailing at right angles boldly into it with two main divisions. While the enemy van was thus cut off and out of touch his centre and rear would be destroyed. After his conference with his captains Nelson wrote, "All approved. It was new, it was singular, it was simple. It must succeed." In a mood of intense exhilaration the fleet prepared for the ordeal ahead. Meanwhile Villeneuve had received orders to sail for Naples in support of Napoleon's new military plans. After learning that he was about to be superseded, he resolved to obey before his successor could arrive. On the morning of October 19 a frigate signalled to Nelson's flagship, "Enemy has their topsail yards hoisted," and some time later, "Enemy ships are coming out of port." On receiving these messages Nelson led his fleet to the southeast to cut off the enemy from the Straits and force them to fight in the open sea. At daybreak on the 21st he saw from the quarterdeck of the *Victory* the battle line of the enemy, consisting of an advance squadron of twelve Spanish ships under Admiral Gravina and twenty-one French ships of the line under Villeneuve. It was seven months since the escape from Toulon, and the first time that Nelson had seen his foes since war had begun again in 1803.

The British fleet lay about ten miles west of the enemy, to

the windward, and at six in the morning Nelson signalled his ships to steer east-north-east for the attack in the two columns he had planned. The enemy turned northwards on seeing the advancing squadrons, and Nelson pressed on with every sail set. The clumsy seamanship of his men convinced Villeneuve that flight was impossible, and he hove to in a long sagging line to await Nelson's attack. The English admiral turned to one of his officers. "They have put a good face on it, but I will give them such a dressing as they have never had before." Nelson signalled to Collingwood, who was at the head of the southern column in the *Royal Sovereign*, "I intend to pass through the van of the enemy's line, to prevent him getting into Cadiz." Nelson went down to his cabin to compose a prayer. "May the Great God whom I worship grant to my country, and for the benefit of Europe in general, a great and glorious Victory. . . . For myself, I commit my life to Him who made me, and may His blessing light upon my endeavours for serving my country faithfully." The fleets were drawing nearer and nearer. Another signal was run up upon the *Victory*, "England expects every man will do his duty." When Collingwood saw the flutter he remarked testily, "I wish Nelson would stop signalling, as we all know well enough what we have to do," but when the message was reported to him cheers broke out from the ships in his line. A deathly silence fell upon the fleet as the ships drew nearer. Each captain marked down his adversary, and within a few minutes the two English columns thundered into action. The roar of broadsides, the crashing of masts, the rattle of musketry at point-blank range rent the air. The *Victory* smashed through between Villeneuve's flagship, the *Bucentaure,* and the *Redoutable*. The three ships remained locked together, raking each other with broadsides. Nelson was pacing as if on parade on his quarterdeck when at 1.15 P.M. he was shot from the mast-head of the *Redoutable* by a bullet in the shoulder. His backbone was broken, and he was carried below amid the thunder of the *Victory's* guns. The battle was still raging. By the afternoon of October 21, 1805, eighteen of the enemy ships had surrendered and the remainder were in full retreat. Eleven entered Cadiz, but four more were captured off the coast of Spain. In the log of the *Victory* occurs the passage, "Partial firing continued until 4.30, when a victory having been reported to the right Hon. Lord Viscount Nelson, K.B. and Commander-in-Chief, he then died of his wound."

The victory was complete and final. The British Fleet, under her most superb commander, like him had done its duty.

*   *   *   *   *

Napoleon meanwhile was attracted to other fields. When Villeneuve that summer failed to break through into the Channel the Emperor made a sudden change of plan. He determined to strike at the European coalition raised against him by Pitt's diplomacy and subsidies. In August 1805 the camp at Boulogne broke up, and the French troops set out on their long march to the Danube.

The campaign that followed wrecked Pitt's hopes and schemes. In the month of Trafalgar the Austrian General Mack surrendered at Ulm. Austria and Russia were broken at the Battle of Austerlitz. Napoleon's star had once more triumphed, and for England all was to do again. About this time the Prime Minister gave audience to a young general home from India. In forthright terms this officer noted his opinion of Pitt. "The fault of his character," he wrote, "is being too sanguine. . . . He conceives a project and then imagines it is done." This severe but not inaccurate judgment was formed by one who was to have many dealings with the armies of the French Emperor. His name was Arthur Wellesley, later Duke of Wellington.

A personal sorrow now darkened Pitt's life. The House

of Commons by the casting vote of the Speaker resolved to impeach his close colleague and lifelong companion, Henry Dundas, now Lord Melville, for maladministration in the Admiralty and for the peculations of certain of his subordinates. The decisive speech against Dundas was made by none other than Wilberforce. The scene in the House of Commons was poignant. Pitt's eyes filled with tears as he listened to Wilberforce attacking his other greatest friend. After the adverse decision the Opposition crowded round him "to see how Pitt took it"; but, encircled by his supporters, he was led from the House. It was this disgrace, rather than the news of Austerlitz, which finally broke the spirit and energy of the Prime Minister. In January 1806 he died. Wilberforce has written a valediction for his friend:

The time and circumstances of his death were peculiarly affecting. I really never remember any event producing so much apparent feeling. . . . For a clear and comprehensive view of the most complicated subject in all its relations; for the fairness of mind which disposes a man to follow out, and when overtaken to recognise, the truth; for magnanimity which made him ready to change his measures when he thought the good of the country required it, though he knew he should be charged with inconsistency on account of the change; for willingness to give a fair hearing to all that could be urged against his own opinions, and to listen to the suggestions of men whose understanding he knew to be inferior to his own; for personal purity, disinterestedness, integrity, and love of his country, I have never known his equal.

"In an age," runs the inscription on his monument in Guildhall, "when the contagion of ideals threatened to dissolve the forms of civil society he rallied the loyal, the soberminded, and the good around the venerable structure of the English monarchy." This is a fitting epitaph.

The Emperor of the French

WILLIAM PITT'S successors were staunch in the prosecution of war, but even less adept at it than he. The three years between the death of Pitt in January 1806 and the rise of Wellington in 1809 were uncheered by fortune. England's military strength was wasted in unfruitful expeditions to the fringes of the Mediterranean coastline. One small victory was won at Maida, in the Kingdom of Naples. There the rush of French attack was first broken by steady British infantry. Accounts of the battle reached Sir Arthur Wellesley in England, and fortified his views on how to meet the French in the field. But Maida was of no strategic consequence. An ambitious plan to gain a permanent foothold in the Spanish colonies of South America led to the temporary occupation of Buenos Aires and the ultimate loss of valuable forces. Thanks to the Fleet, the sea lanes of the world remained open, and in Europe the important islands of Sicily and Sardinia were kept from Napoleon's grasp.

In 1806 and 1807 there was a brief Ministry of "All the Talents" under Lord Grenville. The talent was largely provided by the Whigs, now in office for the first time since 1783 and the last until 1830. Over twenty years of divorce from power had had an insidious and lowering effect upon the party. Their organisation and their programme dissolved in the perplexed bickering of their leaders. The renewal of the European conflict quenched the hopes of Parliamentary reform, upon which they had taken their stand in the early 1790's. The rise of Napoleon destroyed their chance of effective opposition to the war. They had maintained a straggling and futile fire against the strategic proposals of the Government. They hoped now to lift some of the restrictions upon Roman Catholics, for they were much oppressed by the problem of Ireland. But in this they failed. The Secretary of State for War, William Windham, produced admirable paper reforms of the Army. He introduced short-time service, with increased pay. Abolishing the local militia he passed a Training Act, which made universal military service compulsory. The manhood of England would be called to the colours in batches of two hundred thousand at a time. This was a striking piece of legislation. But in practical administration Windham was less successful. "He is a most wretched man of business," remarked Wilberforce. "No precision or knowledge of details even in his own measures." The Government's tenure of office was redeemed by Fox's abolition of the slave trade, a measure which ranks among the greatest of British achievements, and from which Pitt had always shrunk. It was Fox's last effort. For forty years his warm-hearted eloquence had inspired the Whigs. Almost his whole Parliamentary life was spent in Opposition. He died as Secretary of State, nine months after his great rival, Pitt, had gone to the grave.

In 1807 the Whigs fell. They were succeeded by a mixed Government of Tory complexion under the nominal leadership of the Duke of Portland. Its object was to hold together the loyalties of as much of the nation as it could command. In this it was remarkably successful. New figures were appearing in the Tory ranks, trained by Pitt in the daily business of government. George Canning, Spencer Perceval, Viscount Castlereagh, were reaching out for power. Politics centred on the conduct of the War Office and on the personal enmity and rivalry of Canning and Castlereagh.

These restless spirits soon impelled the Government to dis-
card the strategies of William Pitt. Active participation in the
military and naval struggle for Europe became the order of
the day.

*   *   *   *   *

Speed was essential, for Napoleon was reaching the height
of his career. At Austerlitz he had struck down Russia and
Austria. He was already master of the Netherlands, Italy,
and the states of the Rhine. At Jena, a year later, he had
broken Prussia. He became master of the whole country.
For the next seven years French garrisons held Berlin and
all important Prussian places. The Czar was still in the
field, but in June 1807 the Russian Army was defeated on the
Eylau River. There followed the reconciliation of Napoleon
and Alexander. On a raft upon the Niemen, with their armies
gathered on either bank, the two Emperors met and embraced. Peace was made between them. And not only peace,
but alliance. Alexander, estranged from England by the
paltry support he had received, yielded himself to Napoleon's
spell. The two potentates planned Europe according to their
common interests. Alexander had his moments of revolt.
When he reviewed the French Army and at Napoleon's side
watched the Old Guard march past he was struck by the
scars and wounds which many of these veterans bore. "And
where are the soldiers who have given these wounds?" he
exclaimed to Ney. "Sire, they are dead."

The Franco-Russian Alliance, signed at Tilsit on July 7,
was the culmination of Napoleon's power. He dominated all
Europe. The Emperor of Austria was a cowed and obsequious
satellite. The King of Prussia and his handsome queen were
beggars, and almost captives in his train. Napoleon's brothers
reigned as Kings at the Hague, at Naples, and in Westphalia.
His step-son ruled Northern Italy in his name. Spain lent itself
to his system, trusting that worse might not befall. Denmark

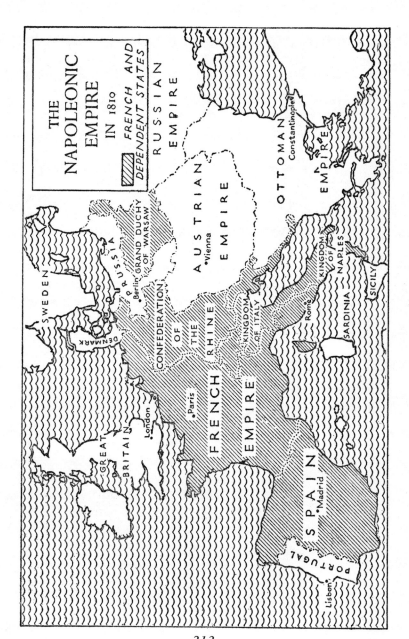

THE
NAPOLEONIC
EMPIRE
IN 1810

*FRENCH AND
DEPENDENT STATES*

RUSSIAN EMPIRE

SWEDEN

P R U S S I A

Berlin

GRAND DUCHY OF WARSAW

DENMARK

CONFEDERATION OF THE RHINE

AUSTRIAN EMPIRE

•Vienna

OTTOMAN EMPIRE

Constantinople

GREAT BRITAIN

London

THE RHINE

KINGDOM OF ITALY

•Paris

FRENCH EMPIRE

Rome•

KINGDOM OF NAPLES

SARDINIA

SICILY

S P A I N

Madrid•

PORTUGAL

Lisbon•

and Scandinavia made haste to obey. Russia, the great counterpoise, had swung over to his side. Only Britannia remained, unreconciled, unconquered, implacable. There she lay in her Island, mistress of the seas and oceans, ruled by her proud, stubborn aristocracy, facing this immense combination alone, sullen, fierce, and almost unperturbed. Some anxious merchants and manufacturers complained of the British blockade, which materially affected their interests. They stirred up Whig politicians to denounce it. But the Government was founded on land, not trade, and turned a deaf ear. Nevertheless Britain owed much of the power that was to bring her victory to her growing industrial supremacy. Industry knew this. The seeds were now sown for a crop of post-war troubles in which industry was to demand a greater share in the councils of the nation. But for the time being patriotism healed all, or nearly all. It was against this contumacious land, which marred and derided the unity of Europe and challenged the French peace, that Napoleon now directed his whole strength. To venture upon salt water, except for cruiser raids on commerce, was to be sunk or captured. The British blockade wrapped the French Empire and Napoleon's Europe in a clammy shroud. No trade, no coffee, no sugar, no contact with the East, or with the Americans! And no means of ending the deadlock! Napoleon had believed that the marshalling of all Europe under his hands would force England to make terms. But no response came from the Island, which throve upon seaborne trade, and whose ruling classes seemed to take as much interest in prize-fighting and fox-hunting as in the world crisis.

Grave and threatening news was conveyed to London from the raft where the two Emperors had met upon the river Niemen. An English secret agent reported that an arrangement had been reached whereby Napoleon was to seize the Danish Fleet and gain control of the entrance to the Baltic. This was to be a preliminary to a joint invasion of England with the help of the Russians. The Cabinet acted with praiseworthy decision. Admiral Gambier was immediately ordered to enter the Baltic with twenty ships of the line and procure, by force if necessary, the surrender of the Danish Fleet. After a heavy action in the harbour of Copenhagen the Danes yielded to this humiliation. This act of aggression against a neutral state aroused a storm against the Government in Whig political and literary circles. But events vindicated the promptitude and excused the violence of their action. Two days after the British Fleet left home waters Napoleon had informed the Danish Minister in Paris that if England were to refuse Russian mediation in the Great War Denmark would be forced to choose sides. Had the British Government not acted with speed the French would have been in possession of the Danish Navy within a few weeks.

At the War Office Castlereagh was busy attempting to reorganise the Regular Army. This was done by drastic and immediate legislation. Thirty thousand men were drawn from the local militia, which had been restored, and formed into regular regiments, and provision was made to raise forty-four thousand recruits for the militia to take their place in home defence.

Secure throughout the rest of Europe, Napoleon turned his attention to the Spanish Peninsula. Powerless at sea, he realised that to destroy his one outstanding rival he must turn the weapon of blockade against the Island. English goods must be kept out of the markets of Europe by an iron ring of customs guards stretching from the borders of Russia round the coasts of Northern Europe and Western France and sealing the whole Mediterranean coastline as far as the Dardanelles. Napoleon proclaimed his policy from Berlin. It was a land blockade of sea-power. The weakest link in the immense barrier of French troops and customs officers was the Peninsula of Spain. To complete this amazing plan it was essential to control not only Spain, but also Portugal, the traditional ally of Britain, whose capital, Lisbon, was an important potential base for the British Fleet.

The crucial point therefore lay in the Peninsula. Slowly the minds of English Ministers turned to this theatre of coming war. Napoleon was determined to strike through Spain at Lisbon before the British Fleet could sail southwards. Canning, in charge at the Foreign Office, displayed the energy of youth. An English squadron sailed to the Tagus, collected the Portuguese ships, and packed off the Portuguese royal family, Government, and society to the safety of Brazil. A few days later Marshal Junot entered the Portuguese capital, and the following day Napoleon declared war on the country he had just occupied.

France and Britain were now locked in their deadliest grip. In reply to Napoleon's Continental System the British Government issued an Order in Council declaring a sea blockade of all French and French-allied ports—in other words, of almost the whole of Europe. Napoleon's decrees and the English Orders wounded the merchant shipping of the neutral countries. The results of this trade war were far-reaching for both sides. The commerce of Europe was paralysed and the nations stirred beneath the French yoke. Interference by British ships with neutral vessels raised with the United States the question of the freedom of the seas. It was a grievous dispute, not to be settled without recourse to war.

Napoleon, insatiable of power, and seeking always to break England and her intangible blockade, resolved to seize the Spanish crown. He enticed King Charles IV of Spain and his son Ferdinand into a trap at Bayonne, and under the threat of a firing squad compelled them to sign documents of abdication. He placed his own brother Joseph on the throne of Spain as a vassal of the French Empire. He was overjoyed with the success of this violence. "Spanish opinion bends to my will. Tranquillity is everywhere reestablished,"

he wrote to Cambacérès; and to his Foreign Secretary Talleyrand on May 16, 1807, "The Spanish business goes well
and will soon be entirely settled." But, happily for human
freedom, things are not so easy as that. As soon as the
Spainards realised what had happened and that their country
was practically annexed to France they rose everywhere in
spontaneous revolt. Between May 24 and 30 in every hamlet
and village throughout the Peninsula they took up what arms
they could find and set out for the capital of the province
or their local centre, where the same process was already
working on a larger scale. Nothing like this universal uprising
of a numerous, ancient race and nation, all animated by one
thought, had been seen before. The tiny province of Asturias,
on the Biscayan shore, separated by the mountains from the
rest of Spain, knowing nothing of what the rest were doing,
drove out the French governor, seized the arsenal with booty
of a hundred thousand muskets, constituted itself an independent Government, declared war upon Napoleon at the
height of his greatness, and sent their envoys to England to
appeal for alliance and aid. The envoys landed at Falmouth
on the night of June 6, and were conveyed by the admiralty to
Canning. Canning understood. From that moment the Peninsular War began. For the first time the forces unchained
by the French Revolution, which Napoleon had disciplined
and directed, met, not kings or Old World hierarchies, but a
whole population inspired by the religion and patriotism
which Joan of Arc had tried in vain to teach to France, and
now Spain was to teach to Europe.

The character of the warfare darkened. In Germany and
Italy and elsewhere there had been pillage and rough deeds,
but the armies had given quarter and the inhabitants had
remained spectators. Now, in Spain, the French troops
found as they marched the corpses of their stragglers and
wounded, often horribly mutilated, sometimes bearing signs

of torture. It was with a chill that they realised they were at grips with a foe who, though incompetent in a set battle, neither gave nor sought mercy. Moreover, this foe lay everywhere. In July King Joseph wrote to Napoleon from Madrid, "No one has told the truth so far. The fact is that there is not a single Spaniard who is for me except the few who came here with me. All are terrorised by the unanimous feelings of their compatriots"; and he called for "plenty of troops and money." The Emperor was very slow to measure the force of the Spanish revolt. He had been warring in Europe for fifteen years, and he thought he understood the sort of things that happened and their values. He conceived himself a liberator, as indeed he was in many parts of the Continent. He could not understand a people who preferred misgovernment of their own making to rational rule imposed from without. Now, at the end of July, news reached him at the Tuileries of an event in Spain, grave in itself, and menacing to the whole structure of his power.

General Dupont, withdrawing to Madrid from Cordova, had been entangled and brought to a standstill at Baylen, in Andalusia. In the burning summer he had to fight for water, and, not gaining it, surrendered to the Spanish insurgents with twenty-two thousand French soldiers. This was a new event in Europe since the Revolutionary wars began. Napoleon felt himself smitten in a manner deadly to his system. The capitulation of Baylen compelled the evacuation of Madrid. The French army, carrying King Joseph with them, withdrew to the north-east behind the Ebro. Marshal Junot, in Portugal, whose people had likewise risen *en masse*, was isolated by hundreds of miles of hostile country and by the salt seas where Britain ruled, and from which she could strike. Napoleon felt in every nerve and fibre the tremor which ran through Europe and jarred the foundations of his Imperial throne. Here and now he was strong enough to quit Spain; his power would still have been enormous; but he feared to retreat from a false and dangerous position. He must move, like all dictators, from one triumph to another. This country, which he had expected to incorporate in his Empire by a personal arrangement with a feeble Government, by a trick, by a trap, without bloodshed or expense, suddenly became his main military problem. He resolved to conquer. He reached out to Germany and drew the flower of his armies to the South. He prepared to fill their places by anticipating the conscription of the year 1809 and moved a hundred and sixty thousand recruits through his depots, gradually forward to their posts in Germany and through Austria, about whose attitude he already felt misgivings. The veterans marched through France into Spain. Their journey was made agreeable. They were officially fêted and feasted in all the French towns through which they passed. The soldiers were cheered by the kindness of the people. The people were impressed by the spectacle of the Emperor's glorious army.

But meanwhile the English had struck a shrewd blow. Canning and his colleagues decided to send an army to the Peninsula to aid the Spanish insurgents. But as the Juntas of Galicia and Andalusia were not as yet willing to accept foreign troops the expedition was sent to Portugal, and in July 1808 disembarked north of Lisbon in the Mondego River. This small British army consisted of thirty thousand well-equipped men. At the head of the first troops to land appeared Sir Arthur Wellesley, whose conduct of the Mahratta war in India had been distinguished. He had gained the Battle of Assaye. He was the younger brother of the Governor-General of India. He was a member of Parliament and of the Tory administration, and actually held office at this time as Chief Secretary to the Lord-Lieutenant of Ireland. He did not wait for the rest of the army, but immediately took the field. At the combat at Roliça Junot received a sharp repulse. At Vimeiro this was repeated on a larger scale. The French columns of assault were broken by the reserved fire of the "thin red line," which now began to attract attention. Junot retreated upon Lisbon.

Sir Arthur Wellesley was superseded in the moment of victory by the arrival of Sir Harry Burrard, who later in the same day made over his command to Sir Hew Dalrymple. Wellesley's wish to seize the pass of Torres Vedras and thus cut Junot's line of retreat was frustrated by his seniors. But the French commander now sent Kellerman to the British camp to negotiate. He offered to evacuate Portugal if the British would carry him back to France. The Convention of Cintra was signed, and punctiliously executed by the British. Junot and twenty-six thousand Frenchmen were landed from British transports at Rochefort. Wellesley in dudgeon remarked to his officers, "We can now go and shoot red-legged partridges." There was a loud and not unnatural outcry in England at Junot's being freed. A military court of inquiry in London exonerated the three commanders, but only one of them was ever employed again.

He was the one that mattered:

> Sir Arthur and Sir Harry,
> Sir Harry and Sir Hew,
> Sing cock-a-doodle doodle,
>   doodle-doodle-doo.

> Sir Arthur was a fighting cock,
> But of the other two
> Sing doodle-doodle-doodle,
>   doodle-doodle-doo.

Napoleon had intended to court-martial Junot, but as the English were trying their own generals he declared himself glad not to have to proceed against an old friend. History has endorsed Byron's line, "Britannia sickens, Cintra! at thy name."

Napoleon now moved a quarter of a million of his best troops into Spain. While the Grand Army was gathering behind the Ebro he organised a mighty display. At Erfurt an imposing reunion of all his tributaries and allies was convened. Thirty-eight princes and rulers assembled at the Emperor's call. When the Czar arrived Napoleon sought to inflame his mind with schemes of a Franco-Russian march to Constantinople and beyond along the historic route to India. Alexander was still fascinated by Napoleon's personality. He liked to dream of world conquest with him. But he was also vexed by the large garrisons Napoleon kept on the Oder. Talleyrand, by subtle whispers, betrayed Napoleon's interest, urging the Czar to unite himself with France rather than with its Emperor. All passed off with pomp and splendour. Alexander and Napoleon kissed each other before the august circle. But Erfurt was only a hollow echo of Tilsit.

The moment had now come for Napoleon to take command on the Ebro. An avalanche of fire and steel broke upon the Spanish Juntas, who, with ninety thousand raw but ardent volunteers, had nursed a brief illusion of freedom regained. The Emperor advanced upon Madrid, driving the Spanish army before him in a series of routs, in which the French cavalry took pitiless vengeance. He astonished his personal staff by his violent energy. Always with the leading troops, he forced the fighting, even at Somo Sierra making his own bodyguard charge the batteries, regardless of loss. In December he entered Madrid, and replaced Joseph, who had hitherto followed with the baggage-train, upon the stolen throne. But the Spanish people were undaunted, and all around the camps of the victorious invaders flickered a horrible guerrilla.

*   *   *   *   *

A new English general of high quality had succeeded the commanders involved in the Convention of Cintra. Sir John Moore advanced from Lisbon through Salamanca to Valladolid. He had been lured by promises of powerful Spanish assistance, and he tried by running great risks to turn Spanish hopes into reality. His daring thrust cut or threatened the communications of all the French armies, and immediately prevented any French action in the south of Spain or against Portugal. But Napoleon, watching from Madrid, saw him a prey. At Christmas 1808, with fifty thousand men, with Ney, Soult, and the Old Guard, he marched to intercept and destroy him. On foot with his soldiers Napoleon tramped through the snows of the Guadarrama. He moved with amazing speed. Moore, warned in time, and invoking amphibious power, dropped his communications with Portugal and ordered his transports to meet him at Corunna, on the northwest tip of Spain. It was a race; but when the French horse crossed the Rio Seco they were hurled back, and their general captured, by the cavalry of the English rearguard. Moore had already passed Astorga and was half-way to his haven.

At Astorga the Emperor sat down on the parapet of a bridge to read dispatches brought apace from the capital. After a few moments he rose, and stood absorbed in thought. Then, ordering up his travelling coach, he handed over the pursuit of the British to Soult, and, without offering any explanation to his officers, set off for Valladolid and Paris. He had known for some months that the Austrian armies were assembling and he must expect an Austrian declaration of war, but his summons home was more intimate. His brother, Lucien, and his step-son, Eugène de Beauharnais, warned him of an intrigue, or even plot, against him by Talleyrand and Fouché, his Minister of Police. Besides, there was now no chance of cutting off the British. The pursuit had become a stern chase. Soult and Ney could have it.

The retreat of the British through the rugged, snow-bound hill country was arduous. The French pressed heavily. Scenes of mass drunkenness where wine stores were found, pillage, stragglers dying of cold and hunger, and the Army chest of gold flung down a precipice to baffle capture darkened the British track. But when, at Lugo, Moore turned and offered battle his army showed so firm a posture that for two days Soult, although already superior, awaited reinforcements. It was now resolved to slip away in the night to Corunna, where the army arrived on January 14, 1809. But the harbour was empty. Contrary winds had delayed the Fleet and transports. There would be a battle after all. On the 16th Soult assaulted Moore with 20,000 against 14,000. He was everywhere repulsed, and indeed counter-attacked. When darkness fell the pursuers had had enough. But both Sir John Moore and his second-in-command, Sir David Baird, had fallen on the field. Moore's death and burial have been recorded in famous prose and verse.

"From the spot where he fell," wrote Napier, who fought in the action,

the General was carried to the town by a party of soldiers. The blood flowed fast, and the torture of his wound increased; but such was the unshaken firmness of his mind that those about him, judging from the resolution of his countenance that his hurt was not mortal, expressed a hope of his recovery. Hearing this, he looked steadfastly at the injury for a moment, and then said, "No, I feel that to be impossible." Several times he caused his attendants to stop and turn him round, that he might behold the field of battle, and when the firing indicated the advance of the British he discovered his satisfaction and permitted the bearers to proceed. Being brought to his lodgings, the surgeons examined his wound, but there was no hope; the pain increased and he spoke with great difficulty. At intervals he asked if the French were beaten, and, addressing his old friend, Colonel Anderson, he said, "You know that I always wished to die this way." Again he asked if the enemy were defeated, and being told they were, observed, "It is a great satisfaction to me to know we have beaten the French." His countenance continued firm and his thoughts clear; once only, when he spoke of his mother, he became agitated. He inquired after the safety of his friends, and the officers of his staff, and he did not even in this moment forget to recommend those whose merit had given them claims to promotion. His strength was failing fast, and life was just extinct, when, with an unsubdued spirit, as if anticipating the baseness of his posthumous calumniators, he exclaimed, "I hope the people of England will be satisfied. I hope my country will do me justice." The battle was scarcely ended when his corpse, wrapped in a military cloak, was interred by the officers of his staff in the citadel of Corunna. The guns of the enemy paid him funeral honours, and Soult, with a noble feeling of respect for his valour, raised a monument to his memory.[1]

Moore's countrymen may well do him justice. By daring, skill, and luck he had ruptured Napoleon's winter campaign and had drawn the Emperor and his finest army into the least important part of Spain, thus affording protection and time for movements to get on foot in all the rest of the Peninsula. He had escaped Napoleon's amazing forward spring and clutch. He died like Wolfe and Nelson, in the hour of victory. His army re-embarked unmolested. His campaign had restored the military reputation of Britain, which had suffered increasing eclipse since the days of Chatham; he had prepared the way for a new figure, destined to lead the armies of Europe upon the decisive field.

*   *   *   *   *

The return of the Emperor to Paris recalled his servants to their treacherous allegiance. He had now to face war with Austria. For this purpose he made demands upon the manhood and youth of France, already drained by so many years

[1] Napier, *The Peninsular War,* vol. i.

of glory, which shocked his counsellors. He drew the class of 1810 to the colours; he compelled the leading families to send their sons to the military colleges from the age of sixteen upwards. He brought some troops back from Spain, and in April, having a flow of life filling his ranks or training on behind him to the number of two hundred and forty thousand men, he marched against Austria. High authorities consider that the opening phase of the campaign of 1809 in the Danube valley ranks among the finest examples of military genius. He found his marshals ill-connected and in disarray. As he approached the front he sent his orders before him to the various corps. In what has been called the Battle of the Five Days—at Thann, Abensberg, Landshut, Eckmühl, and Ratisbon—he unfolded a single theme of war, which at every stage corrected the faulty dispositions into which his subordinates had drifted and was marked each day by a fresh and fruitful victory. The centre of the long Austrian front was pierced, and its fragments retreated with heavy losses. For the second time he entered Vienna at the head of his troops.

But he had not yet disposed of the Austrian army. When he attempted to cross the Danube at Aspern-Essling a sudden rise of the river broke his bridges and he narrowly escaped a decisive defeat at the hands of the Archduke Charles, ablest of the Austrian commanders. In the wooded island of Lobau he lay crouched for six weeks while he gathered reinforcements from every conceivable quarter of his Empire. Meanwhile the Czar, nominally his ally, trembled upon the verge of coming in against him. On July 4 he sallied out from his island and forced the passage of the Danube in the immense Battle of Wagram. Nearly four hundred thousand men fought on this field, and forty thousand fell. Europe was stunned. The Czar Alexander hastened to send his congratulations, and Austria submitted again to the conqueror's sword.

The Peninsular War and the Fall of Napoleon

WHEN the British sailed away from Corunna no organised forces remained in Spain to hinder Napoleon's Marshals. Everywhere Spanish armies were defeated, and only the implacable guerilla continued. In the opening months of 1809 the French were again free to move their armies where they pleased in the Peninsula. Soult now entered Portugal and established himself at Oporto. What was left of the original British expedition still occupied Lisbon, and by successive reinforcements was again raised to a strength of thirty thousand men. These, conjoined with an equal number of Portuguese, organised under a British general, Beresford, were sufficient to keep Soult inert for several months, during which he distracted himself with an intrigue to become King. The Government in London were divided in counsel upon what ought to be done. Should they resume a major campaign in the Peninsula or strike at the Netherlands? They decided to split their effort and make an attempt in both quarters. An expedition was mounted to seize the Dutch island at Walcheren, at the mouth of the Scheldt, and occupy Antwerp. It proved a costly diversion, but it seemed a promising plan. Few observers were then convinced that effective success could be won in distant Spain and Portugal. These doubts were not shared by Arthur Wellesley. In April he was reappointed to take command in Lisbon. He was to spend the next five years in the Peninsula, and return to London in triumph by way of the capital of France.

Wellesley resigned his seat in Parliament and his office as Chief Secretary, and reached Lisbon before the end of the month. He could choose between attacking Soult at Oporto or re-entering Spain to engage one or other of the numerous French Marshals whose corps were widely spread throughout the Peninsula. He decided first to clear Portugal. By a swift and secret march he reached the Douro, passed a division across it by night in boats and barges, and surprised Soult and his army in the town. With very small loss he compelled the Marshal, whose retreat southwards was also compromised by the operations of Beresford's Portuguese, to withdraw into the mountainous regions of the north. Soult was forced to abandon the whole of his artillery, his wounded, and the bulk of his baggage. He arrived at Orense, in Spanish Galicia, six days later, with an army disordered and exhausted, having lost since he entered Portugal over six thousand men. The passage of the Douro, the surprise of Oporto, and the discomfiture of Soult constituted a brilliant achievement for the new British general and paved the way for further action.

Wellesley now resolved to penetrate into the centre of Spain along the valley of the Tagus, and, joining the Spanish army under Cuesta, to engage Marshal Victor. Soult, his troops re-organised and re-equipped, was moving to join Victor, who would give him a decisive superiority. Wellesley's position at Talavera, a hundred miles south-west of Madrid, became precarious, and his soldiers were near starvation. Marshal Victor conceived himself strong enough to attack without waiting for the arrival of Soult. On the afternoon of July 27, 1809, the armies engaged. The French were fifty thousand strong. Wellesley had twenty thousand British and twenty-four thousand Spaniards, but these latter, though brave, could not be counted upon for serious work in a set battle. Their strength lay in harassing operations. The whole severity of the fighting was borne by sixteen thousand British and thirty thousand Frenchmen. Victor's attacks, which began in earnest on the 28th, were ill-concerted, and were repulsed with heavy loss after fierce mass-fighting with the bayonet. In the afternoon the crisis of the battle was reached. The English Guards, elated by the defeat of the French column in their front, were drawn from their place in the line by the ardour of pursuit. The British centre was open, and a French counter-stroke caused widespread disorder. But Wellesley had brought the 48th Regiment to the scene, who, in perfect array and discipline, advanced through the retreating soldiery, and, striking the French column on the flank, restored the day. A wild cavalry charge by the 23rd Light Dragoons, in which half the regiment fell, cut deeply into the enemy's flanks. By nightfall Marshal Victor accepted defeat and withdrew towards Madrid. The ferocity of the fighting may be judged from the British losses. Nearly 6,000 men out of Wellesley's total of 20,000 had fallen, killed or wounded; the French had lost 7,500 and twenty guns. The Spaniards claimed to have lost 1,200 men.

Wellesley was in no condition to pursue. The next morning General Robert Craufurd arrived with his Light Brigade, afterwards the famous Light Division, having marched sixty-two miles in twenty-six hours, the most rapid march by foot-soldiers on record. But Wellesley could no longer place any reliance upon the co-operation of his Spanish allies. They engaged the enemy in their own free way, which was certainly not his. Like Sir John Moore before him, he had run enormous risks, and had been saved only by the narrowest of margins. He withdrew unmolested along the Tagus back to Portugal. Not only had he established the reputation of a highly skilful and determined general, but the fighting quality

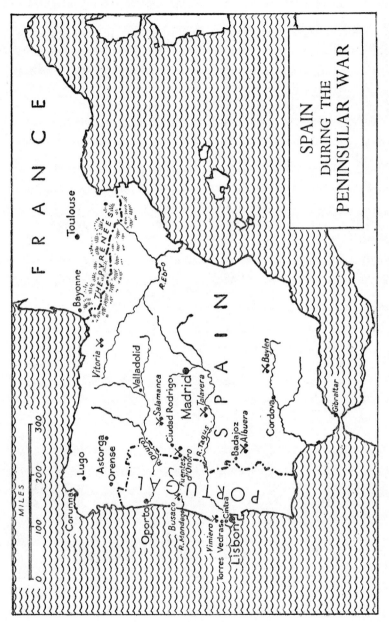

SPAIN
DURING THE
PENINSULAR WAR

FRANCE

Toulouse

Bayonne

THE PYRENEES

R. Ebro

Vitoria ✕

Valladolid

SPAIN

Lugo

Astorga

Orense

Corunna

R. Duero

Salamanca

Ciudad Rodrigo ✕

Fuentes d'Onoro

Madrid

R. Tagus

Talavera ✕

PORTUGAL

Oporto

Busaco

R. Mondego

Vimiero

Torres Vedras

Cintra

Lisbon

Badajoz ✕

Albuera

Beylen ✕

Cordova

Gibraltar

MILES

0   100   200   300

· 329 ·

of the British had made a profound impression upon the French. In England there was unwonted satisfaction. Sir Arthur Wellesley was raised to the peerage as Viscount Wellington, and, in spite of Whig opposition, was granted a pension of £2,000 a year for three years. Nelson was gone; Pitt was gone; but here at last was someone to replace them.

*   *   *   *   *

The close connection between political developments at home and the fortunes of the generals at the front is a remarkable feature of the history of these years. Each military reverse led to a crisis in the personal relations of the Cabinet Ministers in London. The disgrace of the Convention at Cintra had sharpened the rivalry and mutual dislike of Canning and Castlereagh. The former had been anxious to dismiss all the generals involved; the latter was interested in the political and military careers of the Wellesley brothers. Fortunately Castlereagh had prevailed. Now the two Ministers were at loggerheads over the disaster that threatened the expedition to Walcheren. Tempers were sharpened by the ill-defined and overlapping functions of the Foreign Secretary and the Secretary for War. The failing health of the Duke of Portland, the titular head of the Government, increased the rivalry of the two younger statesmen for the succession to the Premiership. A duel was fought between them, in which Canning was wounded. Both resigned office, and so did Portland. Spencer Perceval, hitherto Chancellor of the Exchequer, took over the Government. He was an unassuming figure, but an adroit debater, and in the conduct of the war a man of considerable resolution. Wellington's cause in Spain was favoured by the new administration. Perceval appointed as his Foreign Secretary the Marquess Wellesley, who steadfastly stood up for his younger brother in the Cabinet. The new War Minister, Lord Liverpool, was also well disposed. The Government did their best to satisfy Wellington's requirements, but,

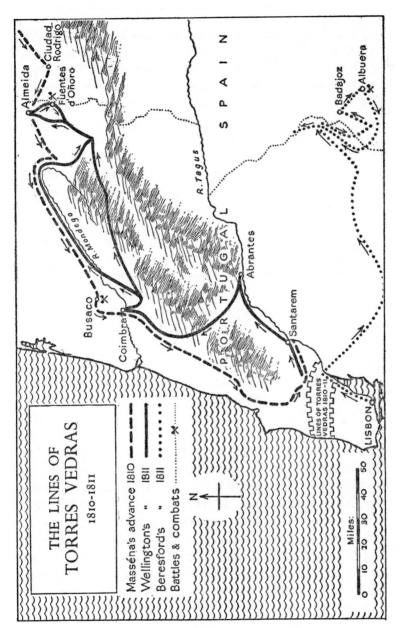

THE LINES OF
TORRES VEDRAS
1810-1811

Masséna's advance 1810 ----
Wellington's " 1811 ——
Beresford's " 1811 ••••••
Battles & combats ·········· ✗

N

Miles:
0 10 20 30 40 50

Almeida
Ciudad Rodrigo
✗ Fuentes d'Oñoro
Busaco ✗
Coimbra
R. Mondego
R. Tagus
SPAIN
PORTUGAL
Abrantes
Santarem
LINES OF TORRES VEDRAS 1810-11.
LISBON
Badajoz
✗ Albuera

· 331 ·

faced with the Whig Opposition and the Tory rebels in the Commons, they were continually obstructed by petty issues. In 1810 the King's renewed madness provoked a fresh crisis. Perceval skilfully averted a change in the political balance of power. George, Prince of Wales, became Regent, but he did not send for his former friends, the Opposition Whigs, as they had fondly hoped. The Prince Regent decided to trust his father's Ministers. It is to his credit that he did so. By frugal finance Perceval was able to maintain supplies and nourish the armed forces. The three years of his Government were marked by quietly growing efficiency.

*   *   *   *   *

These were testing years for Wellington. He commanded Britain's sole remaining army on the continent of Europe. Failure would have been disastrous to Britain, and to the patriots in Spain and Portugal; it would also have liberated large numbers of French troops for the reinforcement of Napoleon's ventures elsewhere. We can only speculate upon what further triumphs the Emperor might have enjoyed, even perhaps in Russia, but for the steady drain on his resources caused by Wellington's presence in the Peninsula. All this was not lost upon the English commander. But for the time being caution must be his policy. "As this is the last army England has," he drily wrote, "we must take care of it." Since the start of the Revolutionary wars many British lodgments had been made on the European continent, but none had long survived. The French had always bent every effort to driving the British into the sea. In 1810 they were massing for a fresh attempt. Wellington was resolved that no hasty evacuation would be forced upon him. All the previous winter he had been perfecting a series of fortified lines around Lisbon on the heights of Torres Vedras. This was to form his final bastion, and on these defences he gradually fell back.

The ablest of Napoleon's Marshals, Masséna, now headed

the French Army of Portugal. Having overwhelmed Spanish resistance, Masséna advanced across the frontier with eighty thousand men. The British numbered about twenty-five thousand, and their Portuguese allies the same. In September there was a stiff battle at Busaco. Sixty thousand French met fifty thousand Allies, only half of whom were British. But the Portuguese were by now well seasoned. The French were badly mauled and beaten. Wellington's withdrawal nevertheless continued. Suddenly the forward flow of the French came to a halt. Ahead of them rose the formidable lines of Torres Vedras, manned by the undefeated British, and all around extended a countryside deliberately laid waste. Masséna saw before him a prospect of bleak, hungry months, with no hope of successful assault. This was the hinge of the whole campaign. The French paused and dug into winter quarters. Wellington hovered about them, determined, as he put it, "to force them out of Portugal by the distresses they will suffer." So it turned out. In the following spring Masséna gave up. He retreated into Spain, leaving behind him seventeen thousand dead and eight thousand prisoners.

Portugal was now free, and Wellington's successes strengthened the position of the Government at home. Rejoicing in London and Lisbon however was mingled with a certain impatience. The British commander had eager critics, even within his own army, who could not appreciate the wisdom of his steadily developing strategy. Wellington himself was unperturbed by cries for haste. Nothing could shake him, and he kept his own counsel. He was determined to secure behind him a broad base and reliable communications before he ventured into the recesses of Spain. He must have in his hands the frontier fortresses of Badajoz and Ciudad Rodrigo, which guarded the roads to Madrid. Two French armies confronted him. Masséna, later replaced by Marmont, held the northern front in the province of Leon. Soult lay to the south in Andalusia. They and their fellow Marshals elsewhere in Spain commanded some quarter of a million men, of whom about a hundred thousand faced Wellington. They were much hampered by the incessant guerrilla. They could no longer count on living off the country, as French armies had hitherto done all over Europe; they quarrelled among themselves; and they were in constant receipt of angry instructions from their Emperor in Paris, based on fancy rather than on fact. For the genius of Napoleon, grappling with the problems of his Continental empire, failed him in his conduct of the distant, remorseless Spanish struggle.

Wellington had gauged precisely the size and scope of the task before him. A war of manœuvre unfolded in 1811 within the Spanish frontiers, and both the French armies blocking his advance were separately met and defeated at Fuentes d'Oñoro and Albuera. These were violent battles. Of Fuentes, which lies to the west of Ciudad Rodrigo, Wellington admitted, "If Boney had been there we should have been beaten." But Napoleon was not there. He was enmeshed in diplomacy and preparations for war elsewhere. Besides, he had just solemnised his second marriage. The Corsican's bride was a daughter of the proud house of Habsburg, the Archduchess Marie Louise. She gave him a long-desired son and heir, but little happiness.

The battles of Fuentes and Albuera, which was fought by Wellington's lieutenant, Beresford, were not decisive, but the British remained masters of the field. As Wellington wrote to Lord Liverpool, "We have certainly altered the course of the war in Spain; it has become to a certain degree offensive on our part." This was a typical understatement. In fact Wellington was already laying his plans for the day when he would drive the French back over the Pyrenees and carry the conflict into their own country. Amid the snows of January 1812 he was at last able to seize Ciudad Rodrigo. Four months later Badajoz fell to a bloody assault. The cost in life was heavy, but the way was opened for an overpowering thrust into Spain. Wellington and Marmont manœuvred about one another, each watching for the other to make a mistake. It was Marmont who erred, and at Salamanca Wellington achieved his first victory on the offensive in the Peninsular War. King Joseph Bonaparte fled from Madrid, and the British occupied the capital amid the pealing of bells and popular rejoicing. But there was still Soult to be dealt with. Coming up from the south, the French Marshal wheeled round Wellington's flank. He outnumbered the British commander by nearly two to one, and he was careful to offer no opening for promising attack. Wellington fell back once more on the Portuguese frontier. In the year's campaign he had shattered one French army and enabled the whole of Southern Spain to be freed from the French. But meanwhile heavier shadows from the East were falling upon Napoleon's Empire. It was the winter of the retreat from Moscow.

*   *   *   *   *

All through the spring of 1812 the Emperor had been gathering forces on a scale hitherto unknown in Europe, and as the summer came he drew them eastward from all his dominions. For two years past his relations with Russia had been growing more and more embittered. The Czar had gradually become convinced that no general European settlement could be made so long as the French Emperor dominated the scene. The amiable days of Tilsit were forgotten, and the Emperors who had sworn friendship on the raft in the river Niemen were now foes. Napoleon determined to get his blow in first, and to make it a shattering one. Although his generals and Ministers were reluctant and apprehensive a kind of delirium swept the martial classes of the Empire. The idea of a campaign larger than any yet conceived, more daring than the deeds of Alexander the Great, which might lead to the conquest of all Asia, took possession of the fighting men. Napoleon marshalled beyond the Vistula a group of armies nearly five hundred thousand strong. His Viceroy and step-son Eugene marched from Italy with fifty thousand Italians. Holland, Denmark, and all the states of the Rhine sent their contingents. Austria and Prussia took the field as Napoleon's dutiful allies, each with thirty thousand men. War-ravaged Europe after all these years of strife had never seen such an array. Among these armies moving eastwards were barely two hundred thousand Frenchmen. They formed the central spearhead of attack under the Emperor's direct command. Thus the great drama reached its culmination.

Many voices had warned Napoleon of the hardships and difficulties of campaigning in Russia. Nor did he disregard their advice. He had assembled what seemed for those days abundant transport and supply. It proved unequal to the event. In June 1812 he crossed the Niemen and headed straight for Moscow, some five hundred miles to the east. He was con-fronted by two main Russian armies totalling two hundred thousand men. His plan was to overwhelm them separately and snatch at the old Russian capital. He confidently ex-pected that the Czar would then treat for peace. All the other sovereigns of Europe in similar circumstances had hastened to bow the knee. But Russia proved a different proposition. In this fateful month of June the Russian Ambassador in London made a startlingly accurate prophecy. It reflected the expectations of the Czar and his advisers. "We can win by persistent defence and retreat," he wrote. "If the enemy be-gins to pursue us it is all up with him; for the farther he ad-vances from his bases of supply into a trackless and foodless country, starved and encircled by an army of Cossacks, his position will become more and more dangerous. He will end by being decimated by the winter, which has always been our most faithful ally." Defence, retreat, and winter—on these resources the Russian high command relied. Napoleon had studied the amazing Russian campaigns of the great Swede, King Charles XII. He thought he had profited by his reading. In the twentieth century another more ruthless dictator was to study Napoleon's errors. He too thought he had marked the lesson. Russia undeceived them both.

Before Napoleon the Russian armies fell back, avoiding the traps he set for them and devastating the countryside through which the French had to pass. At Borodino, some sixty miles west of the capital, the Russians turned at bay. There in the bloodiest battle of the nineteenth century General Kutusov inflicted a terrible mauling on Napoleon. Both the armies engaged, each of about a hundred and twenty thousand men, lost a third of their strength. Kutusov withdrew once more, and Moscow fell to the French. But the Russians declined to sue for peace. As winter drew near it was forced on Napoleon's mind that Moscow, burnt to a shell by accident or by design, was untenable by his starving troops. There was nothing for it but retreat through the gathering snows—the most celebrated and disastrous retreat in history. Winter now took its dreadful toll. Rearguard actions, however gallant, sapped the remaining French strength. Out of the huge Grand Army launched upon Russia only twenty thousand straggled back to Warsaw. Marshal Ney was said to have been the last Frenchman to quit Russian soil.

On December 5 Napoleon abandoned the remnant of his armies on the Russian frontier and set out by sleigh for Paris. Whatever salvaging could be done he left to his Marshals. For himself he was insensible of disaster. He still put trust in his Star. If he had failed to extend his Empire to the East, he could yet preserve it in the West. By tremendous efforts he would raise new forces and fight again. In the spring of 1813 he once more took the field. Half his men were raw recruits, and France was no longer behind him. Reluctant support was all he could get, and even his Marshals began to waver. Germany rose in the hour of his downfall. The spirit of nationalism, diffused by French armies, sprang up to baffle and betray the master of Europe. Coalitions were formed, backed by the finances of Britain. Napoleon was offered the chance of an honourable peace. Thinking that fate could be reversed by genius in battle, he rejected it. One by one his hesitant allies dropped away. Sweden, ruled by the French Marshal Bernadotte; Prussia, Austria, and even Saxony and Bavaria, his own client states, abandoned him. The Czar was resolved upon a march for the Rhine. Central Europe, so long subservient to France, joined the Russian thrust. A series of gigantic engagements were fought in Saxony and Silesia. At last in the three-day battle of Leipzig in October all Napoleon's foes closed in upon him. Nearly half a million men were involved on each side. In this Battle of the Nations Napoleon was overwhelmed and driven west-wards to the frontiers of France. The Allies gathered on the borders of their enemy for the first time since 1793. The great Revolutionary and Imperial adventure was drawing to a close.

* * * * *

On the southern front Wellington's achievement surpassed all expectations. Issuing from his frontier bastions in May 1813, he flourished his cocked hat. "Farewell, Portugal!" he exclaimed. "I shall never see you again." Nor did he. He once more bundled King Joseph Bonaparte out of Madrid. He cleared the whole north of Spain and herded the retreating French into the old mountain kingdom of Navarre. At the bat-tle of Vitoria on June 21 he routed Marshal Jourdan and drove his forces over the Pyrenees. News of this victory heart-ened the Czar and the Allied armies of Europe in Saxony. Little more than a tithe of the forces circling round Dres-den and Leipzig had been engaged at Vitoria. But the effect was signal. Except for Catalonia, Spain was free from the

French. For the first and only time in history the success of British arms was greeted by a *Te Deum* sung in Russian. Tenaciously Wellington pursued his purpose of reducing, as he put it, "the power and influence of the grand disturber of Europe." By the spring of 1814 he was on French soil and had occupied Bordeaux. In early April he sought out and defeated his old antagonist, Soult, at Toulouse.

For Napoleon the end had already come. In the south the front had crumpled; to the east Prussians, Russians, and Austrians were reaching into the heart of France. Napoleon was never more brilliant in manœuvre than during his brief campaign of 1814. In February he beat the allies at Montmirail and Montereau. Rivers which flow between the fronts of opposing armies have never proved a secure shield. In this campaign Napoleon used the much surer advantages to defence of rivers which run parallel to the lines of advance. His manœuvres were a model of the military art, and by crossing and recrossing both the Aisne and the Marne he compelled his superior opponents to withdraw in disorder. But the combined strength of Europe was too much for him. The forces of opposition to his rule in France openly rose against him. Fouché and Talleyrand, long conspiring in doubt, now put it to themselves that France could only be saved by deserting her Emperor. At the end of March Marshal Marmont, defending Paris, gave up and surrendered the capital. On April 3 Napoleon abdicated and retired to the island of Elba. The long, remorseless tides of war rolled back, and at the Congress of Vienna the Powers prepared for the diplomatic struggle of the peace.

* * * * *

Britain was represented at Vienna by Castlereagh. In 1812 the Prime Minister, Perceval, had been shot dead by a madman in the lobby of the House of Commons. His colleague, Lord Liverpool, took over the administration, and remained in power for fifteen years. Castlereagh rejoined the Government as Foreign Secretary, an office he was to hold until his death. The war Governments of these years have received graceless treatment at the hands of Whig historians. Yet Perceval and Liverpool, Canning and Castlereagh, bore the burden with courage and increasing skill. Castlereagh was now to take an influential part in the reconstruction of Europe. His voice was foremost in proposing a just and honourable peace. He had already in March 1814 negotiated the Treaty of Chaumont between the principal Allies which laid the foundations for the future settlement. Castlereagh believed in the Balance of Power. This is a concept that became unpopular in the twentieth century during the interval between the World Wars. We have since learnt the need for a balance when great power is concentrated in the hands of two or three nations. In Castlereagh's day there were five Great Powers in Europe. His object was to concert their interests. Harmony between them was too much to expect. But at least it might be arranged that the jars of international life should not lead inevitably to war.

Castlereagh's principal colleagues at Vienna were Metternich, the Austrian Chancellor, and Talleyrand, the spokesman of France. Metternich was a confirmed believer in the old régime of the eighteenth century; his desire was to put back the clock to pre-Revolutionary days. In his later years, when bereft of power, he was proud to declare that he had always been a "Rock of Order." The supple Talleyrand had served in turn the Revolution, Napoleon, and now the Bourbons; his aim was to salvage for France all that he could from the ruins of the Imperial adventure. Between them Castlereagh held the advantage of disinterestedness.

The most urgent problem was the government of France. Napoleon had gone, but who was to replace him? It was Talleyrand who persuaded the Powers to restore the Bourbons in the person of Louis XVIII, brother of the executed king. After the glories of the Revolution and the triumphs of Napoleon not even the royalist pen of Chateaubriand could invest the shadowy monarchy with prestige or popularity. Louis however represented at least a tradition, a fragment of the political faith of France; above all, he represented peace. He was himself a man of mildness and accommodation. The years of exile had not soured him. The main social changes of the past twenty-five years were tacitly accepted; the system of government and administration created under Napoleon was continued by his successors, with the added novelty of a partially free Press and the beginnings of a Parliamentary constitution.

A politic moderation was displayed in the terms offered to the defeated enemy: no indemnity, no occupation by Allied troops, not even the return of the art treasures which had been looted from the galleries of Europe. The foreign conquests of the Emperor were surrendered, but the essential unity of France remained untroubled and the territory over which Louis XVIII ruled was slightly more extensive than that of Louis XVI. The reason for this moderation is not difficult to comprehend. To disrupt France would add too much weight to one or other of the Continental Powers. Besides, it would kindle a flame of vengeance in the hearts of all Frenchmen.

The British were principally concerned with the colonial settlement. Many conquests were returned, yet the Peace of Paris, which was the outcome of the Congress, marks another stage in the establishment of the new Empire which was replacing the lost American colonies. The captured French colonies were surrendered, with the exception of Mauritius, Tobago, and St Lucia. The Dutch recovered their possessions in the East Indies. Sir Stamford Raffles, who had governed with singular success the rich island of Java, saw this British prize given back to its former owners. It was not until some years later that he founded the trading settlement which is now the city of Singapore. At the price of three millions sterling Britain acquired part of Guiana from the Dutch. The Government however was most concerned with those possessions which had a strategic value as ports of call. For that reason it held on to Malta, and the key of the route to India, the Cape of Good Hope. From this acquisition in South Africa a troubled saga was to unfold. Dutch Ceylon was kept, and Danish Heligoland, which had proved a fine base for breaking the Continental System and smuggling goods into Germany. These gains were scattered and piecemeal, but, taken together, they represented a powerful consolidation of the Imperial structure.

On the Continent the main preoccupation of the Powers was to draw a *cordon sanitaire* around France to protect Central Europe from the infections and dangers of revolution. In the North was established a precarious and uneasy union of Calvinist Holland and Catholic Belgium in the Kingdom of the Netherlands—a union which lasted only until 1830. The Rhineland, mainly at the instance of the British Government, was allotted to Prussia. In the South the King of Sardinia regained Piedmont and Savoy, with the old Republic of Genoa as a further sop. Throughout the rest of Italy the authority of Austria stretched unchallenged. Lombardy and Venetia, Trieste and Dalmatia, were placed under direct Austrian rule. Austrian Archdukes reigned in Florence and Modena. The Empress Marie Louise was allotted the Duchy of Parma, more because she was a Habsburg than because she was Napoleon's wife. It was laid down that her son should not succeed her. Bonaparte blood was to be barred from thrones. At Naples for a while Marshal Murat was left in possession of his stolen kingdom. But not for long. Soon the Bourbons were restored, and over them Austrian influence also reigned supreme.

So much for Western Europe. The root trouble lay in the East. Russia wanted Poland, Prussia wanted Saxony. Left to themselves each might have accepted the demands of the other, but this was far from agreeable to either France or Austria. Castlereagh, as fearful of the expansion of Russia as Metternich was of Prussia, took sides against so sweeping a settlement. An alliance between Britain, France, and Austria was formed to resist these pretensions, if necessary even by war. War did not prove necessary. Russia consented to swallow the greater part of Poland, with many professions from the Czar that Polish rights and liberties would be respected. He did not live up to his promises. Prussia, grumbling, accepted two-fifths of Saxony as well as the Rhineland. This compromise was reached only just in time. For while Congress danced at Vienna and the statesmen of Europe replotted the map Napoleon was brooding and scheming in his new retreat at Elba. Long before the wrangling of the Powers had ended he again burst upon the scene.

Washington, Adams, and Jefferson

THE confused and tumultuous issues of European politics reached America in black and white. Debate on the French Revolution raged throughout the country. Corresponding societies on the Revolutionary model sprang up wherever Jeffersonian principles were upheld, while the Federalist Press thundered against the Jacobins of the New World, and, like Burke in England, denounced them as destroyers of society.

Controversy became less theoretical and much more vehement as soon as American commercial interests were affected. Tempers rose as American ships and merchandise endured the commerce-raiding and privateering of France and Britain. Both parties demanded war—the Federalists against France and the Jeffersonians against England. President Washington was determined to keep the infant republic at peace. His task was smoothed by the antics of the French Revolutionary envoy to the United States, Citizen Genêt, who, finding the Government reluctant to honour the Franco-American alliance of 1778, meddled in American politics, attempted to raise troops, and greatly embarrassed his political allies. In August 1793 Washington demanded his recall. But, knowing the sharp activity of the guillotine in France, Genêt wisely married an American heiress and subsided peaceably in the New World.

Washington prevailed, and it was he who enunciated the first principle of traditional American foreign policy. In April

1793 his famous proclamation of neutrality declared that it was "the disposition of the United States to pursue a conduct friendly and impartial towards the belligerent Powers." Infringements would render American citizens liable to prosecution in the Federal courts. But relations with Britain were clouded by unsettled issues. Hamilton's Federalist Party was deeply committed to maintaining a friendly commerce with Britain. The overseas trade of New England was largely financed by London bankers. The carrying trade between the two countries brought great profit to the shipowners of the Eastern states, and they strongly opposed any suggestion of war on the side of Revolutionary France. The farmers and pioneers of the frontier felt differently. To them Britain was the enemy who refused to honour the treaty of 1783 by evacuating the frontier posts on the Canadian border, and was pushing her fur trade from Canada southwards, inciting the Indians against American settlers, and threatening the flank of their own advance to the West. The British in their turn resented the failure of the American Government to settle the large debts still unpaid since before the Revolution. Meanwhile British interference with American shipping, on the plea that it was helping to sustain France, stung public opinion throughout the United States.

Washington decided that the whole field of Anglo-American relations must be revised and settled, and in 1794 he appointed John Jay, Chief Justice of the Supreme Court, as Envoy Extraordinary to London. The British Government felt little tenderness for their late rebels. They knew their military weakness, and Washington's need of the support of Hamilton's party. Moreover, they were considerably aided by Jay's ineptitude in negotiation. A treaty was drawn up which made few concessions to America. The frontier posts were evacuated, and the way to the West thus lay open and unmolested to American pioneers, but no guarantees were given about future British relations with the Indians. Britain paid some compensation for damage done to American ships on the high seas, but refused to modify her blockade or renounce the right to seize ships and cargoes destined for France and her allies. No satisfaction was obtained about the impressment of American seamen for service in the Royal Navy. Worst of all, Jay was forced to yield on the issue of the debts owing to British creditors, and the United States were bound to compensate British claimants for outstanding losses.

The effect on the Federalist Party was most damaging. The Western states were angered by the incomplete arrangements on the Canadian frontier. The Southerners were threatened with serious injury by the debts clause. The treaty revealed and exposed the superiority of British diplomacy and the weakness of the new American Government. The atmosphere was charged afresh with distrust, and the seeds were sown for another war between Britain and the United States.

Washington's second term of office expired in the spring of 1797, and he prepared longingly for his retirement to Mount Vernon. His last days in power were vexed by the gathering assaults of the anti-Federalists and the din of preparations for the new Presidential election. Washington and many of his associates were alarmed by the growth of party spirit. They clung to the view that the diverse interests of the nation were best reflected in a balanced and all-embracing Government. The notion that two great parties should perpetually struggle for power was foreign and repellent to them. Only Jefferson, who had already resigned from the administration, had a clear vision of the rôle that parties should play. He saw the advantages of directing the strife of factions into broad streams and keeping an organised Opposition before the country as a possible alternative Government. But in Washington's mind the dangers of faction were uppermost when in September he issued his Farewell Address to the nation. This document is one of the most celebrated in American history. It is an eloquent plea for union, a warning against "the baneful effects of the Spirit of Party." It is also an exposition of the doctrine of isolation as the true future American policy. "Europe has a set of primary interests, which to us have none, or a very remote relation. Hence she must be engaged in frequent controversies, the causes of which are essentially foreign to our concerns. Hence therefore it must be unwise in us to implicate ourselves by artificial ties in the ordinary vicissitudes of her politics or the ordinary combinations and collisions of her friendships or enmities. Our detached and distant situation invites us to pursue a different course. . . . 'Tis our true policy to steer clear of permanent alliances with any portion of the foreign world. . . . Taking care always to keep ourselves, by suitable establishments, in a respectable defensive posture, we may safely trust to temporary alliances for extraordinary emergencies."

George Washington holds one of the proudest titles that history can bestow. He was the Father of his Nation. Almost alone his staunchness in the War of Independence held the American colonies to their united purpose. His services after victory had been won were no less great. His firmness and example while first President restrained the violence of faction and postponed a national schism for sixty years. His character and influence steadied the dangerous leanings of Americans to take sides against Britain or France. He filled his office with dignity and inspired his administration with much of his own wisdom. To his terms as President are due the smooth organisation of the Federal Government, the establishment of national credit, and the foundation of a foreign policy. By refusing to stand for a third term he set a tradition in American politics which has only been departed from by President Franklin Roosevelt in the Second World War.

For two years Washington lived quietly at his country seat on the Potomac, riding round his plantations, as he had long wished to do. Amid the snows of the last days of the eighteenth century he took to his bed. On the evening of December 14, 1799, he turned to the physician at his side, murmuring, "Doctor, I die hard, but I am not afraid to go." Soon afterwards he passed away.

* * * * *

John Adams succeeded Washington as head of the American State. He had been nominated by the Federalist Party. Fear of chaos and disorder, a basic distrust of democracy, had cooled his revolutionary ardour and made him a supporter of Hamilton. Of independent mind, he was a thinker rather than a party politician, an intellectual rather than a leader. Though agreeing with Hamilton on the need for strong government and the preservation of property, Adams opposed using the Federal machine for the benefit of particular economic interests and was by no means a wholehearted Federalist. In his judgments he was frequently right, but he lacked the arts of persuasion. He was bad at handling men, and his reputation has suffered accordingly. He was nevertheless one of the ablest political thinkers among American statesmen.

In foreign affairs a new crisis was at hand. The rise of Napoleon Bonaparte dimmed the high regard of Americans for their first ally, France. Fears began to grow that the French might acquire from Spain the provinces of Louisiana and Florida. A vigorous and ambitious European Power would then replace a weak one as a barrier between the expanding United States and the Gulf of Mexico. News also came of extensive French propaganda among the French-speaking inhabitants of Canada. There was a strong reaction, and for the last time the Federalists managed to outdistance their opponents. War hysteria swept the country, and they seized the opportunity to push through legislation which gave the executive extraordinary powers over aliens. The Naturalisation Act of 1798 extended the qualifying period of residence from five to fourteen years, and the Aliens Act gave the President the right to expel foreigners from the country by decree. More pointed was the Sedition Act, which in effect imposed a rigid censorship on the Press and was aimed specifically at the Opposition newspapers. The result was an intense constitutional conflict. It was in vain that Hamilton exhorted his colleagues, "Let us not establish tyranny. Energy is a very different thing from violence." Jefferson was determined to take up the challenge. He drafted resolutions, which were passed both in Kentucky and Virginia, maintaining that a state could review acts of Congress and nullify any measure deemed unconstitutional. This fateful doctrine has been heard since in American history, and these resolves of 1798 became a platform of State Rights in later years.

The Federalists' attack on the liberty of the individual marked the beginning of their fall. Hamilton, who had resigned from the Treasury some years earlier, thought he could now regain power by forcing a war with France. He conceived a vast plan for dividing, in concert with Great Britain, the Spanish colonies in the New World. A grandiose campaign took shape in his mind, with himself leading the American Army southwards to the mouth of the Mississippi. But the person who extinguished these hopes was the President. Although he was no lover of the masses Adams hated both plutocracy and militarism. Until 1799 he had shown no signs of opposition to the Federalists, but he now realised that war was very near. His complete powers as President over foreign affairs made it easy for him to act swiftly. He suddenly announced the appointment of an envoy to France, and on October 1, 1800, an American mission in Paris concluded a commercial treaty with the French. On the very same day France in secret purchased Louisiana from Spain.

Adams's term of office was now expiring and the Presidential elections were due. They present a complicated spectacle, for there were dramatic splits on both sides. The Federalists had not forgiven Adams for stopping them from going to war with France. Nevertheless he was the only Federalist candidate with any hope of success, and so he won the nomination. Real power in the party however still lay with Hamilton, and he in his resentment hampered Adams in every way he could.

Ranged on the Republican side stood Jefferson, flanked for the office of Vice-President by Aaron Burr, a corrupt New York politician. By a curiosity of the American Constitution in those days, which was soon to be remedied, the man who won the largest number of votes became President, while the runner-up was declared Vice-President. Thus it was quite possible to have a President and a Vice-President belonging to opposite parties. Adams was beaten by both Jefferson and Burr, but Jefferson and Burr each gained an equal number of votes. There was little love lost between them. Burr tried to overthrow his chief when the deadlock was referred for decision to the House of Representatives. But here Hamilton stepped in to frustrate him. Local politics have always excited strong loyalties and antipathies in the United States, stronger often than Federal issues. Hamilton and Burr were at grips for power in New York. Hamilton could not stomach the thought of Burr becoming President, and in the House of Representatives he threw his weight behind Jefferson. Thus by a remarkable twist of fortune Hamilton's old opponent became the third President of the United States, and the centre of influence once more shifted from Massachusetts to Virginia. But the significance of the accession to power of Thomas Jefferson must not be exaggerated. The Supreme Court, headed by John Marshall, remained the zealous, impartial guardian and upholder of the rights and authority of the Federal Government. Jefferson himself, though a sincere agrarian democrat, was neither unrealistic nor sentimental, and events soon compelled him to follow the theme and methods of his predecessors.

*   *   *   *   *

The United States in which Jefferson was inaugurated as President on March 4, 1801, had grown fast during their short existence and were still growing. In the twenty-five years since the Declaration of Independence the population had nearly doubled and was now about five and a half millions. Three new inland states had been set up and admitted to the Union: Vermont in the North, Kentucky and Tennessee in the Central South. Red Indian confederacies that blocked the westward migration had been decisively defeated, and their lands divided into territories which were in their turn to form states. The nation was everywhere thrusting outward from its original Atlantic seaboard. Its commerce upon the high seas now flowed from China, round Cape Horn, to the countries of Europe by way of the fast-rising ports of Boston, Baltimore, and above all New York. Philadelphia remained the greatest of American cities, but it was gradually losing its position as the centre of the life of the Union. It now ceased to be the political capital. Jefferson was the first President to be inaugurated in the new city of Washington, for which spacious plans had been drawn up. As yet only one wing of the Capitol, which housed Congress, had been built and the White House was incomplete; there was a single convenient tavern, a few boarding-houses for Senators and Congressmen, and little else except quagmire and waste land. Jefferson was undaunted by the hardships of his backwoods capital. Thought of the fine city that would one day arise kindled his idealism, and its pioneering life suited his frugal, homely manner.

It was impossible for the President to ignore the world struggle. The farmers whom Jefferson represented depended for their markets upon the Old World, and the Western states and territories needed unhindered transport for their produce down the Mississippi to the Gulf of Mexico. At the mouth of the great river lay the port of New Orleans, and New Orleans was still in Spanish hands. Rumours of the secret French purchase of Louisiana were now circulating, and were soon given substance. Bonaparte dispatched an expedition to suppress a Negro rising under Toussaint L'Ouverture in the French island colony of Haiti. This accomplished, it was to take possession of Louisiana in the name of the French Government. Thus while the Treaty of Amiens imposed an uneasy peace on Europe trained French troops had arrived once more off the North American continent, and would shortly, it seemed, proceed to the mainland. This, like the French menace from Canada in the eighteenth century, drew the English-speaking nations together. "The day that France takes possession of New Orleans . . ." wrote Jefferson to the American envoy in Paris, "we must marry ourselves to the British Fleet and nation. We must turn all our attention to a maritime force, and make the first cannon-shot which shall be fired in Europe a signal for . . . holding the two continents of America in sequestration for the common purposes of the united British and American nations. This is not a state of things which we seek or desire. It is one which this measure [the purchase of Louisiana], if adopted by France, forces on us." This was a surprising development in the views of Jefferson, hitherto an admirer of France and opponent of Great Britain. But theoretical opinions must often give way before the facts of international politics. At any rate, it is wise if they do, and Jefferson had his share of practical wisdom.

In the summer of 1802 France compelled the Spaniards to close New Orleans to American produce. The whole West Country was ablaze with anger and alarm. As Jefferson wrote to his envoy in Paris, "There is on the globe one single spot the possessor of which is our natural and habitual enemy. It is New Orleans, through which three-eighths of our produce must pass to market." James Monroe was now sent on a special mission to Paris to try to purchase Louisiana, or at least New Orleans, from the French. While he was on his way American plans were suddenly forwarded by events elsewhere. The French expedition to Haiti ended in disaster, with the loss of thirty thousand men. The renewal of war between France and Britain after the Peace of Amiens was also imminent. With dramatic swiftness Napoleon abandoned all hopes of American empire, and to the astonishment of the American envoy offered to sell all the Louisiana territories which Spain had ceded to France. Monroe arrived in Paris in time to complete the purchase, and for fifteen million dollars Louisiana was transferred to the United States.

At a stroke of the pen the United States had thus doubled its area and acquired vast lands out of which a dozen states later arose. It was to prove the finest bargain in American history. Yet when the news crossed the Atlantic there was a vehement outcry. Had Napoleon the legal right to sign these lands away? Had the United States paid out an immense sum merely to acquire a faulty title-deed? Moreover, there was no express power in the Constitution for the Federal Government to carry out such an act. But it was necessary to confirm it at once lest Napoleon should change his mind. The Senate was called upon to ratify the cession, and Jefferson claimed that the negotiations were valid under his treaty-making powers in the Constitution. The Federalists loudly denounced the new acquisition, with its high purchase price and undefined frontiers. They realised it would provoke an extensive shift of power in the Union and a rapid growth of the agricultural interests of the West. But all the influence and pressure of the Eastern seaboard were marshalled in vain. In December 1803 the American flag was raised upon the Government buildings of New Orleans and the United States entered upon the possession of nine hundred thousand square miles of new territory.

The acquisition of Louisiana brought a new restlessness into American politics and a desire for further advance. West Florida, which stretched along the Gulf of Mexico, still belonged to Spain, and beyond the newly acquired lands the plains of Texas beckoned. Troubles were stirred up between the Western states and territories and the Federal capital. The evil genius of these years is Aaron Burr.

Burr, as we have seen, had missed a chance of becoming President in 1800 largely owing to Hamilton's intervention. Now in 1804 Hamilton's opposition stopped him being selected for the Governorship of New York. He challenged Hamilton to a duel. Hamilton accepted, intending to satisfy honour by firing wide. But Aaron Burr shot to kill, and thus put an end to the life of one of the outstanding figures in the founding years of the American Republic. Discredited in the eyes of all, Burr cast about for means of creating a new American realm of his own. He even sought a large bribe from the British Government. Whether he hoped to detach the Western states from the Union or to carve off a slice of the Spanish dominions is still obscure and disputed, but his career ended abruptly with his arrest and trial for treason. For lack of evidence he was acquitted, and went into voluntary exile.

Jefferson had been triumphantly re-elected President in 1804, but his second term of office was less happy than his first. Under the stress of Westward expansion his party in the East was splitting into local factions. The renewal of European war had also revived the old sinister issues of embargo, blockade, and impressment. Jefferson was faced with the provocations of the British Fleet, which continually arrested ships and took off sailors on the verge of American territorial waters, and sometimes even within them. The British were entitled by the customs of the time to impress British subjects who happened to be serving in American ships; but they also made a practice of impressing American citizens and many sailors whose nationality was doubtful. To this grievance was added another. In retaliation for Napoleon's Berlin Decrees, establishing a Continental blockade of Britain, Orders in Council were issued in London in 1806 imposing severe restrictions on all neutral trade with France and her allies. United States commerce was hard hit by both these belligerent measures. But, as the Battle of Trafalgar had proved, the Royal Navy was much more powerful than the French, and it was at the hands of the British that American shipping suffered most.

Amidst these troubles Jefferson remained serenely determined to preserve the peace. But public opinion was mounting against him. On his recommendation in 1807 Congress passed an Embargo Act which forbade American ships to sail for foreign waters. It prohibited all exports from America by sea or land, and all imports of certain British manufactures. Jefferson hoped that the loss of American trade would oblige the belligerents to come to terms, but in fact his measure proved far more damaging to American commerce than to either the British or French. The economy of New England and all the seaports of the Atlantic coast depended on trade with Britain. From everywhere in the Eastern states protests went up, New England being particularly vociferous. The Federalists were quick to rally their forces and join in the outcry. Jefferson's own party, the Republicans, revolted and divided against him. After it had been in operation for fourteen months he was forced to withdraw the embargo. Three days later his term of office expired and he retired to his Virginian estate of Monticello.

The failure of his policies in the last two years of his Presidency should not obscure the commanding position of Thomas

Jefferson in the history of the United States. He was the first political idealist among American statesmen and the real founder of the American democratic tradition. Contact with the perils of high policy during the crisis of world war modified the original simplicity of his views, but his belief in the common man never wavered. Although his dislike of industrialism weakened in later years, he retained to the end his faith in a close connection between yeoman farming and democracy. His strength lay in the frontier states of the West, which he so truly represented and served in over thirty years of political life.

The War of 1812

THE new President of the United States in March 1809 was James Madison. As Jefferson's Secretary of State he had had much experience of public office, and he was a political theorist of note. There was a stubborn side to his nature, and his practical skill and judgment were not always equal to that of his predecessor. Madison inherited an inflamed public opinion and a delicate state of relations with Great Britain. At first there were high hopes of a settlement. Madison reached a provisional agreement with the British Minister in Washington which was very favourable to British interests. But the Foreign Secretary, Canning, repudiated the document and recalled the Minister responsible for it. He was never so happy in his handling of America as he was in Europe. For three years Anglo-American relations grew steadily worse. Madison was deceived by Napoleon's revocation of the Berlin Decrees which had closed all European ports controlled by France. He now tried to get England to reciprocate by annulling her Orders in Council against trade with ports in French hands. In vain wiser politicians warned him that Napoleon's action was merely a diplomatic move "to catch us into a war with England."

The unofficial trade war with the United States was telling heavily upon England. The loss of the American market and the hard winter of 1811–12 had brought widespread unemployment and a business crisis. Petitions were sent to Parliament begging the Government to revoke the Orders in Council. After much hesitation Castlereagh, now at the Foreign Office, announced in the House of Commons that the

Government had done so. But it was too late. The Atlantic crossing took too long for the news to reach America in time. On June 18, 1812, two days after Castlereagh's announcement, Congress declared war on Great Britain.

In the following week Napoleon began his long-planned invasion of Russia.

The root of the quarrel, as American historians have pointed out, lay not in rival interpretations of maritime law, but in the problems of the Western frontier. The seaboard states, and especially New England, wanted peace. Their main concern was America's foreign trade, which had already gravely diminished. War with Britain would bring it to a stop. But American domestic politics had brought to power representatives of the West and South-West who were hostile to Britain, and it was they, not the merchants of the Atlantic coastline, who forced America into the conflict. On the frontiers, and especially in the North-West, men were hungry for land, and this could be had only from the Indians or from the British Empire.

Trouble with the Indians had been brewing for some time. The pioneers of the early nineteenth century were woodsmen. They had already occupied the forest lands held by Redskin tribes in Illinois and Indiana; they now coveted the forests of British Canada round the Great Lakes, with their unsettled Crown territory and tiny population of Loyalists. As the Western territories of America filled up, pressure mounted for a farther north-westerly move. In 1811 the Red Indians bordering on the Ohio united under their last great warrior leader, Tecumseh. On his orders the tribes now showed themselves impervious to the temptations of liquor and trade. Alarm spread along the frontier. A revival of Indian power would put an end to further expansion. Troops were called out by the Governor of Indiana, William Henry Harrison, who had been largely responsible for the recent westward push, and in November 1811 the Indian Confederacy was overthrown at the Battle of Tippecanoe.

It is one of the legends of American history that the resistance of the Indians was encouraged and organised from Canada—a legend created by the war party of 1812. A new generation was entering American politics, headed by Henry Clay from Kentucky and John C. Calhoun from South Carolina. These young men formed a powerful group in the House of Representatives, which came to be known as the "War Hawks." They had no conception of affairs in Europe; they cared nothing about Napoleon's designs, still less about the fate of Russia. Their prime aim and object was to seize Canada and establish American sovereignty throughout the whole Northern continent. Through the influence of Clay the President was won over to a policy of war. The causes of the conflict were stated in traditional terms: impressment, violations of the three-mile limit, blockades, and Orders in Council. Opinion in America was sharply divided, and New England voted overwhelmingly against the declaration of war, but the "War Hawks" with their vociferous propaganda had their way. The frontier spirit in American politics was coming in with a vengeance, and it was sure of itself. Moreover, the frontier farmers felt they had a genuine grievance. There was some good ground for the slogan of "Free Trade and Sailors' Rights" which they adopted. British restrictions on American shipping were holding up the export of their produce. A short expedition of pioneers would set things right, it was thought, and dictate peace in Quebec in a few weeks. Congress adjourned without even voting extra money for the American Army or Navy.

*   *   *   *   *

On paper the forces were very unequal. The population of the United States was now seven and a half millions, including slaves. In Canada there were only five hundred thousand people, most of them French. But there were nearly five thousand trained British troops, about four thousand Canadian regulars, and about the same number of militia. The Indians could supply between three and four thousand auxiliaries.

The American Regular Army numbered less than seven thousand men, and although with great difficulty over four hundred thousand state militia were called out few were used in Canada. On the American side never more than seven thousand men took part in any engagement, and the untrained volunteers proved hopeless soldiers. Nor was this all. The Seven Years' War had shown that Canada could only be conquered by striking up the St Lawrence, but the Americans had no sufficient Navy for such a project. They were therefore forced to fight an offensive war on a wide frontier, impassable at places, and were exposed to Indian onslaughts on their columns. Their leaders had worked out no broad strategy. If they had concentrated their troops on Lake Ontario they might have succeeded, but instead they made half-hearted and unco-ordinated thrusts across the borders.

The first American expedition ended in disaster. The ablest British commander, General Isaac Brock, supported by the Indian Confederacy, drove it back. By August the British were in Detroit, and within a few days Fort Dearborn, where Chicago now stands, had fallen. The American frontier rested once more on a line from the Ohio to Lake Erie. The remainder of the year was spent on fruitless moves upon the Niagara front, and operations came to an inconclusive end. The British in Canada were forced to remain on the defensive while great events were taking place in Europe.

The war at sea was more colorful, and for the Americans more cheering. They had sixteen vessels, of which three surpassed anything afloat. These were 44-gun frigates, the *Constitution,* the *United States,* and the *President.* They fired a heavier broadside than British frigates, they were heavily timbered, but their clean lines under water enabled them to outsail any ship upon the seas. Their crews were volunteers and their officers highly trained. A London journalist called them "a few fir-built frigates, manned by a handful of bastards and outlaws." This phrase was adopted with glee by the Americans, who gloried in disproving the insult. The British fleet on the transatlantic station consisted of ninety-seven sail, including eleven ships of the line and thirty-four frigates. Their naval tradition was long and glorious, and, with their memories of Trafalgar and the Nile, the English captains were confident they could sink any American. But when one English ship after another found its guns out-ranged and was battered to pieces the reputation of the "fir-built frigates" was startlingly made. The American public, smarting at the disasters in Canada, gained new heart from these victories. Their frigates within a year had won more successes over the British than the French and Spaniards in two decades of warfare. But retribution was at hand. On June 1, 1813, the American frigate *Chesapeake,* under Captain Lawrence, sailed from Boston harbour with a green and mutinous crew to accept a challenge from Captain Broke of H.M.S. *Shannon.* After a fifteen-minute fight the *Chesapeake* surrendered. Other American losses followed, and command of the ocean passed into British hands. American privateers however continued to harry British shipping throughout the rest of the war.

These naval episodes had no effect on the general course of the war, and if the British Government had abandoned impressment a new campaign might have been avoided in 1813. But they did not do so, and the Americans set about revising their strategy. The war was continuing officially upon the single issue of impressment, for the conquest of Canada was never announced as a war aim by the United States.

Nevertheless Canada was their main objective. By land the Americans made a number of raids into the province of Upper Canada, now named Ontario. Towns and villages were sacked and burnt, including the little capital which has since become the great city of Toronto. The war was becoming fiercer. During the winter of 1812–13 the Americans had also established a base at Fort Presqu'île, on Lake Erie, and stores were laboriously hauled over the mountains to furnish the American commander, Captain Oliver H. Perry, with a flotilla for fresh-water fighting. In the autumn Perry's little armada sailed to victory. A strange amphibious battle was fought in September 1813. Negroes, frontier scouts, and militiamen, aboard craft hastily built of new green wood, fought to the end upon the still waters of the lake. The American ships were heavier, and the British were defeated with heavy loss. "We have met the enemy," Perry reported laconically, "and they are ours."

Harrison, American victor at Tippecanoe, could now advance into Ontario. In October, at the Battle of the Thames, he destroyed a British army which had beaten him earlier in the year, together with its Indian allies. The Indian Confederacy was broken and Tecumseh was killed. Thus the United States were established on the southern shores of the Great Lakes and the Indians could no longer outflank their frontier. But the invasion of Upper Canada on land had been a failure, and the year ended with the Canadians in possession of Fort Niagara.

*　　*　　*　　*　　*

Hitherto the British in Canada had lacked the means for offensive action. Troops and ships in Europe were locked in the deadly struggle against Napoleon. Moreover the British Government was anxious not to irritate the New England states by threatening them from the North. Even the blockade was not extended to cover Massachusetts until 1814, and indeed the British forces were almost entirely fed from the New England ports. But by the spring of 1814 a decision had been reached in Europe. Napoleon abdicated in April and the British could at last send adequate reinforcements. They purposed to strike from Niagara, from Montreal by way of Lake Champlain, and in the South at New Orleans, with simultaneous naval raids on the American coast. The campaign opened before Wellington's veterans could arrive from the Peninsula. The advance from Niagara was checked by a savage drawn battle at Lundy's Lane, near the Falls. But by the end of August eleven thousand troops from Europe had been concentrated near Montreal to advance by Burgoyne's old route down the Hudson valley. In September, under Sir George Prevost, they moved on Plattsburg, and prepared to dispute the command of Lake Champlain. They were faced by a mere fifteen hundred American regulars, supported by a few thousand militia. All depended on the engagement of the British and American flotillas. As at Lake Erie, the Americans built better ships for fresh-water fighting, and they gained the victory. This crippled the British advance and was the most decisive engagement of the war. Prevost and his forces retired into Canada.

At sea, in spite of their reverses of the previous years, the British were supreme. More ships arrived from European waters. The American coast was defenceless. In August the British General Ross landed in Chesapeake Bay at the head of four thousand men. The American militia, seven thousand strong, but raw and untrained, retreated rapidly, and on the 24th British troops entered the Federal capital of Washington, President Madison took refuge in Virginia. So hasty was the American withdrawal that English officers sat down to a meal cooked for him and his family in the White House. The White House and the Capitol were then burnt in reprisal for the conduct of American militiamen in Canada. Washington's home on the Potomac was spared and strictly guarded by the British. The campaign ended in an attempt to land at Baltimore, but here the militia were ready; and General Ross was killed and a retreat to the ships followed.

In December the last and most irresponsible British on-slaught, the expedition to New Orleans, reached its base. But here in the frontier lands of the South-West a military leader of high quality had appeared in the person of Andrew Jackson. As an early settler in Tennessee he had won a reputation in warfare against the Indians. When the British now tried to subsidise and organise them Jackson pursued them into Spanish West Florida, and occupied its capital, Pensacola.

Meanwhile eight thousand British troops had landed at New Orleans under Sir Edward Pakenham, who had com-manded a division at Salamanca. The swamps and inlets in the mouth of the Mississippi made an amphibious operation extremely dangerous. All men and stores had to be trans-ported seventy miles in row-boats from the Fleet. Jackson had hastened back from Florida and entrenched himself on the left bank of the river. His forces were much inferior in num-bers, but composed of highly skilled marksmen. On the morning of January 8, 1815, Pakenham led a frontal assault against the American earthworks—one of the most unin-telligent manœuvres in the history of British warfare. Here he was slain and two thousand of his troops were killed or wounded. The only surviving general officer withdrew the army to its transports. The Americans lost seventy men, thirteen of them killed. The battle had lasted precisely half an hour.

Peace between England and America had meanwhile been signed on Christmas Eve, 1814. But the Battle of New Or-leans is an important event in American history. It made the career of a future President, Jackson, it led to the belief that the Americans had decisively won the war, and it created an evil legend that the struggle had been a second War of Independence against British tyranny.

*   *   *   *   *

On the American domestic scene events had been moving fast. New England, dependent upon shipping and commerce, was suffering heavily and her leaders were embarrassed. They had supported the Federalist Party, now in disarray; they resented the predominance of the Western states and territories which had pushed them into war, and they began to contemplate leaving the Union. In the summer of 1814 Massachusetts had been thrown upon her own resources. British troops were in Maine; the harbours were blockaded by British ships. The burden of taxation fell largely upon the New England states, yet the Federal Government seemed incapable of providing even a local defence. In October a Convention of delegates from Massachusetts, Rhode Island, and Connecticut was summoned to meet. They assembled at Hartford in December. They wanted a separate peace with Great Britain and no further connection with the fast-growing West. They believed that the British expedition to New Orleans would succeed and that the West, cut off from the sea, would probably leave the Union on its own initiative. The President was alarmed and the war party feared the worst. Fortunately for the United States the moderate New England politicians gained the upper hand at Hartford and the Convention only drew up a severe arraignment of Madison's administration. For the time being secession was killed. "To attempt," they declared, "upon every abuse of power to change the Constitution would be to perpetuate the evils of revolution."

Andrew Jackson's victory at New Orleans and the success of the peace negotiations produced an outcry against the disloyalty of New England and attached a permanent stigma to the Federalist Party. Yet the doctrine of State Rights, to which the Hartford delegates held, was to remain a vivid force in American politics. The war had also done much to diversify New England's economy. To her shipping and commercial interests were added great and rewarding developments in manufacture and industry.

Peace negotiations had been tried throughout the war, but it was not until January 1814 that the British had agreed to treat. The American Commissioners, among them Henry Clay, reached Ghent in June. At first the British refused to discuss either neutral rights or impressment, and they still hoped for an Indian buffer state in the North-West. It was Wellington's common sense which changed the atmosphere. The previous November he had been asked to take command in America, but he had studied reports of the Battle of Plattsburg and realised that victory depended on naval superiority upon the lakes. He saw no way of gaining it. He held moreover that it was not in Britain's interest to demand territory from America on the Canadian border. Both sides therefore agreed upon the *status quo* for the long boundary in the North. Other points were left undetermined. Naval forces on the Great Lakes were regulated by a Commission in 1817, and the disputed boundary of Maine was similarly settled later. By the time the British Navy went to war again impressment had been abandoned.

Thus ended a futile and unnecessary conflict. Anti-American feeling in Great Britain ran high for several years, but the United States were never again refused proper treatment as an independent Power. The British Army and Navy had learned to respect their former colonials. When news of peace reached the British army in the New World one of the soldiers wrote, "We are all happy enough, for we Peninsular soldiers saw that neither fame nor any other military distinction could be acquired by this type of milito-nautico-guerrilla-plundering warfare."

The results of the peace were solid and enduring. The war was a turning-point in the history of Canada. Canadians took pride in the part they had played in defending their country, and their growing national sentiment was strengthened. Many disagreements were still to shake Anglo-American relations. Thirty years later in the dispute over the possession of Oregon vast territories were involved and there was a threat of war. But henceforward the world was to see a three-thousand-mile international frontier between Canada and the United States undefended by men or guns. On the oceans the British Navy ruled supreme for a century to come, and behind this shield the United States were free to fulfil their continental destiny.

Elba and Waterloo

IN the New Year of 1815 peace reigned in Europe and in America. In Paris a stout, elderly, easy-going Bourbon sat on the throne of France, oblivious of the mistakes made by his relations, advisers, and followers. His royalist supporters, more royal than their King, were trying the patience of his new-found subjects. The French people, still dreaming of Imperial glories, were ripe for another adventure. At Vienna the Powers of Europe had solved one of their most vexatious problems. They had decided how to apportion the peoples of Saxony and Poland among the hungry victors, Prussia and Russia. But they were still by no means in accord on many details of the map of Europe which they had met to redraw. After the exertions of twenty years of warfare they felt they had earned leisure enough to indulge in haggling, bargains, and festivity. A sharp and sudden shock was needed to re-call them to their unity of purpose. It came from a familiar quarter.

Napoleon had for nine months been sovereign of Elba. The former master of the Continent now looked out upon a shrunken island domain. He kept about him the apparatus of Imperial dignity. He applied to the iron mines and tunny fisheries of his little kingdom the same probing energy that had once set great armies in motion. He still possessed an army. It included four hundred members of his Old Guard, a few displaced Polish soldiers, and a local militia. He also had a navy, for which he devised a special Elban ensign. His fleet consisted of a single brig and some cutters. To these puny armaments and to the exiguous Elban Budget he devoted his attention. He would henceforth give himself up, he had told the people of Elba, to the task of ensuring their happiness. For their civic dignitaries he invented an impressive uniform. At Porto Ferrajo, his capital, he furnished a palace in the grand manner. He played cards with his mother and cheated according to his recognised custom. He entertained his favourite sister and his faithful Polish mistress. Only his wife, the Empress Marie Louise, and their son were missing. The Austrian Government took care to keep them both in Vienna. The Empress showed no sign of wishing to break her parole. Family Habsburg loyalty meant more to her than her husband.

A stream of curious foreign visitors came to see the fallen Emperor, many from Britain. One of them reported, perhaps not without prejudice, that he looked more like a crafty priest than a great commander. The resident Allied Commissioner on Elba, Sir Neil Campbell, knew better. As the months went by close observers became sure that Napoleon was biding his time. He was keeping a watch on events in France and Italy. Through spies he was in touch with many currents of opinion. He perceived that the restored Bourbons could not command the loyalty of the French. Besides, they had failed to pay him the annual pension stipulated in the treaty of peace. This act of pettiness persuaded Napoleon that he was absolved from honouring the treaty's terms. In February 1815 he saw, or thought he saw, that the Congress of Vienna was breaking up. The Allies were at odds, and France, discontented, beckoned to him. Campbell, the shrewd Scottish watchdog, was absent in Italy. Of all this conjunction of circumstances Napoleon took lightning advantage. On Sunday night, the 26th of February, he slipped out of harbour in his brig, attended by a small train of lesser vessels. At the head of a thousand men he set sail for France. On March 1 he landed near Antibes. The local band, welcoming him, played the French equivalent of *Home, Sweet Home*.

The drama of the Hundred Days had begun, and a blood-less march to Paris ensued. Royalist armies sent to stop the intruder melted away or went over to him. Marshal Ney, "the Bravest of the Brave," who had taken service under the Bourbons, boasted that he would bring his former master back to Paris in an iron cage. He found he could not resist the Emperor's call; he joined Napoleon. Other Marshals who had turned their coats now turned them again. Within eighteen days of his landing Napoleon was installed in the capital. The Bourbons ran for cover, and found it at Ghent. Meanwhile the Emperor proclaimed his peaceful intentions, and at once started shaping his army. He bid for support by promising liberal institutions to the French people. In fact he dreamed of restoring all the old forms of Empire as soon as he had behind him the consolidation of military victory. But the mood of France had changed since the high noon of Auster-litz, Jena, and Wagram. There was enthusiasm, but no longer at the topmost fighting pitch. The Army and its leaders were not what they had been. The frightful losses of the Russian campaign and of Leipzig could not be made good. Since 1805 a hundred and forty-eight French generals had fallen in battle. Of those that remained only half were now loyal to Napoleon. Marshals like Marmont and Victor had fled to Belgium. Victor in Brussels had taken refuge in the Welling-ton Hotel. It was named after the Duke who had beaten him at Talavera. Marshal Berthier, the Emperor's indispensable Chief of Staff, failed to rally to him, and Napoleon had to rely, as he afterwards complained, on "that idiot Soult." He showed all his usual energy. He abounded in self-confidence. But the flashing military judgment of earlier years was dimmed. The gastric ulcer from which he had long suffered caused him intermittent pain.

Yet the Emperor remained a formidable figure and a chal-lenge to Europe. The Powers at Vienna acted with unaccustomed speed and unanimity. They declared Napoleon an outlaw. He was pronounced a disturber of world peace who had rendered himself liable to public indictment. The Powers, too, set about marshalling their forces. The British Government, which had led the country and the world against the Corsican, realised that they would have to bear the brunt of a whirlwind campaign. It would take time for Russia and Austria to muster their strength. Prussia was the only main ally then in readiness. There was no time to lose. Wellington recommended the immediate transport of an army to the Netherlands, to form bases for a march on Paris and prepare for a clash upon the frontiers. Within a month of the escape from Elba Wellington took up his command at Brussels.

The state of his army did not please the Duke. Many of his best troops from the Peninsula had gone to America, including his Chief of Staff, Sir George Murray. With great difficulty the British Government had collected six regiments of cavalry and twenty-five battalions of infantry, consisting partly of Peninsular veterans and partly of untrained boys. The biggest deficiency was in artillery. On the conclusion of the Peace of Paris in 1814 the British Cabinet had ordered the wholesale discharge of gunners and drivers, and the shortage was now serious. But there were, as in all European wars, the Continental allies and auxiliaries. The King of Great Britain was still King of Hanover. Hanoverian troops, on their way home through the Netherlands, were halted and joined the new army. Wellington, at a loss for numbers, tried to persuade the Portuguese to send a few battalions. He had taught them the arts of war, and he was proud of his "fighting cocks," as he called them. But his efforts were in vain. The Dutch and Belgian troops put under his command by the King of the Netherlands looked unreliable. Their countries had for twenty years been occupied by the French, and the Belgians at least had taken not unkindly to French rule. The sympathies of their rank and file would probably waver towards Napoleon. There were contingents also from Nassau and other German provinces. As the summer drew near Wellington assembled a mixed force of eighty-three thousand men, of whom about a third were British. He bluntly cursed, as was his habit, the quality of his untried troops, while bending all his endeavours to train and transform them. The main support for his new adventure must be Marshal Blücher. The Prussians had a force of a hundred and thirteen thousand men, but nearly half of them were untrained militia. They lay in Eastern Belgium. Wellington, with his staff, planned a large-scale advance into France. He meant to take the offensive. He did not propose tamely to await a Napoleonic onslaught. In his calm, considering way, he worked it all out. Based upon Brussels, he took up a line between Maubeuge and Beaumont, with the Prussians on his left holding the position between Philippeville and Givet. As it happened, the Emperor seized his usual initiative.

*　　*　　*　　*　　*

Napoleon could not afford to waste a day. Nor did he do so. His two main enemies stood on his north-eastern frontier within a few days' march of his capital. He must strike immediately at his gathering foes. The moral value of victory would be overwhelming, and the prestige of the British Government would be shaken. His admirers in London, the pacific Whigs, might replace the Tories and proffer a negotiated peace. Louis XVIII would be driven into permanent exile and the Belgian Netherlands restored to French rule. This achieved, he could face with equanimity the menaces of Austria and Russia. Such were his hopes while he applied his intense power of will to rousing the French nation. Assembling a sufficient army threw a heavy strain upon exhausted France. Five corps of about a hundred and twenty-five thousand men were organised on the frontier fortress

line. The protection afforded by these fortresses, behind which
he could build up at leisure, gave Napoleon the impetus in
the opening phases of the campaign. Wellington was obliged
to canton his troops upon a possible defence line of forty
miles and to guard against a French stroke at the point of
junction between the British and Prussian armies. During the
early days of June tension was heightening. It was plain, or
at least predictable, that Napoleon would attempt to rout
Wellington's and Blücher's armies separately and piecemeal.
But where would he land his first blow? Wellington waited
patiently in Brussels for a sign of the Emperor's intention.
He and his great opponent were to cross swords for the first
time. They were both in their forty-sixth year. Quietly on
June 15 Napoleon crossed the Sambre at Charleroi and
Marchiennes, driving the Prussian forward troops before him
to within twenty-five miles of Brussels. He had struck at the
hinge of the Allied armies. The capture of Brussels would
be a great forward stride. Possession of a capital city was
always a lure for him, and a source of strength.

Liaison between the British and Prussians was mysteriously
defective and hours passed before the news reached Wellington. It seemed as though there was no detailed plan of co-
operation between the Allied commanders. Military intelligence, as so often at the neap of events, was confusing and
contradictory. There were no British troops on the Waterloo-
Charleroi road, which was held thinly by a Dutch-Belgian
division. On the night of the 15th, while the French armies
massed to destroy the Prussians, the Duchess of Richmond
gave a ball in Brussels in honour of the Allied officers.
Wellington graced the occasion with his presence. He knew
the value of preserving a bold, unruffled face. Amid the
dancing he reflected on the belated news which had reached
him. At all costs contact must be maintained with the Prussians and the French advance upon Brussels held. Wellington

resolved to concentrate on the strategic point of Quatre-Bras. In the early hours of the morning of the 16th Picton's brigade rumbled down the Brussels road to join the Dutch troops already covering this dangerous ground lying open between the British and Prussian array.

For the French everything depended upon beating the Prussians before forcing Wellington north-westwards to the coast. Napoleon had in mind the vision of a shattered British army grimly awaiting transports for home in the Flemish ports. At Corunna and Walcheren such things had happened before. Leaving Ney with the French left, the Emperor swung with sixty-three thousand men and ninety-two guns to meet the main Prussian army, centred in Ligny. But the tardiness and sureness of Wellington's movements deceived him. Realising that so far only a small force held the position at Quatre-Bras, he ordered Ney to attack, and then meet him that evening in Brussels. At two o'clock in the afternoon of the 16th the French went into action on a two-mile front. Wellington himself arrived to take command with a force of seven thousand men and sixteen guns. The brunt of the battle fell upon Picton's leading brigade. After having marched for twelve hours from Brussels these Peninsular veterans steadily pressed on. In vain the French cavalry swirled round them while the Allied Dutch and Belgian infantry were edged from the field. There was little tactical manœuvre in the fierce struggle which swayed backwards and forwards on that June afternoon at the cross-roads on the way to Brussels. It was a head-on collision in which generalship played no part, though leadership did. Wellington was always at his coolest in the hottest of moments. In this battle of private soldiers the fire-power of the British infantry prevailed. Out of thirty thousand men engaged by nightfall on their side the Allies lost four thousand six hundred; the

French somewhat less. But Ney had not gained his objective. Brussels was not in his grasp.

On the French side the staff work had hardly been creditable. D'Erlon, under Napoleon's orders, had marched aimlessly about, at one time in the direction of Ligny and at another towards Quatre-Bras. Napoleon had gained the advantage at the opening of the campaign, but he had not intended that both wings of his army should be in action at once. He seems to have departed from his original plan. At Ligny however he won a striking success. Marshal Blücher was out-generalled, his army split in two, battered by the magnificent French artillery, and driven back on Wavre. Again liaison between the Allied armies broke down. Wellington had no immediate information of the outcome at Ligny, nor of the subsequent movements of the Prussians. He had held the French left at Quatre-Bras, but their victory to the east enabled them to concentrate their strength against him and the Brussels road. Wellington's main body had gathered around the village of Quatre-Bras by the time he learnt of the Prussian defeat. Napoleon decided in the small hours of the 17th to send Marshal Grouchy with thirty-three thousand men to pursue the Prussians while he flung his main weight against Wellington. The crisis of the campaign was at hand.

There seems no doubt that in the opening days Wellington had been surprised. As he confessed at the time, Napoleon's movements had "humbugged" him. Years later, when he read French accounts of Quatre-Bras, he declared with his habitual frankness, "Damn them, I beat them, and if I was surprised, if I did place myself in so foolish a position, they were the greater fools for not knowing how to take advantage of my faults." Immediately after the battle his methodical mind was in full command of the situation. His plan was to fall back upon a prepared position at Mont St Jean, which

British engineers had examined before the campaign of the previous year. There he would accept battle, and all he asked from the Prussians was the support of one corps.

Wellington himself had inspected this Belgian countryside in the autumn of 1814. He had noted the advantages of the ridge at Waterloo. So had the great Duke of Marlborough a century earlier, when his Dutch allies had prevented him from engaging Marshal Villeroi there. His unfought battle was now to unroll. Throughout the night of the 16th and 17th a carefully screened retreat began, and by morning the Waterloo position, a line of defence such as Wellington had already tested in the Peninsula, was occupied. Upon the French must be forced the onus of a frontal attack. Wellington knew that time was playing against his adversary. Swift results must be achieved by Napoleon if he was to establish himself again in France. A line of fortified farms and rolling slopes made up the Allied front, held by sixty-three thousand men and a hundred and fifty-six guns. The French troops failed to harass the retreat. Their staff work had again gone awry. Napoleon was unaware of what had happened at Quatre-Bras, and there was an imminent danger that the Prussians would fall back and unite with Wellington. That was indeed their intention. Blücher and his Chief of Staff, Gneisenau, who was the brain of the Prussian army, were retiring north-west from Ligny in the direction of Brussels. Grouchy, mis-informed or misjudging, thought they were moving north-east towards Liége. He remained out of touch and ineffective. Grouchy's was a costly mistake for the French. Meanwhile Napoleon, furious to hear of Wellington's skilful withdrawal, pounded in his carriage down the Brussels road with his advance-guard in a desperate attempt to entrap the British rear. The mercy of a violent storm slowed up progress. The English cavalry galloped for safety through the thunder and torrential rain. An angry scene took place upon the meeting of Napoleon and Ney, who was greeted with the words from the Emperor, "You have ruined France!" As Napoleon reached the ridge of Waterloo and saw the British already in their positions he realised how complete had been their escape.

*   *   *   *   *

Late in the morning of the 18th of June the French attacked both flanks of the Allied position, of which the key points were the fortified château of Hougoumont on the right and the farm of La Haye Sainte in the middle. Napoleon promised his staff they would sleep that night in Brussels. And to Soult, who raised some demur, he said, "You think Wellington a great general because he beat you. I tell you this will be a picnic." Then seventy thousand French troops and two hundred and twenty-four guns were concentrated for the decisive assault. Fierce cannonades were launched upon the Allied posts. The battle swayed backwards and forwards upon the grass slopes, and intense fighting centred in the farm of La Haye Sainte, which eventually fell to the French. At Hougoumont, which held out all day, the fighting was heavier still. In the early afternoon one of the most terrific artillery barrages of the time was launched upon Wellington's infantry as preparation for the major cavalry advance of fifteen thousand troopers under Ney. Under the hail of the French guns Wellington moved his infantry farther back over the ridge of Waterloo to give them a little more shelter. On seeing this Ney launched his squadrons in a series of attacks. Everything now depended upon the British muskets and bayonets. Anxiously Wellington looked eastwards for a sign of the Prussians. They were on their way, for Blücher was keeping faith. But the French cuirassiers were upon the Duke. They never reached the infantry squares. As one eye-witness wrote: "As to the so-called charges, I do not think that on a single occasion actual collision occurred. I many times saw the cuirassiers come on with boldness to within

· 377 ·

some twenty or thirty yards of a square, when, seeing the steady firmness of our men, they invariably edged away and retired. Sometimes they would halt and gaze at the triple row of bayonets, when two or three brave officers would advance and strive to urge the attack, raising their helmets aloft on their sabres; but all in vain, as no efforts could make the men close with the terrible bayonets and meet certain destruction."

No visible decision was achieved. Napoleon, looking through his glasses at the awful *mêlée,* exclaimed, "Will the English never show their backs?" "I fear," replied Soult, "they will be cut to pieces first." Wellington too had much to disturb him. Although the Prussians had been distantly sighted upon the roads in the early afternoon, they were slow in making their presence felt upon the French right. But by six o'clock in the evening Ney's onslaughts had failed and the Prussians were beating relentlessly upon the wing. They drew off fourteen thousand men from the forces assailing Wellington. The French made a final effort, and desperate fighting with no quarter raged again round the farms. The Imperial Guard itself, with Ney at its head, rolled up the hill, but again the fury of British infantry fire held them. The long-awaited moment to counter-attack had come. Wellington had been in the forefront of danger all day. On his chestnut, Copenhagen, he had galloped everywhere, issuing brusque orders, gruffly encouraging his men. Now he rode along his much-battered line and ordered the advance. "Go on, go on!" he shouted. "They will not stand!" His cavalry swept from the ridge and sabred the French army into a disorganised mass of stragglers. Ney, beside himself with rage, a broken sword in his hand, staggered shouting in vain from one band to another. It was too late. Wellington handed over the pursuit to the Prussians. In agony of soul Napoleon followed the road back to Paris.

* * * * *

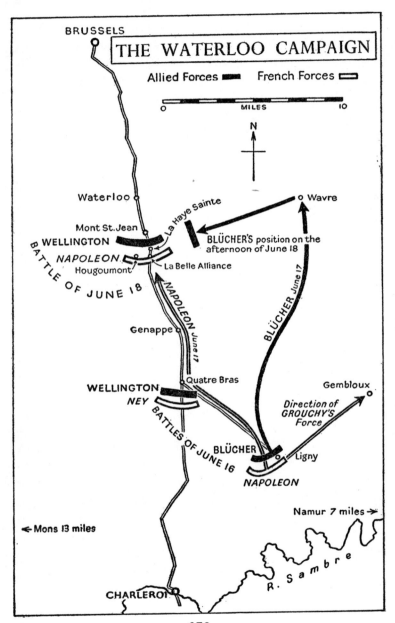

BRUSSELS

THE WATERLOO CAMPAIGN

Allied Forces ▬▬   French Forces ▭▭

0   MILES   10

N

Waterloo
La Haye Sainte
Mont St.Jean
WELLINGTON
NAPOLEON
Hougoumont
La Belle Alliance
BATTLE OF JUNE 18
NAPOLEON June 17
Genappe
BLÜCHER June 17
o Wavre
BLÜCHER'S position on the
afternoon of June 18

Quatre Bras
WELLINGTON
NEY
BATTLES OF JUNE 16
Gembloux
Direction of
GROUCHY'S
Force
BLÜCHER
Ligny
NAPOLEON

Mons 13 miles
Namur 7 miles →

R. Sambre

CHARLEROI

· 379 ·

Late that night Blücher and Wellington met and embraced. *"Mein lieber Kamerad,"* said the old German Field-Marshal, who knew not a word of English, *"quelle affaire!,"* which was about all the French he could command. This brief greeting was greatly to Wellington's laconic taste. It was a story he delighted to repeat in later years when he was Lord Warden of the Cinque Ports, recalling his memories at Walmer. The Duke rode back to Brussels. The day had been almost too much even for a man of iron. The whole weight of responsibility had fallen on him. Only the power and example of his own personality had kept his motley force together. The strain had been barely tolerable. "By God!" as he justly said, "I don't think it would have been done if I had not been there." As he took tea and toast and had the casualty lists read to him he broke down and wept.

Letters of congratulation poured in to the Duke in the days that followed. Prince Metternich, the Austrian Chancellor, conveyed his appreciation of what he cautiously called the "brilliant opening of the campaign." In fact it was all over. Blücher and his Prussians marched steadily and uneventfully upon Paris. Napoleon had reached his capital three days after the battle. He had a momentary surge of hope. He would fight again in France a campaign like that of 1814. But no one shared his optimism. The grand officials of the Empire, who owed him their positions and fortunes, had had enough. On June 22 he abdicated and retired to Malmaison. The treacherous Fouché headed a provisional Government and set about treating with the Allies and with Louis XVIII. There was nothing else to be done. On July 6 Blücher and Wellington entered the capital. One of the Duke's first tasks was to restrain the Prussians from resentful vengeance. Their army in 1806 had been thrashed by the French, their country mutilated and their garrison towns occupied. They nourished a bitterness which the Duke did not share. When

Blücher proposed to blow up the bridge of Jena over the Seine, named after the celebrated Prussian defeat, Wellington posted British sentries to prevent him. Two days after the Allies' arrival Louis XVIII appeared. His second restoration was largely of Wellington's making. Most Frenchmen and many of the Allies would have preferred a monarchy under the Duke of Orleans, a Regency for Napoleon's young son, or a constitutional republic. Wellington had no high regard for the Bourbons, but he was convinced that France under their shaky rule would no longer have the power to disturb the peace of Europe. Louis XVIII was no *Grand Monarque* and could never aspire to become one. Wellington, like many great soldiers when victory is complete, looked forward to an age of tranquillity. Laurels and bays had been won; it was time to cultivate the olive.

*   *   *   *   *

Napoleon left Malmaison at the end of June. He made for Rochefort, on the Biscay coast, narrowly evading capture on the way by Blücher's Prussians. Had they taken him they would have shot him. He had thoughts of sailing for America, and he ordered a set of travel books about the transatlantic continent. Perhaps a new Empire might be forged in Mexico, Peru, or Brazil. The alternative was to throw himself upon the mercy of his most inveterate foe. This is what happened. Captain Maitland in the *Bellerophon* was cruising off Rochefort with orders to prevent any French ships from putting to sea. With him Napoleon entered into negotiation. Maitland offered him asylum on his ship. He could not forecast what the British Government would decide to do with his eminent hostage. Nor did he make any promise. Napoleon hoped he might be kept in pleasant captivity in some English country house or Scottish castle. Marshal Tallard and other French generals a century earlier had enjoyed their forced residence in England. The ex-Emperor wrote a flattering letter to the

· 381 ·

Prince Regent, whom he addressed as "the strongest, the stubbornest, the most generous of my foes." When the Prince read this missive it must have helped to convince him that he and not his generals or his Ministers had really won the war. On this matter he did not need much convincing. The *Bellerophon* anchored in Torbay, and curious Devonshire crowds gazed upon the "Corsican ogre," while Lord Liverpool and the Cabinet deliberated in London. Newspapers clamoured that Napoleon should be put on trial. The Government, acting for the Allies, decided on exile in St Helena, an island about the same size as Jersey, but very mountainous, and far away. Escape from it was impossible. On July 26 the Emperor sailed to his sunset in the South Atlantic. He never permitted himself to understand what had happened at Waterloo. The event was everybody's fault but his own. Six years of life in exile lay before him. He spent them with his small faithful retinue creating the Napoleonic legend of invincibility which was to have so powerful an effect on the France of the future.

*   *   *   *   *

The Congress of Vienna had completed its work in June. It remained for the emissaries of the Powers to assemble in Paris and compose a new peace with France. The task took three months. The Prussians pressed for harsh terms. Castlereagh, representing Britain, saw that mildness would create the least grievance and guard best against a renewal of war. In this he had the hearty support of Wellington, who now exerted a unique authority throughout Europe. The second Treaty of Paris, concluded in November, was somewhat stiffer than that of 1814. Together with the loss of certain small territories, France was to pay an indemnity of seven hundred million francs and to submit to an Allied army of occupation for three years. Yet no intolerable humiliations were involved. In the moderation of the settlement with France the treaty

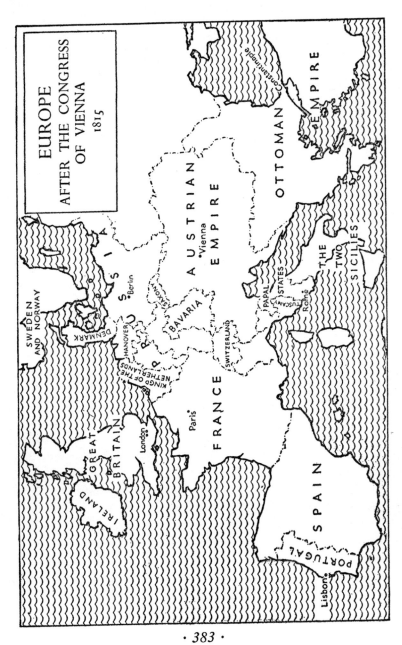

EUROPE
AFTER THE CONGRESS
OF VIENNA
1815

Constantinople

OTTOMAN EMPIRE

AUSTRIAN EMPIRE

•Vienna

SWEDEN AND NORWAY

P R U S S I A

•Berlin

SAXONY

DENMARK

BAVARIA

HANOVER•

KINGD OF THE
NETHERLANDS

SWITZERLAND

GREAT BRITAIN

IRELAND

London•

Paris•

F R A N C E

PAPAL STATES

TUSCANY

Rome•

THE TWO SICILIES

S P A I N

PORTUGAL

Lisbon•

had its greatest success. Wellington took command of the occupying army. For the next three years he was practically a Great European Power in himself. Castlereagh, with his sombre cast of mind, thought the treaty would be justified if it kept the peace for seven years. He had built better than he knew. Peace reigned for forty years between the Great Powers, and the main framework of the settlements at Vienna and Paris endured until the twentieth century.

The treaties drawn up in 1815 were the last great European settlements until 1919–20. Herbert Fisher, the Liberal historian and Cabinet Minister, has thus compared the two settlements: "Talleyrand's formula of legitimacy summed up the spirit of the settlement. It was legitimacy which restored the Bourbons to France, saved Saxony for the Wettins, and confirmed the power of the house of Sardinia. No respect was paid to nationality or to the wishes of the populations concerned. In all essentials, therefore, the statesmen who drew up the settlement at Vienna were sharply opposed in aims and principles to the artificers of the Europe in which we now live. The peace treaties of 1920 constituted a democratic settlement made possible only by the downfall of those very monarchies to which the Congress of Vienna had entrusted the policing of Europe. The settlement of 1920 created new republics, redistributed frontiers, accepted the dissolution of the old Austrian Empire, and built up a Europe on that principle of self-determination which had been preached by the French Revolutionaries, but was afterwards long lost to view. To the Congress of Vienna the principles of President Wilson would have been anathema. Guided by Metternich, Talleyrand, and Castlereagh, it held that the well-being of Europe was to be secured not by compliance with the assumed wishes of the peoples concerned, but only by punctual obedience to legitimate authority." [1]

[1] H. A. L. Fisher, *History of Europe* (1935).

Castlereagh might dismiss the Holy Alliance which was now formed between the three autocratic Powers, Russia, Prussia, and Austria, as "a piece of sublime mysticism and nonsense." It was indeed a product of the Czar Alexander's soaring, cloudy brain. Yet for the sake of stability Castlereagh was prepared to see Romanovs, Hohenzollerns, and Habsburgs re-establish their reactionary authority throughout the greater part of Central and Eastern Europe in defiance of all popular movements for nationality and freedom. Such was the price that Europe paid for the overthrow of Napoleon. Even the principle of legitimacy was discarded when it clashed with the interests of one of the Great Powers. Poland, still independent in 1792, was no longer accounted legitimate in 1814. Part of the kingdom of Saxony and the prince-bishoprics of the Rhine went to Prussia, the Republic of Venice and its Adriatic seaboard to Austria. Legitimacy presented no obstacle to territorial expansion.

So the scene closes on a protracted peace-making after the longest of the world wars. The impetus of the French Revolution had been spread by the genius of Napoleon to the four quarters of Europe. Ideals of liberty and nationalism, born in Paris, had been imparted to all the European peoples. In the nineteenth century ahead they were to clash resoundingly with the ordered world for which the Congress of Vienna had striven. If France was defeated and her Emperor fallen, the principles which had inspired her lived on. They were to play a notable part in changing the shape of government in every European country, Britain not excepted.

INDEX

Abbeville, 75
Abensberg, Battle of, 325
Abercromby, General James, 153
Abercromby, General Sir Ralph, 294
Aboukir Bay, 293
Abraham, Heights of, 155, 185
Acre, 294
Adams, John, 178, 239; Presidency of, 348–50
Adams, Samuel, and stamp duty, 171; creates machinery for revolt, 176–7; attempt to arrest, 180; and Western territories, 239; mentioned, 178, 184
Addington, Henry, 297
Agrarian democrats, 253, 257, 265
Aire, 84
Aislabie, John, 110
Aisne, River, 339
Aix-la-Chapelle, Treaty of, 136, 152, 216
Albany, 195, 197
Albermarle, A. J. van Keppel, first Duke of, 25
Albuera, Battle of, 334
Alexander I, Czar of Russia, at Tilsit, 312, 314–5; at Erfurt, 321; doubtful loyalty of, to Napoleon, 325; at war with Napoleon, 335–6, 338; Holy Alliance of, 385
Alexandria, Battle of, 295
Aliens Act (U. S.), 349
"All the Talents," Ministry of, 310
Alleghany Mountains, 151, 191, 239
Almanza, Battle of, 69
Amazon trading rights, 96
American colonies, capture of Louisburg by, 130; self-government in, 139–40, 143; Parliament claims supremacy over, 139, 143, 175; conflict between Mother Country and, 139–44, 169, 174–81; British planning of trade with, 142; French threat to, 140, 144, 151–3; slow to organise, 144, 152; British officials in, 144–5, 175; economic difficulties in, 145, 170; foundation of last of Thirteen, 146; non-English emigrants to, 146; westward spread of, 147, 169–70; forced labour and slaves in, 147; campaigns against French in, 151–6; soldiery of, 154, 183–4, 208, 210; gain frontier on Great Lakes, 155; British acquire hinterland of, 169; British taxes on, 170–2, 174–5; leaders of Revolution in, 171; Burke's attitude towards, 173–4; duties on imports of, 175–6; resist only on commercial plane, 175, 179; idea of secession takes root in, 176–81; attempts to coerce, 179; Declaration of Rights of, 179; outbreak of war in, 180–1, 182–5; French help for, 180, 197–8, 201–3; raise Army, 184–5; invade Canada, 185; Declaration of Independence by, 186–8; blockade of coast of, 186, 189; opposition to secession in, 188–9, 206; near defeat, 191, 194; Clinton attempts subjugation of South, 200–2; civil war between Patriots and Loyalists in South, 202–4; sign peace preliminaries with Britain, 239; unpaid debts of merchants of, 240, 253, 346. *See also* North America; United States
American Independence, War of—*see* Independence, War of
Amherst, Jeffrey, Lord, 148, 151–6
Amherst, William Pitt Amherst, Earl, 230
Amiens, Treaty of, 297, 352
Andalusia, 318–9
André, Major, 205–6
Anjou, Duke of—*see* Philip V, King of Spain
Anne, Queen of England, surrenders right to succeed Mary, 8; influence of Churchills on, 13, 20, 25, 38–9; breaks with Mary, 13–14; reconciled to William, 20; Tory and Churchwoman, 26, 45; ascends throne, 38–9; attitude of, to Pretender, 45; upholds Marlborough, 47, 57; rewards Marlborough, 53; dislikes Whigs, 65–6; breaks with Sarah, 66–7, 85; and Abigail Hill, 66–7, 70, 77; and Harley, 67, 70–1, 98–9; breaks with Marlborough, 70–1, 77, 84; dismisses Whigs, 85; creates Tory peers, 91; last days of, 97–100; presides over Cabinet meetings, 98, 123
Anson, Captain, 122
Antigua, 303
Antwerp, French in, 35, 285; Marlborough aims at, 46; falls to Marlborough, 60, 64; campaign to occupy (1809), 326
Aragon, 62
Arcot, 218
Argyll, John Campbell, second Duke of, 99, 108
Arleux, 89
Army, Dutch in command of, 6, 12, 17; Tory reduction of, 21–2, 23–4; revival of, 33; refuses battle at Quesnoy, 93; divided, in America, 191, 193–5; conditions in (1793), 288; Windham's reforms of, 310; Wellington's use of infantry in, 310, 320, 374, 377; Castlereagh's reorganisation of, 315; in Peninsula, 319–24, 327–30, 332; and war with America, 366, 371; raising of, in 1815, 371–2; at Waterloo, 377–81
Arnold, Benedict, 181; Canadian expedition of, 185; treachery of, 205–6
Arras, 88
Artois, Count d'—*see* Charles X, King of France
"Asiento contract," 119–20
Aspern-Essling, 325
Assaye, Battle of, 232, 319
Astorga, 322
Asturias, 317
Ath, 64
Atterbury, Francis, Bishop of Rochester, 113
Audit Office, 249

INDEX

Aughrim, 12
Augsburg, 47
Austerlitz, Battle of, 308, 312
Australia, discovery of, 248
Austria, accession of Maria Theresa to throne of, 127; no longer Great Power, 131; allied to France, 137, 150; Republican France at war with, 282; defeated in Italy, 291; comes to understanding with Napoleon, 292–3; in alliance against Napoleon, 299, 322, 338; defeated by Napoleon, 308, 312, 324–5; Army of, in Russian campaign, 336; Italian possessions of, 342, 385; in Holy Alliance, 385
Austrian Succession, War of, 125–31; repercussions of, in India, 216

Badajoz, 333–5
Baden, Prince Louis of (Margrave), in Marlborough's 1704 campaign, 48, 50, 52; fails to support Marlborough, 55–6; defeated by Villars, 57, 69
Baird, Sir David, 323
Balance of Power, 340
Baltic Sea, 314–5
Baltimore, 351, 364
Bank of England, creation of, 20, 23; Tory rival of, 23; and South Sea Company, 110, 112, 114; suspends payment, 236
Barbados, 302
Barcelona, 62, 79, 87
Barham, Lord, 303
Barrier Treaty, 108
Bastille, fall of, 276–7
Bavaria, claim of Electoral Prince of, to Spanish throne, 27–8, 29; in alliance with France, 36, 48; Marlborough attacks, 50; Elector reinstated in, 97; attacks Maria Theresa, 128
Baylen, capitulation of, 318
Bayonne, 316
Beachy Head, Battle of, 11
Beauharnais, Eugène de, 312, 322, 336
Beaumont, 372
Bedford, John Russell, fourth Duke of, 160–1, 165
Belgium, French take barrier fortresses of, 32; Marlborough conquers, 60; unpopularity of Dutch rule in, 71; annexed by France, 286, 292, 372; joined to Holland, 342; Marshals flee to, 370; Army against Napoleon in, 370–2; 1815 campaign in, 372–7. See also Netherlands
Belle Isle, 162
Bellerophon, H.M.S., 381–2
Bengal, war in, 220–2; sale of throne of, 223; famine in, 225; Hastings Governor of, 225–7; money raised in, 226–8; British rule over, 230–1; tribute demanded from, 232
Beresford, William Carr, Viscount, 326–7, 334
Berkeley, James, third Earl of, 100
Berlin, Napoleon in, 312
Berlin Decrees, 314–6, 355; revocation of, 357
Bernadotte, Marshal, 283, 338
Bernstorff, Count von, 106
Berri, Charles, Duke of, 72
Berthier, Marshal, 370

Berwick, James FitzJames, Duke of, son of James II, 13; in Spain, 68–9; in Netherlands, 76; Marlborough negotiates peace with, 77; on Jacobites in England, 106–7
Bingfield, Colonel, 58
Bishops, Bench of, 46
Black Hole of Calcutta, 221
Blenheim, Battle of, 51, 52
Blücher, Marshal, 372–81
Bohemia, accession of Maria Theresa to throne of, 125
Bolingbroke, Henry St John, Viscount, Secretary at War, 48; resigns, 71; and Marlborough, 71, 85, 104; returns to office, 85; Quebec expedition of, 86; estranged from Harley, 87; orders Army not to fight, 93; supplants Harley, 97–9; dismissed by George I, 104; Secretary of State to Pretender, 104; return of, 114, 116–8
Bombay, 216, 225–8; Presidency, 233
Bonaparte—*see* Napoleon
Bonhomme Richard, the, 203–4
Bonn, 46–8
Bordeaux, 339
Borodino, Battle of, 337
Boscawen, Admiral Edward, 151
Boston, Adams fosters trouble in, 177; tea cargoes destroyed in, 178; outbreak of war in, 180–1; British reinforcements arrive in, 182; evacuated by Howe, 186; port of, 351
Bouchain, 88–90, 94
Boufflers, Marshal, 75, 82
Boulogne, invading force at, 298, 300–2, 308; Napoleon at, 304
Bourbon Family Compact, 129
Bourbons, restored to throne of France, 340–1, 381; restored to throne of Naples, 342
Boyne, Battle of the, 12
Brabant, Lines of, 55, 58
Braddock, General, 152, 184
Brandywine, River, 195
Brazil, 316
Breed's Hill, 183–4
Brest, expedition planned to, 18; blockade of French fleet in, 299–300, 305
Britain, at war with Spain, 120–2, 125, 127, 160, 203; at war with France, 126, 137–8, 150, 158, 197–8, 227, 237, 286–290; conflict between colonies and, 139–44, 169, 174–81; acquisitions of, under Peace of Paris (1763), 161–2, 169; Parliamentary system of government of, 163; attempts to regulate new land in North America, 169; colonies taxed from, 170–1, 174; attempts coercion of colonies, 179, 186; hires German troops for America, 188, 198; opposition in, to American War, 192–3, 198; fears invasion, 198, 202, 298, 300–2; no longer in command of sea, 202, 237; coalition against, 203, 207; slow to take over India from Company, 224; without an ally, 237, 299, 314; unpaid American debts to merchants of, 240, 253, 346; shattered complacency of, 242, 244–5; Industrial Revolution in, 244, 314; election in (1784), 245–6; Pitt's reforms in finances of, 248–50; Constitution of,

INDEX

256; foreign policy of, 285–6; no military plan, 294, 310; compulsory military service in, 310; blockades Europe, 314, 316, 354, 357; Napoleon seeks to blockade, 315–6; Asturians appeal to, 317; sends army to Peninsula, 319–20; acquisitions of, under Peace of Paris (1814), 341–2; relations of United States to, 344–6, 354–5, 357; prohibition of U. S. trade with, 355; at war with U. S., 357–66; anti-American feeling in, 366; acts quickly on escape of Napoleon, 371; Napoleon gives himself up to, 381. *See also* England

British Empire, first, 142–3, 161–2; collapse of, 164, 241, 248; in India, 228; French hope to dismember, 238, 240; growth of new, 248–9, 341–2

British Guiana, 342

Brittany, 294

Broad-bottomed Administration, 131

Brock, General Isaac, 360

Broke, Captain, 361

Brooklyn, 190

Brueys, Admiral, 293

Bruges, 64, 71, 76

Brunswick, 150

Brussels, Marlborough aims at, 56; fall of, 60, 64; French attack on, 76; Wellington in, 372–3; Napoleon aims at, 373

Bucentaure, the, 307

Buckingham and Normanby, John Sheffield, first Duke of, 98

Budget, Pitt's reorganisation of machinery of, 249

Buenos Aires, 310

Bunker Hill, 183–5; lesson of, 190, 200

Burgoyne, General John, arrives in America, 182; plan of, 194; advance and surrender of, 196–7

Burgundy, Louis, Duke of, 71

Burke, Edmund, 172–4; on Walpole, 115; attempts organisation of Whigs, 173; American policy of, 173, 179; on American War, 192; epitaph of, to Chatham, 199; and impeachment of Hastings, 229; without influence, 238; opposed to Pitt, 247; and French Revolution, 251, 277, 284; mentioned, 213

Burnet, Thomas, 106

Burns, Robert, 66

Burr, Aaron, 350, 354

Burrard, Sir Harry, 320

Busaco, Battle of, 333

Bute, John Stuart, third Earl of, opposes Pitt, 157–9; in office, 160, 165; and Peace of Paris, 160; and education of George III, 163

Byng, Admiral John, 138, 148

Cabinet, sovereign ceases to preside over, 123; convention of mutual loyalty in, 251

Cadiz, naval expedition to, 43–4; French fleet blockaded at, 151, 306; French fleet at, 302, 308

Cadogan: William Cadogan, first Earl of, at Oudenarde, 72; at turning of "Ne Plus Ultra" Lines, 88–9; mentioned, 97

Calcinato, Battle of, 57

Calcutta, founding of, 215; Black Hole of, 221; recapture of, 221; Governor-General at, 226–7

Calder, Admiral Sir Robert, 303–4

Calhoun, John C., 359

Camden, Battle of, 205, 208

Camden, Charles Pratt, first Earl of, 167

Campbell, Sir Neil, 369

Camperdown, Battle of, 292

Campo Formio, Treaty of, 292–3

Canada, colonies attempt to capture French, 144; colonies attacked from French, 151; conquest of, 151, 153–6, 161; Guadeloupe and, 162; British troops cut off from, 181; American invasions of, 185, 360–2; American refugees in, 186, 240; Burgoyne's advance from, 194–7; menace of invasion from, 212; frontier of, with America, 239, 367; nucleus of new Empire, 248; evacuation of trading posts on frontier of, 253, 345; French propaganda in, 348; U. S. covets, 359, 361–2; effect of war of 1812 on, 367

Canning, George, on Addington and Pitt, 297; enmity between Castlereagh and, 311, 330; and Napoleon's threat to Portugal, 316; and risings in Spain, 317–9; resignation of, 330; U. S. policy of, 357; mentioned, 340

Cape Breton, acquisition of, 130, 151, 161

Cape of Good Hope, 342

Cape St Vincent, Battle of, 292

Caribbean Sea, American privateers in, 203; Nelson misses Villeneuve in, 302–3

Carleton, Sir Guy, 185

Carlisle, 134

Carlyle, Thomas, on Chatham, 159

Carnatic, the, Mahratta warfare in, 215–6, 218; Dupleix and Nawab of, 216; Clive takes, 218; Hyder Ali in, 227; Nawab of, 230; becomes Madras Presidency, 231–2

Carnot, Lazare, 282

Caroline, Queen of George II, 116–8

Cartenet, John, Lord Granville, 106, 126–9

Castlereagh, Robert Stewart, Viscount (later second Marquess of Londonderry), enmity between Canning and, 311, 330; at Congress of Vienna, 339–43; revokes Order in Council, 357–8; at Treaty of Paris, 382–5; mentioned, 297

Catalonia, 78, 274, 62, 96, 338

Catholic Church: in France, 269, 279; concessions in Ireland, 292, 311; emancipation, Pitt and, 295

Ceylon, 342

Champlain, Lake, 363

Chandernagore, 220–1

Charleroi, 96, 373

Charles VI, Holy Roman Emperor (Archduke Charles), claimant for Spanish throne, 27–30; in Lisbon, 60; successes of, in Spain, 62, 68; Catalan adherence to, 62, 96; elected Emperor, 87; continues war, 96; death of, 125

Charles X, King of France, 278

Charles II, King of Spain, 28–30

Charles IV, King of Spain, 316

Charles XII, King of Sweden, 337

· *389* ·

INDEX

INDEX

Detroit, 360
Dettingen, Battle of, 128–9
De Witts, murder of, 4
Dickinson, John, *Letters from a Farmer* of, 175
Diderot, *Encyclopedia* of, 271
Directorate, 290
Dissenters, Tory warfare against, 45; Acts of Indemnity for, 114–5; under George III, 245
Dominica, 161
Douai, 84, 87–8, 94
Douro, River, 327
Downing Street, Number Ten in, 123
Dublin, James II reigns in, 9; independent Parliament in, 291, 295
Dugommier, General, 289
Dumouriez, General, 282
Dundas, Henry (first Viscount Melville), and India Act, 228–9, 247; friend and ally of Pitt, 246–7; in charge of military matters (1783), 288–9; impeachment of, 309; mentioned, 245
Dunkirk, sluices opened at, 75; English in, 94, 97; demolition of fortifications of, 94, 161; attempt to take, 289
Dupleix, Joseph, 216–8
Dupont, General, 318
Dutch, William favours, 5, 12–3; at Malplaquet, 82–3; troops to repel Jacobites in England, 108, 129, 134; American colony taken from, 139; troops against Napoleon, 371–4. *See also* Holland
Dutch East Indies, 341
Dutch Fleet, defeated off Beachy Head, 11; victory of, off La Hogue, 15–16
Dutch Guards, 6, 24
Dyle, River, 58, 72

East India Company, 215; acquisitions of, by Peace of Paris, 161; granted monopoly in tea to colonies, 178; growth of Indian Empire of, 214, 223–4, 230–3; forced to fight the French, 218; corruption in, 224–6; Hastings and, 225, 228–9; Fox's attempt to control, 241–2; supports Pitt, 245–6
Ebro, River, 318–21
Eckmühl, Battle of, 325
Economic Reform Act, Burke's, 243
Eden, William, 250
Edinburgh, Young Pretender in, 133
Egypt, invasion of, 293–4
Elba, Napoleon in, 339, 343, 368–9
Elizabeth Stuart, Queen of Bohemia, 26
Embargo Act (U. S.), 355
England, William III as King of, 5; enters coalition against France, 6; threatened invasion of, 11–2, 15–6, 31, 129, 298, 299–302; reconstruction of credit and finances of, 19–20; at peace with France, 21; disarmament of, 22, 31; Protestant Succession to, 26, 94, 97–100, 123; and Spanish Succession, 31, 94; aroused by French gains, 32–3; at war with France, 35, 79–80, 122, 126–31; governing class in, in Anne's reign, 38; party faction in, 39; union of, with Scotland, 65–6; terms for, at Utrecht, 94; financial speculation in, 109–12; conflict between American colonies and, 139–44; trade between col-

onies and, 142, 145; elections in (1761), 164; Industrial Revolution in, 244; financial policy of, compared with that of U. S., 262–3; Revolution in, 267; repressive measures in, 291. *See also* Britain
English Channel, French in command of, 11, 202; Franco-Spanish fleets in, 237; protection of approaches to, 299–300; Napoleon seeks command of, 301
Erfurt, 321
Erie, Lake, amphibious fighting on, 362
Eugene, Prince, of Savoy, fights in Italy, 34, 42; association of, with Marlborough, 48, 71, 93–4; at and after Blenheim, 50, 52; Marlborough plans to join in Italy, 57; reinforcements sent to, 57, 67; drives French out of Northern Italy, 60; his enterprise against Toulon, 68–9; in Netherlands, 71, 76, 82, 84, 87, 93; at Oudenarde, 74; and Spanish campaign, 79; at Malplaquet, 82; moves to Rhine, 87; British Army fails, 93
Excise: Walpole scheme for duties, 117–9; amalgamation of Customs and, 249
Eylau, Battle of River, 312

Falkirk, Battle of, 134
Falmouth, 317
Federal District Courts, 261
Federalist, The, 257–8
Federalist Party, 257; reactions of, to Revolution, 257; and treaty with Britain, 345; attacks liberty of individual, 349; opposes Embargo Act, 355; stigma of disloyalty on, 365
Ferrol, 303–4
"Fifteen," Jacobite rising of the, 107–9
Finchley Common, troops on, 133
Finisterre, Cape, 303
Five Days, Battle of, 325
Flamborough Head, action off, 203–4
Flanders—*see* Netherlands
Fleurus, Battle of, 11
Florence, 342
Florida, acquired from Spain, 161; Spanish threat to, 203; Spanish ownership of, 240–1, 253; fears of French ownership of, 348; U. S. desire for, 354; Jackson pursues Indians into, 364; mentioned, 140
Fontenoy, Battle of, 129
Forbes, Brigadier, 153–4
Fort Dearborn, 360
Fort Duquesne, 153
Fort Edward, 152
Fort Knocke, 96
Fort Presqu'île, 362
Fort St David, 216
Fort William Henry, 152
"Forty-five," Jacobite rising of the, 130–5
Fouché, Joseph, Duke of, 322, 339, 380
Fox, Charles James, and impeachment of Hastings, 229; opposed to Shelburne, 238; and American Independence, 238; coalition of, with the North, 241–2, 245; Indian Bill of, 241–2; opposed to Pitt, 247; and the French Revolution, 251, 284; in France, 297; abolition of slave trade under, 311; death of, 311; mentioned, 174
Fox, Henry, 137–8, 173

INDEX

France, William III's enmity against, 4; threatens invasion, 11–2, 15–8, 297–8; helps Stuarts, 15, 34, 107, 132; decisively defeated at sea, 16; claim of, to Spain, 27–31; virtual union of Crowns of Spain and, 32; takes over Netherland fortresses, 32; Grand Alliance re-forms against, 28–36; England at war with, 35, 79–80, 122, 137–8, 150, 158, 197–8, 227, 237, 272, 286–90; allies of, 35, 126, 137, 150; early successes of, 47; defeat of, 52, 60, 76–7; driven out of Northern Italy, 60; driven out of Eastern Spain, 63; invasion of Southern, 67–9; invades Germany, 69; Marlborough wishes to march into, 75; great frost in, 77; offers made by, 78; resurgence of national spirit in, 80, 82, 86; secret peace negotiations of, 86–7, 91; concessions of, at Utrecht, 94; makes peace with Emperor, 96; *entente* with, 115; supports Frederick the Great, 125; American colonies threatened by, 140, 142, 144, 151–6; in Seven Years War, 137–8, 150–1; loses Canada, 155–6; need for decisive defeat of, 158, 161; alliance of, with Spain, 159, 203, 238; appeasement of, in Peace of Paris, 161–2; sends gunpowder to America, 180; Americans seek aid from, 192, 197–8; in alliance with American colonists, 197–8, 201–3, 214, 238, 253, 272; Indian adventures of, 216–8, 221–2, 227; helps Indians against British, 231, 237; signs Treaty of Versailles, 240; Britain's Free Trade Treaty with, 249–50; States-General meet in, 260, 273–6; Jefferson looks to, 266; under Louis XVI, 268–73; growing middle class of, 268, 270–1, 275; system of finances in, 268–71; privileged nobility and clergy of, 269–70, 272; administrative chaos in, 271–3; "Terror" in, 274, 285, 290; Third Estate of, 274–5; deliberation upon Constitution for, 278; emigration of reactionaries from, 278; peasant proprietors of, 279; New Régime in, 280; regicide in, 281–2; at war with Austria and Prussia, 282; own armies a threat to, 285; annexes Netherlands, 286–7; victories of, under Napoleon, 292–3; English tourists in, 297; no longer behind Napoleon, 337; defeat of, 339; Wellington's army in, 339; return of Bourbons to, 340, 381, 384; terms offered to, 341; U. S. on brink of war with, 348–9; buys and sells Louisiana, 349, 352, 353; Hundred Days in, 370–82; Wellington plans advance into, 371–2; terms for (1815), 384. *See also* French

Francis, Philip, 227, 229

Franco-Prussian alliance (1740), 126

Franklin, Benjamin, 177; mission of, to France, 192, 197–8; interest of, in Western lands, 239

Frederick II (the Great), King of Prussia, in War of Austrian Succession, 125, 126, 136; in Seven Years War, 137, 150; on Pitt, 148, 157; subsidies to, 150, 157; resentment of, at Peace of Paris, 162

Frederick, Prince of Wales, 118, 122, 136

Free Trade, Pitt's belief in, 248–9; French, in corn, 272

French Army, forced on defensive, 42; destroyed at Blenheim, 52; defends Lille, 75–6; upholds Louis XIV, 80; Revolutionary, 282, 285; under Napoleon, 291, 324–5; in Spain, 321–4; drain on, by Peninsular War, 332; retreats from Portugal, 333; driven from Spain, 338; in the Hundred Days, 370–7; at Waterloo, 377–8, 379

French Navy, at Malaga, 54; defeated in Seven Years War, 151; inactivity of, in American campaign, 156; nursery of, in the St Lawrence, 161; in War of American Independence, 198, 201–4, 211–12; defeated at Nile, 293–4; prevention of junction of fleets of, 299–302, 303–6; poor condition of, 301; defeated at Trafalgar, 306–8

French Revolution, 267–83; British reactions to, 250–1, 285–6, 297; conditions leading to, 267–73; beginning of, 276–7; death of Louis XVI in, 281–2; American reactions to, 344–5; spread of ideals of, 385

Fuentes d'Oñoro, Battle of, 334

Furnes, 96

Gadsden, Christopher, 171

Gage, General Thomas, 180, 182–4

Galway, Henri de Massue, Earl of, 62, 68

Bambier, Admiral, 315

Ganteaume, Admiral, 301, 303–4

Gaspee, H.M.S., 177

Gates, Horatio, 197, 205

Gavre, 72

Genêt, Citizen, 344

Genoa, 342

George, Lake, 53

George I, King of England and Elector of Hanover, 103; Marlborough and, 91, 97–8; accession of, 100, 103–4; Court of, 105; mistresses of, 105, 116; Hanoverian foreign policy of, 107, 113; Walpole keeps favour of, 115; ceases to preside over Cabinet, 123; monarchy under, 163

George II, King, Opposition gathers round, 116; dismisses Walpole, 116; Hanoverian interests of, 126–7; Pitt antagonises, 127, 131, 135–7; at Dettingen, 128–9; and loss of Minorca, 138; death of, 158; monarchy under, 163; mentioned, 133

George III, King, upbringing of, 157, 163; accession of, 158; character of, 158, 172; and Chatham, 158–9, 198; monarchy under, 163–4; disastrous results of rule of, 164, 193, 237; and arrest of Wilkes, 165–6; and American colonies, 170, 172, 176; seeks reconciliation with Whigs, 172–3; war policy of, 193–4; forced to accept Rockingham, 213; and Shelburne, 238; asks Pitt to form Government, 242, 245–6; opposes Parliamentary Reform, 247; refuses assent to Catholic Emancipation, 295; madness of, 332

George IV, King, becomes Regent, 332; Napoleon's letter to, 382

George, Prince of Denmark, 14, 41, 46, 71

Georgia, 147, 207, 210

Germain, Lord George, 194

Germantown, Battle of, 196

· 392 ·

INDEX

INDEX

INDEX

Marat, Jean Paul, 282, 285
Marchiennes, 373
Marengo, Battle of, 294
Maria Theresa, Empress of Germany, 125
Marie Antoinette, Queen of Louis XVI, 272, 275, 278; burnt in effigy, 273; attempts to escape, 281
Marie Louise, Empress, 334, 342, 369
Maritime Powers, 21, 35
Marlborough, John Churchill, first Duke of, influence of, over Anne, 8, 13, 20; created Earl, 9; leads contingent in Flanders (1689), 9; and Godolphin, 10, 67; prepares to meet invasion, 11; Irish campaign of, 12; rift between William and, 12–4, 20, 25; in touch with James, 13; said to have betrayed invasion plans, 19; supports William, 20–1, 26; William reconciled with, 25–6, 33, 37; Governor of Duke of Gloucester, 25–6; Commander-in-Chief and Ambassador Extraordinary to the United Provinces, 33; ten years of victory of, 37, 90; Captain-General of English and Dutch forces, 40–1; turns tide of war, 42–3, 46, 52–3; created Duke, 43; protects Ormonde and Rooke, 44; held back by Allies, 46–7, 55–6, 64; marches to Danube, 49, 50, 52; Prince Eugene and, 48, 50, 71–2, 93; at Blenheim, 50–2; at field of Waterloo, 56, 376; plans campaign in Italy, 56–7, 67, 71; lacks support, 57; at Ramillies, 58–60; supports Sunderland, 65; gets rid of Harley, 70–1; his breach with Anne, 71, 84; illness of, 72; at Oudenarde, 72–5; captures Lille, 76; negotiates for peace, 77, 79–80; controls Army but not policy, 78, 86; plans Spanish campaign, 79; at Malplaquet, 82–3; breaks "Ne Plus Ultra" Lines, 88–90; charged with peculation and dismissed, 91–2, 97; relations of, with George I, 91, 97–8; refuses separate peace, 91; in self-imposed exile, 97; advises Bolingbroke, 104; death of, 106; and "Fifteen" rising, 108
Marlborough, Sarah Churchill, Duchess of, her influence over Anne, 8, 13, 38; dismissed from Court, 14; Anne's letter to, 47; Marlborough's letters to, 52, 83; breach between Queen and, 66–7, 85; last days of, 106
Marmont, Marshal, in Spain, 333, 335; surrenders Paris, 339; in Belgium, 370; mentioned, 283
Marne, River, 339
Marshall, John, 350
Marsin, Marshal, 42–3, 48, 50, 51
Martinique, 156, 162, 246, 302
Mary II, Queen of England, relations with William, 3; accession of, 7–8; Council of (1609), 11–2; rift between Anne and, 13–4; death of, 20
Massachusetts, expedition from, takes Nova Scotia, 94; proposes petition against duties, 175; "Committees of Correspondence" in, 177; "Coercion Acts" against, 179; war starts in, 180; appeals to Congress for help, 184; rebellion in, 253; profits by Hamilton's financial policy, 262; seeks separate peace with Britain, 365

Masséna, Marshal, 268–70, 283, 331–3
Maubeuge, 88, 372
Mauritius, 231, 341
Mediterranean, threat to British communications in, 32, 35, 43, 203; English intervention in, 53; Allied expedition into, 62; English foothold in, 77, 94; British fleet supreme in, 294; Nelson watches for French fleet in, 300–2
Melfort, Jacobite Secretary of State, 31
Melville, first Viscount—see Dundas, Henry
Menin, 64, 96
Merchant Navy, 142
Methodist movement, 245
Metternich, Prince, 310, 340, 380, 382
Meuse, River, 35, 42–3, 46, 55, 64
Milan and Milanese, 96, 97, 292
Military service, compulsory universal, 310
Minden, Battle of, 194
Minorca, Marlborough seeks capture of, 44; capture of, 76, 106; British possession, 94; loss of, 137, 150, 237; restored to Britain, 161; returned to Spain, 241, 300
Minto, Gilbert Elliot, first Earl, 230, 233
Miquelon, 161
Mir Jafar, 221, 222, 223
Mirabeau, Count de, 280
Mississippi, River, French on, 153, 155; British right to navigate, 161; American frontier, 239; trade on, 352; swamps at mouth of, 364
Modena, 342
Mogul Emperor, disintegration of Empire of, 214–6; asks Clive for British protection, 224; Mahrattas seize, 232
Molasses Act, 170
Monmouth, James Scott, Duke of, 4
Monmouth Court House, 201
Monroe, James, 353
Mons, 82–3
Montcalm, Marquis de, 150, 153, 155
Montereau, 339
Montgomery, Richard, 185
Montjuich, 63
Montmirail, 339
Montreal, Amherst takes, 156; Montgomery takes, 185; Burgoyne's advance from, 194; advance into U. S. from, 363
Moore, Sir John, 321–4
Morris, Gouverneur, 254–5, 260
Morris, Robert, 257
Moscow, Napoleon in, 336–7
Moselle, River, 48, 52–6
Mount Vernon, 260, 346, 348
Murat, Marshal, 283, 342
Murray, Lord George, 133–4
Murray, Sir George, 371
Mysore, 227, 230, 231

Nabobs, 226, 229, 243
Namur, falls to French, 16, 32, 35; William recovers, 21; Holland secures, 96; mentioned, 55, 64
Naples, Kingdom of, succession to, 28, 97; Bonaparte King of, 312; Bourbons restored to throne of, 342
Napoleon I, Emperor of French, and India, 231; takes Toulon, 289–90; and 13th Vendémiaire, 291; plans conquest of East, 291–4, 321; European victories

INDEX

Occasional Conformity Bill of, 46, 48; change in leadership of, 47–8; out of office under Anne, 77; and accession of George I, 100, 104; Jacobitism of, 104, 109, 115, 164; hope for revival of, 113; in the shades, 116; and George III, 164; American, 210; support Pitt, 246

Toronto, 362

Torres Vedras, 320; Lines of, 332–3

Toulon, expedition against, 68–70; Boscawen defeats squadron from, 151; Napoleon takes from Royalists, 289, 290; blockade of, 299–300

Toulouse, 339

Tournai, 82, 90, 96, 129

Tourville, Admiral, 11, 15–6

Townshend, Charles, second Viscount, resignation of, 113; dismissal of, 117; and taxation of colonies, 171; imposes duties on colonial imports, 174–5; mentioned, 106

Trade and Plantations, Board of, 140, 143

Trade, Board of, reconstruction of, 249

Trafalgar, Battle of, 303–8

Training Act, 310

Trarbach, 48, 52, 54

Treason Act, 291

Treasury, Pitt's reforms of, 249

Trenton, Battle of, 191

Treves, 35, 48, 52, 54

Trichinopoly, 218

Trieste, 342

Turgot, A. R. J., 272

Turin, 60, 278

Turkey, 21, 36

Tyrconnel, Duchess of, 13

Ulm, 52, 56; Battle of, 308

Ulster, 295

Union, Act of, 66; Scottish dissatisfaction at, 107, 132; with Ireland, 295–6

"United Empire Loyalists," 240

United Irishmen, 295

United States of America, refugees from, in Canada, 185–6, 240; treaty granting independence to, 239, 253; frontiers of, 239, 367; unpaid debts to British merchants, 240, 253; political organisation of, 252–66; conflicting interests in, 252, 258, 262; internal disorder in, 252–3, 259–60; Constitution of, 253–61; problems of Western expansion of, 254, 358; first elections in, 260; Government takes over public debts in, 262; beginnings of political parties in, 263, 266; capital of, 263; Protectionist policy of, 263; Revolution of, 267; British interference with shipping of, 316, 344, 345, 354; reactions to French Revolution in, 344; French interference with, 344; traditional foreign policy of, 344; impressment of seamen of, 346, 359, 361, 366; party spirit in, 346; on brink of war with France, 348–9, 351–3; growth of, 351; commerce of, 351; purchases Louisiana, 353–4; prohibition of trade with Britain, 355; at war with Britain, 358–66; causes of war, 358, 361; invasion of Canada by, 359–62; frigates of, 360; blockade of coast of, 362, 365; risk of secession in, 365; peace terms, 367

United States, the, 360

Utrecht, Treaty of, 94, 96–7, 119

Valencia, 62, 68

Valladolid, 321–2

Valley Forge, 200

Valmy, Battle of, 282

Vanguard, H.M.S., 293

Varennes, 281

Vendôme, Marshal, at Calcinato, 57; Marlborough holds, 68; at Oudenarde, 72–4; at Lille, 76

Vendémiaire, cannonade of 13th, 291

Venetian Republic passes to Austria, 292, 342, 385

Venloo, 32

Vermont, 351

Vernon, Admiral Edward, 122

Versailles, States-General meet at, 260, 274; nobles compelled to live at Court at, 269; King recalled from, 278–9

Versailles, Treaty of, 228, 240

Victor, Marshal, 283, 327, 370

Victory, H.M.S., 304, 306–8

Vienna, French threat to, 48, 50; Napoleon enters, 325; Marie Louise in, 369

Vienna, Congress of, personalities of, 339–40; terms arrived at, 340–3, 385; disagreement at, 368–9; and escape of Napoleon, 370–1; settlement at, compared with that of 1919–20, 382

Vigo Bay, 43–4

Villars, Marshal, at Saarlouis, 54–5; defeats Margrave, 57, 69; upholds Louis, 80; at Malplaquet, 82–3; "Ne Plus Ultra" Lines of, 88–90; successes of (1712), 94

Villeneuve, Admiral, Nelson pursues, 302–4; at Trafalgar, 306–8

Villeroy, Marshal, 50, 55, 58

Vimiero, Battle of, 319

Vimy Ridge, 89

Virginia, agitation for revolt in, 177; Cornwallis in, 207, 210–1; speculation in, on Western lands, 239; opposition to Constitution in, 257; opposes financial policy, 262

Vitoria, Battle of, 338

Vitry, 89

Voltaire, 271

Wade, General, 133, 135

Wagram, Battle of, 325

Walcheren, expedition to, 326, 330

Waldeck, Prince of, 11

Wales, Jacobites in, 133, 134

Walmer, Pitt at, 298; Wellington at, 380

Walpole, Horace, on capture of Martinique, 156

Walpole, Sir Robert (Earl of Orford), opposes Bill to limit peerages, 108–9; attacks South Sea Company, 110; financial policy of, 112, 114; career of, 113, 123–4; head of Government, 113–9; policy of, 114–5; opposition to, 115–24; Excise scheme of, 117–8, 127; "Prime Minister," 117, 124; fall of, 122–4; Johnson on, 138; more than Minister, 163; mentioned, 106

"War Hawks," 359

Warrants, illegality of general, 166, 174, 244

· 401 ·